A Nation of

Millionaires

A Nation of Millionaires

Karl Gittelman

To order additional copies of this book, contact:
Xlibris LLC
1-888-795-4274
www.Xlibris.com
Orders@Xlibris.com
141364

CONTENTS

FOREWORD

This book was researched and written in 2006 and 2007. It has languished as I was distracted by other ventures. The data may be a few years out-of-date, but the ideas remain valid. The stock market has experienced some severe ups and downs, as predicted, in the past few years as the United States and most of the world have suffered through another significant recession. The Dow Jones Industrial Averages dropped dramatically from the 11,000 cited in the text to under 7,000. It has now recovered to over 15,000 at the time I write this Foreword. That only confirms the research and advice cited in the book. As you might imagine, I stayed with my stock and fund investments right through the downturn, did not sell a thing, and am now back near all-time highs. The yearly compound rate of return calculation for my investments has declined slightly for some of the investments cited in the book. But I am convinced that the markets are on the way to returning to the historical returns cited. We have still not fully recovered from the recession and are still a long way from the full extent of the bull market that will ensue if normal growth and employment return. If anything, the added history of the past six years only reinforces the ideas in this book.

Karl Gittelman PhD
October 2013

CHAPTER 1

Why This Book?

Philip Morris, 1957 and Six Million Dollars

1957 was a good year. Ike was the president. The 1950s prosperity was in full swing. The stock market was going up, a bull market; rock and roll was sweeping the country, and I was a carefree, fun-loving, beer-drinking undergraduate at the Wharton School of the University of Pennsylvania. My freshmen course load included all the standard fare: Economics, Accounting, Marketing, and Political Science. I did not take a course in investments until graduate school many years later.

I already had some experience with investing, taking part in my father's Kiwanis investment club, investing $10 a month. I had little interest and no say in how the club invested their money, and to this day, I have no memory of those stocks or what happened to them. By 1962, I did have a nest egg of my own, about $20,000, some of it in bank Certificates of Deposit for safety. I also had a few stocks, and while I can't remember the exact stocks I owned in 1957, I do have a written record of the ones I owned just a few years later. They probably were not much different in 1957. The stocks I did own were not the result of my own research but came from stock tips that my father got from his friends, often top executives and principals of public companies, whom he played gin rummy with. (No one seemed as worried about insider information in 1957 as they are today.) My other source came from my father's brother, an engineer, who was a committed stock chartist. He spent hours hand charting (no computers) prices of the stocks that he followed looking for "support" and "resistance" levels to buy and sell to make a small profit. Both my father and uncle died years later, having made little from their multiyear stock investing.

The stocks that I owned then totaled almost $10,000 and included San Juan Racetrack, Reichhold Chemicals, Smith, Kline & French (a drug company), and Celanese (another chemical company). In looking at my records by 1965, I had disposed of all but the San Juan Racetrack (a strong tip from one of my father's wealthy friends). By 1966, I had sold all four and was on to other ventures. Before I tell you what happened to these early investments, I want to describe another company that most of you are familiar with.

If you are over 45, you probably will remember "Call for Philip Morris." Who can forget that bellhop's piercing chant as he strolled through the hotel lobby paging a phone call for a fictitious or long-dead character in the 1950s TV and radio commercials for Philip Morris cigarettes. We knew Philip Morris, and some of us even tried smoking them, but who knew the potential of a relative small investment in the Philip Morris Company in 1957? I could have easily taken $1,000 from my other stocks or from my bank Certificate of Deposit and invested it in Philip Morris stock. Had I invested my $1,000 and then reinvested all the dividends over the years in added stock, then paid any taxes on the dividends out of other money (hold on to your hat), my investment would be worth $6,076,850 on July 1, 2005 as I write this on my computer. Writing it alone makes me cringe. It may sound incredulous, especially considering all the problems Philip Morris was to face in the coming decades. The Surgeon General's report was only a few years away and told us what many had long suspected, that cigarettes were killing us. This was followed quickly by warning labels on cigarette packages and endless individual and then government lawsuits that dogged Philip Morris and seemed ready to doom an entire industry. If I had invested $1,000 in Philip Morris in 1957, I would have most likely sold it in the early 1960s, fearing the effects on the stock price of the health and smoking disaster that was unfolding.

But my question now many years later is simple: how come no one told me? Not my father, not my uncle, not my teachers at Wharton. No one told me that this spectacular return was even possible investing in stocks. I would be annoyed about it today, but I realize that most of them did not understand it either. They were too caught up in stock tips, short-term movements, and technical analysis to take the time to understand the simple power of compound rates of return. The power of compound rates of return and time were something that I had vaguely heard of but never understood, and I never assumed that it could produce this magnitude of return.

Was Philip Morris unique? In a nutshell, yes. It was, by far, the stellar performer for 48 years of all the stocks in the original S&P 500. The truth is there were many other stocks in which I might have invested had I realized the potential return possible. Many of them would have produced significant returns that would have made me happy and much richer. Had I realized the key to long-term stock investing success was to buy, reinvest all dividends, avoid taxes, and hold and hold and hold and hold, I would have done well indeed. Figure 1A shows the return for a group of companies that almost everyone knew in 1957. Most of them were household names. Not secret information from insiders, not the latest technology breakthrough, not your favorite brokers' hottest tip, no these were, as Jeremy Siegel so aptly named them in his latest book, "The Tried and True."

I am not going to tell you how to find the next Philip Morris. Spectacular returns like that are not easy to come by. One of the obvious facts in Figure 1A is how much better Philip Morris did than any of the other stocks. So don't think you are going to read this book and find out how to turn $1,000 into $6 million by finding the next great company for the next 50 years. But great returns are possible even if you only perform at the market average, which will be the focus of this book. Doubtless, careful stock selection can outperform the average. Remember, the average in stock market investing means that about half the stocks performed worse and half better than the average. I will focus later in this book on picking stocks that will last, "thrive and survive." I will also spend pages showing those of you who don't believe that you can pick stocks yourself, how you can achieve the market average, and perhaps more. And the market average turns out to be spectacular itself.

The amounts in the first column in Figure 1A are what anyone would have achieved if they had invested $1,000 in 1957 in any one of these companies. This assumes that they would have held the stock until today (2005,) reinvesting all dividends, using a tax-deferred account.

FIGURE 1A "The Tried and True"—1957-2005[1]

Stock	Result of	
	$1,000 Invested	**$10,000 Invested**
Altria	$6,076,850	$60,768,500
Abbott Labs	1,228,440	12,284,409
Bristol-Myers	1,006,416	10,064,162
Pepsi	998,331	9,983,311
Tootsie Roll	807,243	8,072,434
Coca-Cola	803,505	8,035,059
Hershey Foods	757,490	7,574,902
Pfizer	738,135	7,381,356
Colgate-Palmolive	697,000	6,970,000
Wrigley	677,051	6,770,514
Fortune Brands	673,116	6,731,166
Merck	625,630	6,256,309
Crane	577,633	5,776,338
Heinz	575,245	5,752,458
Schering-Plough	531,369	5,313,693
Procter & Gamble	502,774	5,027,747
Kroger	459,274	4,982,895
Royal Dutch	498,285	4,592,749
Wyeth	447,238	4,472,388
General Mills	371,851	3,718,516
Total of all 20	$19,052,887	$190,528,875
Total for S&P 500	$216.037	$2,160,370

I know what some of you are thinking. I have to be kidding. I love Tootsie Rolls; they are still my favorite candy today, but who could have imagined that I could have made over $800,000 with a single $1,000 investment in a candy stock? Heck, I drank so much coke that I started a collection of coke bottle tops (remember the cork inserts in the tops). I had so many (50,000 or more) in boxes in the cellar that my mother threw them away, cleaning out the cellar, when I went to college—Coke, Pepsi,

Wrigley chewing gum, Heinz Ketchup, Colgate-Palmolive toothpaste, and Hershey chocolates. I could have turned everything I knew and liked into gold. This was not sophisticated investing. These weren't the recommendations of high-priced *Wall Street* pros. In the end, these stocks are the 20 top performers of the original S&P 500 stocks with 20/20 hindsight, and we all know that everything looks obvious after the fact. But this theoretical portfolio turned $1,000 invested in each stock in1957 into $19,052,887 in 48 years. It is true that picking all 20 of these stocks would have been unlikely. For instance, one of my uncle's favorite stocks was Studebaker, which had he held until today would have returned him a handsome compound 11.64% yearly compound return even though Studebaker, the auto manufacturer, went out of business long ago. But he also owned Pennsylvania Railroad headed for the scrap heap. So picking all winners is not likely in the cards, but finding at least a couple of these was something any one of us might have done, and finding a couple is all we would have had to do. Nobody told me about the power in long-term investing!

Well, that is why I am writing this book. So when you are my age (67 for those of you who are curious), you won't be able to write a book and say, "Nobody Told Me." In this book, I am going to tell you! I am going to tell you how and why it is possible. How you can do-it-yourself. I will give you ideas on how to get the money to invest, how to maximize your return, how to reinvest your dividends, and how to avoid or delay taxes. Instead of saying "Nobody Told Me," you will be able to say "Thank, God" I read that book by (What was his name?).

I included in Figure 1A the result of both a $1,000 investment for each stock and a $10,000 investment for each stock. Now, $10,000 was much money in 1957. You could have bought a small house for $10,000 (I bought my first home in 1964 for $17,500), so I am not implying that a $10,000 investment in 1957 was easy for most people. But it is interesting to see the returns possible. Note, however, if I had taken my $10,000 and invested only as well as the average of the S&P 500 stocks, I would still have had over $2 million today from that one investment alone.

Let us look at some of the stocks I did own in Figure 1B and what would have happened if I had kept them and reinvested all the dividends: where would I be today? I have no idea what happened to San Juan Racetrack. I think that El Comandante Racetrack acquired it, and they are now in bankruptcy. Let's assume that investment would be worthless today. Reichhold Chemicals still survives. A Japanese chemical company, Dainippon Ink and Chemical, bought it in 1987 so there is no easy way to figure my possible return. I imagine that I would have come out well, but it would have depended, in part, on what I invested the funds I received in the acquisition. Three of remaining stocks performed well. Celanese merged with Aventis, and in 1999, Celanese became a separate company again, Celanese AG. It would have returned me over $2.5 million today on my $2,500 investment if I had held it and reinvested all the dividends each year. I remember watching SmithKline for several years, and it did nothing. I was young and wanted action, and SmithKline did not provide it. SmithKline eventually merged to create the giant drug company, GlaxoSmithKline, and would have returned me a cool $447,500 for my $2,500 investment in 1957, below the S&P 500 average but still remarkable. In 1966, I bought some AT&T stock. The stock languished for years, and of course, I disposed of it along the way. But I calculate that had I held that stock, reinvested all the dividends, and held the "Baby Bells," I would have received in the famous AT&T divestiture in the early 1980s that it would be worth a sweet $2,032,804 today. Notice that I didn't have any of the top 20 stocks in Siegel's list. But even the stocks I did own, way back when, would still have produced some fantastic results had I simply understood compound rates of return and long-term investing. I owned some others like Keebler, General Motors, and Sperry Rand that would have produced modest results. Of course, my records show that I owned some real clinkers: Moly B, Ransburg, Ward Foods, Optical Scanning, and a few others. (These stock's value listed as "??" because I cannot determine if that investment, held to today, would be worth anything. I assume they probably should be zero.) But my experience shows, happily and painfully in my case, that you don't have to pick all winners. A few good ones will do nicely, and I hope to show you how to pick them later in this book.

Figure 1B shows what I would have had from my early foray into stock investing in the late 1950s and 1960s if I held until December 31, 2003. It pains me to have to write "hypothetical" in front of Figure 1B. My modest first investments would have produced somewhere over $5 million, maybe closer to $6 million.

FIGURE 1B Karl Gittelman's Stock
Investments 1957-2003 "Hypothetical"

Result of Karl Gittelman's Initial Stock Investments as of December 31, 2003		
Celanese		$2,691,913
Smith, Kline & French		447,500
AT&T		2,032,084
General Motors		87,095
Sperry Rand		22,265
Keebler		122,896
Reichhold Chemicals (acquired in 1987)		NA
San Juan Racetrack	??	
Moly B	??	
Ransburg Electric	??	
Ward Foods	??	

Looked at another way, could I or would I have picked any of the stocks in Figure 1A? Why didn't I? I am positive that if I had read this book, or something like it, then I would have found several of the stocks in Figure 1A. Most of those companies were selling some of my favorite products. But I was chasing rainbows, insider tips, and the latest news, hoping to make a small killing on some stocks' quick move upward. There is no doubt in my mind that I would have converted to a long-term investing philosophy once I understood the power of compound rates of return. (Chapter 5 explores this in more depth.) I could have held the stocks I owned anyway, like a long-term investor instead of a trader, and I would have had a spectacular return on my original stock investments.

There are encouraging things that one finds looking in detail at Jeremy Siegel's list of top returns during the 1957-2003 period. Many of the companies that did not do all that well on their own ended with spectacular shareholder returns as the result of acquisition. Modest companies like Thatcher Glass, Rexall Drugs, Illinois Tool Works, Lane Bryant, CSX, California Packing, Del Monte, and my own Celanese all returned over 16% compounded for years largely as the result of acquisition. So even if your selection isn't the best, you can sometimes luck out if your company is taken over by a high performer. For the record, 16% compounded turns a single $1,000 investment into more than $1.6 million

—

in 52 years. The S&P average stock returned 10.85% from 1957 to 2003, which translates into more than $170,000 for a single $1,000 investment in 50 years. Using the S&P 500 average return, you would need to make a onetime investment of $5,882 at 10.85% compounded for 50 years to become a millionaire. You don't need to find the superstars and you don't need to invest a fortune to significantly upgrade your retirement.

Everyone Can Benefit from This Book

This book evolved initially out of my experience as a volunteer high school teacher of Economics for 14 years. The first year (1992) that I taught the class, several students came to me asking how they might get rich. Could I please tell them? Like it was some inside information that I could give that would make it happen without them having to do much. It was clearly a tough question to answer. I thought and thought about it, trying to come up with some sage advice that might make them all the next Bill Gates. But I realized that any advice I might give them would only apply to certain people and I wanted to come up with a plan that could, potentially, make everyone in my class "rich." Pretty ambitious! I wanted to make the smart, motivated kids rich, and I wanted to make the lazy, careless kids rich. It stimulated me to start, what became famous at our school, my "Millionaires" class. It is one class a semester in which I give everyone the "secret" that they all can use to become millionaires when they retire. Researching this idea led me to compound rates of return and the stock market. I discovered that an investment of $2,000 every year compounded at 8% would make them all millionaires in 50 years (about their retirement age), over $1.2 million. Little did I realize during the first years of my "Millionaires" class that average stock returns over 50 years were more than 11%, making the return even greater, over $3.7 million. In fact, 8% turned out to be conservative; it was close to Jeremy Siegel's 200-year compound rate of return. Everyone in my class could get a job, summer or during college, and earn $2,000 a year if motivated enough by the returns possible. In fact, most of the kids in this prestigious private school probably wasted $2,000 a year on stuff that was burning a hole in their closet. So, for starters, this book is for young people. It will show you the enormous power of investments made early in your life. Many of my kids have come back to tell me that they are setting up an investment plan, stimulated by that one class.

The Importance of Time and Age Differences

There are two other groups, parents of young children and grandparents, for whom this book should be helpful. In presenting the data for 17—and 18-year-old high school seniors, it was painfully obvious to me how much they lost in those 17 years. Had their parents started even a modest investment program for them at birth, the potential returns of 60 or 70 years, as opposed to 50 years, explode. So the second group that this book should help is parents of young children who want to start them on the way to a wealthy retirement at a young age.

Grandparents often spend time and money on their precious grandchildren, lavishing them with presents and attention. A grandparent, who would like to leave a legacy for a beloved grandchild, could set up an investment plan at an early age. A modest investment can make a real impact that their grandchildren will remember and enjoy many years after the grandparent leaves.

What about the middle-aged investor? Is all hope lost? Clearly, the impressive returns in this plan depend on time, and the less time you have, the less the eventual result. I will include sections on 10-, 20-, 30-, and 40-year returns, and the investor will have to make his or her own judgment. But frankly, the shorter time you have until retirement, the lower the expected return and the more volatile that return might be. Volatility and risk both decrease with time.

In Chapters 12 and 14, I will look at the potential for life extension in the 21st century and its impact on investment returns. While no one knows what is going to happen in the future, it is likely that anyone under the age 40 today will have a much longer life span than her parents or grandparents. A longer life may mean an older retirement age, more years in retirement to support, and more of the critical element that makes investment compounding so powerful, time.

Amateurs and Professional Investors

Many "professional" investors turn their noses up at "long-term" investors. It is only natural. *Wall Street* depends on trading, and long-term investors do not trade a lot. The "professionals" will hate it if this book turns traders into long-term investors. It isn't that *Wall Street* tries to hide the power of compound rates of return. On the contrary, they often tout the long-term in stock investing. Most brokers have wall charts that show the dramatic results of $1 invested in some market average, usually the Dow Jones Industrial Averages in 1926, and what it would have grown to by the year 2000. Almost every mutual fund sends out reports and prospectus that include charts of the value of $10,000 invested in their fund at birth or 20 years ago. These charts show exactly how well an investor would have done with an investment in the fund.

There are three major issues they do not highlight. To get the return cited, you must have invested $10,000 to start and reinvested all distributions in added fund shares or stock. That means that you would have had to pay any dividends and capital gains taxes out of other money. The second issue that they do not explain is the impact of inflation on your investment. The $10,000 you invested years ago would have purchased a lot more goods and services at the mall at the start date than it would many years later. You need an increase in value just to keep up with inflation. I don't blame the funds for showing it this way. They can't tell what your individual tax rate was. They are not responsible for inflation, but they do overstate the values described by not, at least, recognizing this fact. This book has many figures that also do not adjust for inflation. You will be able to see the raw pure power of compound rates of return. In Chapter 13, I will show how to adjust those returns to reflect inflation in the past and theoretical inflation in the future. An investor who invested $1,000 in Philip Morris in 1957 is still delighted that his or her investment is worth over $6 million today even if it is not adjusted for inflation.

The final and most critical point that most professionals will ignore is that the returns cited in those charts and graphs depend on an investor who bought and held and held and held. In Chapter 16, I will discuss the impact of trading on total returns. They are significant, and *Wall Street* professionals live from trading. They cannot get rich off investors who buy and hold. They may try to convince you that a well-formed plan of trading would maximize your return, allow you to beat the market averages. Their claims are dubious at best. Every study that I have come across shows that professionals cannot beat the market averages over a long period of time, and this book is about investing over time. Some market professionals can beat the market averages for a few years or during either up or down markets. But the truth is that any professional who can consistently beat the market in good times and in bad would be legend. There are only a few legends in the investment field, and most of them are researchers, not practitioners. Warren Buffett and Peter Lynch are two who are famous precisely because they were able to beat the market averages for many years. But even they have not yet done it for 50, 60, or 70 years. I readily admit that if you can find someone to advise you on some trading system that beats the averages over half century, even if they only do it by a small margin, the rewards would be great. But I am doubtful that it is possible. The real point is that you don't have to look. You can do-it-yourself with the knowledge and techniques that you will learn from this book.

Experienced Investors, Market Trading, and Speculation

If you are an experienced investor who has the funds to afford trying speculative investments or market timing, I have no objection. I do it myself. *But first fund your retirement.* I have been investing for over 50 years, trading, speculating, and trying to find some "system" that beats the market averages. I haven't found it yet, but I admit that I am still looking. I only wish I had discovered the power of compound rates of return years ago. It is the one method that I have found that clearly works over the long haul. I have done all right on my own but nothing to compare to an amateur investor, who bought a good stock or fund, reinvested all the distributions, and held and held and held. I still speculate with some of my capital. I love technology stocks, biotech and nanotech stocks, and I encourage anyone who wants to take a "flyer" on them, just don't do it with your retirement money. That is what this book is about. Fund your retirement first.

It is a good idea for experienced investors to divide their investing dollars into two groups. First, your retirement fund would include, depending on your age, some funds invested for the long run. Second, your normal investment funds would include your speculative investing, your fixed income (bonds) investments using some form of asset allocation described elsewhere. This book is about the power of long-term investing, and it will focus largely on that portion of your investment dollars that you decide to set aside for retirement. Once you are satisfied with your investment retirement plan, be my guest—speculate to your heart's content. If you make millions, your retirement fund may end obsolete, but if you fail in speculative investing, you will have this plan to fall back on. In some ways, it is your backup plan or your insurance policy.

How to Read and Use This Book?

I admit that one purpose of this book is to get you enthusiastic about long-term investing. It is my experience that few people understand its power, even though other authors have described it. Don't buy and read this book unless you are prepared to make some sacrifice to become a millionaire or better someday. Everyone can do it, but you must be willing to act. You must be willing to open accounts, get a job, sacrifice some

—

spending, make some decisions, live through the natural ups and downs of the stock market, maintain discipline, and systematically carry out your plan through thick and thin. If the future resembles the past, it will not take a big sacrifice to make a huge impact on your life someday. But you do have to make a sacrifice.

I hope to motivate young people, like my Economics class students, to begin saving and investing early in life. I want parents and grandparents to start investment programs for their children's and grandchildren's retirements instead of just their college fund. I hope to motivate employees to fund their 401Ks, Individual Retirement Accounts (IRAs), or other retirement plans. I would like this book to stimulate millions of people who have little or no investment experience to begin stock investing and to realize that they can succeed in it without becoming an investment "pro." I hope that they will adopt long-term stock investing and secure for themselves a better future and a richer and more meaningful retirement.

Read the book slowly and carefully. Do not skim. Make sure that you understand each chart or graph before you continue to the next one. I have tried to make them as simple as possible, but some of them do need a careful reading of the text. The reason this is important is that your success in fulfilling this plan will depend partially on your understanding and commitment to the power of compound rates of return. I strongly suggest that those of you who are competent users of computer spreadsheets try to reproduce some of the data yourself on your own spreadsheets. It is easy to do. You can take a 50-, 60-, or 70-year or more models and calculate the return of a $1,000 investment that compounds for 11% using a spreadsheet. I know that for me, doing this was an eye-opener. It is one thing to see the results of investment years presented in a chart, like mutual funds do, but another and more powerful presentation comes when you do-it-yourself on your own computer. If you are not computer literate, you can still reproduce the results with a paper, pencil, and some elementary math skills. Take a columnar pad and write down an initial investment at the top of the first column. Then calculate a percentage return to compound, showing how much the investment would have produced in the first year. Then do the second year. Figure 1C shows you the first 5-year and then 10-year increments in such a chart. You finish it all the way to 70 years and include every single year. Show the return and the total, and you will convert to a committed long-term investor in a way that I could never achieve. Don't delay. Do it now. Read this book carefully and start your own plan. It is your life, your future, and your retirement.

—

FIGURE 1C Compound Rates of Return

Initial Investment, $10,000 Compounded at 11%		
Year	Return	Total
Year 0		$10,000
Year 1	$1,100	$11,100
Year 2	1,221	$12,321
Year 3	1,355	$13,676
Year 4	1,504	$15,180
Year 5	1,670	$16,850
Year 10		$31,060
Year 20		$80,620
Year 30		$228,920
Year 40		$650,010
Year 50		$1,845,650
Year 60		$5,240,570
Year 70		$14,880,019

I want to make every American a millionaire!

CHAPTER 2

Long-Term Investing— What Does It Mean?

Long-Term Investing

There is no formal definition of long-term investing. Investment experts will often talk about long-term as if it is a few years, maybe 5 years. The Internal Revenue Service defines a long-term capital gain as one held for more than 1 year. I am going to stress the really long-term, 50 years or more. It is the focus of this book. There is nothing wrong with short-term investing. There are many sources that an investor can find if he or she is interested in short-term movements in the stock market, and there are many different theories about how to make money using short-term movements in stock prices. In fact, most of the advice that you get from financial sources, newspapers, magazines, television, and the Internet is what I would call short-term advice. They are looking at stock investments that will move in the coming months or a few years at best. Value investors look for stocks that seem undervalued based on inherent aspects of the company right now. If they are right, and the market recognizes that they are right, they are rewarded over the coming months and years with a disproportionate gain in their investment's price. Momentum investors look for shorter moves using short-term historical trends to predict where a stock price might move next.

I watch TV quite a lot, read a lot of print material, and study Internet sources, and I cannot find an investment analyst who looks at potential stock or company performance over the "really" long run. When have you heard a financial analyst comment on the potential of Procter & Gamble over the next 50 years or even 10 years? If I went on a financial channel and talked about the possible return an investor might earn over the next 50 years in General Electric, they would probably laugh me out of the studio. Let's face it; most investors are only interested in a quick profit. One reason for this is that most investors are not aware of the potential return to long-term investors.

It is true that some sources, in the last 10 years or so, have looked at long-term historic returns for stocks, and some of those sources are used in this book. Professor Jeremy Siegel, James P. O'Shaughnessy, and others have produced research looking at long-term returns to stock market investors. What is clear from their work is that what is successful in short—or even medium-term investing is often quite different from what works for a long-term investor.

Alternative Investment Strategies—Why Many Investment Strategies Fail?

There are an infinite number of possible investment strategies that have been proposed and tried over the years. It is interesting that if one particular investment strategy worked consistently, we would probably all know about it. And if it worked, for technical reasons, once we found out about it, it would probably not work anymore. In fact, studies that have compared various strategies or various investment advisers show that almost no one can consistently produce better results than the market averages over a long period. Advisers that do well 1 year often fall by the wayside the next year. Strategies that work better than average in up-markets often do worse than average in down markets. Rarely, do we find a single investment adviser or investor who can consistently get it right. Peter Lynch was one of the best, the famous longtime manager of the Fidelity Magellan Fund. Lynch is famous today precisely because he was able to produce above-average results for over a decade. But even in Lynch's case, it is hard to tell whether he could have kept up his returns for 30 or 40 years or more. After all, remember, there are thousands of investment advisers, gurus, who claim to know all the answers, and, in any given year, the stock market or individual stocks can only go two ways: up or down. If 50% of the investment professionals who forecast future market moves predict the market will go up and 50% predict it will go down, half of them will be right in any given year or time period, even if they just flip a coin. Predicting correctly for 1 year is not that unusual, but being able to do it year after year consistently for many years is very difficult, perhaps impossible. It will behoove investors to remember there has been a long upward bias in stock prices. It is not surprising that more investment pros are "bulls" and advise the market will go up. They know the history.

As you can tell, I am skeptical there is a strategy or an adviser who can consistently beat the market averages. Maybe I will be proven wrong in the future, but I am sure that if such a beast exists, we will all find out. We will all be paying to get him or her to invest our money for us.

Long-Term Stock Investing

If it turns out that I am right and beating the market averages is purely random, then what is a scientific investor to do? The truth is that investors can do very well just achieving the market averages if they are patient and have significant time. Investing for the long-term means committing funds for many years. It means looking for investment vehicles, stocks, and funds that will produce at least average returns for many years, decades. It means staying committed through good times and inevitably through bad times. This book will show investors the importance of preserving their investment plans when the stock market goes down, when there is a "bear" market. In fact, the success of long-term investing depends on the investor doing simple things. A critical one is to maintain your investments, keep investing and reinvesting even when the markets are performing badly.

Long-term investing means that we do not attempt to time the market. We do not attempt to get out of the market when we think it is going down and then get back in when we think it is going up. Statistically, an investor can dramatically improve his or her performance if he or she gets out of the market before the downturns and gets into the market just before the upturns. I don't believe that this strategy works in reality. I have seen no evidence there is anyway or anybody who can do this consistently and make money. I believe that a long-term strategy of buy and hold and hold and hold will always defeat a market timer over time.

History shows, and this book will confirm, that we don't need market timing or other short-term strategies to do very, very well in the stock market. I know there is a gambling attraction to picking stocks for short-term movements or trying to time the market. Many of us love getting a blackjack at the tables in Vegas, and we also love buying a $10 stock that moves to $20. But just like gambling, it doesn't work consistently. Just like gamblers, stock investors, stockbrokers, and others love to brag about their winners and ignore their losers. But in the long run, Vegas gamblers lose and short-term stock investors underperform the market averages, no matter what they tell you. But unlike Vegas, stock investing for most of us is not gambling, it is investing, and results do matter. Intelligent and informed stock investing can make your retirement years much more enjoyable. They can make your children's or grandchildren's lives more comfortable and less stressful. This is important stuff.

The Ultimate and Surest Wealth Creator—Time

There is only one sure wealth creator that I have come across. I didn't discover it myself; others discovered it years ago and led me to it, including Albert Einstein and some high school seniors that I had in Economics class in 1992. The best, ultimate, and surest wealth creator is simply time. Chapter 5 will introduce you to the power of a concept called "compound rates of return." Chapter 6 will show you some results from stock market investing in the past. Other chapters will show you several factors that are ignored or overlooked by short-term investors, like dividend reinvestment, tax avoidance or deferral, patience, and a different criterion for long-term stock or fund selection than is appropriate for short-term investing.

Does *Wall Street* Hide the Power of "Buy and Hold" and Hold and Hold?

It isn't fair to argue that *Wall Street* hides the power of buy and hold. As noted in Chapter 1, almost every stockbroker in the country has a Dow Jones stock chart that shows what a dollar invested in the famous averages would have produced for 60-80 years. Almost every mutual fund shows, in their annual report, what a theoretical investment, usually $10,000, in their fund would have produced since inception or for a long period of time. So *Wall Street* doesn't hide the power of long-term investing; they just don't stress it. They don't make clear how an average investor can take advantage of the returns those wall charts clearly display. After all, most brokers make their money from trading. An investor who invests his or her money once and merely holds his or her investment, patiently reinvesting all distributions, for 50, 60, or 70 years is not very profitable. So, in a sense, *Wall Street* advertises the long-term returns available in the stock market without telling the average investor how these returns were accomplished. Those Dow charts, those mutual fund annual statements show you the power of buying and holding and holding and holding. Trading stocks did not produce the returns on those charts. I will include a chapter on trading and the impact trading costs, even for a successful trader, have on long-term returns. In a nutshell, even small costs like commissions, taxes on distributions, or slightly reduced rates of return can have a big impact on final results for a long-term investor.

So the real reason that *Wall Street* is, at best, ambivalent about long-term results in the stock market is that long-term investing conflicts with what makes *Wall Street* professional's money—trades. No matter how good you think your adviser or broker is, always remember that his or her interests are fundamentally different from yours.

You Don't Have to Be an Expert

One point I want to impress on readers who do not consider themselves investment savvy is that you don't have to be an expert to do well in the stock market. In fact, I would argue that your lack of knowledge and experience might just be a benefit. The truth is that it is easy to get an investment performance that mimics the market average. And the market average, as you will see, has produced great results over the long run. Informed investors always think that they know more than the markets do. At one point in my life, years and years ago, I owned a fast-food franchise. I knew nothing about running a fast-food franchise, and all the other franchisees in our chain were experienced in running fast food. They knew everything. I knew nothing. Because I knew nothing, I followed the franchisor's instructions, their manual, and everything else they told me to do to the letter. I didn't deviate. Unlike most of the other franchisees, I did not think I knew how to run a fast-food franchise better than my franchisor. I followed the book to the tee and ended with one of the best run, most profitable franchises in the entire chain. To some degree, long-term investing may be like my franchise example. Experienced investors can't help themselves. They have to market time, use some form of technical analysis, pick stocks based on short-term information and stock tips, and ignore the principles of long-term investing. If you are an amateur investor, do not despair. You will likely do better than most of the pros. All you need is a little knowledge and some guts and determination. I hope this book will supply it.

There are a lot of tables in this book. Don't let that intimidate you. I wanted to include some redundant information to convince the skeptical.

And there will be many skeptics and critics, I am sure. I try to show multiple examples of return possibilities for both mutual funds and stocks with data at different rates of return and different time periods. This means that this book will inevitably have many graphics. I have tried to make the data as understandable as possible for an amateur. If you are not comfortable reading tables and graphs, don't let that deter you. Read the text materials and even without understanding each and every figure, you will be able to take action. It is not hard, and your judgment in investing is just as good as any professionals or mine.

CHAPTER 3

How Hard Is It to Become a Millionaire?

How Many Millionaires Are There?

One of the interesting questions to ask is just how hard is it to become a millionaire in the United States? One of the problems in answering this question is that there is no clear definition of what constitutes a millionaire. Some use $1 million in assets (things of value that you own), some use $1 million in net worth (your assets minus your liabilities or amounts that you owe), and some use $1 million in income. There are even calculations of millionaires that do not include your home or only include liquid investment assets, assets that you might sell and convert to cash quickly. One issue to address at the beginning when talking about wealth is whether you mean wealth in income or wealth in assets (possibly net worth). They are not the same. It is possible to be wealthy in assets but not in income or to have a large income with little or no assets. Many well-off Americans are in one position or another. We have more reliable information on income than we do on wealth because of the Internal Revenue Service. Every taxpayer must report his or her income to the IRS each year, but no taxpayer is required to report his or her net worth to anyone until he or she dies. It isn't that important for our purposes, but you should realize that definitions vary and one person's millionaire may be in someone else's middle class.

There is an added point that we must keep in mind when measuring the number of millionaires in a country. The numbers used are all based on someone's survey. There are no official counts of all the millionaires in the United States. These figures are not of the same type and quality as stock market numbers or dividends. They are all based on projections from surveys that have ranges and error levels just like political polls in campaigns.

As Yogi Berra said, "A nickel isn't worth a dime anymore," a million dollars is not what it used to be. Millionaires were rare 100 years ago, and the prices of the goods and services that we buy have gone up in the last century. Current prices are about 11 times what they were in 1926, for instance. Again, price data depend largely on surveys, and there are complicated issues with how they are measured that are beyond the scope of this book. For practical purposes, we can assume that it would take roughly $11 million today to be the equivalent of a millionaire in 1926.

Merrill Lynch and Capgemini conduct one of the most widely used surveys of millionaires each year.[2] The latest survey suggests there are almost 2.5 million households in the United States that meet their definition of millionaire. They use a definition of millionaire that includes financial assets, excluding home real estate, at over $1 million dollars. If we accept the Capgemini definition, it means that about 2.3% of American households are millionaires. To show you how difficult wealth calculations are, another well-respected organization, the Spectrem Group, estimates there are 7.5 million millionaire households in the United States.[3] Their survey also excludes the value of one's primary residence but includes other real estate holdings and second homes. Another survey lists 4 million households, and a fourth lists the ranks of millionaires at 3.8 million, and another, TNS Financial Services, lists 8.9 million millionaire households.[4] When you consider there are somewhere between 110 million and 125 million households (depending on how you count households) in the United States, you can see that it is not that common for an American to become a millionaire. The estimated statistics that I used in my Economics class are portrayed in Figure 3A1.

—

FIGURE 3A1 Millionaires in the United States

Percent of Households	Net Worth Exceeds
.76%	$1,000,000
0.42%	$5,000,000
0.20%	$15,000,000

Capgemini's latest world survey in 2005 of millionaires[5] worldwide shows 7.4 million households with financial assets of between $1 million and $5 million. It shows 745,000 households worldwide with financial assets between $5 million and $30 million, and 78,000 households worldwide with financial assets of over $30 million.

For our purposes, this data is as good as we are ever going to get. It is clear that your chances of getting to $1 million, however you want to calculate it, are on the order of 5% or less. Your chances of getting to $5 or $10 million are less than 1%. If you are not in line to become a millionaire already, your chances are even less since a significant number of millionaires, perhaps 20%, are millionaires from inherited wealth. The inherited wealth factor does reduce the average person's chances to become a millionaire. However, in another way, it is comforting to note that most millionaires are self-made, and if they can do it, why can't you?

The Federal Reserve Bank (FED) does a survey of family wealth every few years, and the statistics are excerpted in Figure 3A2.

FIGURE 3A2 Federal Reserve Bank Survey of Consumer Finances, Selected Net WorthData, 2004, United States

Median net worth	$93,100
Mean net worth	$448,200

To understand the data in Figure 3A2, we need to understand the difference between mean and median. It is simple. The median is the midpoint. It is as if you listed every household in the United States in order from poorest to richest and just selected the one in the middle. The median means that exactly half of the households in the country have a net worth of less than $93,100 and half of the households have a net worth of more than $93,100. The mean is a different measure. It adds up all the net worth in our list and divides by the number of households listed to get us an average. Both measurements are trying to get us some idea of where the middle is, and still, they differ significantly. When you think about it, the reason is simple. If your net worth is in the bottom half, below $93,100, there is only so far you can fall. With certain notable exceptions, your net worth can only fall to zero. But if you are in the top half, over $93,100, your net worth can be almost anything, for some that means billions. If there were three people in the country and their net worth's were 0, $93,100, and $1 billion, the median would still be $93,100, but the average of the three or the mean would be a little over $448 million. So what these figures tell us is there are many people in the upper half who have net worth's that are significant and you want to be one of them. They also tell us that a large part of the population has no significant saving and is dependent on social security and employer retirement plans to fund their retirement. This state of affairs is preventable. It is sad when you consider that a small investment made at an early age can leave an investor with a much more comfortable retirement. I am convinced the only reason that most of the households in the lower half do not become millionaires is that they were unaware of the potential returns available. To correct this, all they need is a little knowledge, motivation, and enough time.

A large focus of this book will be on these people, those whose net worth is below average, mean, or median. I want to show them that with time, a little discipline, and a basic amount of information that everyone can become a millionaire by whatever definition.

How Did They Do It?

Trying to figure out the best way to become a millionaire is a tricky business. In fact, trying to figure out how someone became a millionaire is even trickier. I tried to do it for myself, and it is impossible. How much of my current net worth is due to business ownership, real estate, stocks and bonds, or other stuff is almost impossible to calculate even if you are privy to the data. You would have to trace each source of income and see what happened to it. My best estimate would be that I made about 20% of my current net worth from real estate, principally home ownership, and the balance 80% divided about equally between investing and my business, including the sale of businesses.

There are good books about millionaires in the bookstore. Most of them try to use whatever data or information they have on millionaires to tell you how to become one. Thomas Staley and William Danko surveyed American millionaires, and their broad occupation categories were[6]

Business Owner/Entrepreneur	32%
Corporate Executive	16%
Attorney	10%
Physician	9%

Surveys like this tell us only a little about how they got there. Owning your own business, becoming an entrepreneur is clearly one of the favored occupations for millionaires. Corporate executive is another closely related way, and becoming an attorney or a doctor is a third way. One source lists the investment profile of millionaires that is given in Figure 3B1, which I am reproducing directly from his book.

FIGURE 3B1[7] The Investments of Millionaires: Publicly Traded Stock versus Other Financial Assets

Net Worth Average	$1-$2 Million	$5-$10 Million	$10 Million+
Publicly traded stock	16.8%	23.6%	26.4%
Private/closely held	8.5%	15.8%	28.3%
Bonds	8.8%	12.4%	12.4%
Cash/equivalents	7.5%	4.1%	2.3%
Loans/receivables	3.2%	3.8%	3.1%
Equity in other business	2.7%	3.8%	6.1%
Partnerships	1.1%	3.1%	4.1%
Investment real estate	18.1%	15.1%	11.0%
Total	66.7%	82.3%	93.7%
Total minus public stock	49.9%	58.7%	67.3%
Net worth average	$1,471,000	$6,809,000	$27,917,000

The data in Figure 3B1 are out-of-date but still interesting. It looks like the richer you are, the more likely it is that you own publicly traded stock. Over 26% of financial assets of the $10 million net worth millionaires consist of publicly traded stock compared to fewer than 17% for the $1-$2 million crowd. The odds that you have stock in a privately held corporation or take part in a partnership in a business increase dramatically with added wealth. Bond holdings also go up slightly with more wealth.

In general, publicly traded stock accounted for around 25-28% of the financial assets of millionaires. Only 8% of millionaires inherited at least half of their wealth. Most (92%) are married and almost all (97%) own their own home. Almost all (90%) are college graduates and more than half (52%) hold advanced degrees.[8]

You Can Do It, Go for It!

There are many ways to become a millionaire. The easiest and surest way is to inherit it, but many of you may not be in a position to do so. In fact, if you are waiting for a relative to die hoping to become wealthy, be careful. Elderly people do funny things with their money. Sometimes, they simply spend it or make foolish investment decisions; often, they fall prey to hustlers who steal most of it, and sometimes, they change their minds about whom they want to leave their money to. A new marriage, new grandchildren, or a whole host of other things can change people's minds about heirs. I know several wealthy people who simply lost their money through bad investments or bad luck while their heirs waited to inherit. My message is simple—don't depend on it. Implement the investment plan in this book and view any inheritance as your bonus.

Most millionaires get there the old-fashioned way, they work smart and they work hard. Making millions by starting a business is one of the most satisfying ways you can do it. I encourage everyone to try. But you need to be practical about your chances. Hard work and skill alone are not enough to make you rich. You also need some luck. Again, use the plan in this book as your backup plan. This is the plan that will make you a millionaire at retirement if all else fails. While many people have visions of starting a business and making a fortune, it is not easy to do. Many fail and often, beaten down, they give up on making a fortune and settle for a steady job. There is nothing wrong with a job, but most Americans are living from paycheck to paycheck and with a family to support, so starting a business can be an impossible dream.

Another method that can make you millions is to climb the corporate ladder and become a top executive in a major public corporation. CEOs and CFOs make much money in corporate America today, and the rewards for corporate success can be staggering. But, again, remember that for every corporate CEO, there are thousands competing for these plum positions. Also, corporate life is not for everyone, and talented individuals sometimes find it difficult to succeed in the unavoidable bureaucratic atmosphere that exists.

There are investors who get rich through investments. Famous ones like Warren Buffett come to mind. I encourage anyone who wants to make money from investments to pursue it. But again, to be sensible, there are few Warren Buffetts, and the probabilities are not on your side. I am going to advise investors to view the plan in this book as being separate from your regular speculative investments. This is your retirement fund, and you need to treat it differently. Keep a separate record of it, don't mix it in with your regular investments, and always fund this investment plan first. If you want to do some short-term speculative investments, fine. Just fund your retirement plan first, and you will be able to speculate with more confidence. If you don't have enough funds to do both, wait, be patient. Do your retirement plan first and speculate later when you have extra investment funds.

If you want to become a millionaire, there is no best way, only several ways, and you should pursue as many avenues as possible. This book should be viewed as one of those avenues. It is one that almost everyone can aim for and allows an individual another great opportunity to become a millionaire besides the ones listed above.

The truth is that any of the methods listed above can succeed, but all have a low probability of succeeding. No plan is foolproof, but using the one in this book probably has a much higher likelihood of success than any other plan you can come up with. In Chapter 29, I go into more detail about the possibilities that this plan won't work. I want you to be realistic. But if you look at most of the obstacles in Chapter 29, they are all long shots. The truth is that using this plan has the probabilities on your side. You don't need miracles; you don't need luck or special skills. What you need the most is for the U.S. economy to continue along the same road for the next 50, 60, or 70 years that it has for the last 60 years. You are not asking a lot. It might be worse in the future, and some experts are even predicting it. But no one knows for sure, and it is more likely the economy will be better in the future than it has in the past. Personally, I think that it is highly likely that the future for stock investors will be better than the past. If you want to view this plan as gambling, you are gambling with the odds in your favor. You can't do that in Vegas.

Your Backup Plan

Statistically, we have seen that the odds of making millions on your own are stacked against you. That doesn't mean you should not try, but I want you to have an insurance policy, a backup plan. This book describes your backup plan to become a millionaire. Think of it that way. Go about your business, live your life to the fullest, and use this plan to insure you're arriving where you want to be when you reach an age at which you can no longer continue to chase your dreams. In fact, use this plan to free you to be able to follow your dreams and live the life you want now. This plan says that you can live anyway you want, and if you fund this plan, no matter how successful or unsuccessful you are for the rest of your life, you can still end your life as a millionaire.

CHAPTER 4

How You Can Make Yourself, Your Children, or Your Grandchildren Millionaires?

What Does It Mean to Be a Millionaire?

The idea of becoming a millionaire has always been an American dream. When Americans dreamed about becoming millionaires during the earlier part of the 20th century, it implied a standard of living that seemed unimaginable to most. Only the superrich, the Rockefellers, the Morgans, or other famous families, lived a life of elaborate mansions, servants to care for every need, and the ability to have and do everything that money can buy. It was a lifestyle only imagined in the movies or in the novels. In the 21st century, billionaires have taken over from millionaire to represent the truly superrich, and billionaires are few and far between. *Forbes* magazine ranks the world's billionaires, and in 2006, they listed 793 individuals that have a net worth of at least 1 billion dollars.[9] Two Americans, Bill Gates and Warren Buffett, both familiar names in the investment community, top the billionaires' list. Gates was and continues to be the principal shareholder in Microsoft, a company familiar to everyone that uses a computer. Buffett is well known within the investment community and is increasingly known outside of it. Buffett is the principal shareholder in a company called Berkshire Hathaway, which is a holding company for close to 40 operating companies. Buffett's investment philosophy is called value investing, and a few books have been written about him and his philosophy of investing. In fact, Buffett's ideas on investing fit well into the concept of long-term investing. He buys companies or interests in companies that he perceives are undervalued but have great potential. Buffett holds investments for long periods of time, which will be a theme in this book.

Becoming a millionaire or even a multimillionaire in today's world means something different from years ago. It means a more comfortable life but nothing on the order imagined about millionaires by Americans in bygone eras. Inflation and the increasing demands of a more sophisticated lifestyle have changed the idea of being a millionaire substantially. But is it still important? Of course, it is. Most Americans save little during their lifetime. The demands of raising a family in a consumer-oriented, competitive society make it difficult for the average person to take money from their paycheck and do anything except consume it. The motivation to save, even a little bit, seems lacking. The median net worth of Americans in 2004 was only $93,100, not that much money[10]. A luxury car can cost that much in today's world. So most Americans live from paycheck to paycheck and depend for their retirement on company pension plans and social security. Company pension plans are looking more and more problematic, and as we have heard so many times, social security may be in jeopardy in the next 20-30 years. The arrival of IRAs 30 years ago and the increasing popularity of company-sponsored retirement plans like 401Ks that employees can take part in has opened up new possibilities for the average American. Still, most Americans do not fully fund these plans even when they are eligible and are ignoring the potential problems with pensions and social security. A solution to the social security problem does not seem to be happening despite many studies and varied proposals. Voters are not turned on and do not seem worried about it.

I have a theory about Americans' unwillingness to save and invest, fully fund their 401Ks or IRAs. I think that most Americans believe the only way investing can make a significant difference in their lives, especially at retirement, is if they start investing with a whole lot of money. "It takes money to make money" is a common American saying. Investing a few hundred a year or even a few thousand dollars can't make much difference, so why do it? Why deprive myself and my family of things we want, the vacation we want to take, or that more expensive luxury SUV when saving and investing small amounts of money can't make a difference? I hope this book will change this attitude. Readers will find out that you can become a millionaire without investing much money if you just do it the right way and have enough time. If the average American realized the potential of even $1,000 invested over a long period of time, he or she might just be willing to sacrifice some small luxuries now to have a much better lifestyle sometime in the future.

Americans love their children and grandchildren. Parents and grandparents are often willing to sacrifice to give their children and grandchildren the things that they want—luxuries that have almost become necessities in today's world. Many parents and grandparents invest for their children's education or so they can purchase a car when they get to the legal driving age. Only a few, usually the already superrich, ever think or plan about their children or grandchildren's retirement. The truth is that much of the stuff we buy for our children and grandchildren is forgotten quickly, things that were passionately needed at the time become lost memories as the months and years go by. With all the confusion surrounding future retirement plans, investing a modest amount of money for your children and grandchildren would leave them with a legacy that they will come to appreciate as the years go by. Investing for retirement at birth is a powerful, powerful strategy, and it does not take much money to make a significant difference. Ten years ago, there was an article in the *Wall Street Journal* about how to make your grandchildren millionaires. It did not get a whole lot of notice, and it concluded that a parent or grandparent who invested $2,000 a year for just 6 years would make their grandchild a millionaire at retirement. Figure 4A2 shows that a grandparent who invested only $1,000 at his or her grandchild's birth in a mutual fund that tracks the S&P 500 may have given the grandchild a gift of $2,399,095 at age 70. If the grandchild lives to 100 (see Chapter 12), that $1,000 investment could be worth an astounding $67,396,805. About $10,000 invested at birth turns into almost $24 million at age 70 and over $670 million at age 100. This assumes that the grandparent invested the $1,000 in a manner that allowed the investment to avoid or defer taxes, reinvested all distributions from the fund in additional fund shares and that in the next 70-100 years the S&P achieves exactly the same compound rate of return it did from 1946 to 2004. Figure 4A1 shows the investment amounts required for a teenager to become a millionaire by age 70. The second column assumes that they will invest every year for 5 years and then stop and never invest again. The third column assumes that they will invest every year until retirement. The investments in both columns produce a $1 million + retirement. An investor who wants to finish with $2 million or $10 million can simply multiply the investment amount by 2 or 10. As an example, a 13-year-old would have to invest $1,900 every year to be worth $10 million at retirement.

I hope that this book will bring you the motivation to begin a long-term investment plan for yourself, if you have the time, and also for your children and grandchildren.

FIGURE 4A1 Age and Investment Required to Become Millionaire

Age	Invest 5 Years and Stop	Invest Every Year Until Retirement
13	$400	$190
14	$490	$210
15	$550	$240
16	$610	$265
17	$685	$295
18	$765	$330
19	$860	$365

FIGURE 4A2 $1,000 and $10,000 Onetime Investments at Birth

Investment at Birth	Value at Age 70	Value at Age 100
$1,000	$2,399,095	$67,396,805
$10,000	$23,990,950	$673,68,050

You Need Time and Patience

While I can't promise you the riches imagined in those 1930s movies, I am here to prove to you, in many different ways, that long-term investing can make your life much more comfortable and even make you rich. Investors who did not even realize what they were doing have done it in the past. Often investors held their investments for long periods of time out of ignorance or inertia. They weren't smart enough to try to trade stocks with the "big boys." Sometimes, early pension investment plans have made even janitors millionaires. They simply held for many years. Becoming wealthy using long-term investing is possible, and, in fact, I would argue it is probable. You do need to do a few simple things

—

correctly, and I will make them clear later in this book, but you don't need to become an investment pro or expert. You don't need to seek out investment advice from brokers or other professionals. You don't need to talk to anyone; in fact, it is my preferred method. You can do it entirely on the Internet or through the mail. I will lay it out step-by-step to make it easy for you. All you need is a little determination, patience, and the willingness to do it. Patience is so critical that I will include a section on its importance later on in this book.

CHAPTER 5

The Power of Compound Rates of Return

Albert Einstein is reputed to have said that the reality of compound rates of return was the most amazing discovery of all time. The power of compounding is truly astounding as I hope to show in this chapter. If you understand the difference between simple rates of return and compound rates of return, it can change your life. This is the most important concept in this book. The idea is usually well understood by investment professionals and experienced investors, but I often find that even professionals are astounded when they see the actual potential of this simple concept.

Understanding Rates of Return

Whenever you save or invest money, you usually do so with the expectation that you will earn something for your effort. You don't have to save anything; you can simply spend everything you have at the mall. When you save money, you are choosing to deprive yourself of the immediate enjoyment that you would get from spending the money. There are two major reasons you would select saving instead of spending. One is to "save up for a rainy day," save money now in case you might need it at a later time. The second reason you might save money is if you can earn some additional money for the effort. That extra money that you can earn from saving is what is called a return. We can look at the return that you might get for saving and investing $1,000 in simple dollar terms. If you earn $50 on $1,000 of saving during the next year, we might say that your return was $50. But since many people save and invest in many different investments at different rates of return and in different amounts, it can be difficult to compare one investment to another just using dollar returns. Someone else might have invested $200,000 and earned $10,000 in return. The idea of a "rate" of return developed to allow us to compare differing amounts and different investments with each other. The rate of return is simply the money earned divided by the money invested, in this case $50 divided by $1,000 for a return of 5%.

Rates of return are often expressed in yearly terms even if the savings account or investment is for more or less than 1 year. You might put $1,000 into a savings account for 6 months and earn $25 and that still amounts to about a 5% yearly rate of return. Five percent is what you would have earned if you had kept the investment for an entire year. With stock investing, the rate of return often takes two forms. First is any yearly increase in the price of the stock, and second, the cash dividend that a company might pay you as a shareholder out of their earnings. A stock that has returned a total of 10% in the past year might have paid 3% to the shareholders as a cash dividend and the balance, about 7%, occurred because the price of the stock went up.

Simple Rates of Return

The rate of return cited in the last paragraph is called simple interest. When making an investment of $1,000, you might earn a 10% return during the year. At the end of the year, you would have $100 in addition to the $1,000 you started with. You might reinvest the $1,000 again the second year to try to earn the 10% return again and take the $100 that you just "earned" to the mall and buy some new CDs or a sweater. If you invest your $1,000 and do it for years and years and always earn a 10% return, you will have the enjoyment of spending $100, money that you would not otherwise have, every year. Figure 5A1 shows some typical return results using simple interest on the left side. For example, if you invest $1,000 for 10 years and earn 8% each year, you would have $1,800, which includes the $1,000 you started with, at the end. This assumes that you keep the return in your account, your bank, or your mattress. If you earn a higher rate of return, say 14%, you would have $2,400 after 10 years, including the $1,000 you started with. The difference in return, $2,400 – $1,800 = $600, is due to the higher rate of return earned, 14% instead of 8%. If you invest the money for a longer period of time, say 60 years, you will earn a

—

much bigger return in dollars, even though the "rate" of return remains the same. And $1,000 invested at 8% produces $5,200 after 60 years and at 14% produces $9,400. Two obvious characteristics of simple rates of return are the higher the rate, the higher the return and the longer the holding period, the higher the return. This assumes that you take the return each year and simply hold it, spend it, or put it in your mattress.

FIGURE 5A1 Compound and Simple Interest Returns Illustrated: $1,000 Invested Onetime

	Simple Interest Rates			Compound Interest Rates		
Years	8%	11%	14%	8%	11%	14%
10	$1,800	$2,100	$2,400	$2,367	$2,839	$4,046
20	$2,600	$3,200	$3,800	$4,661	$8,061	$13,743
40	$3,800	$5,400	$6,600	$14,974	$64,991	$188,884
60	$5,200	$7,600	$9,400	$57,946	$523,980	$2,595,919
80	$6,600	$9,800	$12,220	$224,234	$4,225,113	$35,676,982

Compound Rates of Return

When I was in elementary school, a friend of mine came up to me one day and asked me if I knew how much money I would have if I took a single dollar and doubled it every day for a month. On the first day, $1 becomes $2, and the $2 becomes $4 on the second day, and so on. I had no idea. He told me that if I double my money every day for just 1 month, 30 days, I would have over $550 million dollars at the end of the month. I didn't believe him, and I went home and tried to take a pencil and paper and produce these results. Finally, my father had to help me, and lo and behold, my friend was right. In fact, I discovered that if you take a single penny and double it every day for 28 days, you are a millionaire. I was flabbergasted, and it made such an impression on me that I remember it clearly almost 60 years later. It seemed easy to get rich.

How can this be possible? Is it some mathematical trick? The secret is in the idea of "compound" rates of return. It is the secret that can make you, your children, or your grandchildren rich. How does this happen? Compounding works like this:

If you invest $1,000 and earn 11%, you have $1,110 at the end of the first year.

If instead of spending or putting the $110 you earned in your mattress, you reinvest the entire $1,110 and earn 11% for the second year, you now have $1,232.

If you then invest the entire $1,232 and earn 11% for the third year, you now have $1,368.

If, on the other hand, you had invested the $1,000 for 3 years and earned 11% but put the earnings in your mattress, you would now have $1,000 from the investment and $330 in the mattress for a total of $1,330, a small but significant difference of $38. Figure 5A2 shows the return for simple and compound returns by year.

FIGURE 5A2 Simple and Compound Returns at 11% Yearly

Year	Simple Interest Rate of Return			Compound Rate of Return		
	Investment	Return	Total	Investment	Return	Total
1	$1,000	$110	$1,110	$1,000	$110	$1,110
2	$0	$110	$1,220	$0	$122	$1,232
3	$0	$110	$1,330	$0	$136	$1,368
4	$0	$110	$1,440	$0	$150	$1,518
5	$0	$110	$1,550	$0	$167	$1,685
6	$0	$110	$1,660	$0	$185	$1,870
7	$0	$110	$1,770	$0	$206	$2,076
8	$0	$110	$1,880	$0	$228	$2,305
9	$0	$110	$1,990	$0	$253	$2,558
10	$0	$110	$2,100	$0	$281	$2,839
20	$0	$110	$3,200	$0	$5,222	$8,061
30	$0	$110	$4,300	$0	$14,828	$22,889
40	$0	$110	$5,400	$0	$42,102	$64,991
50	$0	$110	$6,500	$0	$119,546	$184,537
60	$0	$110	$7,600	$0	$339,443	$523,980
70	$0	$110	$8,700	$0	$963,819	$1,487,799

At the end of 3 years, compounding has earned you an added $38. It doesn't seem that significant. But look what happens to the difference between simple returns and compounding as the years pass. The right side of Figure 5A2 shows that after 20 years, the difference between reinvesting your earnings and "compounding" the return at 11% and using the mattress is now a $4,861($8,061-$3,200.) And in 40 years, compounding produces $64,991 instead of $5,400 using simple interest, and at 60 years compounding produces $523,980 instead of $7,600 for simple interest. And at 70 years, the difference is astounding: compounding a $1,000 investment at 11% produces a whopping $1,487,799 instead of a paltry $8,700 with simple interest. If you looked at 80 years at 11%, you would have over $4.2 million at the end instead of only $9,800 at simple interest. If you use a 14% rate of return, you would have over $35 million instead of $12,200, unbelievable.

Figure 5A3 shows the return on a $10,000 single investment for 70 years at 11.76% compounded. You would end with almost $24,000,000, most of it would have been lost if you spend your return each year instead of reinvesting it. Is a return like this possible? Yes, of course, it is. In fact, James O'Shaughnessy showed in his book, *What Works on Wall Street*, the average return of all stocks from 1951 to 2003, 52 years, was a hefty 11.52%, and Professor Robert Shiller's Standard and Poor's data from his website show a compound return of 11.76% for the S&P composite from 1946 to 2004. Chapter 8 has more details on long-term stock market returns.

FIGURE 5A3 Rate of Return, $10,000 Onetime Investment for 70 Years

Invest $10,000 at 11.76% per year for 70 years at simple interest	= $18,232
Invest $10,000 at 11.76% per year for 70 years compounded	= $23,990,954
Your loss by not reinvesting the return each year	= $23,972,722
Is This Possible?	
Actual compound rate of return for all stocks 1946-2004	= 11.76%[1]

The reason for these numbers is simply that with compounding, you are earning a return on the past returns as well as the return on your original investment. Your investment is "compounding." As the years go by, the return you earn on previous returns gets bigger and bigger and begins to dwarf the return earned on the original investment. We can look at the difference as a penalty that you pay for not reinvesting and compounding the return each year. In fact, as the rate of return you are earning goes up, the penalty that you pay for not reinvesting and compounding all earnings or returns gets bigger and bigger. Figure 5A4 shows the percentage of possible returns lost when you don't reinvest your earnings and let them compound. Notice that at higher rates and longer years, you can lose over 99% of the possible return because you did not reinvest the returns every year. Even after 40 years, you would lose over 90% of your potential return at 11% and almost 75% of your potential return at 8%. Without reinvesting returns for 40 years, a possible $65,001 will turn into only $5,400 at 11% and a possible $14,974 will turn into only $3,800 at 8%. Those are large losses to incur for not reinvesting the modest return each year. (A full table with more compound rates of return and years is included in Table 5A1 in the appendix.)

It is this power of compound rates of return that can make you rich. You don't need much money to become a millionaire. You do need some money, and I will address this in later chapters, but what you need most of all is a good rate of return and time, the more time the better. The rate of return is also critical, and I will deal in detail with both time and rates of return in later chapters. The important thing to consider at this point is how much can be lost if you don't save and then reinvest all returns. Most people think that to make a lot of money investing, you have to have a lot of money to invest. But the reality is with good rates of return and lots of time that saving and investing even $1,000 can mean an enormous amount of money over a long period of time.

FIGURE 5A4 Percentage of Return Lost without Compounding

Years	8% Interest Rate	11% Interest Rate	14% Interest Rate
10	23.97%	32.39%	40.68%
20	44.22%	60.31%	72.35%
40	74.62%	91.69%	96.51%
60	94.27%	98.55%	99.64%
80	98.43%	99.77%	99.97%

Albert Einstein and the Rule of 72

Albert Einstein invented a convenient and simple way to calculate the results of compound rates of return that is in common use still today. It is called the "Rule of 72." It allows you to calculate the estimated number of years that it takes for you to double your investment using only the rate of return and the number 72. It turns out that Einstein discovered that if you divide the rate of return into the number 72, you will get the estimated number of years it would take for you to double your original investment using compounding. If, for example, you are earning a 12% compound rate of return, your original investment will double in 6 years, 72 divided by 12. If you are earning a 6% compound rate of return, your original investment will double in 12 years, 72 divided by 6.

Note that if your investment is doubling in value every 6 years, it means that it will have doubled 10 times in 60 years. One $1,000 investment that doubles every 6 years is worth over $1 million in 60 years. Do the math yourself if you don't believe me. The rule of 72 is an approximate and easy way to compare rates of return and results. Here is a chart that lets you see the power of Einstein's idea.

FIGURE 5A5 Einstein's Rule of 72 Applied to a $1,000 or $10,000 Onetime Initial Investment

Yearly/Rate	Do the Math	Years to Double Investment	Millionaire After One Investment	
			of $1,000	of $10,000
4%	72 divided by 4 =	18	180 years	126 Years
6%	72 divided by 6 =	12	120 years	84 years
8%	72 divided by 8 =	9	90 years	56 years
10%	72 divided by 10	7.2	72 years	50 years
12%	72 divided by 12	6	60 years	42 years
14%	72 divided by 14	5.14	52 years	36 years
16%	72 divided by 16	4.5	45 years	32 years

The importance of the rate of return is obvious from Figure 5A5. With enough time and a high enough rate of return, it is possible to become a millionaire during your or your kid's or grandchildren's lifetime with a modest investment. Most of the rest of this book will be devoted to examining what is the surest ways for you to do it.

The Unique Advantage of Compound Rates of Return

I did not discover the power of compound rates of return. Many others, including Einstein, have commented on its strength. James

—

O'Shaughnessy in his wonderfully detailed book, *What Works on Wall Street*, and Jeremy Siegel in several books including his latest, *The Future for Investors*, confirm the basic idea, compound rates of return can make you wealthy.

The truth is there are many ways to make a million or millions of dollars. Most of them require some skill, often significant capital, a good education, and a lot of luck. The method I am going to give you in this book needs no skill, apart from reading. It might want for a little luck in that it depends on the U.S. and world economies performing in the future pretty much as they have in the past. It does require some money to invest, and the more money that you can invest early, the higher the likelihood of success, but even with a fairly small amount, you will have an excellent chance to make it. Look again at Figure 5A1. A $1,000 invested one time at 11% would bring you over $500,000 dollars in 60 years. What if you could invest more than $1,000? What if you could invest $2,000 or $1,000 a year for 10 years or for 60 years? Is 11% a realistic or likely outcome during the 21st century? What kind of investment can produce 11% or even 14% or more? What happened in the 20th century? Were these kinds of returns ever achieved in the past? All these questions will be answered later on in this book. As Albert Einstein came to realize, the stark reality of compound rates of return is a unique opportunity. Now that you understand the opportunity, all you have to do is seize it. The rest of this book will tell you how to do it.

CHAPTER 6

Why Stocks?

What Are Stocks?

This chapter and Chapter 8 will explain why stock investing provides such a unique long-term opportunity. But before I jump into it, let me be sure that everyone understands what a stock is and some fundamental characteristics of stock and stock investing.

There are many ways in which you can organize a business. You can go into business for yourself and become a sole proprietor. You can go into business with others and form a partnership. Both partnerships and sole proprietorships require little paperwork and expense at the beginning and carry with them some unique tax advantages that are not available to the other main form of business organization, a corporation.

A corporation, however, has unique capabilities. A corporation is a separate entity that is chartered by a state. It can have one owner or many. One of the unique characteristics of a corporation is the method in which it accounts for ownership. It is called stock. In a corporation, the owners of the corporation get stock to evidence their ownership. A corporation can issue any number of shares of stock from one share to millions. As the owner of stock in a corporation, you can find out how much of the business you own by dividing the total number of shares the company has outstanding into the number of shares that you own. If you are the sole owner, then you will own all the shares, no matter how many exist. That could be one share or millions of shares. If there is more than one person involved in owning the corporation, each owner buys a number of shares. Each share represents some proportionate interest in the company. So stock, or a stock certificate, simply shows how many shares that someone owns in a particular corporation. Unlike most partnerships or sole proprietorships, corporations can "go public" and sell their stock (shares) to all of us. All the companies that you see traded on the stock exchanges are corporations that issued stock, sold shares to investors, and went "public." The prices that are quoted in the newspaper or on the financial channels on TV are simply the price to buy one share of that company's stock. Microsoft trading at $30 means that you have to pay $30 for one share of stock in Microsoft. Stock is just an easy and convenient way to divide ownership in a business that is a corporation. If, for example, you own 1,000 shares of stock in a company that has 1,000,000 shares issued and outstanding, then you own 1/10th of 1% of the company, 1,000 divided by 1,000,000. This is often called an "equity" interest in the company.

Stock Market Investing and Other Investments

People have been investing in stocks for several hundred years. In the 17th century, stock investing took place in London coffeehouses. In 1761, 150 "stockbrokers" moved into a single building that was briefly called "New Jonathan's" after the most prominent stock trading coffeehouse, "Jonathan's." So investing in stock of corporations that sell their shares to the public has been around for a while.

There are other investments or investment vehicles that an individual can use with their investment dollars besides stocks. Investments in any of these involve more detailed explanations than I can offer here, but let me just comment briefly on some of the more prominent ones:

Bonds—A bond is evidence of a debt. Unlike a stock, bonds usually return a fixed interest rate each year. Unlike stock, a bond does not suggest any ownership rights. A bondholder does not own part of a company. He or she has simply lent the company money for a period of time. As an enticement to lend, the company pays the bondholder an amount of money each year called interest. Governments as well as corporations sell bonds so you can buy a bond issued by the U.S. Government, a state-issued bond or a corporate bond. Most foreign countries have the same structure in bond issuance.

Real Estate—Real estate investing involves owing property, perhaps a home, raw undeveloped land, or an income property. An investor can invest his or her savings in all kinds of property, and the techniques, advantages, and disadvantages of property ownership are beyond the scope of this book. One can own property, in a way, when you buy stock in a company that owns property.

Precious Metals—Investing in precious metals such as gold, silver, bronze, copper, and some newer metals like platinum have drawn investment interest for hundreds if not thousands of years. There are a number of methods used to invest in precious metals. You can buy and store the metal itself, or you can buy coins made of the metal. You can speculate in the futures or options markets in metals (see below). Or you can buy stock in corporations that own or mine the metals.

Commodities—An investor can invest in all kinds of useful commodities in much the same way one might invest in precious metals. You can buy the commodity outright or use the futures or options market to speculate on price movements in your favorite commodities.

Futures Market—The futures market gives an investor the mechanism to invest in precious metals and other commodities or financial instruments without owning anything. In the futures market, the investor purchases or sells a contract for delivery of the commodity at a fixed price at a given time in the future. The investor hopes to profit when the price of the commodity goes up or down, moving away from the price at which she agreed to trade at the outset. The futures market is not a place for novice investors.

Options Market—The options market gives an investor the opportunity to buy an option on a commodity, financial instrument, or even a stock. In return for the purchase price, the option holder has the right to either buy the item, or sell the item, at the agreed on price for a named period of time. Options are used widely in speculating on stocks, but, again, they are not recommended for a novice investor.

There are obviously many different things in which an investor can invest her money, including real estate. In the last section of this chapter, I will look at some of the evidence from the past that allows us to compare stock investing with some of these other forms of investing. You will see why I recommend the stock market and stocks for the long-term investor.

What Determines the Price of a Share of Stock?

Everyone wants to know what determines the price of a share of stock. There are many theories, but no one really knows the answer to this question. There are many factors that are involved in determining the price of a stock on the exchanges. Investment analysts look at earnings for a guide. The price/earnings multiple is one of the most widely used statistics in analyzing stock prices, but it cannot explain many situations. Should the price of a stock be high or low relative to earnings? Some say a low price-earnings ratio is preferred. It means the shareholder is buying more earnings for each dollar he or she pays for the stock. But a low price-earnings ratio can also mean that investors in the market do not think these earnings are going to grow much in the future. A high price-earnings ratio means that a buyer of a share of stock is paying more for each dollar of current earnings. Why would an investor do this? The answer may be that the price of the stock is high compared to its current earnings per share because the market expects that these earnings are going to grow significantly in the future.

It is clear the market is anticipating the future. The price of a share of a company's stock is a representation or compilation of what investors in the market think about the future earnings of the company. Past performance, sales, and earnings are only important to the market to the degree they represents or tell us something about the company's future. If past earnings are strong but it is clear the company has a limited future, the stock will probably look cheap to the amateur investor. Sometimes, companies with zero profits but a big potential will still sell for high prices. The recent "dot.com" era was a good example as many companies with little or no earnings sold for high prices because the market was expecting great things in the future.

When I took classes in investments back in the 1960s, the most commonly accepted method that academics used to evaluate stock prices was called the dividend stock price model. The idea is that a stock would sell for the total of its expected future dividend payments, discounted to their current value. Simply put, it means that you would sum up all the future dividends a company might pay to a shareholder, valuing the current payments more than the distant future ones. The market would price a share of stock based on its estimate of the "current value" of those future dividends. In fact, the market represents the combined judgment of all investors about what those future dividends might be. In this model, earnings are unimportant to shareholders unless they are paid out to them as dividends. Earnings do matter since it is earnings that usually allow the company to pay the dividends in the first place, but in and of themselves, earnings are meaningless in the dividend model.

No one knows for certain what factor or factors actually determine a stock's price at any given time. Clearly, in a free market, the selling price represents the compilation of supply and demand for the stock. But we also understand that the buyers and sellers in any given market have many different motivations for their actions. As attractive as it seems in theory,

—

most buyers and sellers are probably not calculating their estimates of future company dividends and discounting them to the present when they decide what price they are willing to buy or sell a stock.

A good way to look at stock prices is that stocks reward you for taking risks. Every time you invest in a stock, you are taking risks—risk of loss of capital, risk of return, and risk of volatility. The rewards that you get are the result of your being willing to take a risk. But it also seems clear that stock prices are not always rational. Stock prices tend to overshoot the mark. When things are going well, prices move higher than they should, and when things are going poorly, there seems to be no bottom. No matter what theory you subscribe to, the market is made up of human beings. Any stock price is simply the current result of the judgment of the number of human beings that are willing to buy the stock and the number of human beings that are willing to sell the stock. Sometimes, it looks irrational, but it simply is what it is. Many people thought the 50% drop in stock prices in the final months of 1929 was irrational. They may have been right, but stock prices dropped another 80% in the following 3 years.

What Is Risk? Are Stocks Risky?

An integral part of investing is an understanding of the concept of risk. Individuals view risk in all investments in different ways. One way of looking at risk is to try to understand the potential that you might lose all or part of the money that you invested. Loss of your investment is always a possibility in any investment. Another risk that investors take is the risk of volatility. That is, your investment may move up sharply or down sharply during any period of time. Sometimes, an investment can end right where you would like it to, but during the years of investing, it took you on a roller coaster of ups and downs that made you, the investor, uncomfortable. Another risk is the risk the outcome of the investment will not match the investor's expectations. You may not end with the return that you expected when you made the investment to begin with.

There are many ways in which sophisticated investors try to lessen their risk, but every investment, by definition, carries some risk. Stocks can be risky. We know of companies that failed or performed poorly and caused investors to lose money or earn less than they expected. Stock investing is considered to be riskier than bond investing, but bond investing can be risky as well. History shows that stocks are riskier in the short run than they are in the long run. Professor Jeremy Siegel, in his well-respected and thorough study of stock market returns in the United States for almost 200 years, concluded that stocks were clearly "riskier" in

—

61

the short run than fixed income investments (bonds). But over the long run (10-30 years or more), stocks are not riskier. [12]

In fact, using Siegel's data, two investment professionals wrote a book inferring that stocks were significantly undervalued in 1999 since the cash return (interest) to bondholders was higher than the cash return (dividends) to stockholders. Glassman and Hassett decided that, as Siegel pointed out, stocks in the long run were no riskier than bonds and that stocks should be sold for about 3 times the amount they were then selling for.[13] Unfortunately, the stock market took a significant dive after Glassman and Hassett's book was published.

FIGURE 6A1 MFS Mass Inv. Growth Stock Fund A[14]

Year	Net Value	Compound Rate of Return to 2005	Year	Net Value	Compound Rate of Return to 2005
1924	$10,000	9.23%	1965	$371,101	9.25%
1925	$10,760	9.25%	1966	$409,344	9.23%
1926	$13,607	9.05%	1967	$377,970	9.71%
1927	$15,085	9.03%	1968	$454,244	9.44%
1928	$19,951	8.76%	1969	$501,889	9.41%
1929	$25,649	8.52%	1970	$477,978	9.85%
1930	$23,503	8.76%	1971	$482,280	10.12%
1931	$17,290	9.34%	1972	$526,136	10.15%
1932	$9,820	10.32%	1973	$584,882	10.12%
1933	$9,479	10.53%	1974	$511,211	10.95%
1934	$12,490	10.26%	1975	$380,035	12.44%
1935	$13,902	10.24%	1976	$505,911	11.78%
1936	$18,501	9.94%	1977	$625,462	11.38%
1937	$24,008	9.67%	1978	$556,273	12.31%
1938	$16,201	10.47%	1979	$602,306	12.47%
1939	$20,130	10.27%	1980	$734,757	12.11%
1940	$19,810	10.47%	1981	$959,704	11.40%
1941	$17,990	10.81%	1982	$912,820	12.16%
1942	$16,455	11.14%	1983	$1,085,280	11.87%

1943	$18,904	11.08%	1984	$1,311,994	11.45%
1944	$23,586	10.87%	1985	$1,350,514	11.90%
1945	$28,491	10.71%	1986	$1,682,213	11.27%
1946	$37,705	10.38%	1987	$1,971,695	10.95%
1947	$35,801	10.67%	1988	$2,118,821	11.16%
1948	$36,629	10.82%	1989	$2,338,812	11.20%
1949	$37,054	11.00%	1990	$3,183,633	9.72%
1950	$44,599	10.84%	1991	$3,180,490	10.45%
1951	$56,893	10.55%	1992	$4,060,471	9.23%
1952	$69,949	10.33%	1993	$4,360,301	9.38%
1953	$80,256	10.24%	1994	$4,797,550	9.33%
1954	$80,534	10.45%	1995	$4,748,663	10.42%
1955	$123,116	9.73%	1996	$6,616,924	7.60%
1956	$153,679	9.44%	1997	$8,330,655	5.51%
1957	$171,030	9.41%	1998	$10,970,839	2.22%
1958	$151,003	9.91%	1999	$13,488,722	-0.88%
1959	$216,469	9.27%	2000	$14,427,023	-2.38%
1960	$236,247	9.28%	2001	$14,377,917	-2.88%
1961	$234,293	9.52%	2002	$12,042,968	2.04%
1962	$294,770	9.16%	2003	$9,393,444	16.70%
1963	$266,362	9.66%	2004	$11,472,953	11.51%
1964	$319,983	9.41%	2005	$12,793,272	

As part of my research for this book, I did an analysis of the oldest mutual fund in the United States, an MFS fund that was started in 1924.[15] Figure 6A1 shows the achieved compound rates of return for this long-lasting mutual fund, assuming the investor started with an investment in any given year. From 1924 to 2004, the compound yearly rate of return for the entire period was 9.23%. If our investor had launched his or her investment in 1925 instead of 1924, his or her return would have been slightly higher at 9.25% per year. An investment made in 1950 would have produced a 10.84% annual compound rate of return if held until 2005. All the returns assume the investor reinvested all distributions in added stock and paid any taxes due from other funds.

Once an investor goes back past 1995 (10 years), his or her return is never less than a compounded 8.52% and never more than 12.47%. I would have assumed that starting your investing during a market top, like the summer of 1929, would have greatly lessened the yearly return. And starting your investment during a market trough, like 1932, would have greatly increased your yearly return. An investor who had started his or her investment in 1929 would have achieved an average compound rate of return of 8.52%, while the investor who was fortunate enough to start his or her investment in this fund at the bottom of the depression in 1932 would have achieved a slightly but significantly higher 10.32%. The highest rate of return in stock market investing is reserved for investors who are willing to invest when the market is at its lowest levels. It seems clear that fearing a market top should not be a serious obstacle to investing if the investor has a long-term objective. Stocks dropped almost 90% between 1929 and 1932. Figure 6A1 also shows the weak stock market during the late 1970s and early 1980s. Beginning an investment in these years would have produced a pronounced difference in rate of return than starting one during most of the more prosperous 1990s. If we had looked at these same figures in 1937, the impact of the depression in 1932 and the recovery in 1937 would be more pronounced. As the years go by, time will sharply reduce the difference between an investor's average compound rate of return for investments launched in bull markets than those in bear markets. Figure 6A2 shows the same pattern for the Stratton Growth Fund, the mutual fund that I have held the longest.

FIGURE 6A2 Stratton Growth Fund[16] Compound Rates of Return Calculated for Starting Years 1972-2004

Year	Annual Rate of Return	Year	Annual Rate of Return
1972		1989	12.83%
1973	12.17%	1990	12.13%
1974	12.05%	1991	13.61%
1975	13.56%	1992	12.98%
1976	14.79%	1993	13.52%
1977	14.14%	1994	14.19%
1978	12.79%	1995	14.91%
1979	13.23%	1996	12.63%

—

1980	13.46%	1997	12.44%
1981	12.67%	1998	9.42%
1982	12.06%	1999	9.08%
1983	12.25%	2000	9.08%
1984	12.67%	2001	11.06%
1985	12.06%	2002	11.36%
1986	12.25%	2003	32.53%
1987	12.34%	2004	23.53%
1988	13.38%	2005	

An investor in the start-up of this fund achieved an average compound rate of return of 12.17% over the 33 years of the fund's life. Once you go back to an investment initiated before 1998, the difference in rate of return narrows to a range between 12% and 14%. I suspect that this pattern would hold true for most stock market investments. Your compound rate of return in the long run does not vary as much as you might imagine. The years, time, narrow the early differences in the long run.

The message is clear. Stocks tend to be more risky and more volatile than bonds only in the short run. And the risk in stock investing depends, to a degree, on the style of the investor. Stock market investing can be risky indeed. The good news is that it has not been that difficult to earn a strong return in the stock market and make you wealthy at retirement without taking much risk over the long run. I will give you some ideas for investing that can reduce your risk substantially, but every investor must be prepared to weather some risk of loss and/or significant volatility. An investor who cannot stomach downturns will inevitably miss out on the big benefits of the upturns. In the long run, and this book is only for long-term investors; the evidence we have points out that stock investing is not as risky as we might have imagined.

The Relationship between Risk and Return

One of the most important concepts in investing is the relationship between risk and return. In the previous section, we discussed stock prices as a reward for taking risk. There are many different types of risk, and the size of the risk an investor takes can vary dramatically. The concept of risk and return implies that for an investor to get a bigger return for his or her investment, he or she must be willing to take a bigger risk. The bigger the return you want, the bigger the risk you have to take.

—

Investments can vary all over the lot. An investor can put his or her money to work in U.S. government bonds, considered to be one of the least risky investments. The idea is that a private company, no matter how solid, is still more likely to go under than the U.S. government. If you invest your money in government bonds, the return you get each year will usually be lower than if you invest in stocks. There are two reasons for this. First, the government bond is less likely to cause an investor to lose money. Second, a government bond normally returns a fixed and stable return each year. Stock returns can vary all over the lot. You may get a 50-year average rate of return of 11% in a stock investment, but it will not return 11% every year. The 11% is an average. Some years the stock will lose money, and some years it will earn much more than 11%. This variability or volatility makes stock investing more "risky," in this sense, than a government bond. But if the more volatile and risky stock returns an 11% average each year, the safer government bond might return a stable and sure 6% per year. By buying the bond, an investor is paying (losing) about 5% a year to get a less risky investment. That is sometimes called the "risk premium."

The conclusion is simply the more return you seek, the more risk (risk of loss and risk of volatility) you must endure.

How Volatile (Risky) Are Stocks?

It is important for an investor to understand the likelihood and possible size of major declines in the stock market, often called "bear markets." It is especially important for the long-term investor. During bear markets, the long-term investor's conviction is sorely tested, and many investment plans eventually fail when investors cannot stomach painful and prolonged declines. There are several ways to look at market declines. James O'Shaughnessy in his book, *What Works on Wall Street*, is a good source for this. He looks at the impact of market declines on many different types of stocks. In Figure 6B1, O'Shaughnessy looks at 11 significant market declines (over 10%) since 1962 in his "All Stocks" category.

FIGURE 6B1 Significant Stock Market Declines, 1962-2003[17]

Market Declines, All Stocks, 1962-2003			
Peak Date	**Trough Date**	**Duration in Months**	**Decline (%)**
Apr 1966	Sept 1966	5 months	-15.99%
Nov 1968	Jun 1970	19 months	-42.67%
Nov 1972	Sept 1974	22 months	-50.12%
Aug 1978	Oct 1978	2 months	-17.04%
Jan 1980	Mar 1980	2 months	-16.82%
May 1981	Jul 1982	14 months	-18.34%
Jun 1983	Jul 1984	12 months	-15.56%
Aug 1987	Nov 1987	3 months	-31.66%
Aug 1989	Oct 1990	14 months	-24.58%
Apr 1998	Aug 1998	4 months	-27.28%
Feb 2000	Sept 2002	31 months	-30.04%

Figure 6B1 looks at two important aspects of stock market declines that a long-term investor should be aware of. One is, obviously, the percentage of the decline. During this 41-year period, the two largest declines took place almost back to back, during the 1968-1970 period and during the 1972-1974 period. Both lasted about 2 years, and both had big declines that would have cost an investor around half of his or her capital. A long-term investor needs to be prepared to weather these kinds of losses temporarily. From personal experience, it is not easy to watch your net worth decline so severely and, in addition, to have to keep reinvesting added funds or dividends in a declining market. As you will see later in this book, reinvesting dividends in a down market is a critical part of the strategy that makes a long-term investor successful. It is important not to ignore the smaller but more sudden declines such as those that occurred during 1987 and 1998. In retrospect, these bear markets look more tolerable, but declines of 32% in 3 months and 27% in 4 months can be even more disconcerting to the long-term investor than larger percentage declines over longer periods of time. It is clear the only way a long-term investor will succeed in producing the kind of returns outlined in this book will depend on his or her ability to survive both the short sudden and the long steep downturns with his or her strategy intact.

Figure 6B2 looks at market declines yearly. I am going to advise long-term investors to look at their portfolios rarely, maybe only once a year. So let's look at the 1899-2005 period using the Dow Jones Industrial Averages on June 26, or the closest trading day, of each year. There is nothing magical about June 26. It just happened to be the day I did this analysis. I am also using the Dow since it more closely represents the kind of stock I am going to recommend long-term investor look to for their retirement investing. It turns out there were 22 significant year-to-year market declines from 1899 until 2005. Figure 6B2 shows some interesting things. Out of the 22, 16 market declines of more than 10% occurred in the first half of the century. Only 6 have taken place since 1950. There were 7 back-to-back yearly declines of more than 10%, all of which occurred between 1900 and 1950. There have been no back-to-back yearly declines of more than 10% in the last 55 years. The average depth of a yearly market decline in the first half of the century was 22% compared with 16.8% in the second half. There were 8 year-to-year market declines of more than 16% during the early half of the century and only one in the latter. From 1900 to 1950, the longest period without a 10% decline was 5 years. From 1950 to 2005, there have been five prolonged periods without a 10% net decline in one year: 1950-1961, 1962-1969, 1974-1981, 1982-1987, and 1988-2001. It seems clear that the number and depth of significant market declines was lower in the last 55 years than in the 50 years preceding. In fact, the last large year-to-year market decline occurred during the 1969-1970 recession when Dow stocks sank a grueling 33% in 1 year.

This analysis gives a long-term investor an idea of what she must live with and survive to succeed in any long-term investing plan. It is critical the investor be prepared for the inevitability of downturns. The good news is that stock market volatility to the downside has been significantly less in the last 55 years than it was in the first half of the 20th century. There may be fewer downturns, and they may be less severe, but they will still occur and they will still be punishing, and a successful investor cannot let them surprise her or alter her strategy.

For investors worried about risk in stock investing, I want to include a paragraph from Siegel's 2002 edition of *Stocks for the Long Run*.

> *No one denies that in the short run stocks are riskier than fixed-income assets. In the long run, however, history has shown that this is not the case. The inflation uncertainty that is inherent*

in the paper money standard the United States and the rest of the world have adopted suggests that fixed income does not mean "fixed purchasing power." Despite the dramatic gains in price stability seen over the past decade, there is still much confusion about what a dollar will be worth two or three decades from now. Historical evidence indicates that we can be more certain of the purchasing power of a diversified portfolio of common stocks 30 years hence than we can of the final payment on a 30-year U.S. government bond.[18]

FIGURE 6B2 Significant Year-to-Year Declines in the Dow Jones Industrial Averages[19]
Dow Jones Yearly Declines of More Than 10%

1899-1900	-18.5%	1961-1962	-12.1%
1903-1904	-21.6%	1969-1970	-33.3%
1906-1907	-14.9%	1973-1974	-12.3%
1912-1913	-11.7%	1981-1982	-15.8%
1914-1915	-20.7%	1987-1988	-14.4%
1917-1918	-15.7%	2001-2002	-12.9%
1919-1920	-13.2%		
1920-1921	-16.9%		
1929-1930	-10.9%		
1930-1931	-51.1%		
1931-1932	-62.4%		
1937-1938	-37.7%		
1939-1940	-16.3%		
1941-1942	-14.1%		
1946-1947	-15.3%		
1948-1949	-10.0%		

Stock Returns and Compounding

One of the components of stock investing is the investor has the opportunity to take advantage of the power of compound rates of return that I described in Chapter 5. I want to begin to look at the results of long-term investing in the stock market in this section and continue with a more detailed analysis of individual stocks in Chapter 8.

It is important to understand the hazards in trying to calculate the returns to stocks. In calculating stock market averages, many analysts look at what are called indexes. These are groups of stocks that are weighted and averaged to get a representation of what the entire stock market is doing. There are even some newer "Total Market Indexes" that try to consider all stocks traded on the exchanges. The most commonly used indexes are the Dow Industrial Averages, the Standard and Poor's 500, and the NASDAQ composite. There are many others, but let me comment briefly on these three.

The Dow was started in 1896 and is still the most widely watched index of stock activity although it includes only 30 stocks. One big advantage of the Dow is that it has been around for so long. Most serious analysts studying long-term stock movements use the S&P 500 since it also has existed for a longtime and includes 500 stocks, including all those in the Dow. The NASDAQ composite was created in 1971 and includes all the stocks traded on the NASDAQ exchange. Although it has merit as a broad-based index, it is of limited value to the long-run stock investing described in this book.

There are several difficulties that need to be overcome in comparing long-run returns. Let me point out a few of them. First, returns to stocks include both price increases and dividends paid. To get the full effect of compound rates of return, the investor needs to reinvest his or her dividends each period in the stock of the issuing corporation. Any examination of stock investing must consider both capital appreciation and dividends to be accurate. Second, an index must account for the unavoidable turnover in stocks within the index. Some companies fail and are dropped from an index; sometimes, they disappear altogether, and others are added to replace them. The Dow index is always 30 stocks, and the S&P 500 is always 500 stocks. Accounting for this turnover without distorting, the index value is critical. Third, stocks trade at many different price levels. There are stocks that trade for pennies per share, and there is one stock, Warren Buffett's Berkshire Hathaway, which trades for almost $100,000 per share. The index must account for these differences without giving a disproportionate role to any particular stock.

Investing in stocks allows an investor to take advantage of the power of compounding since he or she can reinvest any dividends paid to him or her each year and pick up added shares of stock. To the degree the price of the stock appreciates, it is almost like automatic compounding. The investor does not have to take any action to get the benefits of compounding. As we have seen, over long periods of time, this capacity to reinvest dividends accounts for a substantial amount of the return to stocks. Chapter 10 will deal with this idea in more detail.

There are several calculations of the returns to a long-term investor that I find reliable and whose data I will use to explain the points made in this book. Jeremy Siegel calculated the average compound rate of return to stock investors from 1802 to 2001 at 8.3%[20] annually. In calculating the rate of return on all stocks from 1926 until 2001, Siegel found the average yearly return was 10.2%, and the post-WWII return, 1946-2001, was 11.6%.[21] The summary of this data in Figure 6C1 suggests something interesting. Since the return to stocks for the 55-year period, 1946-2001, was higher than the total return, 1802-2001, one must assume that stock returns from 1802 to 1946 were less than average. This is important for two reasons. First, in trying to predict the future, it seems logical to me to use later data as more reflective of what an investor might expect today or in the future. The period 1946-2001 includes all or part of several long and significant downturns in the stock market, 1929-1954 and 1969-1982, as well as some remarkable upturns or bull markets. The 19th century data reflects a different economy, largely agrarian, with the beginning of the industrial revolution making a growing impact on economic affairs. If we assume the current data is more appropriate in trying to project stock market returns, we might use any of the three results calculated by Siegel, 1926-2001, 1946-2001, or 1982-2001. Each period shows a larger and larger rate of return.

FIGURE 6C1 Hypothetical Stock Returns Using Siegel Data[22]
Calculated Compound Rate of Return
Result of $10,000 Invested for Different Periods

Years	Rate	40 Years	50 Years	60 Years	70 Years
1926-2001	10.2%	$486,703	$1,285,523	$3,395,437	$8,968,331
1946-2001	11.6%	$806,432	$2,416,628	$7,241,886	$21,701,693
1982-2001	14.1%	$1,956,256	$7,316,144	$27,361,422	$102,328,147

Figure 6C1 shows us the power of compound rates of return using returns that have been achieved during different past periods of the modern era. These are results that could be achieved if an investor had $10,000 to invest, reinvested all the dividends in added shares, and had the opportunity to use a tax advantage vehicle to make their investment. Remember, these are average returns which mean that approximate half of the stocks an investor might have invested in would have produced better than these averages and half would have achieved below the market averages. Notice the dramatic increase in dollar returns for added years. Hypothetically, holding for 50 years is worth about $800,000 more than holding for 40 years for the investor who earned 10.2% compounded. And holding for 60 years earned our theoretical investor another $2 million plus. It is important to notice the dramatic difference if you earn a larger rate of return. Compounding at 11.6% instead of 10.2% almost doubles your return at 40 and 50 years and more than doubles it at 60 and 70 years.

To confirm the reality for an investor of Siegel's data, I turn to two other sets of comprehensive data: the well-respected book by James O'Shaughnessy, *What Works on Wall Street,* and the detail data used by Robert Shiller in his book, *Irrational Exuberance.* O'Shaughnessy calculated rates of return using many different assumptions, but for now, I want to look at the most broad based of his calculations, "All Stocks" and the S&P 500. "All Stocks" should roughly compare with Siegel's data, and the S&P 500 is the widely used broad-based index of 500 stocks that Siegel used.

—

FIGURE 6C2[23] Hypothetical Stock Returns Using O'Shaughnessy Data
Calculated Compound Rate of Return
Assumed Result of $10,000 Invested for Different Periods

Years	Rate	40 Years	50 Years	60 Years	70 Years
1951-2003 "All Stocks"	13.00%	$1,327,820	$4,507,360	$15,300,530	$51,938,706
1951-2003 S&P 500	11.52%	$783,629	$2,331,514	$6,936,903	$20,639,219

FIGURE 6C3 Hypothetical Stock Returns Using Shiller's Data[24]

Years to December 31, 2004	Compound Rate of Return
134 Years	9.05%
100 Years	9.77%
75 Years	9.65%
60 Years	11.76%
50 Years	11.45%
40 Years	10.34%
30 Years	13.60%

Figure 6C2 uses O'Shaughnessy's calculated returns from past years and projects them into the future. In comparing Siegel's data to O'Shaughnessy's, the closest set time wise is Siegel's from 1946 to 2001 and O'Shaughnessy's 1951-2003. Siegel shows an 11.6% compound return for this period, and O'Shaughnessy shows an 11.52% compound return, quite close.

Shiller used the S&P composite along with O'Shaughnessy's data, and my derived calculations in Table 6A1 in the appendix shows the S&P compound return from 1951 to 2004 was 11.35% and from 1946 to 2004 was 11.76%. In trying to coordinate return calculations between O'Shaughnessy and Shiller, I recalculated Shiller's return from 1951 to 2003, to try to make it compatible by year. Shiller's data produce an

11.33% compound return for the same period. Figure 6C3 shows Shiller's annual compound rate of return for the S&P for 134, 100, 75, 60, 50, 40, and 30 years. The appendix includes Shiller's compound rates of return for every year since 1871.

FIGURE 6D1 Summary of Calculated Returns Using S&P 500 Composite

	Calculated Compound Return	Net Result $10,000 Investment for 50 Years	Net Result $10,000 Investment for 60 Years	Net Result $10,000 Investment for 70 Years
Siegel 1946-2001	11.60%	$2,418,628	$7,241,886	$21,701,693
O'Shaughnessy 1951-2003	11.52%	$2,331,514	$6,936,903	$20,639,219
Shiller 1946-2004	11.76%	$2,596,089	$7,891,937	$23,990,954

Figure 6D1 shows a summary of the calculated returns for about 50 years beginning after the end of WWII for the three authors. They are close considering that they all use a slightly different set of years. The reason they are close lies in the remarkable stability of stock returns when looked at from the long-term. We looked at this earlier, and I will discuss this in more detail later. The important point is, there have been significant returns to investors who just achieved the market average and who invested small amounts of money over a long period of time. You can easily convert a $10,000 investment into a $1,000 investment by dividing the result by 10. And $1,000 invested using Siegel's compounding for 60 years produces $724,188.60. You can also multiply the result by the multiple of any amount over $10,000 that you might be able to invest. A $20,000 investment would have produced double the returns cited in Figure 6D1.

Measuring rates of return is never perfect, and differences can occur from assumptions that must be made about things like timing of dividends and reinvestment of shares. But by whatever measure one wants to use, the potential returns to an investor who invests for a long period of time is sizeable.

It is interesting to look at Figure 6E1 and the entire 130-year period in which we have Shiller's recalculated results for the Standard and

Poor's composite. There is a distinct difference between the pre-WWII period (1870-1945) and the post-WWII period (1946-2004). The earlier period was one of great turmoil both politically and economically. The earlier period featured the Spanish American War, two World Wars, and the Russian Revolution. Economically, the early period was dominated by economic crisis, severe depressions, persistent deflations, monetary instability, and foreign economic crisis like the German inflation in 1923. If we look at one issue like inflation, we find that during the 134 years from 1811 to 1945, prices declined by roughly 16%. But from 1945 to 1970, commodity prices exactly doubled.[25] And since 1970, producer prices have increased about 3½ times.[26] From the standpoint of inflation alone, it was a different era. The postwar period has, with all its problems, been much more stable, both politically and economically, with economic development taking the center stage. Jeremy Siegel's research of stock returns going back 200 years is interesting, but much of the 200-year period was in a completely different economic environment with a completely different set of issues and problems.

The reader can judge for himself. I like the odds of continuing the post-WWII experience, and I think that it is more sensible to use a post-WWII rate of return as something of a norm. It is a long enough period, 58 years, to give an investor some confidence, and it avoids some of the dramatic changes that occurred during the prewar period. I will use the compound rate of return of 11.76% per year, the calculated return for the S&P composite from 1946 to 2004. Figure 6E2 shows the returns possible to a $10,000 investment for different periods using 11.76% as the assumed compound rate of return. To repeat, Figure 6E2 assumes that an investor had invested his or her $1,000, $5,000, $10,000, or $20,000 onetime in the S&P 500 stocks and reinvested all dividends in added stock and paid no taxes on any gains. This simple analysis does not take inflation and its potentially corrosive effect on returns into account. I will deal with it in some detail in Chapter 13.

FIGURE 6E1[27] Standard and Poor's Composite Return: Pre-WWII to Post-WWII

Period	Annual Compound Rate of Return
1870-1945	7.26%
1946-2004	11.76%

FIGURE 6E2 Final Return at 11.76% Compounded

Invested	For 40 Years	For 50 Years	For 60 Years	For 70 years
$1,000	$85,400	$259,609	$789,194	$2,399,095
$5,000	$426,998	$1,298,045	$3,945,968	$11,995,477
$10,000	$853,996	$2,596,089	$7,891,937	$23,990,954
$20,000	$1,707,922	$5,192,179	$15,783,873	$47,981,908

A $10,000 investment for 50 years can bring you $2,596,089 if it compounds at 11.76%, the achieved return in the S&P 500 for the last 58 years. If you wish to use a different compound rate than 11.76% consult Tables 24, A2-A8 in the appendix. These tables allows you to select any return from 7% to 13% and calculate the dollar returns for $1 invested for different years. Just multiply by your planned investment and you can calculate your own return.

It is these returns using the power of compound rates of return over long periods of time that can make you, your children, or your grandchildren wealthy. In later chapters, I will outline alternative plans for investing small amounts of money that can make you millions if you have enough time and are willing to stick to the plan. It isn't hard, you don't have to become an expert investor, and you don't have to invest huge amounts of money to get rich. Just read the rest of this book and take action.

Returns on Other Forms of Investments

The reason that I recommend that a long-term investor use stocks as his or her preferred investment vehicle is that stock returns have been significantly higher than the obvious alternatives. There are many alternatives. Let us look briefly at three major alternatives: real estate, bonds, and precious metals (gold and silver).

Gold and Silver

Investing in gold and silver, the two precious metals that most investors have historically preferred, presents different opportunities and different challenges to an investor than stock market investing. Both metals have commercial use as well as investment interest. Both metals are traded on commodity markets and are easily accessed by investors. Unlike stocks, investing in gold and silver does not provide an investor with any dividend return. Investing in them is all about capital appreciation, prices going up. In fact, if you buy gold and silver bullion or coins, you may have a yearly storage cost to safely hold and protect the metals.

If we look at gold prices since 1926 to April 2005, an investor in gold would have earned a 4.3% annual compound return, far below the 10.26% compound rate earned on the Standard and Poor's Composite.[28] The US government fixed the price of gold until the early 1970s. The compound rate of return to gold investors since 1970, when the gold price was freed, was a more competitive 8.27% compounded compared with 11.42% for the Standard and Poor's composite stocks. Jeremy Siegel calculated the compound rate of return on the S&P 500 from 1957 to 2003 was 10.85%.[29] The matching compound rate of return for gold during the same period was 6.23% (Figure 6F1).

FIGURE 6F1 Comparison of Compound Rates of Return: Gold, Silver, and S&P Composite

Years	Gold	Silver	S&P Composite
1926-2004[2]	4.30%	4.38%	10.26%
1970-2004[3]	8.27%	5.71%	11.42%
1957-2003[4]	6.23%	5.60%	10.85%
1930-2004[5]	4.54%	4.64%	10.36%

The price of silver shows a similar return characteristic to gold. Silver has returned a compound rate of return since 1957-2005 of 5.69%, compared with 11.88% for the S&P composite averages.[34] Even looking at gold and silver from 1930, during the depression, silver prices have only compounded at an annual rate of 4.64% and gold prices at 4.54%. The S&P composite since 1930 has compounded at 10.36%.[35]

So the data clearly show that an investor fared much better in stocks over the long run than he or she did in precious metals. If we look at the S&P composite return since 1930 and exclude dividend reinvestment, the S&P compounded only at 6.09% yearly, making gold and silver more competitive. This explains a key point that I will stress later in Chapter 10, the importance of dividends and dividend reinvestment to investors. If gold and silver paid a respectable dividend, they would look much more attractive as an investment alternative to stocks for a long-term investor.

Bonds

Probably the most common alternative to investing in stocks is bonds. Bonds are debt. They do not represent any form of ownership. As an investor, you simply lend your money to the entity issuing the bond. You can buy many different types of bonds. As indicted earlier, there are government bonds, both US, foreign, and state bonds, and there are corporate bonds. Unlike stocks, bonds promise a fixed return every year, called interest, but they do not pay dividends out of profits and normally do not provide the same kind of capital gain potential as stocks. Under normal circumstances, investors in bonds are looking to recover their investment at the end of the holding period with periodic interest payments along the way. Let's look at how some different types of bonds have compounded. Here, we assume no taxes are paid (taxes must be paid each year on interest payments at ordinary rates) and that all returns are reinvested in added bonds.

FIGURE 6F2 Comparison of Compound Rates of Return: Bonds and S&P Composite

Data Source	Years	Long-Term Debt	Short-Term Debt	S&P Composite
O'Shaughnessy[36]	1963–2003	7.53%	6.03%	10.61%
Siegel[37]	1946–2001	5.50%	4.90%	11.60%
Siegel[38]	1802–2001	4.90%	4.30%	8.30%

Figure 6F2 shows O'Shaughnessy's calculations of compound returns for stocks and various bond categories for the 1963-2003 period. Stocks clearly outperform bonds, both long-term and short-term bonds, by a significant amount. Jeremy Siegel's data cover several periods, but I am most interested in the 1946-2001 period as most relevant for current day long-term investors. During this period, long-term government bonds returned a compound annual return of 5.5%, short-term government bonds returned a compound annual return of 4.9%, and stocks returned a compound annual return of 11.6%. Looking at Siegel's 200-year data, stocks outperformed both short-term and long-term bonds by a significant amount, 8.3% yearly for stocks, 4.9% yearly for long-term bonds, and 4.3% yearly for short-term bonds.

Real Estate

The other investment that most of us are familiar with is real estate. Most investors own their homes, and most of us have seen notable appreciation in our home prices especially if held for a long period of time. Looking at the median home price data from the Statistical Abstract of the United States, median home prices in the entire United States for existing one-family homes have moved from $23,400 to $139,000 from 1970 to the year 2000.[39] The annual compound rate of return for this period for single-family homes was 6.12%. The annual compound rate of return to stocks, using the S&P composite for the same period, was 13.19%. O'Shaughnessy, in his latest book, *Predicting the Markets of Tomorrow*, points out the median price of a new house in the United States in 1963 was $17,200. And the median price of a new house in 2004 had risen to $206,300. That represents a 6.25% annual compound rate of return. The stock market, using the S&P composite again, showed a 10.49% annual compound rate of return for the same period.

If we take a longer look using census data, the median house price in the United States compounded at an annual rate of 6.37% from 1940 to 2000. Robert Shiller in *Irrational Exuberance* builds an index of home prices in the United States from 1890 to 2004 and concludes that home prices compounded at an annual inflation-adjusted rate of just 0.4% per year in 114 years.[40] Comparing inflation-adjusted home prices with inflation-adjusted stock prices, using Shiller's S&P composite data, stocks compounded at an inflation-adjusted rate of 6.62% per year compared to 0.4% for home prices. While most of us are happy with what has happened to our home values, especially in the last few years, the fact is that stock market averages beat home price averages consistently. But we are all governed by our own experience, so let's look at my own experience and see if the averages bear out in my case. I have owned four homes in my lifetime. Home values and compound returns on homes are tricky to calculate. You have to consider more than just the initial purchase price and the final sales price. You also have to consider any improvements made to the property and any taxes paid. So my figures here are just educated "guesstimates." I improved every home I lived in. I don't have the data or remember accurately how much I did spend on improvements or taxes. So I am going to look at only the purchase and selling prices of each home, understanding the compound rates of return we are looking at are clearly overstated for my homes.

**FIGURE 6G1 Annual Compound Rate of Return:
Gittelman's Homes and S&P Composite**

Years	My Home	S&P Composite Average[41]
1964-1968	11.96%	9.43%
1968-1978	10.55%	2.93%
1979-1987	5.00%	15.36%
1987-2004	6.68%	12.34%
Overall average	7.64%	10.34%

Considering the annual compound rate of return on all four of my homes is overstated by at least the physical improvements that I put into each property between buying it and selling it, the results are instructive. First, my results are better than the national medians cited in Figure 6F2. Part of the explanation obviously lies in my inability to include improvements. The last two homes were both California properties, both with either ocean views or water orientation in expensive Orange County. The first two properties were in southern New Jersey across the bridge from Philadelphia. It is interesting that in my case, the compound rates for the Philadelphia area homes were higher than the California homes. It is not important for our purposes, and I don't have a good explanation for this except timing. In the first two periods cited, my home outperformed the S&P averages. The 1968-1978 period was a poor one for stock investing. In the last two periods, 1979-2004, the stock averages beat my home averages significantly. Overall, investing my money in the S&P

averages would have produced a better result during these 40 years than actual home investing did. Imagine that I started with exactly $100,000 invested in homes using the rates of return shown in Figure 6G1. Then assume another $100,000 invested in the S&P using its rate of return. The home investment would have produced $1.9 million in 40 years, and the S&P investment would have produced $5.1 million during the same 40 years. In my case, I would have been significantly better off if I had simply invested all the money in an S&P index fund.

The idea that real estate is such a good investment is so pervasive that I did a comparison of two theoretical investors who both invested $17,775. One in the average American home in 1964, while the other investor put the same $17,775 into the stock market. Each achieved the average annual return calculated using the average American home price and the S&P average. Both investments were closed at the end of 2004. Figure 6G2 shows the result and compound annual rate of return for our two investors.

FIGURE 6G2 Comparable Returns to Real Estate and Stock Market Investors: 1964-2004

Investment in 1964	Real Estate (Home)[42]	Stock Market (S&P Composite)
Invested	$17,725	$17,725
Value in 2000	$218,000	$910,919
Compound Annual Return	6.47%	10.35%[43]

The returns are startling. I used $17,725 as the starting investment because that was the median home price in the United States in 1964. Our stock market investor ended with over 4 times as much final value as did the real estate investor, and this is an era that most consider great for real estate. The annual compound return for our real estate investor was 6.47% compared with 10.35% for an investor in the Standard and Poor's.

Real estate may be considered the best investment by all those so-called experts who write those real estate investment books in the bookstore. But over almost any period of time you want to measure or any market you want to use, stock market returns have consistently outperformed real estate returns.

A Further Note about Volatility in the Stock Market

In Figure 6H1, we look at the Standard and Poor's composite averages assuming investments were made in eight 10-year periods starting in 1904 running through 1983. The data assume each investment was held until 2004, and the shortest investment time period we are looking at is 20 years, not long for a long-term investor. If you had invested in the S&P composite during any of these 10-year periods, reinvested all distributions, avoided taxes, and held until 2004, this figure shows the maximum, minimum, and mean (average) compound rates of return that you would have achieved.

FIGURE 6H1 S&P Composite Annual Compound Rate of Returns. Highest, Lowest, and Median for 10-Year Initial Investment Periods[44] Ended in 2004

Starting Years	Highest Rate of Return	Lowest Rate of Return	Median Rate of Return
1904-1913	10.29%	9.67%	9.99%
1914-1923	10.82%	10.21%	10.59%
1924-1933	11.68%	9.65%	10.30%
1934-1943	12.17%	10.63%	11.42%
1944-1953	11.96%	11.24%	11.45%
1954-1963	12.07%	10.29%	10.82%
1964-1983	13.60%	12.52%	13.16%

Assume that you made an investment in the S&P composite averages during one or any of these periods. The highest possible compound rate of return, the lowest possible compound rate of return, and the median (middle) compound rate of return are given. For instance, if you made an investment in the S&P composite between 1934 and 1943, the best your compound return might have been was 12.17% per year held to 2004. The worst it could have been was 10.63%, and the median or midpoint year would have been 11.42% also held to 2004. The surprising aspect of these figures is, given at least a 20-year time horizon, how stable they are. The differences between the high and lows for each period are always within 2%. A 2% difference does make a significant difference in results, but the variability seems much lower than most investors might have been expected. The high point, a 13.60% annual return, occurred for an investment made in 1974, a depressed time for the markets, and that investment only considers a 30-year time horizon, much less than recommended in this book. A long-term investor should not consider returns of less than 20 years as meaningful. The analysis used in Figure 6H1 starts more than 20 years prior to 2004. Once you go back using an investment horizon of at least 40 years, the returns get even more stable.

While stocks can be unstable in the short run, as shown in Figures 6B1 and 6B2, if we take a longer view, the instability is greatly reduced. Even a 9.67% compound return, the lowest year in Figure 6H1, produces over $2.5 million on a $10,000 investment in 60 years. Looking at stocks on a month-to-month or year-to-year basis gives you a deceptive view of the volatility of stock market investing.

How Individual Stocks Can Achieve 11-12% Compound Returns Over Time?

Stock prices tend to vary with earnings over a long period of time. In the short-term, stock prices can move around a lot, but in the long run, any stock an investor owns is likely to mimic its earnings in investment return. That means, for a company to compound its return to shareholders at 11% or 12% or more it will likely have to produce long-term earnings growth that compound at 11-12%. Earnings come from sales, and there is a strong relationship between sales and earnings in a typical large corporation. In most large companies, the earnings on additional sales can produce a higher profit rate than on the original sales. If a company has sales of $100,000,000 in a year and earns $5,000,000 net profit or 5% on those sales, it is likely that adding $10,000,000 of additional sales will produce more than a 5% profit on the added business. While not always true, it is likely that $110,000,000 in sales next year might produce something like $5,600,000 in profits. In Economics, we would call this marginal analysis. Added sales mean profits at a higher rate on those sales. A 10% increase in sales produced a 12% increase in profits. In addition, many large corporations in America today are reaping the pervasive and varied benefits of technology to lower costs. For instance, the computer revolution has allowed substantial cost savings in inventory management that has improved the profitability of many companies. It is highly likely that the next 50-70 years will see substantial reductions in costs associated with many companies that are not themselves considered technology entities. Over the long-term, large public corporations may be able to

—

produce larger increases in earnings than their sales might indicate. For instance, a corporation whose sales compound at only 8% or 9% over the next 50-70 years might well compound earnings at 11-12%. To illustrate this idea, I looked at a couple of corporate earnings and sales reports for the last few years, which is given in Figure 6H2. Corporate earnings may grow faster than sales improving investor's rates of return.

FIGURE 6H2 Illustration of Sales and Earnings Growth

Company	Latest Year Sales Growth	Earnings Growth	Prior Year Sales Growth	Earnings Growth
Procter & Gamble	20.2%	25.4%	10.4%	12.4%
Johnson & Johnson	6.1%	22.4%	13.1%	18.2%

CHAPTER 7

The Plan

Millionaire or More at Retirement

In this chapter I will outline the beginnings of a specific investment plan that can make the reader a millionaire at retirement. I will also give you guidelines about how you could become a multimillionaire. (Chapter 28 has more information on how to become a multimillionaire.) This chapter will focus on several different types of investment plans that an investor can use to achieve his or her goals. I will use the ideas of compound returns and historical returns to show an investor what to expect, predicated on different levels of investment and different formats and timing of investments. Later in this book, I will give you more detailed advice about how to structure your investments and what to invest in. This chapter outlines modest investment objectives that almost everyone can take part in and get the benefits outlined in this book. If you are fortunate enough to be able to invest more than the amounts indicated, you can usually calculate your returns by multiplying the results by the multiple of the investment that you start with. For example, a $10,000 onetime investment will produce 10 times the results of a $1,000 onetime investment. Investments of different amounts and for multiple years are more difficult to calculate using only these charts. Using Table 22B1 in the appendix, you can calculate investment results based on compound rate of return, years, and amount invested.

Note that all results suggested here depend on structuring your investments in specific ways discussed in later chapters.

Use Stocks

In Chapter 6, we looked at the three most authoritative studies of stock market returns since WWII. Siegel's, O'Shaughnessy's, and Shiller's data differ only slightly in the achieved postwar (WWII) compound rates of return for the S&P. They show compound returns for the S&P of 11.50-11.76% annually. These differences are largely due to slightly different timing, but all three represent long time periods, 50-60 years. Siegel's complete data from 1800 suggest a lower rate of return (closer to 8%) for stocks. Shiller's data since 1871 shows slightly more than a 9% compound rate of return and roughly 10.5% if we use 1925 as a starting date. It might seem more conservative to use the older data as a standard. But I think the likelihood of stock market returns reverting to the 19th century or to the pre-depression era is unlikely. Of course, anything is possible, and I will deal later with some of the possible events that might cause future returns to be lower than post-WWII returns. The data in this chapter show long-term compound returns from 7% to 13% yearly, to allow an investor to look at many possible alternative results. It is also just as likely that returns will meet or exceed the post-WWII returns as it is that they will fall short of postwar returns. It is also possible that an individual investor may make poor selections and produce inferior results or good selections and superior results. This book will try to help an investor avoid the former outcome and achieve the latter.

One Time Investment Plan—$1,000, $2,000, $5,000, $10,000, or More

I am going to examine two basic forms of investment plans; the onetime investment plan and a multiyear investment plan. Use either one or, better yet, both if you are able. Figure 7A1 shows the result of a onetime investment of $1,000, assuming various compound rates of return over time periods of 10-80 years. I consider long-term investing to be at least 50 years so I am including the shorter periods for those who do not have as long a time horizon. For most investors using my long-term plan 10-, 20-, 30-, even 40-year horizons are just too short. (Chapter 27 includes information for investors who don't have 50+ years.)

An investor using these charts must follow the investment advice given in later chapters. You will see that reinvesting dividends and avoiding or deferring taxes are essential in any investment plan that will achieve these results.

Figure 7A1 shows that if you just make a $1,000 onetime investment, your returns over a long period of time can be significant. The post-WWII approximate compound rate of return is closer to 12%. A $1,000 onetime investment for 60 years will make an investor worth more than half million dollars at 11% and held for 70 years will produce almost $1.5 million. Even at 50 years, an 11% rate of return produces $184,565 for a $1,000 initial onetime investment.

There are a couple of important characteristics about this figure and later figures that I would like to mention. Added years produce dramatically improved results, higher return rates produce dramatically improved results, and added years coupled with higher return rates produce even more dramatically improved results. What does this mean to an investor? First, it pays to take some time to try to improve your rate of return. I will give you some ideas on how to do this, but each investor should think about this issue on his or her own and try to find ways to improve on the average return. As you will see later, it is easy to get average returns or at least almost average returns. Second, time has an enormous impact on returns at every level but even more at higher rates of return. At a 7% compound rate of return, the difference between holding an investment for 50 years and holding it for 60 years is about double. At 12%, that difference becomes almost triple. Third, the holding period is critical. For almost any long-term investment (over 50 years), the lion's share of the return in dollars comes during the last 10 years. At 11% compounded, a $1,000 investment cumulates about $500,000 in the first 60 years and almost another $1 million in the next 10 years. This means that an investor must be patient in his or her planning and have as long a time horizon as possible. I will discuss this issue in some detail in Chapters 12 and 14, but for now, it may be that you will have more time than you currently might calculate.

—

FIGURE 7A1 Investment Results
Compound Returns Based on Rate and Years

| | Assumed One Time Investment | | | | | | |
| | $1,000 | | | | | | |
Compound Rate of Return	7%	8%	9%	10%	11%	12%	13%
Years							
10	$1,967	$2,159	$2,367	$2,594	$2,839	$3,106	$3,395
20	$3,870	$4,661	$5,604	$6,727	$8,062	$9,646	$11,523
30	$7,612	$10,063	$13,268	$17,449	$22,892	$29,960	$39,116
40	$14,974	$21,725	$31,409	$45,259	$65,001	$93,051	$132,782
50	$29,457	$46,902	$74,358	$117,391	$184,565	$289,002	$450,736
60	$57,946	$101,257	$176,031	$304,482	$524,057	$897,597	$1,530,053
70	$113,989	$218,606	$416,730	$789,747	$1,488,019	$2,787,800	$5,193,870
80	$224,234	$471,955	$986,552	$2,048,400	$4,225,113	$8,658,483	$17,630,940

Figure 7A2 shows the same results for a $2,000 investment. It is easy to calculate Figures 7A2, 7A3, and 7A4 given Figure 7A1. A onetime $2,000 investment will produce exactly double the results of a onetime $1,000 investment, and a onetime $5,000 investment will produce exactly five times the results and a onetime $10,000 investment exactly ten times the results of a $1,000 investment.

FIGURE 7A2 Investment Results
Compound Returns Based on Rate and Years

| | Assumed Onetime Investment | | | | | | |
| | $2,000 | | | | | | |
Compound Rate of Return	7%	8%	9%	10%	11%	12%	13%
Years							
10	$3,934	$4,318	$4,735	$5,187	$5,679	$6,212	$6,789
20	$7,739	$9,322	$11,209	$13,455	$16,125	$19,293	$23,046
30	$15,225	$20,125	$26,535	$34,899	$45,785	$59,920	$78,232
40	$29,949	$43,449	$62,819	$90,519	$130,002	$186,102	$265,563
50	$58,914	$93,803	$148,715	$234,782	$369,130	$578,004	$901,472

—

60	$115,893	$202,514	$352,063	$608,963	$1,048,114	$1,795,194	$3,060,107
70	$227,979	$437,213	$833,460	$1,579,494	$2,976,038	$5,575,600	$10,387,739
80	$448,469	$943,910	$1,973,103	$4,096,800	$8,450,226	$17,316,966	$35,261,881

If you have $5,000 or $10,000 and don't want to bother with making additional yearly investments, your results can still be spectacular. A $5,000 onetime investment (Figure 7A3) for 50 years at 11% is almost $1 million dollars and held for 60 years is more than $2.5 million. A $10,000 onetime investment (Figure 7A4) held for 50 years produces over $1.8 million and held for 60 years totals over $5.2 million.

FIGURE 7A3 Investment Results
Compound Returns Based on Rate and Years

	Assumed Onetime Investment						
	$5,000						
Compound Rate of Return	7%	8%	9%	10%	11%	12%	13%
Years							
10	$9,836	$10,795	$11,837	$12,969	$14,197	$15,529	$16,973
20	$19,348	$23,305	$28,022	$33,637	$40,312	$48,231	$57,615
30	$38,061	$50,313	$66,338	$87,247	$114,461	$149,800	$195,579
40	$74,872	$108,623	$157,047	$226,296	$325,004	$465,255	$663,908
50	$147,285	$234,508	$371,788	$586,954	$922,824	$1,445,011	$2,253,680
60	$289,732	$506,285	$880,156	$1,522,408	$2,620,286	$4,487,985	$7,650,267
70	$569,947	$1,093,032	$2,083,650	$3,948,735	$7,440,096	$13,938,999	$25,969,348
80	$1,121,172	$2,359,774	$4,932,758	$10,242,001	$21,125,564	$43,292,416	$88,154,702

FIGURE 7A4 Investment Results
Compound Returns Based on Rate and Years

			Assumed Onetime Investment				
			$10,000				
Compound Rate of Return	7%	8%	9%	10%	11%	12%	13%
Years							
10	$19,672	$21,589	$23,674	$25,937	$28,394	$31,058	$33,946
20	$38,697	$46,610	$56,044	$67,275	$80,623	$96,463	$115,231
30	$76,123	$100,627	$132,677	$174,494	$228,923	$299,599	$391,159
40	$149,745	$217,245	$314,094	$452,593	$650,009	$930,510	$1,327,816
50	$294,570	$469,016	$743,575	$1,173,909	$1,845,648	$2,890,022	$4,507,359
60	$579,464	$1,012,571	$1,760,313	$3,044,816	$5,240,572	$8,975,969	$15,300,535
70	$1,139,894	$2,186,064	$4,167,301	$7,897,470	$14,880,191	$27,877,998	$51,938,696
80	$2,242,344	$4,719,548	$9,865,517	$20,484,002	$42,251,128	$86,584,831	$176,309,405

Longer periods and earning larger compound rates of return can increase investor's results in a spectacular fashion.

Yearly Investment Plans

Figures 7B1, 7B2, and 7B3 show the compound returns for investments made every year. I assume that most investors will adopt a plan like these, although some of you may adopt a combination of plans. Figure 7B1 shows the results for a $1,000 investment made every year at compound rates from 7% to 13% and for terms of 10-80 years. In this case, a $1,000 investment made every year for 60 years at 11% produces over $5 million as opposed to slightly over $500,000 if invested only once. Although the early year investments inevitably produce the largest return, investing consistently for long periods of time is an excellent strategy. Even $500 per year for many years will produce some dramatic results.

FIGURE 7B1 Investment Results
Compound Returns Based on Rate and Years

Assumed Yearly Investment
$1,000

Compound Rate of Return Years	7%	8%	9%	10%	11%	12%	13%
10	$14,784	$15,645	$16,560	$17,531	$18,561	$19,655	$20,814
20	$43,865	$49,423	$55,765	$63,002	$71,265	$80,699	$91,470
30	101,073	122,346	$148,575	$180,943	$220,913	$270,293	$331,315
40	213,610	279,781	$368,292	$486,852	$645,827	$859,142	$1,145,486
50	434,986	619,672	$888,441	1,280,299	1,852,336	2,688,020	$3,909,243
60	870,467	1,353,470	$2,119,823	$3,338,298	$5,278,123	$8,368,238	$13,291,003
70	$1,727,124	$2,937,686	$5,034,953	$8,676,217	$15,005,375	$26,010,132	$45,138,021
80	$3,412,297	$6,357,890	$11,936,126	$22,521,402	$42,625,138	$80,803,176	$153,244,867

Figures 7B2 and 7B3 show the result for yearly investments of $2,000 and $5,000, respectively.

A consistent annual investment plan works best for many reasons. One reason is that it avoids the possibility of investing all your funds at some interim high point and getting a lower compound rate of return than average. Investing yearly is more productive, the results more likely to be consistent with the general market averages, but it does require some discipline. As far as I am concerned, it is the best plan.

FIGURE 7B2 Investment Results
Compound Returns Based on Rate and Years

Assumed Yearly Investment
$2,000

Compound Rate of Return Years	7%	8%	9%	10%	11%	12%	13%
10	$29,567	$31,291	$33,121	$35,062	$37,123	$39,309	$41,629
20	$87,730	$98,846	$111,529	$126,005	$142,530	$161,397	$182,940
30	$202,146	$244,692	$297,150	$361,887	$441,826	$540,585	$662,630
40	$427,219	$559,562	$736,584	$973,704	$1,291,654	$1,718,285	$2,290,972

50	$869,972	$1,239,344	$1,776,882	$2,560,599	$3,704,672	$5,376,041	$7,818,486
60	$1,740,934	$2,706,941	$4,239,647	$6,676,596	$10,556,246	$16,736,476	$26,582,007
70	$3,454,247	$5,875,373	$10,069,907	$17,352,433	$30,010,750	$52,020,263	$90,276,041
80	$6,824,594	$12,715,781	$23,872,252	$45,042,805	$85,250,276	$161,606,351	$306,489,734

FIGURE 7B3 Investment Results
Compound Returns Based on Rate and Years

Assumed Yearly Investment $5,000							
Compound Rate of Return Years	7%	8%	9%	10%	11%	12%	13%
10	$73,918	$78,227	$82,801	$87,656	$92,807	$98,273	$104,072
20	$219,326	$247,115	$278,823	$315,012	$356,326	$403,494	$457,350
30	$505,365	$611,729	$742,876	$904,717	$1,104,566	$1,351,463	$1,656,576
40	$1,068,048	$1,398,905	$1,841,459	$2,434,259	$3,229,135	$4,295,712	$5,727,429
50	$2,174,930	$3,098,359	$4,442,205	$6,401,497	$9,261,680	$13,440,102	$19,546,215
60	$4,352,334	$6,767,352	$10,599,117	$16,691,490	$26,390,615	$41,841,190	$66,455,016
70	$8,635,618	$14,688,432	$25,174,766	$43,381,083	$75,026,874	$130,050,659	$225,690,103
80	$17,061,485	$31,789,451	$59,680,629	$112,607,012	$213,125,689	$404,015,878	$766,224,335

Multiple Plans

For many investors, having both onetime and yearly investment plans makes sense. Some investors have a onetime lump sum ready to invest. For instance, if you have $10,000 that you are ready to commit to making you a millionaire at retirement but may only have $1,000 that you can invest in later years, you can use both plans. If down the road you inherit some extra funds, you can start another onetime plan. If you use an annual plan, it is important that you do not fail in making your annual investments. Plan to do it at the same time each year—January 1, your birthday, anniversary, or the 4th of July. Put it on the calendar. It is critical that you contribute every year, particularly in years in which the stock market is depressed, which inevitably it will be at times. Preserving your discipline and continuing to invest even when the markets look bleak will multiply your return in the long run. I will explore the reasons for this in Chapters 10 and 23.

Invest Early and as Often as Possible

You should study the various charts in this chapter. Get a feel for the pattern of returns. One of the most obvious factors in any long-term investment plan is how much of the dollar return comes in the later years. So you must start as early as possible. Do not put off starting your investment plan for any reason. If you don't have as much money as you would like to start, start anyway with a lesser amount. You can try to make up the shortage in later years. If you wait 5 years or 10 years, you will suffer enormous losses. You can figure it out for yourself. A 50-year potential return becomes a 40-year return if you wait for 10 years to start, and so forth.

You must be willing to stick with the plan through thick and thin. Later in this book, I will advise exactly how to invest your funds, what investment vehicle to use, and exactly what to invest in. But no matter how you do it, there will be periods, sometimes years or even a decade, in which the returns are negative or below normal. To succeed, you must have faith that the markets will return to normal rates of return and continue to invest, reinvest dividends and maintain your investment. The early years won't look phenomenal; you have to build a base, and the down years in poor markets will test your patience and resolve. You will be tempted to give up, liquidate your investments, and spend the money on something that you want. In a nutshell, long-term investing requires one critical characteristic: long-term patience.

CHAPTER 8

Long-Term Stock Market Returns

What Is the Record?

In Chapter 6, we looked at several different measures of stock market average returns over the past half-century. In this chapter, we will look at several individual stocks and see what return you might have achieved in the past if you had invested in these companies. I selected three US companies to analyze in detail: General Electric (with about average returns), Altria (with above-average returns), and Union Carbide (with below-average returns) and one foreign company, Nestlé (also with below US average returns).

General Electric

Let's start with an enduring favorite and one of the most respected companies on the New York Stock Exchange, General Electric (GE). GE was incorporated in 1892, and it was one of the original 12 companies included in the first Dow Jones Industrial Averages in 1896. Thanks to the General Electric Investor Relations department, I have stock price and distribution statistics for GE since 1940, 64 years. Adjusted for stock splits, an investor could have bought one share of GE stock in 1940 for 11.654 cents per share and GE stock closed on December 2004 at $36.50 well off its all-time high the equivalent of $58.63 in August 2000.[45]

Note that GE never sold for 11 cents in 1940. GE, like many successful companies, has split its stock numerous times over the years. Each time they split the stock, an existing investor gets more shares of stock. Eleven cents is the amount GE would have sold for considering all the stock splits. If you buy 1,000 shares of GE at $35 and next year they split the stock 2 for 1, you now have 2,000 shares of GE. You still only paid $35,000 ($35 per share) for the original 1,000 shares. This means that your cost per share, for the 2,000 shares you now own, for GE is now reduced from $35 per share to $17.50 per share. As in GE's case, enough splits over a long period of time can reduce your average cost per share to pennies.

A $1,000 onetime investment in GE in 1940 held to 2004 without any reinvestment of distributions would be worth a cool $304,661 at the end of 2004. That turns out to be a compound rate of return of 9.35% per year, not bad at all. But look at the difference if our GE investor had invested his or her $1,000 in GE in 1940 and reinvested all distributions, dividends, in added GE stock. Now our $1,000 investment produces $2,340,056 by the end of 2004 for a compound rate of return of 12.89%. Was this an unusual return? GE is one of the most prominent companies in the world, and their return was somewhat better than the return achieved on the average S&P 500 stock. If you bought a share of every company in the S&P 500 in 1940, your total return would have been a compound 12.12%, which would have produced $1,601,309 for a $1,000 investment by the end of 2004.

FIGURE 8A1 General Electric[46]

General Electric Stock from 1940	Return	Value of $1,000	Investment of $10,000
Compound rate of return GE (no distribution reinvested)	9.35%	$304,661	$3,046,610
Compound rate of return GE (all distributions reinvested)	12.89%	$2,340,056	$23,400,560
Compound rate of return S&P 500 (all distributions reinvested)	12.12%	$1,601,309	$16,013,090

In the next chapter, we will look at the dramatic impact of both time and rate of return on investor outcomes. Figure 8A1 shows you how spectacular actual returns can be over the long run, in this case 64 years. It shows the dramatic difference if an investor reinvests all distributions. Those distributions look small each year, but by reinvesting them instead of taking them in cash, the return, in GE's case, is over 7 times larger. And it also shows the difference that a relatively small increase in your rate of return can make on total return. The difference between investing in GE and the S&P 500 average stock was only 0.77% (12.89-12.12) per year, and that doesn't sound like a lot. But in dollars, that small percentage increase in your average annual return nets an investor an additional 46%. I will examine this in more detail in the next chapter.

Figure 8A2 details the net value by year for an investor who invested $1,000 in GE stock in 1940 and who reinvested all distributions in added stock.

FIGURE 8A2[47] General Electric Detail

	Dollars	$1,000 Shares	Distributions per Share	Distributions Dollars	Distributions in Shares	Total[48] Shares	Total Value
1940	0.1165	8,581	0.0054	$46	396	8,977	$1,046
1941	0.1040	8,977	0.0049	$44	420	9,397	$977
1942	0.0907	9,397	0.0049	$46	503	9,900	$898
1943	0.1226	9,900	0.0049	$48	392	10,292	$1,262
1944	0.1372	10,292	0.0049	$50	365	10,657	$1,462
1945	0.1658	10,657	0.0054	$57	346	11,003	$1,824
1946	0.1246	11,003	0.0056	$61	491	11,493	$1,432
1947	0.1241	11,493	0.0056	$64	515	12,008	$1,490
1948	0.1350	12,008	0.0059	$71	525	12,533	$1,692
1949	0.1463	12,533	0.0069	$87	595	13,128	$1,921
1950	0.1727	13,128	0.0132	$173	1,003	14,131	$2,440
1951	0.2066	14,131	0.0099	$140	677	14,807	$3,059
1952	0.2526	14,807	0.0104	$154	611	15,418	$3,895
1953	0.3038	15,418	0.0139	$214	705	16,123	$4,898
1954	0.4870	16,123	0.0153	$246	506	16,629	$8,098
1955	0.6016	16,629	0.0167	$277	461	17,090	$10,281
1956	0.6276	17,090	0.0208	$356	567	17,657	$11,081
1957	0.6406	17,657	0.0208	$368	574	18,231	$11,679
1958	0.8164	18,231	0.0208	$380	465	18,696	$15,264
1959	1.0326	18,696	0.0208	$390	377	19,074	$19,695
1960	0.7760	19,074	0.0208	$397	512	19,586	$15,198
1961	0.7839	19,586	0.0208	$408	521	20,106	$15,761
1962	0.7995	20,106	0.0208	$419	524	20,630	$16,494

1963	0.9076	20,630	0.0208	$430	474	21,104	$19,154
1964	0.9714	21,104	0.0229	$484	498	21,601	$20,984
1965	1.2292	21,601	0.0240	$518	421	22,023	$27,070
1966	0.9219	22,023	0.0271	$596	647	22,669	$20,899
1967	1.0000	22,669	0.0271	$614	614	23,283	$23,283
1968	0.9779	23,283	0.0271	$631	645	23,928	$23,399
1969	0.8073	23,928	0.0271	$648	803	24,731	$19,965
1970	0.9779	24,731	0.0271	$670	685	25,416	$24,854
1971	1.3047	25,416	0.0286	$728	558	25,974	$33,888
1972	1.5182	25,974	0.0292	$758	499	26,473	$40,191
1973	1.3125	26,473	0.0302	$800	609	27,082	$35,546
1974	0.6953	27,082	0.0333	$903	1,298	28,381	$19,733
1975	0.9609	28,381	0.0333	$946	985	29,365	$28,217
1976	1.1589	29,365	0.0344	$1,009	871	30,236	$35,041
1977	1.0391	30,236	0.0417	$1,260	1,212	31,449	$32,678
1978	0.9818	31,449	0.0500	$1,572	1,602	33,050	$32,449
1979	1.0547	33,050	0.0573	$1,894	1,795	34,845	$36,752
1980	1.2760	34,845	0.0604	$2,105	1,650	36,495	$46,568
1981	1.1953	36,495	0.0646	$2,356	1,971	38,467	$45,979
1982	1.9766	38,467	0.0688	$2,645	1,338	39,805	$78,678
1983	2.4427	39,805	0.0750	$2,985	1,222	41,027	$100,216
1984	2.3646	41,027	0.0833	$3,419	1,446	42,473	$100,431
1985	3.0313	42,473	0.0917	$3,893	1,284	43,757	$132,640
1986	3.5833	43,757	0.0967	$4,230	1,180	44,937	$161,024
1987	3.6771	44,937	0.1075	$4,831	1,314	46,251	$170,070
1988	3.7292	46,251	0.1167	$5,396	1,447	47,698	$177,875
1989	5.3750	47,698	0.1367	$6,519	1,213	48,911	$262,896
1990	4.7813	48,911	0.1567	$7,663	1,603	50,513	$241,520
1991	6.3750	50,513	0.1700	$8,587	1,347	51,860	$330,611
1992	7.1250	51,860	0.1867	$9,681	1,359	53,219	$379,187
1993	8.7396	53,219	0.2100	$11,176	1,279	54,498	$476,290
1994	8.5000	54,498	0.2400	$13,080	1,539	56,037	$476,312
1995	12.0000	56,037	0.1367	$7,658	638	56,675	$680,099
1996	16.4792	56,675	0.1533	$8,690	527	57,202	$942,647
1997	24.4583	57,202	0.1733	$9,915	405	57,608	$1,408,985
1998	34.0000	57,608	0.2000	$11,522	339	57,947	$1,970,181
1999	51.5833	57,947	0.2333	$13,521	262	58,209	$3,002,593

2000	47.9400	58,209	0.2733	$15,910	332	58,540	$2,806,432
2001	40.0800	58,540	0.6400	$37,466	935	59,475	$2,383,769
2002	24.3500	59,475	0.7200	$42,822	1,759	61,234	$1,491,045
2003	30.9800	61,234	0.7600	$46,538	1,502	62,736	$1,943,564
2004	36.5000	62,736	0.8000	$50,189	1,375	64,111	$2,340,056

I include the detail in Figure 8A2 so an investor can see the yearly march from $1,000 to over $2.3 million in 64 years. GE's stock price and dividends are adjusted for the many stock splits during GE's 64-year history. One share of GE stock in 1940 turned into 288 shares in 2004 because of the 7 times during the 64-year period that GE has split its stock. Companies split their stock by issuing added shares to existing shareholders periodically to keep the share price from becoming so high that an average investor could not afford to buy 100 shares.

In looking at the year-by-year results, it becomes clear how important long-term investing is. Almost 60% of the dollar return occurred in the last 8 years of the 64-year investment.

If you look at the return in sections, you see some variance in how the return was achieved. Figure 8A3 shows how many years it took to approximately triple an investor's total value. It turns out that it varied from a high of 14 years to at least triple your value to a low of 4 years.

**FIGURE 8A3 Distribution of GE Total Return
Years to Approximately Triple Total Value**

Year	Total Value	Approximate Years
1940	$1,046	
1951	3,059	11
1955	10,281	4
1971	33,888	14
1983	100,216	12
1991	330,611	8
1996	942,647	5
2004	2,340,050	8

Despite how well GE has done in the last 20 years, its fastest tripling occurred in the 4-year period between 1951 and 1955. It took 14 and 12 years, respectively, for GE to triple shareholder value the next two times.

GE's 2004 stock price is about 30% below its all-time year-end high in 1999, so we are not looking back from some interim market high in GE's case.

One of the obvious challenges for an investor is to be able to withstand the down years like 1969, 1974, and 2002 in Figure 8A2, which can be severe. Just recently in the year 2002, a GE shareholder lost 37% of his or her total value. There are also some prolonged periods in which an investor in GE must have been wondering about his or her investment as his or her total value moved sideways or dipped. The 1959-1969 stagnant period stands out in which the total value did not change much for 10 years, and look at the current period, 1999-2004, for a significant decline in value. Like every investor, a GE investor has to have patience and confidence that GE will eventually exceed the 2004 high and go on to triple shareholder value at some future date. On paper, it may look unrealistic to you to expect a triple of GE's 1999 $3 million value to $9 million, especially because of the estimated 30% decline in GE value since 1999. But look at similar declines from 1945 to 1946, 1959 to 1960, and 1972 to 1974. It took 8, 22, and 14 years respectively until the previous high tripled, but tripled it was if the investor was willing to be patient.

Altria

The second company that I want to analyze in some detail is Altria, the old Philip Morris that I mentioned in the first chapter. Like GE, Altria has had its ups and downs in the past 35 years.

FIGURE 8B1 Altria[49]

Altria Stock from 1970 to 2005		Value of Investment	
Compound rate of return (no distributions reinvested)	14.69%	$121,015	$1,210,148
Compound rate of return (all distributions reinvested)	18.71%	$404,427	$4,044,268
Compound rate of return on S&P 500 (all distributions reinvested)	11.42%	$44,026	$440,260
Project value at 60 years (all distributions reinvested) (assuming the same rate of return)	18.71%	$29,460,377	$290,460,3770

Figure 8B1 shows the value of both a $1,000 investment and a $10,000 investment in Altria for only 35 years, much shorter than the investment time frame that we are looking for in this book. Altria returned a significantly higher rate of return than the average of the Standard and Poor's 500. Even for this relatively short period of time for a long-term investor, the difference between reinvesting all distributions and spending them is significant. It more than triples results. I have also projected what an investment in Altria might produce if Altria continues to maintain the same rate of return for the next 25 years that it did in the past 35 years. This may be a stretch for Altria, but the Siegel data show, with some updating, that for 52 years Altria achieved a higher yearly return than that projected here.

For those of you who are middle aged, Figure 8A2 shows what is possible with a little luck. And you do need a little luck to pick an Altria. As you can see, a $10,000 investment would have produced over $4 million with all distributions reinvested in added stock in just 35 years. There may be hope for those in middle age who want to invest for retirement but don't have 50 or 60 years or more. Two periods stand out in what was an otherwise record-breaking performance for shareholders in Altria. In 1993, a shareholder would have seen the value of his or her Altria stock drop almost 26% from its high the previous year, and even worse, in 1999, Altria stock plummeted 54% from its 1998 high (Figure 8B2). Altria recovered nicely, doubling in 2000, and has continued to perform well for the last 5 years. But imagine an investor who initiated his or her investment in Altria at the high in 1998 as he or she watched shareholder value fall more than 50% in 1 year. If he or she held on until 2005, he or she more than doubled his or her money in 6 years.

FIGURE 8B2 Altria Detail[50]
Invested $10,000

Year	Actual Stock Price	Adjusted Stock Price	Shares	Distributions per Share	Distribution Dollars	Distribution in Shares	Total Shares	Total Value
1970	50	0.52	19,394	0.01092	$212	411	19,805	$10,212
1971	70	0.73	19,805	0.01259	$249	341	20,145	$14,742
1972	118	1.23	20,145	0.01315	$265	215	20,360	$25,079
1973	115	1.20	20,360	0.01466	$298	250	20,610	$24,636
1974	96	1.00	20,610	0.01616	$333	333	20,943	$20,943
1975	106	1.10	20,943	0.01928	$404	366	21,309	$23,529
1976	124	1.29	21,309	0.02396	$511	397	21,706	$27,924
1977	124	1.29	21,706	0.03251	$706	547	22,253	$28,688
1978	141	1.47	22,253	0.04268	$950	647	22,900	$33,634
1979	144	1.50	22,900	0.05202	$1,191	794	23,694	$35,541
1980	173	1.80	23,694	0.06668	$1,580	877	24,571	$44,278
1981	195	2.03	24,571	0.08332	$2,047	1,008	25,579	$51,956
1982	240	2.50	25,579	0.1	$2,558	1,023	26,602	$66,504
1983	285	2.97	26,602	0.12084	$3,215	1,083	27,685	$82,188
1984	322	3.36	27,685	0.14168	$3,922	1,168	28,852	$96,919
1985	353	3.68	28,852	0.16668	$4,809	1,306	30,158	$111,045
1986	575	5.99	30,158	0.20626	$6,220	1,039	31,197	$186,843
1987	683	7.11	31,197	0.2625	$8,189	1,151	32,348	$230,129
1988	766	7.98	32,348	0.3375	$10,917	1,368	33,716	$269,027
1989	1,332	13.88	33,716	0.417	$14,060	1,013	34,729	$481,928
1990	1,656	17.25	34,729	0.517	$17,955	1,041	35,770	$617,037
1991	2,568	26.75	35,770	0.637	$22,786	852	36,622	$979,641
1992	2,468	25.71	36,622	0.7837	$28,701	1,116	37,739	$970,132
1993	1,736	18.08	37,739	0.867	$32,719	1,809	39,548	$715,158
1994	1,840	19.17	39,548	1.01	$39,943	2,084	41,632	$797,945
1995	2,888	30.08	41,632	1.217	$50,666	1,684	43,316	$1,303,093
1996	3,616	37.67	43,316	1.467	$63,545	1,687	45,003	$1,695,118
1997	4,344	45.25	45,003	1.6	$72,005	1,591	46,594	$2,108,397
1998	5,136	53.50	46,594	1.68	$78,279	1,463	48,058	$2,571,080
1999	2,208	23.00	48,058	1.84	$88,426	3,845	51,902	$1,193,750
2000	4,224	44.00	51,902	2.02	$104,842	2,383	54,285	$2,388,538

—

2001	4,402	45.85	54,285	2.22	$120,513	2,628	56,913	$2,609,704
2002	3,891	40.53	56,913	2.44	$138,868	3,426	60,339	$2,445,628
2003	5,224	54.42	60,339	2.64	$159,296	2,927	63,267	$3,442,760
2004	5,866	61.10	63,267	2.82	$178,412	2,920	66,186	$4,044,268

Figure 8B3 shows the number of years that an investor had to wait to triple her investment in Altria. The slightly longer period (9 years) that just occurred may suggest that Altria's spectacular growth in value may be slowing slightly. However, even a triple of one's investment every 9 years makes a $10,000 investment worth over $1 million in 45 years and almost $10 million in 63 years, nothing to sneeze at.

FIGURE 8B3 Distribution of Altria Total Return Years to Approximately Triple Total Value

Year	Total Value	Approximate Years
1970	$10,212	
1978	33,634	8
1985	111,045	7
1989	481,926	4
1996	1,695,118	7
2005	$5 million+	9

Union Carbide/Dow Chemical

I include in the detailed analysis two companies which performed below the market averages. Investors should look at what kind of return expectations they might achieve if an individual stock selection was not as good as GE, Altria, or the S&P averages. Of course, there are always companies that fail completely and for whom the compound return turns out to be zero. I picked a couple of those in my younger days, and I have tried later on in this book to give you some guidelines to try to avoid the real clinkers. I selected Union Carbide, a long-lived chemical company that merged into Dow Chemical in 2001. The results assume the Union Carbide investor would have taken Dow Chemical stock after the merger and continued to hold and reinvest distributions until 2004. Price and dividend data back to 1926 are available with a couple of years unreported.

—

I simply smoothed out an adjusted price for these few years, and it should make little difference in the 78-year analysis. I do have complete data on distributions.

FIGURE 8C1 Union Carbide/Dow Chemical[51]
$10,000 Invested

	Share Price	Adjusted Share Price (Splits)	$10,000 Shares	Distributions per share	Distributions Dollars	Distributions in Shares	Total Shares	Total Value
1926	100.38	5.5764	1,793	0.2917	$523	94	1,887	$10,523
1927	145.00	8.0556	1,887	0.3333	$629	78	1,965	$15,830
1928	197.00	10.9444	1,965	0.3333	$655	60	2,025	$22,162
1929	79.00	4.3889	2,025	0.2389	$484	110	2,135	$9,371
1930	51.13	2.8403	2,135	0.1444	$308	109	2,244	$6,373
1931	31.00	1.7222	2,244	0.1444	$324	188	2,432	$4,188
1932	26.75	1.4861	2,432	0.0778	$189	127	2,559	$3,803
1933	47.50	2.6389	2,559	0.0667	$171	65	2,624	$6,924
1934	47.13	2.6181	2,624	0.0722	$189	72	2,696	$7,059
1935	71.50	3.9722	2,696	0.0861	$232	58	2,755	$10,942
1936	103.75	5.7639	2,755	0.1278	$352	61	2,816	$16,230
1937	73.50	4.0833	2,816	0.1778	$501	123	2,938	$11,998
1938	89.63	4.9792	2,938	0.1111	$326	66	3,004	$14,957
1939	86.75	4.8194	3,004	0.1111	$334	69	3,073	$14,811
1940	69.63	3.8681	3,073	0.1278	$393	102	3,175	$12,280
1941	74.00	4.1111	3,175	0.1667	$529	129	3,303	$13,581
1942	81.00	4.5000	3,303	0.1667	$551	122	3,426	$15,416
1943	79.75	4.4306	3,426	0.1667	$571	129	3,555	$15,749
1944	79.63	4.4236	3,555	0.1667	$593	134	3,689	$16,317
1945	85.00	4.7222	3,689	0.1667	$615	130	3,819	$18,034
1946	95.00	5.2778	3,819	0.1667	$637	121	3,940	$20,792
1947	110.00	6.1111	3,940	0.2083	$821	134	4,074	$24,896
1948	123.88	6.8819	4,074	0.2766	$1,127	164	4,238	$29,163
1949	44.63	7.4375	4,238	0.3333	$1,412	190	4,427	$32,929
1950	55.13	9.1875	4,427	0.3333	$1,476	161	4,588	$42,153
1951	63.63	10.6042	4,588	0.3333	$1,529	144	4,732	$50,182
1952	71.63	11.9375	4,732	0.4167	$1,972	165	4,897	$58,464

1953	74.25	12.3750	4,897	0.4167	$2,041	165	5,062	$62,647
1954	86.25	14.3750	5,062	0.4167	$2,110	147	5,209	$74,882
1955	110.13	18.3542	5,209	0.5000	$2,605	142	5,351	$98,214
1956	115.75	19.2917	5,351	0.5250	$2,809	146	5,497	$106,040
1957	95.00	15.8333	5,497	0.6000	$3,298	208	5,705	$90,329
1958	126.13	21.0208	5,705	0.6000	$3,423	163	5,868	$123,346
1959	147.00	24.5000	5,868	0.6000	$3,521	144	6,012	$147,282
1960	118.88	19.8125	6,012	0.6000	$3,607	182	6,194	$122,710
1961	120.00	20.0000	6,194	0.6000	$3,716	186	6,379	$127,587
1962	121.50	20.2500	6,379	0.6000	$3,828	189	6,568	$133,010
1963	122.00	20.3333	6,568	0.6000	$3,941	194	6,762	$137,498
1964	127.00	21.1667	6,762	0.6000	$4,057	192	6,954	$147,191
1965	68.50	22.8333	6,954	0.5000	$3,477	152	7,106	$162,258
1966	47.25	15.7500	7,106	0.6667	$4,738	301	7,407	$116,660
1967	49.00	16.3333	7,407	0.6667	$4,938	302	7,709	$125,919
1968	45.25	15.0833	7,709	0.6667	$5,140	341	8,050	$121,422
1969	37.00	12.3333	8,050	0.6667	$5,367	435	8,485	$104,651
1970	39.88	13.2917	8,485	0.6667	$5,657	426	8,911	$118,440
1971	42.50	14.1667	8,911	0.6667	$5,941	419	9,330	$132,178
1972	50.00	16.6667	9,330	0.6667	$6,220	373	9,703	$161,724
1973	34.13	11.3750	9,703	0.6750	$6,550	576	10,279	$116,926
1974	41.38	13.7917	10,279	0.7250	$7,452	540	10,820	$149,220
1975	61.13	20.3750	10,820	0.8000	$8,656	425	11,244	$229,105
1976	42.00	14.0000	11,244	0.8333	$9,370	669	11,914	$166,792
1977	44.00	14.6667	11,914	0.9333	$11,119	758	12,672	$185,853
1978	46.00	15.3333	12,672	0.9333	$11,827	771	13,443	$206,128
1979	48.00	16.0000	13,443	0.9667	$12,995	812	14,255	$228,086
1980	50.25	16.7500	14,255	1.0667	$15,206	908	15,163	$253,983
1981	51.38	17.1250	15,163	1.1000	$16,679	974	16,137	$276,349
1982	52.88	17.6250	16,137	1.1333	$18,288	1,038	17,175	$302,706
1983	62.75	20.9167	17,175	1.1333	$19,464	931	18,105	$378,704
1984	36.75	12.2500	18,105	1.1333	$20,519	1,675	19,780	$242,309
1985	70.88	23.6250	19,780	1.1333	$22,417	949	20,729	$489,728
1986	22.50	22.5000	20,729	5.0200	$104,061	4,625	25,354	$570,468
1987	21.75	21.7500	25,354	1.5000	$38,031	1,749	27,103	$589,484
1988	25.63	25.6250	27,103	1.1500	$31,168	1,216	28,319	$725,675
1989	23.25	23.2500	28,319	1.0000	$28,319	1,218	29,537	$686,736
1990	16.38	16.3750	29,537	1.0000	$29,537	1,804	31,341	$513,206
1991	20.25	20.2500	31,341	1.0000	$31,341	1,548	32,889	$665,993
1992	16.63	16.6250	32,889	0.8750	$28,777	1,731	34,620	$575,549

—

1993	22.38	22.3750	34,620	0.7500	$25,965	1,160	35,780	$800,576
1994	29.38	29.3750	35,780	0.7500	$26,835	914	36,693	$1,077,871
1995	37.50	37.5000	36,693	0.7500	$27,520	734	37,427	$1,403,525
1996	40.88	40.8750	37,427	0.7500	$28,071	687	38,114	$1,557,913
1997	42.94	42.9375	38,114	0.7500	$28,586	666	38,780	$1,665,109
1998	42.50	42.5000	38,780	0.9000	$34,902	821	39,601	$1,683,044
1999	66.75	66.7500	39,601	0.9000	$35,641	534	40,135	$2,679,011
2000	53.81	53.8130	40,135	0.9000	$36,121	671	40,806	$2,195,906
2001	54.42	54.4200	40,806	1.1739	$47,902	880	41,686	$2,268,578
2002	47.85	47.8500	41,686	1.3400	$55,860	1,167	42,854	$2,050,557
2003	66.97	66.9700	42,854	1.3400	$57,424	857	43,711	$2,927,347
2004	79.76	79.7600	43,711	1.3400	$58,573	734	44,446	$3,544,988

The first issue to notice about Union Carbide is while a $10,000 investment produced over $3.5 million compared with a little over $4 million for Altria, Altria accomplished this result in 34 years, and it took Union Carbide 78 years. If we compare Union Carbide to Altria for the same 34 years, 1970-2004, Union Carbide would have returned $299,307 on a $10,000 investment compared with the slightly more than $4 million for Altria.

Figure 8C2 shows the rate of return comparison. Notice the Union Carbide compound rate of return per year averaged 7.82%, less than half the Altria compound return of 18.71% per year and significantly below the S&P average return for the 1926-2004 period of 10.26%. Figure 8C3 shows the estimated number of years it took to triple your investment in Union Carbide. Note there are two long periods in which Union Carbide took 23 and 27 years to triple shareholder value, which largely accounts for the significant difference in overall return.

FIGURE 8C2 Union Carbide/Dow Chemical Rate of Return

Union Carbide/Dow Chemical	Yearly Return	Value of $1,000	Investment of $10,000
Compound rate of return Union Carbide (no distribution reinvested)	3.47%	$14,303	$143,032
Compound rate of return Union Carbide (all distributions reinvested)	7.82%	$354,499	$3,544,988
Compound rate of return S&P 500 (all distributions reinvested)	10.26%	$2,033,469	$20,334,688

—

FIGURE 8C3 Distribution of Union Carbide Total Return Years to Approximately Triple Total Value

Year	Total Value	Approximate Years
1926	$10,523	
1949	32,929	23
1955	98,214	6
1982	302,706	27
1994	1,077,811	12
2004	3,544,988	10

Nestlé

The fourth company that we will look at in some detail is the giant Swiss company, Nestlé. Nestlé, founded back in the 1860s, owns some of the world's best-known foods, beverages, cereals, snack foods, dairy products, and pet care products. They are a company with a true worldwide imprint with an aggressive business in the United States, Europe, South America, Asia, Oceania, and Africa. Like Union Carbide, Nestlé shows the dramatic difference that dividend and distribution reinvestment can make over a 50-year analysis.

FIGURE 8C4 Nestlé[52]

Nestlé Stock from 1954 to 2005*	Value of Investment		
	Return	$1,000	$10,000
Compound rate of return (no distributions reinvested)	7.3138%	$36,596	$365,955
Compound rate of return (all distributions reinvested)	9.7555%	$115,276	$1,152,760
Compound rate of return on S&P 500 (all distributions reinvested)	11.42%	$248,382	$2,483,824
Project value at 60 years (all distributions reinvested) (assuming the same rate of return)	9.7555%	$266,427	$2,664,266

*September 2005.

Figure 8C4 shows that Nestlé has had a solid but unspectacular return, especially when compared with Altria and some of the glamorous performers and even compared with the S&P 500 average. I like to analyze a solid but more pedestrian stock like Nestlé or Union Carbide so the reader can understand that Altria type returns are wonderful but not always the norm. It is likely that many investors will select some solid performers like Nestlé for some of their stock investments. It is rewarding to find top performers, but you can be highly successful without them.

Like Union Carbide, Nestlé shows the dramatic difference dividend and distribution reinvestment makes over a 50-year analysis. Reinvesting dividends tripled an investor's return in Nestlé over a 50 year-period. Looking at Nestlé's performance in detail, the results show three serious declines, which an investor would have had to endure. The worst was an approximate 47% decline during the bear market from 1972 to 1974, an approximate 36% decline from 1958 to 1959, and a more modest 19% decline during the recent market break from 2000 to 2002 (Figure 8C5).

Figure 8C6 shows that Nestlé made investors wait for 18 and 13 years to triple their investment value during the 30 years beginning with 1954. But since 1985, Nestlé's return has tripled twice in 8 and 7 years, respectively. This may bode well for Nestlé as an investment potential in the early part of the 21st century. Nestlé, being a Swiss company, is a little more difficult to invest in than an American company. Nestlé does trade a type of share called an ADR (American Depository Receipt) on the Over-the-Counter Exchange. Many brokers can buy foreign stocks in the origin country for American investors. A stock like Nestlé gives an investor some diversification outside the United States. I will deal with things like diversification and asset allocation in Chapter 30.

FIGURE 8C5 Nestlé Detail[53]

Year	Dollar Stock Price	$10,000 Shares	Distributions Per Share	Distribution Dollars	Distribution in Shares	Total Shares	Total Value
1954	12.79	782	0.45	$352	28	809	$10,352
1955	15.05	809	0.53	$429	29	838	$12,610
1956	18.98	838	0.6	$503	26	864	$16,406
1957	17.07	864	0.6	$519	30	895	$15,273
1958	21.55	895	0.6	$537	25	920	$19,819
1959	13.61	920	0.23	$212	16	935	$12,728
1960	18.45	935	0.26	$243	13	948	$17,497

1961	26.8	948	0.26	$247	9	958	$25,663
1962	21.15	958	0.29	$278	13	971	$20,530
1963	21.85	971	0.32	$311	14	985	$21,520
1964	20.25	985	0.32	$315	16	1,000	$20,260
1965	17.1	1,000	0.35	$350	20	1,021	$17,458
1966	13.47	1,021	0.4	$408	30	1,051	$14,161
1967	18.15	1,051	0.47	$494	27	1,079	$19,575
1968	21.75	1,079	0.51	$550	25	1,104	$24,007
1969	20.2	1,104	0.55	$607	30	1,134	$22,904
1970	20.25	1,134	0.55	$624	31	1,165	$23,584
1971	19.55	1,165	0.6	$699	36	1,200	$23,468
1972	25.3	1,200	0.65	$780	31	1,231	$31,150
1973	21.8	1,231	0.65	$800	37	1,268	$27,641
1974	12.4	1,268	0.65	$824	66	1,334	$16,547
1975	16.4	1,334	0.65	$867	53	1,387	$22,752
1976	19.6	1,387	0.72	$999	51	1,438	$28,190
1977	22.05	1,438	0.72	$1,036	47	1,485	$32,749
1978	22.95	1,485	0.72	$1,069	47	1,532	$35,155
1979	22.4	1,532	0.75	$1,149	51	1,583	$35,461
1980	20.6	1,583	0.75	$1,187	58	1,641	$33,799
1981	19.15	1,641	0.85	$1,395	73	1,714	$32,815
1982	23	1,714	0.96	$1,645	72	1,785	$41,057
1983	30.2	1,785	1.09	$1,946	64	1,850	$55,855
1984	33	1,850	1.15	$2,127	64	1,914	$63,161
1985	49.5	1,914	1.45	$2,775	56	1,970	$97,516
1986	48.3	1,970	1.45	$2,857	59	2,029	$98,009
1987	39.5	2,029	1.5	$3,044	77	2,106	$83,196
1988	66.9	2,106	1.75	$3,686	55	2,161	$144,592
1989	86.8	2,161	2	$4,323	50	2,211	$191,925
1990	69.9	2,211	2	$4,422	63	2,274	$158,980
1991	86	2,274	2.15	$4,890	57	2,331	$200,487
1992	116	2,331	2.35	$5,478	47	2,378	$275,903
1993	128.3	2,378	2.5	$5,946	46	2,425	$311,105
1994	124.7	2,425	2.65	$6,426	52	2,476	$308,801
1995	127.6	2,476	2.65	$6,562	51	2,528	$322,545

1996	143.7	2,528	3	$7,583	53	2,581	$370,825
1997	218.9	2,581	3.5	$9,032	41	2,622	$573,915
1998	299	2,622	3.8	$9,963	33	2,655	$793,885
1999	291.7	2,655	4.3	$11,417	39	2,694	$785,920
2000	378	2,694	5.5	$14,819	39	2,733	$1,033,254
2001	354	2,733	6.4	$17,494	49	2,783	$985,145
2002	293	2,783	7	$19,480	66	2,849	$834,868
2003	309	2,849	7.2	$20,516	66	2,916	$900,974
2004	297.5	2,916	8	$23,326	78	2,994	$890,769
2005	377	2,994	8	$23,953	64	3,058	$1,152,760

FIGURE 8C6 Distribution of Nestlé Total Return
Years to Approximately Triple Total Value

Year	Total Value	Approximate Years
1954	$10,352	
1972	31,150	18
1985	97,516	13
1993	311,105	8
2000	1,033,251	7

Seven Selected Companies

Figure 8D1 includes yearly data results for 7 different additional companies. I included Professor Jeremy Siegel's calculated compound rate of return for an accuracy check. They are not entirely comparable since his term was 1957-2003 and my data is for 1962-2004. Figures 8D1 and 8D2 will give an investor some added confidence in the kinds of long-term returns that are possible with individual stock selection.

The S&P 500 compounded at 10.34% from 1962 until 2004, four of the seven companies had higher returns than average and three had poorer returns than average.

FIGURE 8D1 Total Compound Return—7 Selected Companies[54]
$10,000 Initial Investment, All Distributions
Reinvested and No Taxes Paid

	Total Value						
Year	IBM	Alcoa	Boeing	Caterpillar	DuPont	GM	Coca-Cola
1962	$10,021	$10,220	$10,635	$10,541	$10,376	$11,032	$10,862
1963	$13,056	$13,086	$9,578	$14,465	$11,911	$31,360	$16,410
1964	$13,223	$11,934	$10,940	$13,468	$14,787	$40,853	$21,663
1965	$16,164	$15,140	$11,963	$17,286	$15,055	$45,437	$14,133
1966	$18,092	$15,792	$11,667	$13,199	$9,266	$30,541	$15,920
1967	$30,592	$16,574	$11,657	$17,654	$10,364	$39,782	$24,881
1968	$31,215	$15,400	$26,296	$18,952	$11,034	$40,471	$14,499
1969	$36,961	$15,411	$27,629	$19,859	$7,389	$37,555	$17,525
1970	$33,422	$12,772	$28,548	$20,524	$9,756	$44,662	$19,126
1971	$36,433	$10,135	$25,170	$22,664	$10,972	$46,549	$28,821
1972	$44,973	$12,760	$24,185	$31,904	$13,809	$49,480	$36,425
1973	$28,828	$17,929	$22,195	$32,099	$12,794	$31,340	$32,462
1974	$26,352	$11,538	$21,522	$23,247	$7,906	$23,031	$15,379
1975	$37,455	$15,439	$20,062	$33,460	$11,248	$44,961	$25,978
1976	$49,448	$23,428	$24,074	$41,728	$12,416	$65,768	$27,877
1977	$52,202	$19,778	$65,740	$39,394	$11,565	$58,504	$29,477
1978	$61,396	$21,059	$72,068	$42,215	$12,658	$55,592	$39,043
1979	$58,340	$25,350	$56,863	$38,810	$12,974	$57,351	$35,874
1980	$67,370	$29,023	$77,039	$41,728	$14,378	$54,368	$41,749
1981	$62,500	$26,472	$62,977	$39,880	$13,796	$49,415	$51,491
1982	$112,121	$33,736	$98,748	$33,363	$14,307	$83,145	$88,818
1983	$148,984	$50,147	$131,596	$42,717	$21,692	$103,392	$104,151
1984	$157,942	$42,683	$174,549	$30,598	$21,838	$115,904	$135,337
1985	$208,068	$45,798	$288,896	$42,843	$31,265	$111,467	$200,426
1986	$169,246	$41,730	$283,526	$42,149	$40,101	$112,465	$287,010
1987	$171,771	$58,899	$212,935	$66,510	$43,285	$113,112	$308,639
1988	$190,249	$72,191	$355,543	$70,292	$45,554	$164,011	$385,583
1989	$156,668	$100,191	$358,475	$67,132	$65,738	$177,760	$696,913
1990	$198,246	$81,462	$423,840	$57,764	$61,521	$154,326	$873,427
1991	$166,359	$93,569	$682,973	$57,361	$80,873	$134,979	$1,555,354
1992	$104,454	$106,499	$588,287	$71,945	$84,758	$155,457	$1,671,935
1993	$120,747	$105,532	$648,684	$121,584	$89,937	$268,398	$1,843,366

—

1994	$159,391	$134,209	$719,927	$153,623	$108,017	$210,444	$2,202,234
1995	$200,467	$166,653	$1,215,757	$171,382	$138,366	$271,135	$3,263,936
1996	$335,412	$204,087	$1,669,048	$230,114	$190,805	$295,080	$4,726,487
1997	$465,925	$228,401	$1,378,806	$309,045	$201,630	$348,485	$6,100,573
1998	$825,137	$245,652	$948,624	$308,114	$196,912	$421,968	$6,241,966
1999	$969,854	$552,224	$1,239,164	$332,460	$207,442	$521,964	$5,549,804
2000	$768,977	$452,424	$2,016,022	$357,230	$214,715	$380,146	$5,953,906
2001	$1,099,424	$488,213	$1,223,398	$417,673	$243,489	$377,608	$4,716,134
2002	$709,893	$321,081	$1,082,626	$389,200	$219,583	$301,931	$4,544,226
2003	$854,796	$544,061	$1,435,454	$737,099	$405,451	$453,798	$5,464,534
2004	$915,713	$458,300	$1,819,737	$896,963	$483,054	$357,430	$4,695,908

Figure 8D1 shows what each of these seven companies would have produced yearly for a theoretical investor who invested $10,000 and reinvested all distributions and avoided paying any taxes (more about this in Chapter 11). These differences are significant. General Motors was the worst performer producing $357,430 during the 43-year period, and Coca-Cola performed the best producing over $4.6 million on the same investment. It is interesting to compare the two investments year by year. For the first 18 years, General Motors outperformed Coca-Cola. Then, starting in the 1981-1982 recession, Coca-Cola simply smoked GM for the last two decades. DuPont lagged significantly behind GM until the last few years when it caught and surpassed the giant automaker.

IBM, Alcoa, and Boeing lagged behind GM for the first dozen or so years, and in the 1977-1978 period, both IBM and Boeing caught GM in total value and never looked back. Alcoa only caught GM during the boom market of 1999. An investor in all six of the better-performing stocks would have been disappointed in their performance relative to GM for the 20 years from 1962 to 1982. Patience was the key for these investors. Those that lost patience missed out on the big moves.

FIGURE 8D2 Rate of Returns and Projected Totals
$10,000 Investment

	IBM	Alcoa	Boeing	Caterpillar	DuPont	GM	Coca-Cola
Yearly rate							
of return							
(1962-2004)	11.08%	9.30%	12.86%	11.02%	9.44%	8.67%	15.38%
Siegel							
(1957-2003)[55]	11.94%	8.06%	12.31%	10.55%	8.30%	8.28%	16.02%
Projected totals							
$10,000 invested							
50 Years	$2,121,964	$933,686	$4,791,544	$2,070,528	$993,795	$695,275	$14,749,718
60 Years	$6,066,820	$2,272,558	$16,071,591	$5,891,348	$2,448,633	$1,597,215	$61,675,666
70 Years	$17,345,396	$5,531,320	$53,906,644	$16,762,866	$6,033,238	$3,669,193	$257,895,633

Figure 8D2 shows the compound yearly rate of return for the seven companies from 1962 to 2004 and Professor Siegel's calculation for the 1957-2003 period. In this book, I have been talking largely about longer investment terms than 43 or 47 years. We have been looking at 50, 60, or 70 years as the potential time horizon for a true long-term investor. At the bottom of Figure 8D2 is the "projected" final totals for a $10,000 investment in each company if they continue with the same rate of return for the years left. Figure 8D3 shows the same projected results for an investor of $1,000 in each company.

FIGURE 8D3 Projected Total Values
Assuming a $1,000 Initial Investment in Each Company

Projected Totals	Total Value						
	IBM	Alcoa	Boeing	Caterpillar	DuPont	GM	Coca-Cola
50 Years	$212,196	$93,369	$479,154	$207,053	$99,380	$69,527	$1,474,972
60 Years	$606,682	$227,256	$1,607,159	$589,135	$244,863	$159,722	$6,167,567
70 Years	$1,734,540	$553,132	$5,390,664	$1,676,287	$603,324	$366,919	$25,789,563

The Future and the Past

In Chapter 29, I discuss many of the possible obstacles to the success of the investment plan presented in this book. It may seem odd to look at the ways in which my plan for you may fail. But the reality is that nothing is guaranteed in life, no plan is foolproof, and as optimistic as I am about the future, I believe that it is important for you to understand as many of the gloomier possibilities that exist as well.

We are living in an era of dramatic and fast-paced change. Many authors have documented this, and our own experience in the last two decades has confirmed it. It is likely the next few decades will see change, and a pace of change that occurs on a scale that is hard to imagine.

Our plan does not require the economy to jump through hoops. It does want a performance over the next 50-70 years that is something close to what has occurred in the past 50-70 years. Some believe the prospects for the US and world economies cannot be as good in the future as it has in the past. If they are right, your returns will be reduced from the levels denoted in this book. While I recognize this possibility, I believe the highest likelihood is the economy of the world and the United States are entering an even more prosperous century than the past one.

There are always people who doubt everything and look at the future only with pessimism. In my lifetime, there have always been big issues to worry about. I was born in 1938, so let me briefly review a few of the "big" worries of the past 7 decades to help you realize there is always something big to worry about. Personally, I think that some of the concerns of the present, while substantial, actually lag in magnitude and potential when viewed with the concerns of the past.

The 1940s saw a world war for which the outcome was in doubt for a few years. After the war, the division of the world into communist and non-communist blocs, coupled with the development of the atomic bomb, was a serious concern.

The 1950s saw the Korean War and its aftermath and the "Cold" War, which at times seemed ready to blow up the entire world. The capacity of both sides to launch atomic weapons on intercontinental missiles that could destroy entire cities or countries in minutes was more than disconcerting. The Soviet Union's launch of the first space satellite, Sputnik, combined with the Soviet's faster gross domestic product (GDP) growth during the 1950s made many in the West question whether our economic system of capitalism and even our form of government was not falling behind. One of the most interesting economics courses that I took at the University of Pennsylvania was Comparative Economic Systems.

The professor challenged us to think about the possibility that the Soviets would, given their then current growth rate, exceed the United States in economic size and success by the early to mid-1970s. What if the Soviet system was a better economic system? Would the United States give up its political system and corresponding freedoms to gain the benefits offered by a richer Soviet Union? These were serious questions that we worried about.

The 1960s saw the Kennedy assassination that caused many Americans to question, for the first time, the society in which they always had such confidence. This followed by an almost revolutionary attitude assumed by many young people who questioned and opposed many conventional aspects of our society that the rest had taken for granted and assumed correct for decades. Coupled with the divisive Vietnam War, it seemed at times the country was about to come apart.

The 1970s saw a continuation of the increasingly hostile debate about Vietnam coupled with gas lines and oil shortages that pointed out, for the first time, our increasing vulnerability to unstable Middle East fossil fuels. A disgraced president resigned, and the balance of the decade was dominated by a sluggish economy and stock market and some of the worst inflation in modern American history. Many feared a disastrous runaway inflation as 1980 approached.

The 1980s saw a moderation of our inflation fears but a growing federal debt and a seemingly unstoppable Japanese economy that threaten to own the world. The end of the decade saw the beginning of a severe economic challenge in the Savings and Loan crisis that threatened economic stability.

The 1990s ushered in a solution to the S&L crisis and with it a strong growing economy. Economic optimism lead to unprecedented stock values by the end of the decade that resulted in steep stock price declines, which many have described as a classic bubble.

The first decade of the 21st century saw the World Trade Center terrorism disaster and the controversial war in Iraq. By 2005, the economy was growing nicely and the stock market regained much of its loss from the post-"bubble" headache. But in 2005, many stock price averages still have not penetrated back to their all-time highs in 2000. Federal deficits, worsened by some natural disasters, threaten to explode least temporarily. An expanding trade shortfall resulting from growing levels of cheaper imports threatens the value of the dollar and many worry about "outsourcing" jobs to places like China and India. Despite the outsourcing, unemployment rates remain historically low. Others worry about the middle class losing its position in the United States as some evidence points out the middle and lower middle 20% of the population may be losing their historic share of the economic pie.

So the markets always have serious issues to worry about, but somehow the US economy and political system have always found a way to pull things through, and I am confident that we will find the same in the future as well.

The Future Might Not Be as Good as the Past

Some well-respected authors and stock market experts have predicted a bleaker future for stock investors than occurred in the past. These predictions center on both global economic trends and the US stock market experience. I will deal with some of their arguments in more detail in Chapter 29, but let me make a few general comments about some of these broad issues.

The future can be scary. Some observers fear the results of the technological revolution that we are seeing all around us. This revolution combined with an unstoppable globalization of world economies is cause for alarm. Globalization will cause disruption. The entire idea of work and job skills is changing so quickly that it is hard for many to comprehend. Technological skills have a short shelf life, and this increases the anxiety of the average American. No longer can one go to school, graduate, and begin a traditional career with the security that existed in prior decades. Careers today are multifaceted; most will have several different careers during their lifetime, and the skills that we will need must be constantly upgraded if we are to preserve competency in a fast-changing environment. The new economy will not be a worry-free or secure one, and this is understandably frightening for many. The ability of foreign countries with cheaper skilled labor to compete with US workers is becoming painfully obvious. Global competition in every field means the United States will probably not be able to dominate the world's economy in the 21st century in the way it did for most of the 20th century.

The economic "problem" of the baby boom retirement is starting to be recognized by many authors, particularly financial authors. I will deal with it in more detail in Chapter 29, but the demographic shift from this large population bulge's retirement will be dramatic, and it is not possible to rule out significant economic dislocations as a result.

Experts who believe the market is overvalued compared with historic valuation measures have questioned the stock market itself. Ideas such as "mean reversion" make some believe future stock market returns must be lower than past returns as the markets responded to higher than "average"

—

returns during the last two decades of the 20th century. The reader should understand clearly that there will always be stock market pundits who are pessimistic about the future of the markets. There is always a reason to believe the markets must go down or at least sideways for long periods of time. Credible pundits that believe the markets are headed for disaster will always test a long-term investor. As a student of historical data, I can confirm that you can always find some statistics that support your view. And the truth is there are times in history when the pessimists have been right. The Great Depression of the 1930s is a prime and obvious example, but also a long period from 1965 until 1982 saw an inflation-adjusted market decline that was most painful for investors. There are periods when the stock market is not the best place to invest money, but it is difficult for anyone to predict these periods consistently.

International threats are always on the horizon. In the first decade of the 21st century, the dominant threat we face comes from terrorists and rogue states. I am no expert on these topics, but global terrorism could mushroom and present severe challenges to the world economic system, which could threaten our investments. I do not find it likely to end there. In a global economic sense, terrorism may never amount to a global economic threat. If the threat intensifies and begins to threaten economic systems, I believe that much of the world will join and vigorously stamp it out. It is hard to imagine that the developed world and the developing world would not decide, at one point, that severe action would be needed. I have no doubt in the ability of the world to solve it once it is resolved to do so. Terrorism, as I see it, may have some temporary and severe effects on markets. It is not likely to have a long-term one, and a long-term investor should not be dissuaded from investing in stocks for fear of terrorism.

The Future Might Be Better Than the Past

I cannot predict the future for you, but I want to make a few broad comments not just about some of the general threats but also the opportunities that face the markets.

First, it is likely the technological revolution that we face will be much more powerful and dramatic than most of us expect. We live in the present, and we have great trouble trying to understand a future much different from today. This fact will lead to much confusion but also to unprecedented opportunities for everyone. I am convinced that the stock markets are undervaluing the implications of this revolution and that it is, in fact, a good time to begin a long-term investment program. Large companies around the world face opportunities that have never existed for them in the past. Globalization has its downsides but also almost seemingly unlimited upsides. American companies that used to be limited by the American and Canadian markets now have almost the entire world as a market for their goods and services. Huge populations in countries with expanding economies like China and India present options that were not around for the past 50-70 years. Many American companies are positioning themselves and are poised to take advantage of them. The market opportunities for established companies like Procter & Gamble, Nestlé, or Coca-Cola to sell their recognized brand-name products worldwide have never been bigger. The ability to capitalize on technology and globalization will present profit opportunities for companies unheard of in past decades. And the potential of the newer technology companies like Microsoft, Apple and Intel has never been brighter in their short history. Globalization and technology present opportunities for profit to companies that position themselves to capitalize on them. This is a positive trend for stock market investors.

The baby boom retirement is a much more difficult one to deal with. It is clear the retiring of this large population sector will be both an opportunity and a threat, like most things in economics. If the baby boomers sell their assets, real estate, stocks, and bonds to fund their retirement, will that depress asset prices, stocks included? Some experts worry, others do not believe, the impact will be significant in the global economic system. No one knows for sure, but betting against the capacity of our economy and the world economy to handle this problem is, in my view, a long shot. I would not stay up nights worrying about it.

The arguments about stock market valuations go on and on and on. I have watched this for 50 years. There are always people who believe that they have good reasons to forecast a declining or stagnant market. I deal with this idea of mean reversion elsewhere in Chapter 29. Later in this chapter, I look at ideas about optimistic and pessimistic stock market returns. But I do believe the world economy is on the threshold of a potential expansion of health, wealth, and living standards never previously imagined. Pick a year, study the political and economic situation, and tell me when the prospects and the chances for investors were better. I can't tell you if the market is over or undervalued in the short run, but I do think the potential for the stock market today may be better than it ever has been. And I am not convinced that this attitude is reflected in current stock market valuations and prices (October 2005). In the long run, these arguments should not matter to you. Long-term investors should not be concerned about whether the market is overvalued or undervalued at any given time. The real question is: where do you believe the markets will be in 50, 60, or 70 years? It seems hard not to argue that prospects for long-term economic growth in the world have never been better.

Dow 36,000, Dow 100,000, Reality or Fantasy

Earlier, I briefly touched on a couple of books published a few years ago with what some thought were outlandish predictions about where stock market averages might go. One of them, mentioned in Chapter 6, argued that, based on Siegel's research, the Dow should have been 36,000 then.[56] That book was criticized by many based on some alleged technical calculation errors. Another book by Charles Kadlec predicted that the Dow would hit 100,000 sometime in the future.[57] Assume the Dow will continue to grow at an average 11.76% compound rate of return including the current dividend rate on the Dow of 2.26%. I calculate that the Dow (11,120 on April 9, 2006) could exceed 36,000 in 2019 and 100,000 in 2030. If we look at the S&P with the same assumptions (current dividend yield on the S&P is 1.85%), the S&P (1,296 today) could hit 5,000 in 2021 and 10,000 in 2028. These are the numbers the indexes must hit, assuming current dividend yields, to meet a projection of 11.76% compound rate of return. If dividend yields in either index increase, a smaller increase in the index price will achieve the projected target. For instance, for the S&P to compound at an annual rate of 11.76%, assuming current dividend yields, the index price itself would have to compound at 10.12% yearly. If the dividend yield on the S&P should increase to 2.00%, then the index itself would have to compound at only 9.97% yearly. Dividends are part of the return that investors receive. A higher dividend means a lower required increase in the index's price to return the same compound rate. So the answer is that a Dow at 36,000 could be just 13 years away and 100,000 due in about 24 years. These are well within the realm of probabilities. But I want to caution readers that long-term returns from the past show that rarely in any particular year did an index finish exactly on its long-term compound rate of return. Investors should expect to see periods, sometimes long ones, where the yearly compound rates exceed or are less than the long-term rate.

Optimistic and Pessimistic Stock Market Returns

It is often difficult to try to understand what someone means by optimistic or pessimistic positions about stock market returns. As we just examined, optimistic predictions from credible sources of where the market averages may go in the future are around. The pessimists look at several possibilities. One is the valuation or overvaluation of stocks based on current stock prices.

Benjamin Graham is considered the guru of conservative value investing in many circles today. His books are still in the bookstores. In this principal works published in the 1950s and 1960s, he analyzed securities market valuations from many different standpoints. Many who oppose "high" valuations or "high" price/earnings multiples point to Graham to justify their position. It so happens that my first class in investments in 1965 used one of his books, *Security Analysis,* published in 1962 as the textbook in the class, and I happen to still have the book. In Chapter 39, Graham and his colleagues recommend several techniques for valuing growth stocks. They define growth companies as stocks that have a higher than 7½% projected growth rate. If we adopt Graham's "preferred" method (he suggests several alternatives) for these 11 widely held stocks, even using this conservative valuation system, it is hard to decide that these stocks are grossly overvalued.

FIGURE 8E1 (July 7, 2005)
Benjamin Graham's "Preferred" System for Valuing Growth Stocks[58]

Graham System for Valuation of Growth Stocks		1962			July 5, 2005	
Stock	Symbol	Earnings per Share	Expected Growth Rate	Graham Calculated Multiple	Valuation	Current Price
Altria	MO	4.75	8.50	21.625	102.72	64.2
Citigroup	C	3.29	11.50	26.125	85.95	46.27
McGraw-Hill	MHP	1.97	12.00	27	53.19	43.13
Hershey's	HSY	2.367	10.00	23.5	55.62	60.52
Procter & Gamble	PG	2.6	11.00	25.25	65.65	52.9
Pfizer	PFE	1.23	8.00	21	25.83	26.75
General Mills	GIS	2.77	8.00	21	58.17	45.87
Anheuser-Busch	BUD	2.76	9.00	22.25	61.41	45.42
Johnson & Johnson	JNJ	2.977	10.00	23.5	69.96	63.92
General Electric	GE	1.65	10.50	24.375	40.22	34.18
United Tech	UTX	2.86	12.00	27	77.22	50.74

Figure 8E1 shows 11 stocks, their current market price, earnings, expected earnings growth rate for the next 5 years taken from Yahoo's "Analysts Estimates" and the current multiplier of earnings and valuation suggested by Graham. Of the 11 stocks suggested, only 2 are "overvalued" by the Graham-preferred system. Graham's system assumes that a company whose earnings are not growing at all would justify only a stock price 8.5 times its current earnings. That is an investor should be willing to pay 8.5 times the current earnings with no growth prospects. A 3.5% projected growth rate should justify a price 15 times its current earnings, and a company whose earnings are growing at 10% per year should have a price 23½ times its current earnings. I am not suggesting that you rush out and mortgage your house to buy these stocks. Graham's valuation system looks reasonable to me, but it certainly isn't conservative based on current market valuations. The price/earnings calculations using Graham's system all turn out to be in the 20s plus, not unreasonable but certainly not conservative. It should give us some confidence that we are not entering the market at unreasonably or wildly high prices. Part of the reason for this is the brighter future prospects for a typical US company than in Graham's 1960s. Many more companies in 2006 qualify as "growth" companies than Graham envisioned in 1962. As you will see later in this chapter, a long-term investor (50-70 years) has little to fear, from possible market tops, but it does not look like we are in one in any case.

The second market concern lies in the belief that the market has performed so well during the past two decades that it cannot continue that performance into the future. Stocks must return to some theoretical market average return, which means that it must achieve below-average returns for some years to make up for the boom years. Using price/earnings ratios to justify the current market is overvalued supports the idea. Chapter 29 addresses this idea in more detail.

Market Timing

Markets, and particularly stock markets, do not move up in a smooth linear fashion. They move in fits and starts. They go down, they go up, and sometimes they can move violently in either direction. Market timing is an investing technique that tries to identify market tops and market bottoms and have the investor take advantage of them to improve his or her rate of return. If you knew when the market has reached a high point, you could sell your stocks or mutual funds and wait for a low point to buy back in at a handsome profit. This strategy, if successful, would allow an investor to increase his or her rate of return. As we will see in the next chapter, even a small increase in annual compound return can make a big difference in results. Unfortunately, I have not seen any evidence that anyone has developed a system that can predict the market time successfully over many ups and downs in the market. In Chapter 25, I demonstrate the loss possible for a long-term investor who happens to be out of the market even for a brief period. I do not encourage investors to try to use market timing to improve their returns, especially with their retirement plan. If you want to try it with other money, be my guest. If someone had such a system, it would be well known in the market and its knowledge would probably erase any value it held.

Investing at the Market Top?

Novice investors, and sometimes even experienced investors, worry about entering the market at an interim market top. If I buy stock now and it turns out that this is an interim market high, I will suffer as the market enters the next downturn and experience large losses right off the bat. It is true that buying at a high point can be punishing and even a little humiliating to an investor. However, for a long-term investor, the difference between investing at a market top and any other time is not nearly as great as you might think. Look at Figure 8F2 for the S&P composite with a 2004 ending and assume an investor began an investment anytime between post-WWII and 1994 (10 years before the end point, 2004). Figure 8F2 shows the variance in the compound rate of return was not as great as imagined and investing in any year would have returned pretty spectacular results.

FIGURE 8F2 S&P Compound Rates of Return from Starting Year to 2004[59]

Year	Compound Rate to 2004	Year	Compound Rate to 2004
1946	11.76%	1971	11.35%
1947	11.88%	1972	11.04%
1948	11.96%	1973	12.07%
1949	11.89%	1974	13.60%
1950	11.60%	1975	12.85%
1951	11.35%	1976	12.52%
1952	11.24%	1977	13.26%
1953	11.45%	1978	13.48%
1954	10.84%	1979	13.30%
1955	10.40%	1980	12.67%
1956	10.49%	1981	13.37%
1957	10.96%	1982	13.16%
1958	10.45%	1983	12.71%
1959	10.38%	1984	13.13%
1960	10.64%	1985	12.26%
1961	10.23%	1986	11.65%
1962	10.75%	1987	12.34%
1963	10.49%	1988	11.95%
1964	10.34%	1989	10.84%
1965	10.29%	1990	11.84%
1966	10.82%	1991	11.10%
1967	10.56%	1992	10.75%
1968	10.44%	1993	10.84%
1969	11.14%	1994	11.92%
1970	11.42%		

Figure 8F2 shows the actual compound annual rate of return in the S&P that was achieved for investments initiated in every year from 1946 to 1994, assuming the investment was terminated in 2004. Once you move your investment horizons out, in this case at least 10 years since we are not considering any investment made within the last 10 years, the differences in compound annual rates of return narrow dramatically. Once your horizon is long-term, it turns out to be less relevant when you started and much more relevant than you did it. The worst annual return achieved during this 48-year period was an annual compound return of 10.23% if you initiated your investment in 1961. The best you could have achieved would have occurred with an investment made in 1974 (an interim low point in the stock market) of 13.6%. Don't get me wrong; there is a big difference in final return between 10.23% and 13.60%, but a 10.23% return is still handsome. A 10.23% rate of return for 60 years produces almost $3.5 million for a $10,000 investment. In fact, 10.23% would have been the worst rate of return all the way back to 1929. The longer the period, the narrower the range of returns possible.

This Is an Interim High!

If 2004-2006 are high points in stock market history, then using these years as end points for a return analysis might bias the results. It is accurate to state that the ending year used in an analysis will influence the results, but not as much as you might imagine. Figure 8F3 changes the ending year from 2004 to 1981, a low point in market history. What if we did the same postwar analysis pretending that this was 1981?

FIGURE 8F3 Result Using Bear Market End Point/Current End Point $10,000 One Time Investment

Ending Year	Compound Annual Rate of Return from 1946[60]	Result of $10,000 Investment for 60 years
1981	10.71%	$4,479,309
2004	11.76%	$7,891,937

An investment in the S&P in 1981 compounded at 13.37% until 2004, well above the postwar average of 11.76%. If we assume that 1981 was the end year for a $10,000 investment made in 1946, the compound rate of return was 10.71% yearly instead of 11.76% yearly. If 10.71% turns out to be the actual compound rate for the next 60 years, the result for a onetime $10,000 investment is $4,479,309 instead of $7,891,937. And that is assuming the worst possible ending year since 1946. This analysis tacitly assumes that 2004 is an interim high point in the stock market. We do not know if this is true. It is more likely a midpoint since the S&P was 330 points lower at the end of 2004 than it was at the end of 1999, a 16% decline.

The result initiating an investment in the worst ending year since the war is less but still impressive.

Why Not Trade, Buy Low and Sell High?

You will hear, if you stick around stock market investing, the adage to buy low and sell high. The statement itself is a truism, but I disagree that it is a strategy that any investor could follow and make money. The simple answer is there is no evidence that you can actually improve overall results by trying to buy low and sell high than by simply buying and holding. It is also clear that if you try to time the market and make a mistake, it can be punishing indeed. The reality is you don't have to time the market. Any market timer would be bragging about a long-term rate of return of 10.23% and that is the worst result that any buy-and-hold investor in the S&P averages achieved in 70 years of investing, assuming they held until 2004, reinvested distributions, and avoided taxes. It is the one strategy that has clearly worked in the past. Buy and hold and hold and hold.

Investment Required to Assure My Retirement

Figure 8G1 shows you what an investor would need to invest today to become a millionaire at retirement. The columns represent the number of years that you estimate you have left until retirement. The left column gives you alternative assumptions about compound rate of returns on your investment. For instance, if we use an 11% return, less than the average for the past 50 years, you will need to invest $5,418 today to have $1,000,000 in 50 years. It improves if you have more years left until retirement or can keep your investment growing through retirement. You need only to invest $1,908 today to become a millionaire in 60 years and that number drops to only $672 invested if you have 70 years left. You do need to use a tax-deferred or tax-avoidance vehicle to avoid paying taxes while the returns compound. Chapter 11 tells you how to do this. And you must reinvest all distributions and dividends in added fund shares or stock depending on which plan you select later in this book. Chapter 10 tells you how to do this.

—

You don't have to invest the full amount right now. You can plan to invest the amount required over the next few years. If you need to choose a 5-year investment plan to fund the amount needed in Figure 8G1, that will lengthen you retirement years about 2½ years. For instance, investing $5,418 at 11% over 5 years instead of right now will put your retirement age to become a millionaire back to 52½ years instead of 50 years. And investing it over a 10-year period will push your retirement date roughly 5 years to 55 instead of 50 years. Conversely, if you can invest more money than Figure 8G1 requires, your return will multiply by the amount. Investing $10,836 now at 11% for 50 years will make you worth $2 million.

It is interesting that it is possible to become very, very wealthy if you earn a high rate of return and have many years left. Had you invested $12,196 in Philip Morris 50 years ago, you would be worth $100,000,000 today, and with a 60-year time horizon, it would have taken only a little more than $2,000. Chapter 28 has more information on finishing with $10 to $100 million.

FIGURE 8G1 Dollar Investment Required to Be Worth $1,000,000

Amount Needed to Invest Now to Be Worth $1,000,000				
Compound Return	40 Years	50 Years	60 Years	70 Years
8.00%	$46,031	$21,321	$9,876	$4,574
9.00%	$31,838	$13,449	$5,681	$2,400
10.00%	$22,095	$8,519	$3,284	$1,266
11.00%	$15,384	$5,418	$1,908	$672
12.00%	$10,747	$3,460	$1,114	$359
13.00%	$7,531	$2,219	$654	$193
14.00%	$5,294	$1,428	$385	$104

CHAPTER 9

The Dramatic Impact of
Time on Returns

Time, a Powerful Ally

Time is a powerful force in investments, arguably the most powerful force. As long as an investment return is a positive return, it is increasing the investor's total value. In Chapter 5, we looked at the power of compound rates of return over time. In this chapter, I want to look at the impact of time on returns and in particular the dramatic impact of time on compound rates of return.

We have all heard the phrase "time is money." The phrase is an attempt to encourage us to stop wasting time and get busy doing a job. In the investment field, the expression takes on an even more significant role because most investments produce returns over some period of time. Usually, the longer that period of time, the bigger the returns. Suppose you loan your money to the bank and receive interest in a savings account or a certificate of deposit. You know implicitly the longer you leave your money with the bank, the bigger will be your return in total dollars, even if the interest rate remains the same. Investing in stocks does not normally involve a fixed rate of return, and the return you do earn can vary significantly. However, the basic principle still applies to stocks. The longer you leave your investment, the bigger your return.

The Time Value of Money

I want to start by looking at the returns an investor might have received had he or she invested in the S&P over a long period of time. I am going to start by looking at the yearly rate of return on the S&P composite since the end of WWII (1946). That rate was 11.76%. It is significantly higher than the rate calculated by Jeremy Siegel for 200 years, and I have explained in Chapter 5 why I favor the post-WWII rate for investors for the future. I will also look at alternative returns including the rate Siegel calculates for nearly 200 years.

In looking at the impact of time on returns, let us assume no compounding, that the investor invested $10,000 and earned an average return of 11.76% per year and never reinvested any of his or her returns. As before, we assume an investment vehicle that allows deferral or elimination of taxes on the return. Taxes are covered in detail in Chapter 11. Figure 9A1 and Graph 9A1 show us the total value at the end of each year to an investor of $10,000 who earns a steady yearly 11.76% per year, does not reinvest anything, and holds his or her investment for 70 years. I use the longer range in years because it explains the ideas about time that I want the reader to understand.

FIGURE 9A1 Total Return, $10,000 Investment for 70 Years No Compounding

Rate of Return 11.76%	Onetime Contribution $10,000	Not Compounded	
Year	Total Value of Investment	Year	Total Value of Investment
1	$11,176	36	$52,336
2	$12,352	37	$53,512
3	$13,528	38	$54,688
4	$14,704	39	$55,864
5	$15,880	40	$57,040
6	$17,056	41	$58,216
7	$18,232	42	$59,392
8	$19,408	43	$60,568
9	$20,584	44	$61,744
10	$21,760	45	$62,920
11	$22,936	46	$64,096
12	$24,112	47	$65,272

13	$25,288	48	$66,448
14	$26,464	49	$67,624
15	$27,640	50	$68,800
16	$28,816	51	$69,976
17	$29,992	52	$71,152
18	$31,168	53	$72,328
19	$32,344	54	$73,504
20	$33,520	55	$74,680
21	$34,696	56	$75,856
22	$35,872	57	$77,032
23	$37,048	58	$78,208
24	$38,224	59	$79,384
25	$39,400	60	$80,560
26	$40,576	61	$81,736
27	$41,752	62	$82,912
28	$42,928	63	$84,088
29	$44,104	64	$85,264
30	$45,280	65	$86,440
31	$46,456	66	$87,616
32	$47,632	67	$88,792
33	$48,808	68	$89,968
34	$49,984	69	$91,144
35	$51,160	70	$92,320

Figure 9A1 shows the progression from the original $10,000 investment in year 1 to $92,320 at year 70. Notice in Graph 9A1 how smooth and steady the progress is as this investor's total value goes up over 9 times the original investment.

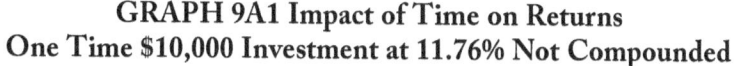

GRAPH 9A1 Impact of Time on Returns
One Time $10,000 Investment at 11.76% Not Compounded

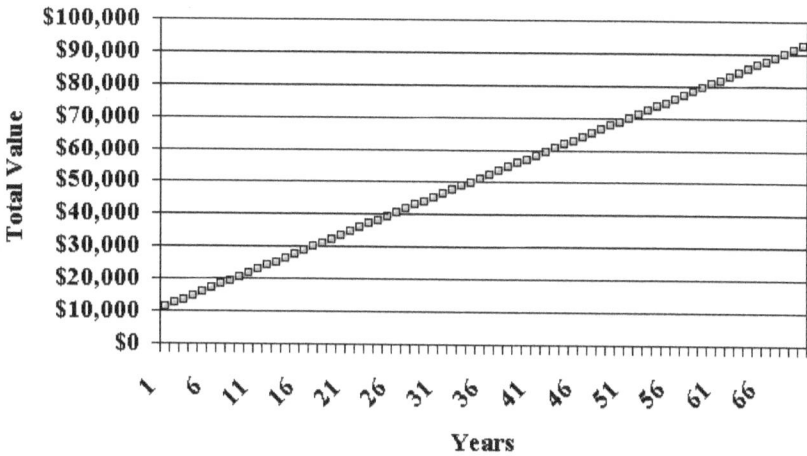

Figure 9A1 and Graph 9A1 explain a few characteristics about time and returns. Assuming a steady yearly rate of return, time always increases the result. If the return never varies, the amount by which the investor's total value increases each year is always the same, $1,176. Each year our investor's total value goes up by the same amount, assuming no reinvestment and the same rate of return every year. This example is unrealistic for several reasons. If the investor is not reinvesting, he or she is doing something else with the money. He or she might be spending his or her $1,176 and getting some immediate enjoyment from it. In that case, his or her investment remains $10,000 for all 70 years. He or she might be investing the return in some other investment, returning more or less than the 11.76% assumed here. Our calculation tacitly assumes that he or she is putting the proceeds away in a safe-deposit box, a home safe, or his or her mattress each year. Only if we accept that assumption as correct, will the returns outlined in Figure 9A1 and Graph 9A1 be accurate.

Assume that we are placing our savings in the mattress. One observation that we might make from looking at the data is that, while the rate of return on our original investment is always 11.76%, the rate on our total investment is declining each year. A return of $1,176 on an investment of $10,000 is 11.76% only for the first year. If we put our first year's return in the mattress, the $1,176 we earn the second year is only 10.52% on our new total value (now $11,176). Looking at the 11th year,

—

129

our return on total value is now only 5.4% earned on our 10th-year total value of $21,760. And looking at the 70th year, our return on total value drops to just over 1.2%. One observation we might make about simple returns (returns that are not compounded) is the percentage rate, and the dollar amount of the return stays the same each year. But the dollar return as a percentage of our total value is declining steadily.

The reason for this is simple. Each year we are increasing our total value (net worth) by the same amount. But each year we are taking the return and putting it in the mattress, where it belongs to us but cannot earn a return. So the dollar return remains the same each year on the original investment ($10,000), but the percentage return on total value is declining. We are increasing our total value but only earning a return each year on our original value. The more time you have, the more your total value increases. Over the course of 70 years, you have increased your total value over 9 times. However, note that you doubled your total value to over $20,000 in 9 years. The next double of total value takes 17 years to $40,576, and the next double of total value takes 35 years to $81,736 in year 61. The reader should understand that steady returns in the stock market do not exist. If an investor actually averages 11.76% per year over a long period of time, the individual yearly returns will vary dramatically, even though it may end up averaging 11.76%. Assuming that the return is the same rate every year allows us to illustrate more clearly certain characteristics about time and return.

Next, we will look at the same two graphics, assuming the investor compounded by reinvesting his or her 11.76% returns each year. Figure 9A2 and Graph 9A2 show the results.

FIGURE 9A2 Total Return, $10,000 Investment for 70 Years Compound Rate of Return

Rate of Return 11.76%	Onetime Contribution $10,000		
Year	Total Value of Investment	Year	Total Value of Investment
1	$11,176	36	$547,407
2	12,490	37	611,782
3	13,959	38	683,727
4	15,601	39	764,134
5	17,435	40	853,996
6	19,486	41	954,426

7	21,777	42	1,066,666
8	24,338	43	1,192,106
9	27,201	44	1,332,298
10	30,399	45	1,488,976
11	33,974	46	1,664,080
12	37,970	47	1,859,775
13	42,435	48	2,078,485
14	47,425	49	2,322,915
15	53,002	50	2,596,089
16	59,236	51	2,901,390
17	66,202	52	3,242,593
18	73,987	53	3,623,922
19	82,688	54	4,050,095
20	92,412	55	4,526,386
21	103,280	56	5,058,689
22	115,425	57	5,653,591
23	128,999	58	6,318,454
24	144,170	59	7,061,504
25	161,124	60	7,891,937
26	180,072	61	8,820,028
27	201,248	62	9,857,264
28	224,915	63	11,016,478
29	251,365	64	12,312,016
30	280,926	65	13,759,909
31	313,963	66	15,378,074
32	350,885	67	17,186,535
33	392,149	68	19,207,672
34	438,266	69	21,466,494
35	489,806	70	23,990,954

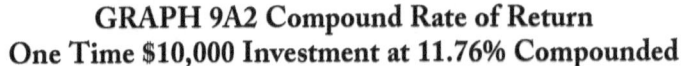

GRAPH 9A2 Compound Rate of Return
One Time $10,000 Investment at 11.76% Compounded

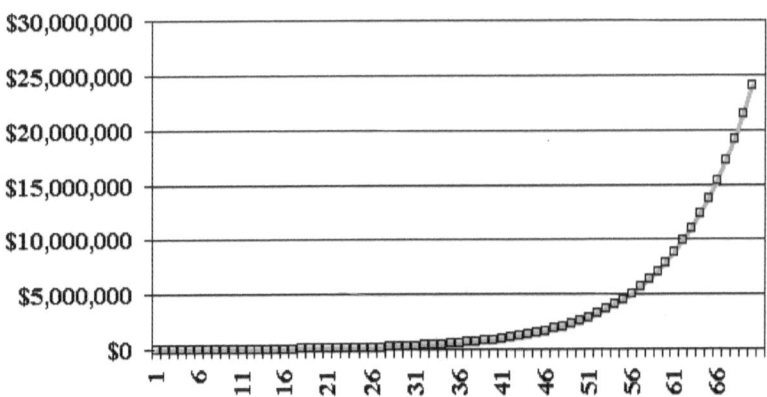

The most obvious difference between Figures 9A1 and 9A2 and Graphs 9A1 and 9A2 is the total return for the same $10,000 investment is so different. The final result to our investor after 70 years is $23,990,954 if he or she reinvested his or her returns each year and only $92,320 if he or she did not. We now know that this difference is due solely to the effects of compounding returns on prior returns. Time increases our return but has an even more dramatic effect with compounding. No longer do we have a steady increase in our total value. As the years go by, the total value begins to climb. Looking at Graph 9A2, the total value increases more and more as the years go by. During the early years, it is difficult to see much difference (Figure 9A3 and Graph 9A3), but as the years go by, the difference becomes more and more pronounced.

FIGURE 9A3 Simple and Compound Returns Compared

Rate of Return	Onetime Contribution				
11.76%	$10,000				
Year	Total Value		Year	Total Value	
	Compound Return	Simple Return		Compound Return	Simple Return
1	$11,176	$11,176	36	$547,407	$52,336
2	$12,490	$12,352	37	$611,782	$53,512
3	$13,959	$13,528	38	$683,727	$54,688
4	$15,601	$14,704	39	$764,134	$55,864

—

132

5	$17,435	$15,880	40	$853,996	$57,040
6	$19,486	$17,056	41	$954,426	$58,216
7	$21,777	$18,232	42	$1,066,666	$59,392
8	$24,338	$19,408	43	$1,192,106	$60,568
9	$27,201	$20,584	44	$1,332,298	$61,744
10	$30,399	$21,760	45	$1,488,976	$62,920
11	$33,974	$22,936	46	$1,664,080	$64,096
12	$37,970	$24,112	47	$1,859,775	$65,272
13	$42,435	$25,288	48	$2,078,485	$66,448
14	$47,425	$26,464	49	$2,322,915	$67,624
15	$53,002	$27,640	50	$2,596,089	$68,800
16	$59,236	$28,816	51	$2,901,390	$69,976
17	$66,202	$29,992	52	$3,242,593	$71,152
18	$73,987	$31,168	53	$3,623,922	$72,328
19	$82,688	$32,344	54	$4,050,095	$73,504
20	$92,412	$33,520	55	$4,526,386	$74,680
21	$103,280	$34,696	56	$5,058,689	$75,856
22	$115,425	$35,872	57	$5,653,591	$77,032
23	$128,999	$37,048	58	$6,318,454	$78,208
24	$144,170	$38,224	59	$7,061,504	$79,384
25	$161,124	$39,400	60	$7,891,937	$80,560
26	$180,072	$40,576	61	$8,820,028	$81,736
27	$201,248	$41,752	62	$9,857,264	$82,912
28	$224,915	$42,928	63	$11,016,478	$84,088
29	$251,365	$44,104	64	$12,312,016	$85,264
30	$280,926	$45,280	65	$13,759,909	$86,440
31	$313,963	$46,456	66	$15,378,074	$87,616
32	$350,885	$47,632	67	$17,186,535	$88,792
33	$392,149	$48,808	68	$19,207,672	$89,968
34	$438,266	$49,984	69	$21,466,494	$91,144
35	$489,806	$51,160	70	$23,990,954	$92,320

Figure 9A3 shows that during the early years the difference between compounding and not compounding seems small. By year 15 compounding doubles the investor's total value. By year 30, it increases his or her total value by more than 6 times and by year 50 almost 38 times and by year 60 almost 98 times. By year 70, our investor's total return is almost 260 times the value achieved without compounding.

GRAPH 9A3 Simple and Compound Returns Compared

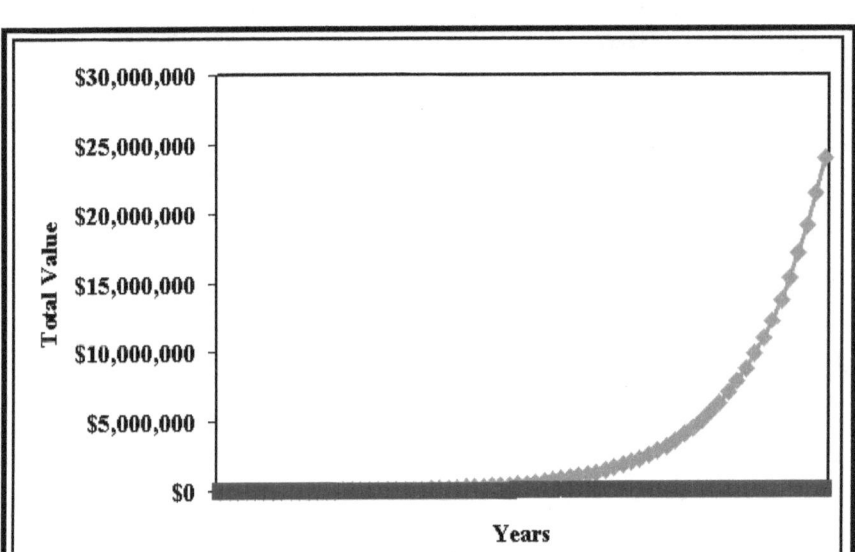

Notice that our compounding investor's value doubles every 6+ years unlike a simple return investment that takes longer and longer to double as the years pass. Investors understand that returns will never be steady and smooth as implied in these graphs. Real stock market returns may end in the same place but will undoubtedly be characterized by large gyrations (see Chapter 25).

In Graph 9A3, we see how dramatic the difference becomes. The horizontal black line represents the total value of an investor who received the same rate of return but did not reinvest his or her return each year. The red line shows the result for an investor who did reinvest his or her return each year. While it is difficult to tell from the graph, the black line does increase in value each year, but because of the scale and size of the compound return, it is hard to see.

Graph 9A3 shows the increasing effect of time on the different compound returns for an investor who compounds returns and one who does not. The compounding curve simply accelerates upward, increasing the difference in returns as the years go by.

The Importance of Escalating Returns To An Investor

The impact of time is clearly obvious in these charts and graphs. Each year that goes by means the return an investor earns in dollars is going up.

—

The longer you hold your investment, the greater the yearly dollar return. Figure 9A2 shows us that in the 70th year, the increase in return alone to our $10,000 investor was more than $2.5 million in just that 1 year alone. How can this be? It is simply the result of compounding. As the years go by, there are simply more and more returns from previous year's returns until the returns from previous returns far outstrip any return from our original investment.

This is a key issue to grasp and a central point of this book. The longer you hold your investment, the more compounding magnifies the return. If we looked at 80 or 90 or 200 years, the results would continue to escalate. To achieve a result similar to the one outlined in Figure 9A2, an investor must invest his or her money for a long period of time, and he or she must reinvest all his or her returns. He or she must hold on for a long time with what looks like modest returns until the curve in Graph 9A2 turns sharply upward and returns step up dramatically. Figure 9A4 shows the dollar increase, every 10 years, in total value experienced by an investor who invested $10,000 compounded at 11.76% for 70 years.

FIGURE 9A4 $10,000 One Time Investment Value Increase in 10-Year Increments at 11.76% Compound Rate of Return[61]

Year	Yearly Increase
1	$1,176
10	$3,198
20	$9,724
30	$29,561
40	$89,862
50	$273,174
60	$830,433
70	$2,524,460

Figure 9A4 is an important one for the reader to understand. It explains better than anything the dramatic impact of time on returns. In year 1, our investor found that his total value on his $10,000 onetime investment went up $1,176. By year 10, his total value increased $3,198 in 1 year, by year 30 his total value increased $29,561 in 1 year, and so on. In year 70, our investor's total value *increased* by $2,524,460 in that year alone. Compounding rate of return and time are the critical elements in your investment plans.

Siegel Return Illustrated

Jeremy Siegel in his landmark book *Stocks for the Long Run* calculates compound stock market returns from 1802 to 2001 at 8.3% per year.[62] As indicated in Chapter 6, I prefer using the S&P returns from post-WWII. For those of you who want to be ultra-cautious, Figure 9A5 shows the compound return for 70 years for a $10,000 investment at 8.3%.

As described in Chapter 5 and throughout this book, there is a dramatic difference in total value depending on the rate of return assumed. At 8.3%, a $10,000 investment produces a total value after 70 years of over $2.6 million, a good amount but nothing like the almost $24 million produced by the 11.76% compound return that the S&P composite actually achieved since the end of WWII. The impact on final result of even slightly higher compound rates of return spirals with added years. It is no accident that over a long period of time, total value would be significantly less if the rate of return earned were less. A small change in rate of return can cause a large change in total value.

Even with this reduced return, the impact of time is still dramatic. Figure 9A6 does the same 10-year analysis of the increase in total net value. Year 1 produced an increase of $830, year 10 an increase of $1,702, year 30 an increase of $8,381, and year 70 an increase of $203,442. While the numbers are not as dramatic as in the 11.76% compound example, the effect of time is similar. As the years go by, the yearly increase in net value increases significantly until it dwarfs the return on the original investment. In either case, the rewards for holding for the long-term are extraordinary.

FIGURE 9A5 Total Return, $10,000 Investment for 70 Years Compound Rate of Return

Rate of Return 8.30%	Onetime investment $10,000		
Year	Total Value of Investment	Year	Total Value of Investment
1	$10,830	36	$176,451
2	$11,729	37	$191,097
3	$12,702	38	$206,958
4	$13,757	39	$224,135

5	$14,898	40	$242,738
6	$16,135	41	$262,886
7	$17,474	42	$284,705
8	$18,925	43	$308,336
9	$20,495	44	$333,927
10	$22,197	45	$361,643
11	$24,039	46	$391,660
12	$26,034	47	$424,168
13	$28,195	48	$459,373
14	$30,535	49	$497,501
15	$33,069	50	$538,794
16	$35,814	51	$583,514
17	$38,787	52	$631,946
18	$42,006	53	$684,397
19	$45,493	54	$741,202
20	$49,268	55	$802,722
21	$53,358	56	$869,348
22	$57,786	57	$941,504
23	$62,583	58	$1,019,648
24	$67,777	59	$1,104,279
25	$73,403	60	$1,195,935
26	$79,495	61	$1,295,197
27	$86,093	62	$1,402,698
28	$93,239	63	$1,519,122
29	$100,978	64	$1,645,210
30	$109,359	65	$1,781,762
31	$118,436	66	$1,929,648
32	$128,266	67	$2,089,809
33	$138,912	68	$2,263,263
34	$150,441	69	$2,451,114
35	$162,928	70	$2,654,556

FIGURE 9A6 $10,000 One Time Investment Value Increase in 10-Year Increments at 8.3% Compound Rate of Return[63]

Year	Yearly Increase
1	$830
10	$1,702
20	$3,775
30	$8,381
40	$18,603
50	$41,293
60	$91,656
70	$203,442

The discussion in this chapter shows how important both rate of return and time are on any individual's final total return. The message is clear—time is on your side. An investor must be patient and use the benefit of time if he or she wants to truly get rich using long-term stock investing. The examples of actual returns cited in Chapters 6 and 8 show that we have to remember that returns that are uniform every year, as in some of the examples in this book, do not exist. So besides being patient and weathering the ups and downs and erratic nature of stock market returns from year to year, the data in this chapter stress the need for patience over long periods of time.

Your Age and Your Return

If you are investing for yourself, not a child, grandchild, or legacy descendants, you may not have 70 years of investing horizon to look forward to. You can use Figure 9A7 to calculate your expected return based on the number of investment years that you do have left. Calculating the number of years of investing that you have left can also be more difficult than it seems. You may be able to hold your long-term investment beyond normal retirement age, especially if you have a pension, retirement, or other investments to live from. It is obvious that the longer you can avoid using your long-term investment dollars, the reward in total return escalates significantly.

—

If you only have 20 years left until you need to use your investment dollars, then your investment of $10,000 will reach $280,926 if 11.76% turns out to be the average compound rate of return. Figure 9A7 shows you what a $10,000 investment should produce based on the assumed rate of return by decade.

FIGURE 9A7 $10,000 One Time Investment
Total Value Based on Years Left at 11.76% Compound Rate of Return

Years Left	Total Value
10	$92,412
20	$280,926
30	$853,996
40	$2,596,089
50	$7,891,937
60	$23,990,954

FIGURE 9A8 Initial Investment Required to Produce Result
Compound Rate of Return 11.76%[64]

Years	Initial Investment				
	$1,000	$10,000	$20,000	$30,000	$50,000
10	$3,040	$30,399	$60,798	$91,197	$151,995
20	$9,241	$92,412	$184,824	$277,236	$462,060
30	$28,093	$280,926	$561,852	$842,778	$1,404,630
40	$85,400	$853,996	$1,707,992	$2,561,988	$4,269,980
50	$259,609	$2,596,089	$5,192,178	$7,788,267	$12,980,445
60	$789,194	$7,891,937	$15,783,874	$23,675,811	$39,459,685
70	$2,399,095	$23,990,954	$47,981,908	$71,972,862	$119,954,770

Figure 9A8 allows the investor to select the number of years that he or she calculates he has left to invest and then figure out how much he needs to invest in a onetime, long-term investment program now to achieve a desired result. For instance, you calculate that you have 40 years of investing left and want to have at least $2 million. The figure shows that you need to invest $30,000 now if you earn the 50-year S&P average compound rate of return of 11.76%. Chapter 27 and Figure 27A1 give you similar information in another format, and several tables in the appendix allow easy calculation of expected returns given different parameters. It is important to remember that even if the markets do achieve an 11.76% compound annual return over 70 years, assuming that exact return rate for 20 or 30 years is problematic. The shorter your time horizon, the more variable the return, both upward and downward. At 20 years, it is very likely that your achieved return will be either higher or lower than the long-term return, whatever that may turn out to be.

A "Real" Example

I want to sketch the dramatic impact of time on investments, with a real example from my personal investing. This example not only shows the power of time but it explains how returns are "back-loaded." The lion's share of long-term investment returns come in the later years.

I own shares in a small mutual fund called the Stratton Growth Fund. The fund owned and managed by an ex-neighbor and friend of mine named Jim Stratton. When Jim started his fund in 1974, he asked me to invest some money in it, and as a favor, I invested $10,000 in this fund. I have held it since then, not adding any additional money, but I did give away some of the shares as charitable gifts, around $35,000. My initial investment is worth roughly $600,000 today as the fund has grown at a compound rate of 13.65% for the 32 years that I have owned it. I intend to continue to hold this fund for at least another 13 years, for a total of 45 years, and hope that Jim continues to grow the fund at exactly 13.65%. Then I will have around $3.2 million for my $10,000 investment in 45 years. Figure 9A9 shows this potential result.

FIGURE 9A9 Stratton Growth Fund[65]
Actual Investment at 13.65% Compound Rate of Return

Initial investment 1974	$10,000
Total value in 2006	$606,441
Estimated value by 2019	$3,200,304
Compound rate of return	13.65%

There are two points worth noting. First, look at the powerful result that is possible with an above-average return. The second point to note is that I held this investment ($10,000) for 32 years to see it move up about $600,000. All I have to do is to hold it for another 13 years, assuming Jim does not retire and earns the same rate of return, and I will make an extra $2.5 million. The returns are back-loaded. The longer the investor holds the investment, the more dramatic the returns become. The reason for this is simple. A "simple" return rate of 13.65% on $10,000 earns the investor $1,365 in a year. A return rate of 13.65% on $1,000,000 earns the investor $136,500 in 1 year. You need to build a large base to show these kinds of returns. Right now I am at the point where a 13.65% return this year means an increase in my investment value of over $81,000. However, if I hold the investment until 2019, the increase in my value if I earn 13.65% will be over $400,000 in just 1 year.

Obviously, I do not expect to earn 13.65% every year. As explained elsewhere in this book, returns to stocks vary greatly with down years, stagnant years, and boom years. It is important to understand the impact of added time, on your investment result. Time is your biggest ally.

CHAPTER 10

The Spectacular Impact of Dividends

What Are Dividends?

There are usually two ways an investor can earn a return investing in stock. The one that most people talk about is capital gains. Simply put, a capital gain occurs any time you buy a share of stock for a specific price and then sell for a higher price. For many, perhaps most investors, capital gains (higher prices) are what stock investing is all about. But there is another way an investor can earn a return on a stock investment. A corporation can make payments to their shareholders that are called dividends. Some companies pay dividends, and some do not. Some companies pay a small dividend relative to their share price, and some companies pay a larger dividend relative to their share price.

The Board of Directors is usually the group that decides to pay or not to pay a dividend. If the Board decides to pay a dividend, it normally, but not always, comes from the profits the company earned the previous year. Companies have varied motivations in their consideration of whether and what dividend to pay to shareholders. Often, newer companies that are growing quickly will decide not to pay dividends and to keep those funds in the company to foster quick expansion and make the company even more profitable in future years. In this case, the Board believes that it can increase the shareholder's total return by not paying dividends and improving the company's future. Other companies are simply not profitable or have weak financial statements and fear paying out any more of their most precious resource (cash) than they have to. Often, successful companies will begin to pay out dividends when the Board sees the company is creating more cash each year than it needs for its expansion plans. Companies that pay out dividends can still be growing rapidly and successfully, creating lots of excess cash that they just have no real profitable use for. Other companies that pay dividends may be in a more mature phase of their life, and they are reaping the benefits of the growth phase in plentiful cash for which they have no other use. So companies have many possible motivations for paying dividends to shareholders. Stock dividends are different from cash dividends since often the motivation for declaring a stock dividend is entirely different from the motivation for paying cash dividends. In theory, the Board makes the decision by selecting the dividend philosophy that it believes will bring the maximum long-term return (capital gain plus dividends) to its shareholders.

Shareholders have as many different motivations for owning shares as companies have for paying dividends. Some shareholders want only stock price increases and are not interested in small cash payouts from company profits. They would prefer the company use the cash to grow the company rapidly so the stock price increases even more and they can sell the stock for a large capital gain. Other shareholders need income and may shun stocks in favor of bonds or other investments that promise a steady yearly payout. Corporations do not have to pay dividends to shareholders. A shareholder who needs income on which to live but also wants some chance at a capital gain, an increase in their company's stock price, will often buy stock in companies that have a history of paying steady dividends each year.

During most of the history of the United States, there has been a tax bias against dividend payments. The Internal Revenue Service taxes corporate earned income initially. If the company then takes some of its income, after paying its own taxes, and pays it out to shareholders, the shareholders must then pay a second tax on the amount they receive as well. This is often called a double tax. Corporations pay tax on total income, and the shareholders pay another tax on the dividend part. If a corporation chooses not to pay dividends, the second tax is avoided entirely. If the company decides to keep the money in the company for expansion, the shareholders pay no extra tax. In addition, for most of our tax history, dividends were taxed to shareholders at the maximum rate under the current income tax law in place. The reason that this is important is that gains on the sale of stock at a profit have usually been taxed at much lower rates. They have often been taxed at half of the regular rate that investors pay on dividends. So for shareholders, there has been a historic bias toward receiving their returns from stock investing in the form of capital gains or stock price increases rather than dividends. Also, shareholders pay no tax on the appreciation of their stock until they choose to sell it. This means the shareholder chooses when to pay his or her tax. Paying dividends is largely out of the control of shareholders. The 2001 tax revision makes the tax treatment of dividends much more favorable. Today (2006), dividends are still taxed twice, but they are now taxed at essentially the same rate as capital gains, making them much more attractive for both shareholders and corporations. This favorable tax treatment will expire at the end of 2010. There is no way of knowing whether Congress and the next president will extend it, but for now, dividends look more attractive from a tax standpoint than they have in many years.

Dividends Are Misunderstood

This chapter will show you, despite its historically unfavorable tax treatment that the role of dividends in investor returns has been significant and the role of dividends to a long-term investor is critical. Figure 10A1 shows a breakdown of the total return for an investor who purchased 1 share of the S&P composite in 1870, assuming no reinvestment of dividends. An investor who purchased 1 share of the entire S&P (which would have been impossible) would have paid $4.74 in 1870 and sold it for $1,199.21 at the end of 2004.[66] His or her capital gain is $1,194.47. However, our investor would have received cash payouts of dividends each of the 134 years of his or her investment. Those cash dividend payments would have totaled $420.70, making his or her total profits $1,615.17 on his or her $4.74 investment. Calculated this way, dividends accounted for 26% of the total return that our shareholder received.

FIGURE 10A1 Total Return to Shareholder[67]
S&P 500 1870-2004

Price of 1 share of S&P 500 in 1870	$4.74
Price of 1 share of S&P 500 in 2004	$1,199.21
Gain on 1 share of S&P 500	$1,194.47
Cumulative dividend payments 1870-2004	$420.70
Total gain or profit from this investment	$1,615.17
Percentage of total gain represented by dividends	26.05%

Dividends are important to all investors but are especially important to two types of investors. The first are those that need income to pay their expenses. Many retirees depend on dividends for all or a large part of their income in retirement. These investors look for steady earnings and consistent dividend payments before investing in a stock. As mentioned, some companies that pay dividends make it a habit to pay them on a consistent long-term basis so investors who need income can depend on them. Others pay dividends that vary from year to year depending on their earnings results. Better earnings mean higher dividends, but lower earnings can mean lower dividends. Dividend investors who are interested in current income should check the company's history of dividend payments before committing. Sometimes, consistency and dependability are more important than the amount or rate of dividend payment. But even investors who are in stocks for capital gains need to understand that at least 25% of their direct return comes from dividend payments.

The second investor that depends on dividends is the long-term investor, the focus of this book. Long-term investors understand the critical role of dividends and dividend reinvestment to their investment goals. In the long, long run, dividends and dividend reinvestment turn out to be almost the entire return. Figure 10B2 shows the difference in return for an investor of $10,000 in the S&P in 1870 if he or she reinvested all his or her dividends in added shares or if he or she took the dividends in cash and spent them. If you had invested $10,000 in the S&P in 1870, and taken the dividends in cash instead of reinvesting them in added shares, you would have a portfolio of $2,529,973 at the end of 2004. If, instead, you had reinvested all the dividends in extra stock, allowing them to compound with the original $10,000 investment, you would have an astounding $1,106,347,348. Yes, over $1 billion dollars. In 1870, $10,000 was a lot of money, and I am not implying that an average investor would have been able to make this investment. But Figure 10B2 illustrates the enormous power of compounding over long periods of time.

FIGURE 10B2 Total Return to Shareholder[68] Who Invested $10,000 S&P 500 1870-2004

	Value by December 31, 2004
$10,000 Invested in S&P 500 in 1870 (no dividend reinvestment)	$2,529,973
$10,000 Invested in S&P 500 in 1870 (all dividends reinvested)	$1,106,347,348
Percent of gain due to dividend reinvestment	99.782%

Figure 10B2 also shows the critical role of dividends to a long-term investor. Later in this chapter, I will look at some real examples using an MFS[69] fund, the oldest mutual fund in the United States, and you will see the impact of dividends and dividend reinvestment to investors who have different time horizons. Even if you have a 10-or 20-year horizon, dividend reinvestment is still critical in your total return.

There are other reasons to look at dividend-paying stocks besides their heavy impact on returns. We have just come through an era of accounting scandals and even some fraud. Investors should understand that earnings reported by public companies are accounting products. It is difficult even for a professional to understand the implications of the thousands of accounting rules that control what a company reports as "earnings." We have learned in recent years that big companies with big accountants have sometimes been able to "fudge" the numbers to reflect earnings that may not be there. There is not a lot the average investor can do to protect himself except to rely on government regulators to police these renegades. One strategy is that an investor might look for a company that pays dividends. Dividends, except for a stock dividend that is a special case, are almost always paid to shareholders in cash. Dividends are usually paid out of earnings. If a company reports earnings and pays cash dividends from those earnings, you may be able to rely on the earnings reports with more confidence. Although it has happened, a company is not likely to be able to pay cash dividends out of fictitious earnings. And dividends have to be paid in cash, not inventory or some other asset, which means you can usually depend, at least, on the earnings represented by the dividend paid.

For a long-term investor, I like to look for companies that have steadily increased earnings and dividends for years. A company that can steadily increase earnings and dividends is more likely to survive over the long run. A company that produces good earnings and dividends but the amounts jump around from year to year or from business cycle to business cycle is more likely to succumb.

Importance of Dividends to a Long-Term Investor

I cannot stress enough the role of dividend reinvestment to the long-term investor. The data in Figure 10C1 is from MFS Mass Investors Trust A. Figure 10C1 shows the actual results of a $10,000 investment in this fund from July 1924, its initial start-up, to June 30, 2005. It shows the difference to an investor who had invested $10,000 and reinvested all dividends or an investor who had invested $10,000 and received the dividends in cash. Figure 10C1 is hard to believe. Assume twin brothers, age 17, both invested $10,000 in this new idea of a mutual fund in 1924 and both held their shares until 2005, their 98th birthday. The only difference is that Brother A reinvested all his distributions in added shares of the fund and Brother B took his distributions in cash and spent them.

FIGURE 10C1[70] MFS Mass Inv. Growth Stock Fund A
(Achieved a compound rate of return of 9.23% per year for 80 years)

	Invested on July 1, 1924	Total Actual Value on June 30, 2005
Brother A (reinvested all distributions)	$10,000	$12,731,934
Brother B (did not reinvest distributions)	$10,000	$44,597
Percent of value lost through not reinvesting		99.65%

I know that it seems hard to believe that so much of Brother B's potential return disappeared simply because he did not reinvest the small distributions, mostly dividends, he received each year, but it is a fact. It is also true that if the two fictional brothers had invested their $10,000 in 1924, they would have had to pay income taxes on the distributions every year. I will explore the impact of taxes in the next chapter. Our two fictional brothers did not have IRAs, 401Ks, or variable annuities to shelter or defer taxes, but you do. Assuming current tax laws, you could have achieved almost exactly the returns in Figure 10C1. I say almost since today you are limited to $4,000 a year contributed into an IRA. You would have had to make a $10,000 investment over several years. In fact, an investment made to comply with current IRA rules: $4,000 in 1924, $4,000 in 1925, and $2,000 in 1926, and your return would have dropped to only $10,523,559. It is a significant drop for delaying part of your $10,000 investment for 1 year and another part for 2 years. Part of the reason lies in the fact that 1925 and 1926 were good years in the stock market. Your money would simply have bought fewer shares in those years than it would have in 1924 and compounded on less shares for 80 years. I will deal in more detail with the impact of taxes in Chapter 11 and the use of IRAs in Chapter 17, annuities in Chapter 18, and other forms of tax-advantaged investing in Chapter 19.

The impact of dividends gets more and more spectacular as time goes by. Examining returns for this ancient MFS fund for shorter periods reveals that dividends are still important but not as spectacular as when looking at the full 84 years. Figure 10C2 shows this impact for selected periods. The difference in the first years of investing is significant but relatively small. But once you look back using this fund for 20 years, by failing to reinvest distributions, you have lost over 80% of your possible return. And in 30 years, the investor lost well over 90% of his or her possible return, advancing to 99%+ as the years go by. So for all but the short-term investor, reinvesting distributions is the key that allows for such spectacular returns. Figures 10C1 and 10C2 show clearly that any investor who ignores the impact of dividends on his or her return does so at his or her own peril.

The role of dividends to long-term investors is illustrated in the debate over those books written during the bull market of a few years ago. These books were speculating about when the Dow, then around 11,000, would reach 36,000 or 100,000. Since the market declines in 2001-2003, some have criticized the authors of these books as absurd or worse. However, Carla Pasternak, coeditor of the newsletter *High-Yield Investing*, calculated that had dividends been reinvested in the Dow Jones Industrial Averages from its start, the Dow would be over *750,000* today.

FIGURE 10C2 The Importance of Dividends over Time[71]
MFS Mass Inv. Growth Fund A
Assumes $10,000 Investment at the Beginning of Period

Investment Periods		Total Return		% Lost
		No Distribution Reinvestment	Distributions Reinvested	Due to Lack of Distribution Reinvestment
10 Years	1994-2004	$17,144	$26,944	36.4%
20 Years	1984-2004	$15,663	$94,763	83.5%
30 Years	1974-2004	$22,711	$336,658	93.3%
40 Years	1964-2004	$10,129	$344,825	97.1%
50 Years	1954-2004	$18,499	$1,040,081	98.2%
60 Years	1944-2004	$44,256	$4,568,929	99.0%
70 Years	1934-2004	$54,967	$9,137,858	99.4%

The Overlooked Importance of Dividends during Downturns or Weak Markets

Reinvesting dividends is also important to investors because that gives investors the ability to mitigate some of the pain of unavoidable periodic downturns in the stock market. In Figure 10D1, I use the data from our oldest mutual fund, MFS Mass Investors Trust A, to show the impact of the Great Depression on an original investor in the fund. The Great Depression dropped the S&P 500 almost 72% from 1928 until 1932. No one was immune, but there was a way to mitigate this loss and guess what it was: dividend reinvestment. Figure 10D1 shows that an investor who did not reinvest his or her distributions in the Mass Investors Trust Fund from 1924 until 1928 suffered a 39% loss by the end of 1932, substantially better than the general market. This was significantly less than the 72% loss suffered by the S&P composite. But an investor who reinvested his or her distributions each year lost only 5.2% from his or her initial investment.

—

FIGURE 10D1 The Value of Dividend Reinvestment in Downturns
The Great Depression Experience
MFS Mass Inv. Trust A[72]

	Invested July 1, 1924	Value December 31, 1928	Value December 31, 1932	% Decline
				From 1924
No dividend reinvestment	$10,000	$20,286	$6,104	39.0%
All dividends reinvested	$10,000	$25,649	$9,479	5.2%

Perhaps an even more spectacular turnaround occurred due to distribution or dividend reinvestment in the 1968-1981 stock market move sideways. From the end of 1968 until the end of 1981, the S&P increased only about 16%, not including dividends, a compound rate of return of less than 1% per year. In Figure 10D2, an investor in the Mass Investors Trust A would have suffered a decline of 34.2%, a compound rate of loss of 3.4% per year, if he or she did not reinvest distributions. (the market averages outperformed the MFS fund from 1968 to 1981.) But he or she enjoyed an 91.2% increase, a compound rate of return of over 5% per year, if he or she simply reinvested all distributions in more shares of the fund.

FIGURE 10D2 The Value of Dividend Reinvestment in Downturns
The 1968-1981 Experience
Mass Inv. Trust A[73]

	Invested December 31, 1968	Value December 31, 1981	% Change
			From 1968
No dividend reinvestment	$10,000	$6,585	(34.2%)
All dividends reinvested	$10,000	$19,122	91.2%

Figures 10D2 and 10D3 show the same effect for an investor in the S&P 500 during these two periods.

FIGURE 10D3 The Value of Dividend Reinvestment in Downturns
The Great Depression Experience
S&P Composite[74]

	Invested December 1, 1900	Value December 31, 1932	% Increase
			From 1900
No dividend reinvestment	$10,000	$10,073	0.0073%
All dividends reinvested	$10,000	$55,911	559.1%

In Figure 10D3, I assume an investor who invested $10,000 in the S&P in 1900 and held through until the bottom of the depression in 1932. This investor saw almost all his or her gains for 3 decades wiped out without reinvesting his or her distributions. The investor who reinvested all dividends and distributions also saw the same dramatic declines from the 1920s booming stock market highs. But instead of ending about even in 1932, with his or her initial investment in 1900 of $10,000, he or she still had a large gain of over 5 times his or her original investment.

Dividends and Individual Stocks

General Electric

In looking at individual stocks and funds, the importance of distributions and reinvesting becomes clear to a long-term investor. Many investors dismiss dividends and distributions as "small potatoes" and long for big increases in share price. Figure 10E1 shows the total value for a $10,000 investment in General Electric, with all distributions reinvested by 10-year increments. It also shows the part of total value represented by the initial investment (assumes the investor did not reinvest distributions) and the part represented by the distributions.

FIGURE 10E1 General Electric Total Value[75]
$10,000 Initial Investment
All Distributions Reinvested

	Total Value			Distributions
	$10,000	Original Shares	Distributions	As % of Total
1940	$10,462	$10,000	$462	4.41%
1950	$24,404	$14,819	$9,585	39.28%
1960	$151,985	$66,587	$85,398	56.19%
1970	$248,543	$83,911	$164,632	66.24%
1980	$465,681	$109,490	$356,191	76.49%
1990	$2,415,200	$410,271	$2,004,929	83.01%
2000	$28,064,315	$4,113,609	$23,950,706	85.34%
2004	$23,400,556	$3,131,972	$20,268,584	86.62%

Notice how the part of the total value represented by reinvesting distributions increases dramatically with time. By the end of the first year, the investment distributions represent only 4.41% of the investor's total value. But 64 years later, in 2004, distributions represent over 86% of the total value amassed by our investor. It took about 20 years for reinvesting distributions to make up more than half of the total value.

Altria

FIGURE 10E2 Altria Total Value[76]
$10,000 Initial Investment
All Distributions Reinvested

	Total Value			Distributions
	$10,000	Original Shares	Distributions	As % of Total
1970	$10,212	$10,212	$0	0.00%
1975	$23,529	$21,868	$1,661	7.06%
1980	$44,178	$35,690	$8,488	19.40%
1985	$111,045	$72,922	$38,123	33.43%
1990	$617,037	$341,631	$275,406	44.63%
1995	$1,303,093	$595,790	$707,303	54.28%
2000	$2,388,538	$871,405	$1,517,133	63.52%
2004	$4,044,268	$1,201,148	$2,843,120	70.08%

Figure 10E2 shows the same data for Altria, but in this case, we only have 35 years of detailed data. Still, the pattern is obvious. A 35-year investor of $10,000 in Altria enjoyed a spectacular result, finishing the end of 2004, with over $4 million for his or her investment. But even in only 35 years, about 30% of his or her return was because of stock price increase on his or her original investment. About 70% or $2.8 million occurred from reinvesting dividends and distributions.

Alcoa

FIGURE 10E3 Alcoa Total Value[77]
$10,000 Initial Investment
All Distributions Reinvested

		Total Value		Distributions
	$10,000	Original Shares	Distributions	As % of Total
1962	$10,220	$10,000	$220	2.2%
1972	$12,760	$9,725	$3,035	23.79%
1982	$33,736	$17,023	$16,713	49.54%
1992	$106,935	$39,328	$67,607	63.07%
2004	$458,300	$137,984	$320,316	69.89%

Alcoa, the giant aluminum company, was not a spectacular performer during this period. It performed well below market averages, returning a compound annual rate of return of 9.25% from 1962 to 2004. Alcoa returned $458,300 to a $10,000 investor after 42 years. But even with a lower than normal rate of return, dividends and dividend reinvestment were critical making up almost 70% of the total return to shareholders. As you can see from Figure 10E3, from 1962 to 1972, the stock price of Alcoa declined (the total value of the original shares). An investor who neglected to reinvest dividends ended losing almost 3% of his or her initial investment after 10 years. But the investor who reinvested Alcoa's dividends ended almost 25% ahead for the period.

Dividends are critical to long-term investing success. Find stocks that pay dividends and reinvest all dividends in added stock. Most American companies now allow automatic reinvestment of dividends without any trading cost to shareholders. Previously, shareholders had to take their dividends in cash and buy the added stock through a broker and pay commissions, usually high commissions on small odd lots. Every shareholder interested in long-term investing should be sure to select automatic reinvestment of dividends.

My Personal Experience—Nestlé

I purchased Nestlé stock in 1979. My original investment of $22,676 in 1979 has turned into just below $350,000 in 27 years. Nestlé is a Swiss company that does not allow automatic reinvestment of dividends. Unaware of the power of dividends in the long-term, I took all my dividends and distributions in cash and did not reinvest them in added Nestlé stock. Had I reinvested all dividends, my investment in Nestlé would be worth $737,148 today, over double my actual return in just 27 years. If I hold my Nestlé stock for another 27 years, I estimate that my investment, based on past history, will be worth over $5.4 million if I continue to take my dividends in cash and over $11 million if I reinvest all distributions. It has been an expensive lesson to learn.

How to Reinvest All Distributions?

If you have invested in an index mutual fund, dividend reinvestment is easy. In fact, most domestic mutual funds allow investors to reinvest all distributions. Cash distributions on mutual funds ordinarily come in two forms: dividends and capital gains. If you use a tax avoidance method (Chapters 17-19) to invest, these distributions are not taxable to an investor now. Most index funds do little trading, and there is not a significant amount of capital gains distributions. Investors should always select reinvestment of all distributions in added stock.

Exchange-traded funds (ETFs) are more complicated. Some automatically reinvest all dividends in additional shares, some will not reinvest dividends in additional shares, and some give the investor the option. Long-term investors should never invest in funds that do not give them the option of reinvesting all distributions in added stock.

For investors in individual stocks, many American companies allow investors to reinvest distributions automatically. If you purchase your stock through a stockbroker, inquire if the company has a dividend reinvestment plan. If you purchase stock online through a discount broker, they will normally give you the option of selecting automatic reinvestment of all distributions when you enter the purchase order. If you own existing stock or fail to make the request at purchase of a stock, you can give or enter the instruction at any time.

You may have difficulty finding dividend reinvestment programs with foreign stocks. Most do not have automatic reinvestment of distribution options. In this case, if you want the advantages of reinvestment of all distributions, you must enter an order to purchase the shares yourself. There are two disadvantages to this. You must pay a commission on the purchase, and the price you are forced to pay for an odd-lot (less than 100 shares) order may be high.

The Dow and Dividends

The wall charts from Ibbotson Associates[78] that most stockbrokers have posted on the wall in their offices are accurate but misleading. They show that $1 invested in the large capitalization stocks in 1926 was worth $2,587 by the year 2000. Most investors think that the individual stock prices simply went up that much. They don't bother to tell you how much of that return was due to dividend reinvestment. In fact, a $1 invested in the Dow in 1926 was only worth approximately $69.60 at the end of 2000, without any dividend reinvestment. Over $2,500 of the return, more than 97%, was earned by reinvesting dividends and other distributions.

Always Select Reinvestment of All Distributions in Added Stock!

CHAPTER 11

The Devastating Impact of Taxes

The Impact of Taxes on Stock Market Returns

The impact of small and innocuous-looking taxes on the long-term results from your investments can be devastating. The reason for this should be obvious. When part of your income is taxed away, you lose that income immediately out of your result. But even more important, you lose the capacity of the amount taxed away to compound indefinitely for many years. It is this compound return on the taxed amount that has such a serious impact over many years.

Let's look at Robert Shiller's data on the S&P composite. I calculated the total return on a $10,000 investment made in 1871, in which the investor held his or her investment for 133 years, reinvested all distributions, and was successfully able to avoid all taxes on those distributions. Since it was not possible to avoid all taxes on distributions in those years, this example is strictly theoretical, but it does explain clearly the long-term impact of taxes. Figure 11A1 shows that our theoretical investor who did everything else correctly still lost 91.49% of his or her total return if he was unable to avoid taxes. This analysis applies the maximum current tax rates on dividends each year to our investor's results. Please note that there was no tax on dividends until 1913. Since 1913, maximum tax rates on ordinary income (includes dividends) has varied upward as high as 94% but only for 2 years. Currently, the maximum tax rate on "qualified" dividends is 15%. You can see that without taxes, our investor's $10,000 turned into $1,106,347,348 in 133 years. With the then current tax rates applied, our investor's return on his or her $10,000 investment turned out to be only $94,176,174. While $94 million is a large amount, the loss attributable to taxes was more than $1 billion.

FIGURE 11A1 S&P Composite, Robert Shiller's Data[79]
Net Results Comparing Tax and No Tax Examples (1871-2004)

$10,000 Initial Investment	Result Assuming No Taxes Paid on Distributions	Result Assuming Normal Taxes Paid on Distributions	Percent of Total Value Lost to Taxes
1871 Original investment	$10,000	$10,000	
2004 Net result	$1,106,347,348	$94,176,174	91.49%

If we look at the Shiller's data for more recent times, we get results that are not as dramatic but still close. We can analyze the same set of data assuming that our investor made his or her $10,000 investment in 1946 (post-WWII) instead of 1871. Figure 11A2 shows that we would have lost 88.7% of our total return during this 58-year period applying the maximum tax rates applicable.

FIGURE 11A2 S&P Composite, Robert Shiller's Data[80]
Net Results Comparing Tax and No Tax Examples (1946-2004)

$10,000 Initial Investment	Result Assuming No Taxes Paid on Distributions	Result Assuming Normal Taxes Paid on Distributions	Percent of Total Value Lost to Taxes
1946 Original investment	$10,000	$10,000	
2004 Net result	$6,599,145	$745,568	88.70%

A single $10,000 investment made by a grandparent or parent in the Standard and Poor's Composite Averages for a baby born in 1946 would have produced a result for that baby, now 58 years old, of $6,599,145. This assumes that he reinvested all distributions in added shares and avoided paying taxes on the distributions. If he paid taxes each year on the

—

distributions at the then current maximum tax rate and reinvested only what was left after taxes, the result drops to a mere $745,568 for a loss of 88.7%.

Assume that our investor was not subject to the maximum tax rate for all or part of the period. His or her results would improve, but even if we assume a tax rate of one half the maximum rate, our investor would still have lost 51.3% of his or her total value.

I looked at results for General Electric stock. Figure 11A3 shows the results were almost as dramatic as for the S&P. It turns out a $10,000 investment in GE stock in 1940 would have produced $23,400,556 by the end of 2004 if the investor had reinvested all distributions and avoided or deferred taxes on the distributions. Assume that our investor had been unable to avoid taxes and reinvested only the distribution amount after tax each year, our investor would have finished with $5,713,856 for a loss of 75.6% due solely to his or her inability to avoid taxes.

FIGURE 11A3 General Electric Data[81]
Net Results Comparing Tax and No Tax Examples

$10,000 Initial Investment	Result Assuming No Taxes Paid on Distributions	Result Assuming Normal Taxes Paid on Distributions	Percent of Total Value Lost to Taxes
1940 Original investment	$10,000	$10,000	
2004 Net result	$23,400,556	$5,713,856	75.60%

Tax rates on dividends are at historic low rates as I write this chapter in early 2006. The Internal Revenue Service maximum rate on "qualified" dividends, which includes most stock dividends held for long periods of time, is 15%. However, it is likely that such low rates will not last forever. Already there are moves in Congress to repeal or adjust this low tax rate. But even if the 15% rate lasts, the penalty for the long-term investor who does not find a tax deferral or avoidance plan is significant. Figure 11A4 shows the difference for an investor who earns an 11.76% compound rate of return for 60 years with a 15% maximum income tax on dividends. We assume that he or she averages either 2% or 3% dividends per year and uses or does not use a tax-deferred or avoidance technique for investing.

FIGURE 11A4 Assumed $10,000 Investment with Compound Return of 11.76% Per Year
Hypothetical Net Results Comparing Tax and No Tax Examples for 60 Years

$10,000 Initial Investment	Result Assuming Normal Taxes Paid on Dividends (Assume 3%)	Result Assuming Normal Taxes Paid on Dividends (Assume 2%)
Net result assuming tax deferral	$9,085,373	$8,998,295
Net result assuming 15% tax on dividends	$6,925,419	$7,496,329
Percent lost to taxes	23.77%	16.99%

Even if we make the unlikely assumption of the favorable tax rates somehow survive the next 60 years, the loss for an investor who does not use a tax avoidance vehicle when investing is significant. Assuming an average dividend rate of 3% means that our investor loses almost 24% of his or her net return over 60 years by paying taxes and 17% if the average dividend rate is 2%. (An 11.76% compound rate of return produces a slightly higher result if dividends make up 3% of the return each year rather than 2%.) It should not be surprising that taxes on dividends are this important since we saw in Chapter 10 how critical dividends and dividend reinvestment are to total returns.

I have emphasized this issue of taxes. I know that many young people reading this book have never paid a dime in taxes directly, and even if they do file a tax return, they probably pay little in taxes. The important point for you to realize is that even though the tax implications of investing may not impact you currently or even for years into the future, at some point they will become important. How you begin your investment plan will be critical in fixing the impact of taxes on your investments. While not impossible, it may be difficult and costly to change the tax structure of your investment account in later years. Long-term investing often results in large dividends paid especially in the later years when you are approaching retirement age and just when the higher tax rates impact you. For instance, an investor who invested $10,000 in General Electric stock in 1940 and reinvested all distributions using a tax avoidance or deferral scheme received over $500,000 in dividends in 2004. Obviously, even at 15%, using a tax deferral or avoidance system at the beginning now becomes critical.

Delay or Avoid Taxes

The beauty of the current tax circumstances is that, unlike prior years, today most investors are almost always able to defer or avoid some or all taxes on distributions if they use the correct investment vehicle to initiate the investment. Although there were no taxes on income until 1913, our long-time investor would have found it difficult, if not impossible, to avoid or defer taxes on his or her distributions. Even our 1946 investor would probably have found it impossible to defeat the taxman. But today (2006), it is easy to at least defer taxes until age 70½, and it is even possible, under some circumstances, to avoid paying any taxes on any of your investment distributions ever.

There are methods for deferring or avoiding taxes, which I will go over in Chapters 17-19. These investment vehicles are the result of acts of Congress supported by Congress for 30+ years. In fact, Congress has seen fit to add new wrinkles and improve the tax avoidance methods every decade. The government wants all of us to save and invest more. Americans are a consuming society. Most economists and other experts think that it would be better for us as a country if we saved and invested more. So Congress passed laws that allow us to save and invest, under certain circumstances and with certain limits, funds using tax deferral or tax avoidance techniques. But you must follow the rules, and I strongly suggest that every reader who intends to set up a tax avoidance strategy familiarize themselves with the techniques outlined in Chapters 17-19. I include chapters covering IRAs, single premium deferred annuities, 401Ks, SEPs, Keoghs, and other investment vehicles that avoid or defer taxes.

The Power of Delaying Taxes

It is attractive to avoid taxes altogether, and for many of you, it is legal under current tax laws. But for many, delaying or deferring taxes may be all that you can achieve. Delaying taxes until a future (distant) date allows you to compound returns on money that would normally go to taxes. The power of compounding is huge even if you must eventually pay taxes on your return at some later date. The key is that you have many years to compound tax-free. This allows the investor to amass a much larger result even if it means paying some taxes as you take the money and use it in retirement. Even at current maximum tax rates of 15% on dividends, avoiding taxes until retirement can potentially be worth millions to a long-term investor. Delaying taxes for many years is a powerful tool, but in a low tax dividend environment with higher taxes on income, it is not as powerful today as it was in the past. I would still advise that you take the tax deferral steps explained in Chapters 17-19 since I have little confidence that low tax rates on dividends will be preserved. I have much greater confidence that the techniques outlined in those chapters will continue and be improved.

The Power of Avoiding Taxes

The power of avoiding all taxes on any income is substantial. There are few ways in which you can legally earn untaxed income in the United States. One of the most lucrative is the Roth IRA detailed in Chapter 17, named after the long-time senator William Roth of Delaware, who sponsored the original legislation. It allows an individual to earn compound returns on dividends and capital gains without paying any taxes at all. Unlike traditional IRAs that require payment on all distributions at regular income tax rates, Roth IRAs require no tax payment ever. All funds withdrawn by investors pass complete tax-free. I cannot overstate this advantage. An investor of $10,000 in Figure 11A4 with an assumed 2% dividend payout amassed almost $9 million in 60 years. If, at age 70½, the investor decides to take the entire $9 million out of his or her IRA, he or she would pay regular income tax rates on the entire amount. At current rates, this would be roughly 35% plus any state income tax that may be applicable. In a high-tax state like New York or California, it could easily amount to 40% of $9 million or $3.6 million. An investor who qualified for a Roth IRA could withdraw the entire $9 million without paying any tax at all. Unfortunately, there are limits on who can contribute to a Roth IRA and not everyone will qualify. Read Chapter 17 and use the Roth IRA if you qualify.

CHAPTER 12

The Fantastic Impact of Possible Life Extension

Life Extension

A book on investments may seem like a strange place to include a chapter on possible life span extension. The essence of this book is to allow the individual investors to take advantage of time in their investments. The time that an investor has to preserve his or her investments and follow the other advice given is critical and central to the return achieved. The longer you have to live, the more profitable your investment return, and human life span can become critical in your long-term plan.

Historic Rate of Change in Life Span[82]

For most of human history, life span had changed little. While there were a few people who lived past 80, the average life span for most of human existence was usually fewer than 30 years. By the beginning of the 19th century, the best information we have is that average life span at birth was roughly 25 or 30 years. At the beginning of the 20th century, the average life span at birth in the United States was just short of 50 years, 48.23 for males and 51.08 for females to be exact. By the beginning of the 21st century, average life span at birth in the United States had increased to 77.1, 74.2 for males and 79.9 for females. In 1900, a male's odds of surviving until age 65 was 39.2%. By the year 2000, that number had increased to 70.6%. A female's odds of surviving until age 65 went up even more, from 43.8% in 1900 to 83.5% in 2000. After stagnating for most of human existence, life span at birth has increased about 25 years in each of the last two centuries. If this trend continues, we may see another increase in life span in the 21st century, bringing average life span at birth to more than 100 years.

There are many scientists who believe that we may be on the verge of some dramatic increases in life span that may even change our understanding of what it means to be human. It is difficult to predict the future in any field and particularly in this one. While there are dramatic breakthroughs in medicine and perhaps aging on the horizon, it is true that much of the life span extension in the past two centuries occurred by reducing infant and childhood mortality. Life span for Americans has increased about 17 years for men and 20 years for woman during the first half of the 20th century. In the last 50 years, life span for both men and women has continued to increase but only about 8 years each. Childhood mortality was so high that many families had ten or more children because the odds of survival until adulthood were so low. Without dramatic breakthroughs, it seems safe to assume that at the minimum we should be able to increase life span about 16 years during the 21st century. That assumes no unusual breakthroughs. As you will see, even 10 or 15 years can mean a dramatic difference for a long-term investor.

FIGURE 12A1 American Life Spans[83]

Year	Male Life span	Female Life span
1900	48.2	51.1
2000	74.2	79.9
2100 (Est. minimum)	90.2	95.9
2100 (Est. maximum)	???	???

Any increase in life span is significant once the investor understands the dramatic impact that time has on long-term investing. If life span increases in the 21st century only as much as it did in the 20th and 19th centuries, it could be profitable for long-term investors. Another 20 or 25 years of life can mean another 20 or 25 years of investing until withdrawal. And that would have a dramatic impact on your returns.

Two Ways Your Life Span May Increase

I will not waste a lot of time on this subject, but a few paragraphs might be helpful to the investor. There are two general ways in which life span might increase in the coming years. The first would occur with the development of cures or therapies for many of the diseases of aging like, cancer, heart disease, Alzheimer's, and Parkinson's. Curing these diseases and others would extend our life but would not be an extension of life span. We would simply not be dying early. While we don't know if there is a "maximum" life span, curing most of the diseases of aging might increase average life span by 10 or 20 years. Most of us would live healthy lives well into our 90s, and a significant number of us would live beyond the century mark. We would not have increased human life span, just be taking better advantage of what seems naturally available to us already. If that is all that occurs, or even some reduced version of it, the impact on investing will be significant.

However, there is an increasing body of scientific knowledge that suggests that in the 21st century, we may be able to do more than just cure diseases of aging. We may be able to actively extend human life span, perhaps dramatically. The combination of the computer, biotech research, and new fields like nanotechnology, coupled with our greater understanding of the mechanism of aging, may lead to dramatic results in the next few decades.

As I write this chapter, my weekly issue of *Barron's*[84] has on its cover the headline, "Live to 150." The article discusses the depth of research into the "secrets of longevity" and includes some interesting opinions that are much more aggressive than those expressed in this chapter. Aubrey de Grey, a Cambridge University geneticist, is quoted as follows, "The first person to live to be 1,000 years old is certainly alive today: indeed, he or she may be about to turn 60." This opinion may be extreme, but it is clear that the biology of aging is under severe scrutiny from any number of institutions.

If you are interested in these possibilities, I suggest that a good place to start is with Michael Fossel's book, *Reversing Human Aging*.[85] Dr. Fossel, who holds both a PhD and MD in Neurobiology from Stanford University, has written a book that outlines some of the possibilities. Dr. Fossel discusses not only the possibility of dramatic life span extension (hundreds of years) but also the potential to reverse the aging process so human beings could live their life using a true fountain of youth. Anything that could lead to a "real" extension of maximum life spans would lead to dramatic windfalls for long-term investors.

Potential Impact of Life Span Extension

As I emphasize over and over in this book, stock investments are time dependent. I assume that any 21st-century life extension would mean some extension of the retirement age. Investors may have an added 10, 20, or more years available to invest before needing to use their investment funds. If people live longer, they may choose to still retire at the same age (say around 70) and simply have more years in retirement to use up their wealth. A longer life span may lead to more work years or some combination of added work years and added retirement years. The impact for an investor who starts early, reinvests all distributions, avoids or defers taxes, and holds and holds and holds could be amazing.

Some readers might have noticed by now that, although I use many different investment spans, I use 60 years as a sort of standard. I arrived at 60 years from my experience as a high school teacher trying to motivate 17-year-olds to begin an investment program. Initially, I used 50 years, the estimated retirement age, for a 15-to 17-year-old teenager. My reading into the history and potential for life extension led me to assume that using 60 years as the norm for anyone under 20 was, in reality, conservative. Sixty years assumes the only life span extension we will get in the 21st century is the same approximate 16 years per century that we achieved in the last 50 years. Assuming only 16 years of added life span led me to assume another 10 years of average-investing life.

I am personally convinced that it is likely that it will turn out to be much more than that. The current arguments over social security will, in the end, probably mean little in the long run. The only real long-term answer to social security reform is to index retirement age to average life spans. Sixty-five was the original retirement age when social security was first launched in the 1930s. The average American lives at least 18 more years than they did in the 1930s, and yet we are just beginning to adjust the retirement age that we use to begin participation in social security payments. I believe there is a high likelihood of extended life spans within the next 100 years. It would not surprise me to see the average American living to 120 (instead of today's 80), some to 150 by the year 2100. The extra years will undoubtedly be divided in some way between retirement and work. Just the potential of increased life span for young people in the

—

21st century should be strong motivation to begin a retirement investment plan like the one favored in this book. If life span is extended, reliance on social security is problematic, and the rewards of extra years of investing for those who have the foresight to begin now can be phenomenal. Any life span increase will produce a difference in investment result for a young—or middle-aged investor who follows a long-term investing plan that will be huge. Failure to invest now may doom you to a dramatically substandard but greatly extended life in retirement in the year 2100.

The Impact of Life Extension or Holding Periods on Long-Term Returns

We can look at the potential impact of added investment time on our fortunes as investors. Figure 12A2 shows how dramatic just a few years of life extension might be.

FIGURE 12A2 Investment Returns on $10,000 Initial Investment Calculated by Year Return and Years

Years	Compound Return 11.76%	Compound Return 10.00%
60	$7,891,936	$3,044,016
70	$23,990,954	$7,897,470
80	$72,930,580	$20,484,002
90	$221,704,945	$53,130,226

Figure 12A2 is interesting. The first point to note is that the returns just about triple every 10 years. For an assumed 11.76% compound return used as the standard estimate in this book, they slightly more than triple every 10 years, and for the more conservative 10% compound return, they slightly less than triple every 10 years. That means that a life extension of even 10 years in the next century will about triple your result. Remember that life span in the 19th and 20th centuries increased around 25 years each century. A 20-year increase in your investment life span would mean increasing your result somewhere between *7 and 10* times our original calculation. Now you see why I thought it important to point out this possibility.

Suppose our investor has 70 years of investment life instead of 60 and invests at an 11.76% compound rate of return, His or her return at the end of the period moves from just under $8 million to just under $24 million. If we add another 10 years it moves that return on the same $10,000 initial investment to just under $73 million. Because compound returns are so "back-loaded," any life extension can be a real bonanza to a long-term investor.

There are many excellent sources on the possibility of expanded life spans for those who are interested. I have included some of them in Table 12A1 in the appendix.

CHAPTER 13

The Corrosive Impact of Inflation on Returns

Historic Inflation

Most Americans have experienced nothing but inflation for their entire lifetimes. Only the oldest of us can remember the deflation of the 1930s when many people kept their money under their floorboards, in their mattress, or in the walls. Unlike inflation, in a deflation, money gets more valuable the longer you hold it. If prices are declining, the dollar in your pocket will buy more at the mall next week, next month, or next year. Why not hold it if you can? In deflation, you get a return for doing nothing. The truth is that deflation was more common than inflation in the 19th century, although we had periodic episodes of both.

For most of the 20th century, after 1940, the United States has experienced constant inflation; prices always go up. The U.S. Bureau of Labor Statistics has been keeping data on inflation since 1913. The Consumer Price Index provides monthly data on the changes in prices paid by consumers for a "basket" of goods and services. The Bureau sets prices that existed on the basket of goods at 100, say for the 1982-1984 period, and then calculates the relative prices that existed before and after this period. A number of 110 would mean that prices in that year were 10% higher than in 1982-1984, and a number of 90 would mean that prices in that year were 10% lower than in 1982-1984.

Inflation and Stock Market Returns

When I first took a course in investments, we learned that stocks were the best investment "hedge" against inflation. The theory was that business would be able to adjust to inflation by increasing prices to offset inflation's devastating impact. Increased prices would mean that, at the minimum, business would be able to increase its dollar profits at least as much as the inflation rate. Stocks might not be a good investment during recessions and especially depressions, but they just might be fine during inflation.

The other argument says that inflation means higher interest rates, and since bonds and other debt investments pay interest, stocks will not look as attractive an alternative to investors when inflation and interest rates are high. I will briefly look at the history of inflation and the stock market in the next section to see if we can detect any obvious trends.

One point is clear. Inflation eats away at raw stock market returns. If your stocks go up 5% this year and inflation is 5%, you are no better off at the end of the year than you were at the beginning. Your investment has grown 5%. But if you sell it and try to spend the money, you will only be able to buy the same amount of goods and services at the end of the year that you could at the beginning. Inflation, higher prices, has eaten away all your gains. Let's look at the effect of inflation on your projected stock market returns in Figure 13B1.

Inflation Devastates Returns

Inflation has a significant negative impact on the value of any investor's returns, especially for a long-term stock market investor. Must mutual funds make no effort to take inflation into account when bragging about their compound yearly returns. Much of the data presented so far in this book has also not been adjusted for inflation. If you invest now for 50, 60, or 70 years, the money you invested will almost surely buy more goods and services in the year the investment is initiated than it will in the year the investment is liquidated. The investor who invested $1,000 in Philip Morris stock in 1957 and cashed out $6 million plus in 2003 may be happy. But he or she should realize that $1,000 in 1957 bought a lot more goods and services in 1957 than it will today.

FIGURE 13B1 Actual Returns Adjusted for Inflation
Assumes a $10,000 Investment

Data Series	Nominal Return	Inflation/Adjusted Return	Percent Lost to Inflation
Shiller's S&P data[86] from 1871	$1,106,347,348	$73,568,853	93.35%
Shiller's S&P data[87] from 1946	$6,599,145	$745,568	88.70%
General Electric[88] from 1940	$23,400,556	$1,711,477	92.69%

Using the three data series noted in Chapter 6, the "nominal" return column shows the return in the current dollars that year. In other words, if you invested $10,000 in General Electric stock in 1940, reinvested all dividends, and avoided taxes, you would have received $23,400,556 in 2004. That is still much money, but to be accurate, we need to adjust the return to reflect any increases in prices of goods and services that we buy. After adjusting for inflation, our investor would have only $1,711,477 in 1940 dollars to spend if he or she chooses to spend it all in 2005. To be clear, our investor would have over $23 million in funds in 2003; it is just that each dollar would not buy as much as it did in 1940. While we cannot know the future, it seems reasonable to assume that we will continue to have some inflation eating away at our spectacular returns in the future. Do not let this fact deter you in your investment planning. In the next chapter, I will look at the impact of possible life extension on inflation.

Table 13A1 in the appendix allows the reader to calculate the impact of inflation on his or her return using annual inflation rates from 0.05% to 4% and years from 1 to 70. Determine the inflation-adjusted return by multiplying the factor located in Table 13A1 by the nominal return. A 2% inflation rate for 20 years requires you to multiply 0.668 times your nominal return to get the inflation-adjusted return.

Can Inflation Be Good for the Stock Market?

What about inflation? Is it good for the stock market? For this analysis, I have chosen to look at an index called the Producer Price Index (PPI) as the benchmark for inflation. The PPI has increased slightly less over a long period of time. The PPI increased about 10.4 times from 1890 until 1985 while the consumer price index increased about 12.9 times during the same period.

—

Figure 13C1 shows us some clear periods of both inflation and deflation. First, let's look at deflation in the right side of Figure 13C1. As I pointed out, we have had some significant deflations in the United States. The deflationary 1870-1900 period saw an almost 50% drop in prices and an anemic 9.9% increase in stock prices. (This is just raw stock prices and does not include dividends or reinvestment of dividends.) The second long period of deflation occurred from 1920 until 1940. It included one decade of stock market increases (1920s) and one decade of stock market declines (1930s). The big deflation took place in the 1930s, although there was some deflation in the PPI in the 1920s. Taking the two decades together, stock prices showed a moderate increase if an investor was able to hold on all the way from 1920 until 1940.

The periods of inflation show two periods (1950-1970 and 1990-2000), in which inflation was moderate and there were strong stock market gains. In one period (1970-1990), stock gains and inflation were about the same, and during one period (1900-1920), inflation roared but the stock market was tame. What are we to make of this?

FIGURE 13C1 Inflation/Deflation and Stock Prices[89]

Periods of Inflation			Periods of Deflation		
1900-1920	PPI	Stocks	1870-1900	PPI	Stocks
	+179.0%	+44.8%		−48.5%	+9.9%
1950-1970	PPI	Stocks	1920-1940	PPI	Stocks
	+40.9%	+488.0%		−49.6%	+39.3%
1970-1990	PPI	Stocks			
	+214.8%	+233.2%			
1990-2000	PPI	Stocks			
	+6.9%	+267.3%			

FIGURE 13C2 Inflation/Deflation and Stock Prices Percent per Year[90]

Periods of Inflation			Periods of Deflation		
1900-1920	PPI +5.55%	Stocks +1.97%	1870-1900	PPI (1.66%)	Stocks +0.33%
1950-1970	PPI +1.82%	Stocks +9.77%	1920-1940	PPI (3.54%)	Stocks +1.76%
1970-1990	PPI +6.22%	Stocks +6.52%			
1990-2000	PPI +0.35%	Stocks +7.09%			

We can look at the annual rate of return and annual inflation rate in Figure 13C2. We see that in two periods (1990-2000 and 1950-1970) when inflation existed but was fairly tame (averaging somewhere around 1% per year), the stock market roared ahead far faster than inflation. In the two periods in which inflation averaged over 5% yearly, the best the stock market could do was to just barely keep up with inflation in one period (1970-1990) and fall behind substantially in the other (1900-1920). Remember, we know that dividends are a big portion of the return to stocks, and they are not in this analysis.

A surface analysis might draw the following conclusions:

The stock market loves it when inflation (at least as measured by the PPI) is moderate. It does not thrive in deflation, and it had mixed results during higher inflation, defined here as over 5%.

But we should look at the numbers more carefully. We want to know if the stock market performs better during inflation. For instance, the 1920-1940 period saw an estimated 3.5% per year drop in prices of goods and services in the PPI. Yet the stock market (as poorly as it did during the 1930s) still gained an average of 1.76% per year. That means that a stock investor was getting richer at a rate of about 5.3% per year. If he or she invested $1,000 in 1920 and grew at 1.76% per year, it was worth $1,390 in 1940. Our mythical investor was able to sell his or her stock and buy goods and services that were almost half the price that they were in

1920. He or she could buy about $2,700 worth of goods in 1920 dollars for his or her $1,390, not bad.

But wait, let's look a little further and compare our periods of inflation and deflation in a slightly different way in Figure 13C3.

**FIGURE 13C3 Inflation/Deflation and Stock Prices
Net Stock Market Returns[91]**

Periods of Inflation		Periods of Deflation	
1900-1920	Net Stock Returns -3.58%	1870-1900	Net Stock Returns +1.99%
1950-1970	Net Stock Returns +7.95%	1920-1940	Net Stock Returns +5.30%
1970-1990	Net Stock Returns +0.32%		
1990-2000	Net Stock Returns +6.74%		

Here, we can look at the appropriate "net" return a stock investor achieved. If stocks go up moderately and prices of goods and services go down, that can be as good or better than if stocks go up more quickly than inflation. Analyzed in this way, it is even clearer that the stock market does not like periods of high inflation (1900-1920 and 1970-1990). The market clearly likes periods of moderate inflation much more, and periods of deflation fall somewhere in the middle. So the idea that inflation is good for the stock market may be partly true. It may be good, but only when inflation is modest. It looks as if the stock market performs the worst when inflation heats up. Despite the greatest depression in history, the stock market performed better in the 1920-1940 period than it did in the 1870-1900 period. In both cases, it seems, the market likes moderation, moderate inflation, or moderate deflation, better than the extremes.

FIGURE 13C4 Total Returns Adjusted for Inflation—7 Companies[92]

	IBM	Alcoa	Boeing	Caterpillar	DuPont	GM	Coca-Cola
Final value unadjusted for inflation	$915,713	$458,300	$1,819,737	$896,963	$483,054	$357,430	$4,695,908
Final value adjusted for inflation (in 1962 dollars)	*$193,597*	*$96,892*	*$384,722*	*$189,633*	*$102,126*	*$75,567*	*$992,792*

Figure 13C4 shows the returns calculated in Figure 8D1 in Chapter 8 in the first row. In the second row, those returns adjusted for the inflation that existed using the PPI. The dollars mentioned in row one are the dollars that an investor received in 2004 for his or her $10,000 investment in 1962. However, a dollar, returned in 2004, was not worth as much in 2004 as it was in 1962. The second row calculates what the actual dollars received in the first row would have been worth in 1962 dollars. The $10,000 that an investor made in Coca-Cola in 1962 earned him or her $992,792 in the same 1962 dollars by 2004. Looked at another way, each dollar investment in Coca-Cola in 1962 returned an investor enough dollars to buy $99 dollars worth of 1962 goods and services. The investor could have simply spent his or her $10,000 in 1962 on as much goods and services as it would buy. By investing it for 42 years, our investor can now buy 99 times as much goods and services. This is adjusting the return to express it in 1962 dollars.

Figure 13C5 reproduces Figure 6D1, which is one of the key return calculations in this book. Figure 6D1 shows the compound rates of return and results for a $10,000 investment in Siegel's, O'Shaughnessy's, and Shiller's data unadjusted for inflation. Figure 13C5 shows the original results and the inflation-adjusted results, using the post-WWII inflation rate from the *Statistical Abstract of the United States* of 3.23%[93] yearly. Figure 13C5 shows the devastating impact of inflation on potential returns. We can use the average compound rates of return for Shiller's, Siegel's, and O'Shaughnessy's data as base returns for the next 50, 60, or 70 years. Figure 13C5 looks at both the unadjusted dollar return and the inflation-adjusted return, assuming an average inflation rate of 3.23% per year. An investor of $10,000 for 60 years, assuming Siegel's calculated annual rate of return of 11.60% occurs, will have $7,241,886 in 60 years, assuming he or she reinvested all distributions and used a tax-advantaged account for his or her investment. But in current dollars, the $7.2 million will only buy $1,076,346 worth of 2006 goods and services in 2066 (assuming the investment began in 2006). To be clear, the investment will return $7.2 million to the investor in 2066. It just won't buy $7.2 million worth of today's goods and services if we have a 3.23% inflation, on average, every year. Chapters 9, 12, 14, and 15 give investors some possibilities to offset the corrosive impact of inflation, but the impact is still significant.

FIGURE 13C5 Summary—Calculated Nominal and Inflation-Adjusted Returns Using S&P 500 Composite

	Calculated Compound Return	Net Result $10,000 Investment for 50 Years	Net Result $10,000 Investment for 60 Years	Net Result $10,000 Investment for 70 Years
Siegel, 1946-2001[94]				
Nominal return	11.60%	$2,418,628	$7,241,886	$21,701,693
Inflation-adjusted	8.11%	$493,487	$1,076,346	$2,347,528
O'Shaughnessy[95],				
1951-2003				
Nominal return	11.52%	$2,331,514	$6,936,903	$20,639,219
Inflation-adjusted	8.03%	$475,712	$1,029,586	$2,228,981
Shiller, 1946-2004[96]				
Nominal	11.76%	$2,596,089	$7,891,937	$23,990,954
Inflation-adjusted	8.26%	$529,695	$1,169,719	$2,586,793

Dealing with Inflation

In the next few chapters and later in this book, I will deal with ways to handle the inflation problem. If inflation worries you, and it should, the simplest method of handling it is as follows:

- Calculate what you would like to have invested in current dollars if you were retiring this year.
- Estimate an inflation rate (2%-3%).
- Calculate what you will need at retirement to meet your goal in current dollars.

Your choices to defeat inflation are as follows:

- Invest more now.
- Increase or add additional yearly investments.
- Plan to hold your investments longer.
- Hope that life extension bails you out.
- Postpone or limit earlier retirement year withdrawals.
- Try to get a higher-than-average return (see Chapter 22).
- Accept it. It is good enough as it is.

Inflation is a fact of modern day life that we just have to deal with it. The investor who put $1,000 into Philip Morris in 1957 is probably not that upset about the $6 million that he or she has in the bank. Continued inflation is one of the obstacles we face in long-term investing, but unlike some other obstacles, there are ways to mitigate it.

Chapter 14

The Interaction of Inflation and Life Extension

While inflation eats away at a long-term investor's return, time makes dramatic additions to the same return. Figure 14A1 tries to look at the trade-off between inflation and time. The first row, labeled 60 years, shows the return in nominal terms for an investor of $10,000 who held his or her investment for 60 years. There is no adjustment for inflation in the first row. The second and third rows show the number of added years needed to restore the nominal return to an inflation-adjusted return based on 2% and 3% inflation assumptions. This suggests that an increase of 11.6 years in investment time horizon would roughly compensate an investor for the amount lost to inflation if the inflation rate was 2% per year. If we assume a 3% annual inflation rate, then our investor would want an added 19.4 years of investment time horizon to completely offset inflation.

FIGURE 14A1 Interaction between Inflation and Years Invested
$10,000 Invested at Compound Rate of 11.76%[97] per Year

Years	Compound Return	Inflation Rate	Final Result
60	11.76%		$7,891,937
71.6	11.76%	2%	$7,866,787
79.4	11.76%	3%	$7,864,197

Assume an 11.76% compound rate of return (the historic post-WWII rate used in this book). An investor investing now for this century would need either an 11.6-year or a 19.4-year increase in life span to completely overcome the effects of inflation. Life span increased around 27 years in the last century. If we only get the same amount of life extension in the 21st century that we had in the 20th century, our investor will more than overcome the impact of inflation with added investment years. While inflation can have a significant impact, it should not deter a long-term investor from carrying out his or her investment plan immediately.

The 20th century began with life spans for most Americans of under 50 years. The 60-year investment horizons were not sensible. But as the century progressed and life spans expanded, a typical investor had more and more years of productive investing to produce more spectacular results. While inflation did eat away at investment returns, those added years more than compensated the dedicated investor for the reduced inflation-adjusted returns.

We can look at a real example of life expectancy and inflation interacting. Assume that someone invested $10,000 in the S&P composite for a baby born in 1928 (before the beginning of the Great Depression). The aim is the baby would continue to keep the funds invested for 60 years (probably a long assumption given the life span expectations in 1928) when he or she would begin to use the money. Figure 14A2 shows the nominal return in dollars at the actual compound rate of 9.04% from 1928 to 1988 when planned retirement should begin. It also shows the inflation-adjusted return using actual inflation data from 1928 to 1988. The $1,797,691 the original investment produced in the 60 years calculates at $255,108 in 1928 dollars. That means that inflation reduced the value of a dollar by about 7 times during the 60 years. Assume that our investor, because he or she lived longer than expected, continued his or her investment portfolio. The question is, how many years would he or she have had to continue his or her investing, without using the funds, to restore the return to $1,797,691 in 1928 dollars? It turns out that it would have taken him or her 11 extra years of investing to make at least $1,797,691 in 1928 dollars. Of course, the nominal dollars in 1999 would have been much greater. Looking at life extension from 1928 to 1999, it turns out that average life span increased exactly 17.88 years, roughly 60% more than needed to offset the impact of inflation. Had our investor held his or her investments for exactly 17.88 years beyond the original plan, he or she would have overcome and exceeded the inflation effect for 60 years. The positive impact of a longer life and a longer investment horizon until retirement overwhelmed the negative impact of inflation during much of the 20th century. It is likely that it will do even better in the 21st century. Most investors faced with expanded years of life will probably want to use some of those years for extra retirement. The statistics in Figures 14A2 and 14A3 suggest that under the most likely conditions, it will be possible for an investor to divide her extra years between earning and investing and still defeat the negative impact of inflation.

FIGURE 14A2 Calculation of Added Years Required to Offset Inflation, 1928-1999

1928	Invested	$10,000 in S&P composite
1988	Nominal value	$1,797,691
1988	Inflation-adjusted value	$255,108 (value in 1928 dollars)
1999	Inflation-adjusted value	$1,881,926 (value in 1928 dollars)

Actual number of additional years required to offset inflation = 11

Look at the interaction between inflation rates and compound rates of return. Figure 14A3 shows us the estimated number of extra years that a 60-year investment would need to offset alternative inflation rates in the left most column, correlated with alternative possible compound rates of return across the top row. The resultant numbers in the table are the number of years of added investing, on average, an investor might need. Obviously, the most favorable result is for an investor to achieve a high return coupled with a low inflation rate. A 12% or 13% rate of return coupled with a 1% inflation rate would force the investor to hold his or her investments only an extra 5 years to offset inflation. But a high inflation rate coupled with a lower rate of return would force the investor to hold his or her investments for more years, sometimes significantly longer.

—
179

To be realistic, an investor might look at a 10% or 11% compound rate coupled with a 2 or 3% inflation rate to see what would seem a more likely result.

FIGURE 14A3 The Interaction of Rates of Return and Inflation
Approximate Years Required to Offset Inflation

Inflation Rate	9% Rate of Return	10% Rate of Return	11% Rate of Return	12% Rate of Return	13% Rate of Return
1%	7 Years	6 Years	6 Years	5 Years	5 Years
2%	16 Years	14 Years	13 Years	11 Years	10 Years
3%	29 Years	24 Years	21 Years	19 Years	17 Years
4%	46 Years	38 Years	33 Years	28 Years	25 Years

Investors should watch inflation carefully but not excessively distress themselves over the impact of inflation on their returns. The 1957 investor of $1,000 in Altria is thrilled that this investment produced over $6 million in current 2003 dollars. He or she would probably accuse us of nitpicking if we suggested that his or her $6 million wasn't worth as much in 2003 as it would have been in 1957. But the reality is that take away 10 years from his or her investment return in Altria and it would have the same effect as calculating the inflation adjustment. Looked at another way, let us assume that our investor in Altria, because of added life span, can hold his or her investment for an extra 10 years, until 2013. The probable effect would be to restore the nominal return over 46 years (1957-2003) to an inflation-adjusted return after 56 years. Added time can offset a destructive inflation.

Even a conservative assumption about life extension, 16 years in a century, will probably offset a moderate inflation. So, yes, some of the results in this book overstated the returns by the compound inflation rate, but they also understated the returns by the impact on investing of historical life span extension. And if we get the dramatic increase in life spans predicted by some experts, the investment result could be mind-boggling. I hesitate to even try to calculate the returns to shareholders who buy and hold and hold if we get some significant life extension beyond that of the last two centuries. Those results would run into the billions.

—

Life Extension and Stock Market Returns

It is possible to speculate on what significant life extension might do for overall stock market returns, but speculation is all it is. A stock investor should not rely on this speculation. The returns available under normal circumstances are significant enough. A significantly longer life span for human beings will undoubtedly have a multiple impact on everything including the stock market. On the one hand, it will mean more current investors holding investments for longer periods of time as we work and save for more years. It will obviously provide more customers for more years for the companies that we invest in to sell goods and services, and it will provide a bigger, more experienced labor force to support the bigger economy and larger population. On the other hand, many of the institutions that we depend on will probably fail. Social security, defined pension plans, and other financial retirement tactics may not be sustainable in an environment with even a modest increase in life span. We may change the entire meaning of retiring, and the nature and meaning of work itself may be altered. Certainly, there will be a dramatically larger difference between the lifestyle available in retirement to long-term investors and those that do not start a retirement investment plan. We may have many more years in whatever form non-work takes in the future, and saving and investing for it should increase dramatically.

Summary

The fact is that if we look at the major ways, the investment plan outlined in this book could fail or produce less than expected; inflation is the only one that can be recoverable.

- If the investor fails to start a long-term investment plan, it is not recoverable.
- If the investor fails to fully fund his or her investment plan, it is not recoverable.
- If the investor fails to hold and hold and hold his or her investments, it is not recoverable.
- If the investor makes poor investment decisions that fail or underperform the market averages, it is not recoverable.
- If the investor fails to reinvest all dividends and distributions in added stock, it is not recoverable.
- If the investor fails to avoid or defer taxes on distributions and dividends, it is not recoverable.

—

- If inflation eats away at our investment return, it is recoverable. Extra time or added dollar investments can and probably will recover any loss of buying power because of inflation.

I am a perfect example. Had I read this book and followed its advice as a young person, I would be much, much richer today than I am in reality. Just like my results, those theoretical results are impacted by inflation. However, I would probably have been able to overcome the impact of the inflation that occurred by simply holding my investments for a longer time period. The real failure of not carrying out the plan parameters is not recoverable by me now. Had I known about and carried out this plan, I would be happy to be "struggling" now with the "problem" of holding some or all my investments for a few more years to overcome the effects of past inflation.

I would strongly advise the investor to pay close attention to the first six possible pitfalls and not excessively worry about the impact of inflation on returns.

CHAPTER 15

The Interaction of Rates of Return and Inflation

The Impact of Increasing or Reducing Compound Rates of Return

Chapter 5 demonstrated that rates of return have a significant impact on total return. Even small changes in the assumed or actual rate of return can produce dramatically different results, especially for a long-term investor. Whether you get 8%, 11%, or 13% will mean significant differences in your outcome. Table 15A1 shows the theoretical result of a $10,000 investment for years up to 90 and for yearly compound rates of return from 8% to 14%.

FIGURE 15A1 Compound Rates of Return/Years
$10,000 One Time Investment

	8%	9%	10%	11%	12%	13%	14%
20 Years	$46,610	$56,044	$67,275	$80,623	$96,463	$115,231	$137,435
30 Years	$100,627	$132,677	$174,494	$228,923	$299,599	$391,159	$509,502
40 Years	$217,245	$314,094	$452,593	$650,009	$930,510	$1,327,816	$1,888,835
50 Years	$469,016	$743,575	$1,173,909	$1,845,648	$2,890,022	$4,507,359	$7,002,330
60 Years	$1,012,571	$1,760,313	$3,044,816	$5,240,572	$8,975,969	$15,300,535	$25,959,187

70 Years	$2,186,064	$4,167,301	$7,897,470	$14,880,191	$27,877,998	$51,938,696	$96,236,450
80 Years	$4,719,548	$9,865,517	$20,484,002	$42,251,128	$86,584,831	$176,309,405	$356,769,818
90 Years	$10,189,151	$23,355,266	$53,130,226	$119,968,738	$268,818,342	$598,494,155	$1,322,624,674

I include in Figure 15A1 returns on a onetime $10,000 investment for 20-90 years in 10-year increments. While 90 years may seem like an unrealistic time frame, I suggest the reader to look at Chapter 12 to understand why I included this long a time. You can see the impact of different rates of return by looking at any specific year length. Let us say 50 years. Notice that a $10,000 investment for 50 years at 8% compounded produces a respectable $469,016. However, if the investor can find a mutual fund or stocks that produce even a 9% compound return instead of 8%, his or her result goes up almost 60% to $743,575. A compound yearly return of 11% instead of 8% produces almost 4 times the result. In fact, the more years we hold the investment, the more magnified the result is by rate of return. At 80 years, the difference between 11% and 8% is around 9 times. Clearly, the longer we hold our investment, the more important the rate of return becomes. For instance, the difference between 10% and 11% for 20 years is only about 20%. If we extend the time period to 50 years, the difference is almost 60%, and looking at 80 years, it is over 100%.

The message here is crystal clear. Small differences in rates of return can produce vast differences in results, especially if we hold our investment for long periods of time. It is important that an investor consider carefully the investment vehicles that he or she intends to use. Chapter 22 gives you my advice on how to find superior long-term stock market returns. It is actually easy to invest and assure yourself that you will achieve close to or at the market averages (see Chapter 22). Every investor should realize that no one is able to predict with certainty what is going to happen over a long period of time. My suggestions are simply my best judgment, but smarter experts than me have been wrong in the past about investment ideas. In the end, every investor must make his or her own judgment even if that means simply following the advice in Chapter 22.

The Interaction of Rates of Return and Inflation

I discussed the impact of inflation on returns in some detail in Chapter 13. I want to look at the interaction between inflation rates and return rates. Inflation will clearly impact the value of your return. We looked at the possible impact of life extension in the 21st century in Chapters 12 and 14, examining possible added years of preserving investments as a potential offset to the impact of inflation. Here, I want to look at rates of return and what effect they have on inflation. Can earning a higher rate of return offset the corrosive impact of inflation on total return?

Figure 15A2 shows the inflation-adjusted returns for the results in Figure 15A1 for 11%, 12%, and 13% rates of return. This figure converts the absolute returns in Figure 15A1 to inflation-adjusted returns.

FIGURE 15A2 11%, 12%, and 13% Compound Rates of Return/Years/Inflation Rate $10,000 One Time Investment

Inflation-adjusted 11% Compound Rates							
Inflation Rate	0.5%	1%	1.5%	2.00%	2.5%	3%	3.5%
Years							
20	$72,933	$65,942	$59,591	$53,825	$48,591	$43,842	$39,537
30	$196,962	$169,334	$145,471	$124,874	$107,109	$91,800	$78,616
40	$531,915	$434,837	$355,114	$289,709	$236,104	$192,216	$156,319
50	$1,436,491	$1,116,628	$866,883	$672,129	$520,451	$402,472	$310,824
60	$3,879,391	$2,867,414	$2,116,180	$1,559,349	$1,147,244	$842,719	$618,041
70	$10,476,692	$7,363,294	$5,165,884	$3,617,711	$2,528,900	$1,764,534	$1,228,911
80	$28,293,375	$18,908,360	$12,610,629	$8,393,138	$5,574,521	$3,694,682	$2,443,562
90	$76,409,148	$48,555,184	$30,784,268	$19,472,195	$12,288,065	$7,736,137	$4,858,769

Inflation-adjusted 12% Compound Rates							
Inflation Rate	0.5%	1%	1.5%	2.00%	2.5%	3%	3.5%
Years							
20	$87,261	$78,898	$71,299	$64,399	$58,137	$52,456	$47,305
30	$257,770	$221,614	$190,383	$163,427	$140,178	$120,141	$102,887
40	$761,455	$622,485	$508,359	$414,729	$337,991	$275,163	$223,776
50	$2,249,340	$1,748,481	$1,357,415	$1,052,458	$814,952	$630,214	$486,706
60	$6,644,560	$4,911,261	$3,624,559	$2,670,828	$1,964,981	$1,443,396	$1,058,571
70	$19,628,054	$13,795,111	$9,678,270	$6,777,771	$4,737,887	$3,305,849	$2,302,362
80	$57,981,343	$38,748,722	$25,842,841	$17,199,977	$11,423,813	$7,571,476	$5,007,568
90	$171,277,103	$108,840,256	$69,005,354	$43,648,453	$27,544,662	$17,341,159	$10,891,313

—

Karl Gittelman

Inflation-adjusted 13% Compound Rate							
Inflation Rate	0.5%	1%	1.5%	2.00%	2.5%	3%	3.5%
Years							
20	$104,239	$94,248	$85,171	$76,929	$69,448	$62,662	$56,509
30	$336,547	$289,340	$248,565	$213,371	$183,017	$156,858	$134,330
40	$1,086,578	$888,271	$725,416	$591,808	$482,306	$392,651	$319,323
50	$3,508,134	$2,726,980	$2,117,063	$1,641,444	$1,271,022	$982,899	$759,081
60	$11,326,388	$8,371,789	$6,178,463	$4,552,722	$3,349,528	$2,460,428	$1,804,452
70	$36,568,462	$25,701,275	$18,031,306	$12,627,470	$8,827,021	$6,159,032	$4,289,464
80	$118,065,208	$78,902,551	$52,622,796	$35,023,660	$23,261,876	$15,417,509	$10,196,721
90	$381,186,210	$242,229,720	$153,575,047	$97,141,930	$61,302,096	$38,593,663	$24,239,191

Look in Figure 15A1 at the results of a $10,000 investment for 60 years at an 11% compound rate of return. It turns into $5.2 million. However, adjust that result in Figure 15A2 for an inflation rate of just 1.5%, for example, and you get an inflation-adjusted return of approximately $2.1 million. While the dollar return after 60 years is still $5.2 million, the dollars you get buy less goods and services after 60 years than they did when you made the investment. A 1.5% annual inflation rate would lessen the value of those dollars to $2.1 million in inflation-adjusted dollars. What rate of return would an investor need to receive more than $5.2 million in nominal dollars, enough to offset inflation? It turns out that a 13% rate of return would give our investor over $15 million in nominal dollars. But it would translate into just over $6.1 million in inflation-adjusted dollars (see the third table in Figure 15A2). That means that a 2% increase in annual compound rate of return would more than offset the impact of inflation on our total return. A 12% (or 1% increase) rate of return would not fully offset the impact of inflation (inflation-adjusted return of just over $3.6 million). A compound rate of return increase of something between 1% and 2% per year would fully offset the impact of a 1.5% per year inflation.

Figure 15A3 shows the added rate increase and the new rate of return for an investor who was seeking an 11% compound rate of return for 60 years.

186

**FIGURE 15A3 Increase Compound Rate of Return Required
60-Year Investor—11% Annual Return Objective**

Yearly Inflation Rate	New Compound Rate of Return Required	Rate Increase over 11% Required
0.5%	11.06%	0.06%
1.0%	12.12%	1.12%
1.5%	12.69%	1.69%
2.0%	13.27%	2.37%
2.5%	13.85%	2.85%
3.0%	14.43%	3.43%

Figure 15A3 shows that an investor seeking an 11% compound annual rate of return, that is adjusted for inflation, who could not use additional time (as illustrated in Chapter 14), could offset the impact of inflation with higher nominal return rates. If an investor experienced a 1.5% inflation rate over 60 years, he or she would need a 1.69% increase in compound yearly rate of return to offset the impact of a 1.5% annual inflation. This would mean a required 12.69% rate of return to "net" an 11% rate of return adjusted for 1.5% inflation. Looked at it from a different perspective, an 11% investor who could not offset the effects of a 1.5% inflation rate really achieved an inflation-adjusted compound annual rate of return of 9.33%.

Figure 15A4 shows the inflation-adjusted compound rates of return for an investor who achieved an annual compound rate of return of 11% for 60 years unadjusted. The higher the annual inflation rate in Figure 15A4, the lower the inflation-adjusted compound rate of return. An investor who achieved an 11% compound rate of return before inflation must reduce the return rate to reflect inflation.

Picking stocks and mutual funds to achieve the highest compound rate of return over many years is a critical part of this investment plan. In Chapter 22, I will present some ideas and a system that I believe will work to achieve that objective.

FIGURE 15A4 Actual Inflation-Adjusted Compound Rate of Return
11% Annual Nominal Return for 60 Years

Yearly Inflation Rate	Inflation-adjusted Compound Rate
0.5%	10.94%
1.0%	9.89%
1.5%	9.33%
2.0%	8.78%
2.5%	8.22%
3.0%	7.67%

CHAPTER 16

The Impact of Trading on Returns

Many *Wall Street* professionals make their money on trading not investing. Investors make money by investing, on capital gains and dividends. Trading for an investor is a cost and actually reduces their long-term result. The professionals will argue that they can more than make up what they cost investors by improving the investors' return. That may or may not be true, but for a long-term investor who is trying to mimic or improve on the market averages, stockbrokers and other professionals have little to offer and usually represent nothing more than a significant added cost. Even if you are trying to improve on market averages, a good idea if it works, investors need to understand the long-term cost of trading with a broker.

Cost of Trading—Commissions

Most stockbrokers and many other professionals on *Wall Street* will recommend that investors need to trade periodically to get the maximum out of their investments. They argue that buying and holding one stock or even many stocks is not productive. There is a significant cost in trading for a long-term investor. Looking at long-term results for stocks in Chapters 6 and 8 makes one wonder just how much better an investor might do by trading as opposed to following a strategy of buy and hold. Remember that a trader has to improve performance enough to more than cover the costs associated with trading. There is a time and place to change investments, and I will discuss this in Chapter 26, but those times and places come few and far between in my estimation. For an amateur investor, even for an experienced investor, I am skeptical that he or she can improve overall results with trading.

Let us look at the cost of trading. There are many different kinds of stockbrokers from full-service to discount brokers. They all have different fee structures. Figure 16A1 tries to show you a theoretical set of examples using a $2,000 annual investment strategy with an 11% compound rate of return. The figure looks first at the compound return for 50-80 years, assuming no trading. You bought and held funds or stocks for the full period with no intermediate trading commissions or other costs. The second section looks at results using discount and full-service brokers and assumes 2, 5, or 10 trades yearly. I assume that the discount broker charges $20 per trade or $40 to sell one stock and then buy another, and the full-service broker charges $50 per trade, $100 to sell one stock, and then buy another. There are discount brokers that charge less than $20. I have found some as low as $6.99 per trade, but there are others that charge more than $20, $29.99, $35, or even $45, for example. Full-service brokers are much harder to classify. Some charge much more than $50 per trade. In fact, at my full-service broker, they charge $50 for online trading and much more ($200 and up) if I call my broker to make the trade for me. So the figures here, especially for full-service brokers, are probably conservative.

The cost to an investor for trading also depends on how many trades he or she makes per year. I assume three possibilities: 2 trades (a trade defined as selling one stock and buying another), 5 trades, or 10 trades a year. Obviously, some investors trade their portfolio much more than 10 trades a year, to the benefit of their stockbroker. But even with these rather conservative trading habits, the costs in lost value over many years can be significant.

The loss is more than the commission costs themselves. If an investor makes 10 trades a year with a discount broker who charges $20 per trade, he or she is incurring a $400 per year direct cost. But, just as we noted with dividend distributions, the long-term impact of losing the ability to compound that $400 over many years is significant.

An investor who makes 10 trades a year, as I defined them, using a discount broker will lose roughly 20% of his or her net value after 50, 60, 70, or 80 years. Figure 16A2 shows the dollars lost. A 50-year investor at 11% compounded loses almost $750,000, and an 80-year investor at 11% compounded loses a whopping $17 million.

—

FIGURE 16A1 Investment Results—Trading Commission Assumptions

Compound rate of return =		11%		
Assumed annual investment =		$2,000		
Years	**50**	**60**	**70**	**80**
No trading/no commissions	$3,704,672	$10,556,246	$30,010,750	$85,250,276
Discount broker ($20 per trade)				
2 trades per year	$3,556,485	$10,133,996	$28,810,320	$81,840,264
5 trades per year	$3,334,205	$9,500,622	$27,009,675	$76,725,248
10 trades per year	$2,963,738	$8,444,997	$24,008,600	$68,200,220
Full-service broker ($50 per trade)				
2 trades per year	$3,334,205	$9,500,622	$27,009,675	$76,725,248
5 trades per year	$2,778,504	$7,917,185	$22,508,062	$63,937,707
10 trades per year	$1,852,336	$5,278,123	$15,005,375	$42,625,138
Percent lost to trading commissions				
Discount broker				
2 trades per year	4.00%	4.00%	4.00%	4.00%
5 trades per year	10.00%	10.00%	10.00%	10.00%
10 trades per year	20.00%	20.00%	20.00%	20.00%
Full-service broker				
2 trades per year	10.00%	10.00%	10.00%	10.00%
5 trades per year	25.00%	25.00%	25.00%	25.00%
10 trades per year	50.00%	50.00%	50.00%	50.00%

The percent and dollar amount lost by an investor using a full-service broker is even more significant. Here, an investor loses 10% of his or her total value if he or she makes just two trades per year and 50% of his or her final value with 10 trades a year. This assumes modest full-service commissions of $50 per trade. Extensive trading defeats the entire theory of compound rates of return. It takes away much of the advantage of

—

reinvesting distributions and compounding them for many years. Much or all the distributions get eaten in commissions. If all your dividend distributions are lost to trading commissions, you end like the examples given previously, in which the investor did not reinvest dividends, a sorry state of affairs.

FIGURE 16A2 Dollars Lost to Trading Commission

Compound Rate of Return =		11%		
Assumed Annual Investment =		$2,000		
Years	**50**	**60**	**70**	**80**
Discount broker ($20 per trade)				
2 trades per year	$148,187	$422,250	$1,200,430	$3,410,011
5 trades per year	$370,467	$1,055,625	$3,001,075	$8,525,028
10 trades per year	$740,934	$2,111,249	$6,002,150	$17,050,055
Full-service broker ($50 per trade)				
2 trades per year	$370,467	$1,055,625	$3,001,075	$8,525,028
5 trades per year	$926,168	$2,639,062	$7,502,687	$21,312,569
10 trades per year	$1,852,336	$5,278,123	$15,005,375	$42,625,138

Assuming a full-service broker would trade a $2,000 investor 10 times a year for a total yearly cost of $1,000 is probably unrealistic. Although examples like this have filled the courts for years, they call it "churning." It might be much more sensible for a high-volume trader to look at an investor who invests say $100,000 for a long period of time, both with and without trading. Figure 16A3 looks at just such an example. Here, we assume an investor invests $100,000 for 60 years. He or she adds $2,000 extra each year and is fortunate to find an investment or investments that produce 11% compound return on average, slightly less than the post-WWII average we are assuming in this book. If he or she avoids all trading, he or she will have almost $63 million dollars in 60 years. If he or she spends $400 in trading 10 times a year with a discount broker, his or her result will be just shy of $61 million for a loss of over $2 million dollars. That loss increases to over $5 million using a full-service broker who charges $50 per trade and is more than $36 million for a full-service broker who charges on average $250 per trade.

192

This analysis assumes no difference in compound rate of return results using trading rather than buy and hold. I do not believe there is any evidence that any system of trading will defeat the rate of return earned by the market averages over a long period of time.

FIGURE 16A3 Cost of Trading—Broker Commissions

11% Compound Return	60 Years
Total return—No trading	$62,961,970
10 trades per year—Discount broker ($20 per trade)	$60,850,721
10 trades per year—Full-service no. 1 ($50 per trade)	$57,783,847
10 trades per year—Full-service no. 2 ($250 per trade)	$36,571,355

The costs of trading can be large, and your broker had better be able to justify every trade. Even a $40 turnaround trade, sell one stock and buy another, has a big impact over many years. If you make just one $40 per year trade every year at 11% compounded, it will cost you $211,125 at the end of 60 years and $600,216 in 70 years. In fact, just one $40 cost to trade during the first year costs you $59,521 at 11% in 70 years, so either you or your broker better have a good reason for each trade. You can justify the costs of trading only if you assume that the trades increase your normal compound rate of return, not a likely assumption in my opinion.

Management Fees and Other Charges

I hope many of you will start a plan by buying a mutual fund. Mutual funds do incur expenses for investors. A mutual fund usually has to pay commission to a broker to buy or sell a stock in its portfolio, although the commission is normally much less than an individual would pay. Nevertheless, mutual funds that trade many stocks over the years without improving results can substantially reduce the net return to shareholders. One of the strategies that I am going to suggest is to invest part of your capital in an index mutual fund. An index fund invests in a basket of stocks intended to mimic an index. This also means that trading costs are less than in traditionally managed mutual funds. This is good for investors. There is not much evidence that actively managed mutual funds,

—

in general, outperform the market averages over a long period of time. At least, part of the reason for this is the cost of increased trading. In the long run, a mutual fund manager must make trading decisions that increase his or her funds rate of return enough to overcome the cost of trading. While it might seem logical to amateurs that professionals can do this, I repeat, there is little evidence that suggests that over the long run mutual fund managers can produce results superior to the market averages.

Besides, trading costs mutual funds incur expenses. They pay large salaries to the fund managers, incur expenses for reports to shareholders and the government and for keeping records of shareholders and their holdings. Those expenses are charged yearly to the fund shareholders. The effect of this is to reduce the dollar amount of distributions paid to shareholders and thus lessen the number of added shares that a shareholder gets when he or she reinvests his or her distributions in additional shares each year. The management fees and other fees that mutual funds charge to shareholders can dramatically reduce the overall return to a long-term investor. This is true unless the fund managers, like the stockbroker, can increase the overall return above normal market averages. If the S&P is going to compound at 11% yearly for the next 50 years, a fund manager must improve on that average to overcome the cost of fees and trading for the shareholder. Figure 16A4 shows that an 11% return on a $100,000 investment, with no trading and no management fees, will produce almost $179 million in 70 years. Using a mutual fund that charges just 1% in trading and management fees per year, a conservative assumption, reduces that return to just under $97 million, a 47% loss. For a mutual fund to maintain his or her performance at market average, the fund manager must increase the yearly compound return over the market average by at least the percentage of management fees and trading costs. So an 11% compound rate of return must increase to about 12% to overcome the extra costs incurred. And many mutual funds impose charges far more than 1%.

FIGURE 16A4 Return Results Using Mutual Fund, With Fees and Trading and No Trading

Assumed 11% Compound Return	
Net result—70 years, no trading or fund fees	$178,812,663
Net result—70 years, assumed 1% per year total mutual fund costs	$96,327,129

If we use data for the oldest mutual fund MFS Mass Investors Growth Stock Fund A, the return for 81 years was 9.23% yearly, less than many of the assumptions included here. A large part of that difference occurred because of the Great Depression. Stock prices did not recover to their 1929 levels for 25 years. If we use 1946 as a starting date, the compound rate of return until 2005 for this conservative fund was 10.56% yearly. If we use the average current expense ratio on MFS domestic stock funds of 1.33%[98] for the entire 81-year period, the fees and expenses for this fund reduced the overall result by an unbelievable $21 million dollars. If an investor had invested in the S&P composite averages in 1924 and avoided trading, he or she would have had a 10.51% return, exactly 1.28% more than the MFS fund. That would have produced a return of almost $30 million for a $10,000 investment, close to $17 million more than the MFS fund produced. It is no accident that the calculated 1.33% yearly fees for MFS almost exactly equal the difference in return of 1.28% between the fund and the S&P. (Please note that I do not have the actual fees and expenses incurred by MFS and charged each year to shareholders. That data is not available. For illustrative purposes, this example uses the current average expense ratio for MFS Domestic Stock Funds to explain the point.) It turns out that MFS actually produced slightly better results than the S & P composite average returns for the 81-year period, and the dramatic loss in total return may be almost entirely due to the management fees and expenses. Figure 16A5 shows this data.

—

FIGURE 16A5 Mutual Fund Returns—Impact of Management Fees[99]

Compound Rate of Return MFS A 9.23%	
Actual return 2005—MFS fund A	$12,793,277
Calculated return 2005—MFS A—No fees	$33,996,987
Calculated return 2005—S&P composite—No trading	$29,747,708

Figures 16A4 and 16A5 show the dramatic importance of mutual fund fees for the long-term investor. One reason that most studies show that fund managers cannot beat the market averages over long—periods of time is that market averages are calculated without consideration of any fees. Buying the Dow, the NASDAQ 500, or the S&P composite in theory and holding them for 50-80 years incur no trading fees on paper. A mutual fund manager that invests in stocks and changes course periodically incurs trading costs and fees, and they have a big impact on long-term results. If most managers cannot beat the market averages year after year in the long run, then they certainly cannot beat the averages by enough to overcome the costs incurred. This idea goes back to Chapter 5 on compounding. Every management fee paid and every trading commission incurred is money, no matter how small, that does not get the magical benefit of compounding over many years. Investors should be wary about any costs of trading.

Sales and Redemption Charges

Some mutual funds impose sales charges to allow an investor to buy shares in their fund. Others do not have sales charges but have redemption fees when an investor sells shares. The value of investing in a load (mutual fund that has a sales charge) or no-load (mutual fund that has no sales charge) mutual fund has been a hot topic in the investment community for many years. Many funds and many fund families have no sales charge, and investors do seem to be aware and concerned about sales charges, unlike management fees that fly by the radar unnoticed. Mutual funds that have sales charges also have yearly management fees, and while the sales charges can be large, they are usually onetime charges that do not reoccur like management fees. We can look at a mutual fund that charges a 5.75% onetime fee and try to analyze the impact of this fee, without considering management fees. Figure16A6 shows the result for a $10,000

—

investment compounded at different rates of return for 50-80 years. Figure 16A7 shows the result for a $10,000 investment at different rates of return for 50-80 years assuming a 5.75% sales charge, a commonly used charge in the load mutual fund industry. As you can see, sales charges, while not as significant as the yearly management fee, can still be big. An 11% investment compounding for 60 years means that the 5.75% sales charge alone cost the investor around $320,000, and for 70 years, it costs the investor over $850,000.

The message here is that an investor needs to be sure that a mutual fund with a sales charge can outperform a mutual fund without a sales charge by enough to cover the long-term cost of the sales charge. This includes the lost compounding on the 5.75% in this case. The combination of sales charges, trading costs, and management fees in investing in traditional mutual funds may be difficult to calculate, but they are significant.

FIGURE 16A6 Investment Results
Compound Returns Based on Rate and Years

Assumed Onetime Investment						
$10,000						
Compound Rate of Return	7%	8%	9%	10%	11%	12%	13%
Years						
50	$294,570	$469,016	$743,575	$1,173,909	$1,845,648	$2,890,022	$4,507,359
60	$579,464	$1,012,571	$1,760,313	$3,044,816	$5,240,572	$8,975,969	$15,300,535
70	$1,139,894	$2,186,064	$4,167,301	$7,897,470	$14,880,191	$27,877,998	$51,938,696
80	$2,242,344	$4,719,548	$9,865,517	$20,484,002	$42,251,128	$86,584,831	$176,309,405

For purposes of this analysis, I ignored the impact of redemption fees. Most redemption fees will probably not impact a long-term investor since they usually disappear after a few years of investment. Redemption fees punish investors who go in and out of mutual funds often. Long-term investors do not exit a mutual fund during the time period to which the fee normally applies. However, the investor should note that redemption fees are a deterrent to an investor who is not happy with the results or strategy of the fund and wishes to switch investments in the early years.

**FIGURE 16A7 Investment Results with Sales Charge of 5.75%
Compound Returns Based on Rate and Years**

Compound Rate of Return Years	7%	8%	9%	10%	11%	12%	13%
			Sales Charge 5.75% $9,425				
50	$277,632	$442,048	$700,820	$1,106,409	$1,739,523	$2,723,846	$4,248,186
60	$546,145	$954,348	$1,659,095	$2,869,739	$4,939,240	$8,459,851	$14,420,754
70	$1,074,350	$2,060,365	$3,927,681	$7,443,365	$14,024,580	$26,275,013	$48,952,221
80	$2,113,409	$4,448,174	$9,298,249	$19,306,172	$39,821,688	$81,606,203	$166,171,614

Trading and the Roulette Wheel

Another way to look at trading stocks is to compare investing in the stock market with gambling on a roulette wheel in Las Vegas. I don't believe that investing in stocks is like gambling, although in some respects it is similar. If we look at it from a strictly statistical standpoint, it might be helpful for some people to understand the impact of trading.

A roulette wheel in Vegas has 38 slots in which the ball can fall: 18 are red, 18 are black, and 2 are green. If you bet on red, on the average you will win 18 times for every 38 spins of the wheel, or 47.37% of the time. If you won 50% of the time, if there were no green slots (0 and 00), you would break even. The fact that you win, on average, 47.37% of the time and lose 52.63% of the time is the house's edge. If you bet on black, the averages are the same. Assume that you are betting on the stock market averages, specifically the Dow Jones Industrial Averages, and you make an investment, a bet, every month on the 1st and sell your investment on the 31st. You just keep repeating this "bet" every month. Since 1928, you would have made money 524 times and lost money 392 times for a win percentage of 57.2% in 916 tries, much better than the 47.37% at the roulette wheel. To be accurate, we would need to know how much your average winnings were and how much your average losses were. For our purposes, let us assume that they are even, that is, just like the roulette wheel, you lose the same amount each time that you win, assume $1,000. The stock market, according to this analysis, is a much better "gamble" than the roulette wheel. Hold on, we did not consider trading costs or commissions. On the roulette wheel, the casino does not usually charge you to make a bet. They make their money on the known likelihood that you will lose 52.63% of the time. Investing in the stock market requires an extra cost, a commission.

Assume that you bet $1,000 on the roulette wheel 916 times and you "bet" $1,000 on the Dow Averages once a month for 916 months (1928-2004). Let us assume that every time the Dow went up, you made exactly $1,000, and every time it went down, you lost exactly $1,000.

FIGURE 16A8 Roulette Wheel/Dow Monthly Averages Impact of Trading Costs

	Wins	Losses	Gross	Net
Roulette wheel	434	482	-$48,000	-$48,000
Dow averages monthly	524	392	$132,000	$132,000
Transaction costs				
$20 per trade			$36,640	$95,360
$50 per trade			$91,600	$40,400

Analyze the odds on the roulette wheel and the historical data in the stock market. You would assume that the Dow would have been a much better place to put your money for these 916 times. Looking at the raw data in Figure 16A8, with no trading commissions, it turns out to be true. A gambler who bet $1,000 on red 916 times would lose $48,000. Our investor in the Dow makes $1,000 in every month the Dow advances and loses $1,000 for every month the Dow declines. He or she would have made $132,000 during the 916 months during which he or she made his or her "bet." However, we did not consider commissions on buying and selling stock. If we assume that our investor used a discount broker at $20 per trade (2 trades per month, one buy and one sell, for 916 months), the investors profit trims to $95,360 after commissions. If he or she used a full-service broker that charged $50 per trade, our investors profit drops to $40,400, *even though the Dow advanced over 57% of the months.* And that is assuming only one round trade per month, one buy and one sell, or 12 trades per year. What about the investor who invests or gambles at the roulette wheel each month with either $10,000 or $100,000?

Figure 16A9 shows a more realistic example of trading costs with a full-service broker. Our $100,000 investor, who trades 12 times a month with a full-service broker charging $250 per trade, loses $5,496,000 or about 42% of his or her return. A $10,000 investor who trades 12 times a month loses a fortune as well.

—

Trading costs are critical to a stock market investor, and I am going to advise you to avoid them whenever possible. You can see from this theoretical example why stockbrokers love investors who trade stocks and hate investors who buy and simply hold for years and years.

FIGURE 16A9 Roulette Wheel/Dow Monthly Averages Impact of Trading Costs

	Wins	Losses	Result of $10,000 Bet	Result of $100,000 Bet
Roulette wheel	434	482	–$480,000	–$4,800,000
Dow averages monthly	524	392	$1,320,000	$13,200,000
Transaction costs (916 trades, 1 trade per month):				
$20 per trade		$36,640	$1,283,360	$13,163,360
$50 per trade		$91,600	$1,228,400	$13,108,400
$250 per trade		$458,000	$862,000	$12,742,000
Transaction costs (12 trades per month)				
$20 per trade		$438,680	$881,320	$12,761,320
$50 per trade		$1,099,200	$220,800	$12,100,800
$250 per trade		$5,496,000	–$4,176,000	$7,704,000

Chapter 17

Individual Retirement Accounts

IRA—The Best and Simplest Way to Avoid or Delay Taxes

In Chapter 11, we looked at the devastating impact of taxes, even small taxes, on a long-term investor's total return. We saw that an investor in the S&P composite in 1871 would have lost over 91% of his or her result by 2004 if he or she could not avoid or defer taxes. This occurred despite the fact that during the early years there were no taxes at all. Today (2006), we have relatively low tax rates historically on dividends and capital gains, the two most common distributions enjoyed by stockholders. If today's tax rates hold for the next 60 years, then our investor would only lose something less than 25% of his or her total return (see Figure 11A4). To a $10,000 onetime investor, this would still mean a loss of over $2 million in his or her result, and to an investor fighting the inflation battle and struggling to get his or her rate of return up even slightly, this loss is unnecessary. I am dubious that these low rates on dividends and capital gains will hold through future Democrat and even Republican administrations. We only need to look at history to see the excessive tax rates to which the government can resort to disabuse ourselves of the idea that low tax rates on investors are lasting.

The good news is that paying these kinds of taxes and worrying about future government taxes are avoidable with a little planning. You don't have to change your investment strategy much. You only have to change the manner in which you invest to defer or avoid all taxes. And, politically, the likelihood of changes to the tax laws that currently allow us to use tax avoidance is much less (although always possible) than the likelihood of increases in tax rates on investment income in the future. In this chapter and in the following two chapters, I will discuss the most common methods for stock investors to erase or mitigate the impact of taxes. Most of the strategies I will propose are well known and available in the investment community. Unlike low tax rates on investment returns, most are popular with both political parties. Most of them are relatively new, started within the last 30 or 35 years to encourage low-saving Americans to save and invest more of their income.

A word about deferral versus avoidance in taxes: it is always better to avoid taxes altogether, and there are some methods that allow an investor to avoid all taxes. However, not all investors will be able to take advantage of total avoidance, and some of you will have to use a tax deferral mechanism to make your stock investments. Unfortunately, this is the category that I currently fall into. Deferral, in the tax sense of the word, means that you do not pay taxes on returns until some date in the future. At that point, usually retirement when the investor begins to withdraw funds, taxes will have to be paid. So what is the advantage? There is still a huge advantage to long-term investors in deferring taxes even if avoidance is unavailable. Deferring taxes to a later date under current law usually means deferring until the investor reaches the age 70½, and it allows an investor to cumulate investment dollars tax-free for years and years. Because of the effect of compounding, you get to use the money that you might otherwise have paid in taxes each year to compound your return even more. In the first few years, this impact is nominal, but for a long-term investor, the ability to compound all of his return instead of just part of it multiplies his or her outcome significantly. Once you reach retirement using a tax deferral scheme, taxes will have to be paid as you withdraw the funds. But you will pay taxes on a much larger stock of capital and only on the minimum amount that you are required to withdraw. It is critical that long-term investors use a tax avoidance or tax deferral scheme. The nice part is that it is easy to do.

What Is an IRA?

The most popular and easiest tax avoidance investment vehicle is an Individual Retirement Account. The law authorizing IRAs was originally passed in 1974 as a means to encourage Americans to save and invest more for their retirement. The two most common IRAs are the traditional IRA and the newer, Roth IRA. There are two other types of IRAs: a SIMPLE

IRA and a SEP IRA that require your employer to offer them as a plan. The rules are a little complicated, but if you take part in a retirement plan at work, you are limited or barred from investing in an IRA on their own. There are some conditions under which you can participate in an employee retirement plan (IRA or otherwise) and still invest using an IRA in a more limited way.

The main characteristic that interests investors is that any investments made through any IRA can compound tax-free until withdrawal. Under current law, withdrawal cannot begin before age 59½ and must begin when the investor reaches 70½ years of age. You are not required to withdraw all your accumulated funds at age 70½. Every investor aged 70½ and older should leave as much as allowed in your IRA for as many years as possible. It is tax-free compounding that makes IRAs such a powerful tool for investors.

Advantages of IRAs Not Clearly Understood

Many investors do not clearly understand the advantages of IRAs. They are not familiar with the impact of compounding over long periods of time. Investors look at a 15% yearly tax on a dividend of 1%, 2%, or even 3% as being small. They are focused on stock price appreciation. They do not understand what readers of this book now know. Over time, most of the return to shareholders comes from otherwise taxable distributions that are reinvested in added stock not in stock price appreciation. If taxes take even a small percentage of an investor's yearly dividend return, it reduces the number of reinvested shares acquired each year. The long-term impact of this can be significant.

The second misunderstanding comes from the fact that traditional IRAs have their returns tax-deferred until withdrawn. When withdrawals occur, compulsory at age 70½, those withdrawals all occur at regular income tax rates not the preferred rate on dividends and capital gains. That may seem like a high price to pay for tax deferral. The truth is that the impact of tax-free compounding may allow an investor to cumulate millions of dollars of extra capital in his or her investment portfolio that makes paying normal tax rates at retirement not such a large burden. Look at Figure 11A3 once again. An investor in General Electric stock in 1940 that retired in 2004 at age 70½ had over $23 million dollars from his or her initial $10,000 onetime investment if he or she used a tax-deferred system to invest. This compares with just under $6 million for the same GE investor who paid taxes on all distributions (normally dividends). I don't think our first investor is complaining as he or she begins

—

203

compulsory yearly withdrawals from his or her $23 million pot even if it means paying normal tax rates on the withdrawals each year. If you can use a Roth IRA, it is obviously preferable. As we will see, even distributions after age 70½ under Roth are untaxed. But you may not qualify for Roth or you may find other terms of the traditional IRA more attractive, and you should not let the eventual tax on a much bigger fund of money deter you. The important thing is to find some way to avoid paying taxes on distributions each investing year.

Traditional IRA

The original and traditional IRA is the most common form of the Individual Retirement Account. It allows an investor to open an account called an IRA and deposit investment funds in that account and then invest the funds from the account in pretty much anything you can invest in a normal brokerage account. So you can invest in stocks, bonds, options, real estate, or almost anything. You can use a self-directed IRA, or you can appoint a bank, savings and loan, or other qualified person as the trustee or custodian. A long-term investor wants to have a self-directed IRA. You can open this account at any brokerage firm, most mutual funds and most banks. You can do it over the Internet without even talking to anyone. If you are under 18, you will need to get a parent or guardian to sign as custodian until you are of age.

There are two big advantages to a traditional IRA. The first and main one that we looked at is tax-free compounding until you begin withdrawals. The second advantage of a traditional IRA is that any money that you contribute each year is deductible from income on your income tax return during the year of the contribution. If you contribute $4,000 to a traditional IRA this year, that is $4,000 less in taxable income, you will have to report and pay tax on to the IRS. Both husband and wife can contribute in separate accounts, and they both get a deduction that year.

There are some limits.

Roth IRA

There is a second, more powerful, IRA that is important to many long-term investors. It is similar to the traditional IRA with a couple of important differences. It is called a Roth IRA, and it allows an investor to compound returns for many years and never, I repeat *never*, pay any taxes on the returns at all. It is the Roth IRA that I recommend, if possible, for younger investors or for parents and grandparents investing for young people. Contribution limits apply to a Roth, $4,000 in 2006 and $4,500 if you are over 50. But unlike the traditional IRA, Roth IRA contributions are limited by the MAGI rules. That means that if you have a high income, over $150,000 of MAGI if you are married and $95,000 if you are unmarried, you may not be able to contribute to a Roth IRA. If your income is higher than the phase limits, you may be limited to a traditional IRA.

There are two major additional differences between the traditional IRA and the Roth IRA. The bad news is that, unlike the traditional IRA, contributions to a Roth IRA are not tax deductible at the year of the contribution. Under a traditional IRA, a contribution of $4,000 allows the taxpayer to deduct that $4,000 (possibly $8,000 for a joint return) from gross income before calculating their taxes. A $4,000 contribution to a Roth IRA does not allow such a deduction and has no effect on the taxpayer's taxes at the year of the contribution.

The second major difference is potentially powerful for a long-term investor. Like a traditional IRA, a Roth IRA allows tax-free compounding of returns with an added twist at the end. All distributions from a Roth IRA for an investor who has reached the age of 59½ are *completely tax-free*. There is no tax on capital gains and no tax on dividends or distributions, and our investor can take funds out of his or her investment account and use the money without ever having paid any taxes on the return. A traditional IRA, just like a Roth IRA, allows tax-free compounding of your investment as long as you do not violate the distribution rules. But in a traditional IRA, since you were able to take a tax deduction at the year of the contribution, you must pay taxes at ordinary income tax rates on all distributions. That tax rate can be as high as 35% in Federal taxes alone in 2006. Roth IRA investors pay zero tax on any income. Assume that you qualify for both a Roth and traditional IRAs. And assume that your investment return compounded at the same rate on each investment, you will be able to distribute without paying taxes using Roth as opposed to paying income tax at full income tax rates using a traditional IRA.

For almost any young investors who can qualify for a Roth, the Roth is the way to go. Usually, young investors have little income and pay little or no taxes to start with or, at least, pay taxes at low rates. For these investors, the tax deductibility of the traditional IRA is not that valuable, but the tax-free nature of the Roth IRA will be extremely valuable someday. For older investors, it can be a more difficult choice. They may not qualify, but even if they do, the tax deduction saves them immediate money on their tax returns, and they may not have enough time left before retirement or age 70½ to allow for the dramatic effects of compounding that we have seen. Older investors who pay at higher tax rates should get advice from their tax adviser based on their individual situation.

There are a couple of other characteristics and differences in the Roth IRA. Under certain circumstances, you can convert a traditional IRA to a Roth IRA before retirement. You must have MAGI income of less than $100,000 and still pay the taxes due on the traditional IRA as if it were a normal distribution. But, once carried out, from that year on, it is a full Roth IRA. The distribution rules to avoid a penalty are slightly different from a traditional IRA. In a Roth, you can distribute after age 59½, but any distributions must be at least 5 years after the first Roth contributions to avoid penalties. This would impact investors starting an IRA after age 54½. There is no limit for setting up and contributing to a Roth IRA after age 70½, as in a traditional IRA. The MAGI phase-out rule for contributions still applies. Your entire investment in a Roth can continue to compound tax-free after age 70½, a potentially big benefit to investors in a century that may see some serious life extension, and a great asset to long-term investors. Almost everyone should have a Roth IRA if they can qualify.

All You Need Is a Job

As you can see, IRAs are powerful and almost perfect tools for a long-term investor. A long-term investor doesn't need to invest millions to make millions. We have seen that rather modest investments can amount to huge sums over long periods of time. The limits placed on contributions to an IRA, $5,000 per year starting in 2008, are sufficiently high that an investor can make a fortune with this size investment. Figure 17A1 shows the total returns for yearly investments from $1,000 to $5,000 compounded at our postwar standard of 11.76% for 50, 60, and 70 years. Even a $1,000 per year investment can produce lucrative results, and $5,000 per year can produce amazing results. The IRA limit on yearly investments is not an obstacle to getting rich in the long run.

**FIGURE 17A1 Net Result Using Yearly Investments
within IRA Limits
Compounded at 11.76% Yearly**

Yearly Invested	50 Years	60 Years	70 Years
$1,000	$2,457,665	$7,490,521	$22,790,064
$2,000	$4,915,329	$14,981,041	$45,580,126
$3,000	$7,372,994	$22,471,562	$68,370,189
$4,000	$9,830,658	$29,962,083	$91,602,252
$5,000	$12,288,323	$37,462,603	$113,950,315

Retirement Age Limits under IRAs

I have discussed retirement age as if an investor must terminate his or her IRA, or any other retirement account, at age 70½. In calculations, I have assumed that investors will completely terminate investments at that age, and this assumption means that most of the calculations in this book are too conservative. It is true that investors must *begin* to withdraw investments from tax-advantaged retirement accounts by April 1 in the year following the year in which they become 70½. But investors are not required to withdraw all the funds. An investor is only required to remove and pay tax on a portion of his or her investments. An individual who reached the age 71 needs only to withdraw and pay tax on approximately 3.8% of his or her fund. The balance can and should remain in his or her IRA investment account, accumulating without taxes. Each year, the percentage of his or her account an investor must withdraw increases. The second year our investor must withdraw about 3.9% of his or her IRA. At age 80, the percentage goes to 5.4%, and by age 90, it is a little over 10%. Assuming continued compounding at the historic postwar rate of 11.76%, an investor with $1 million in an IRA at age 70½ who makes the minimum withdrawal every year until age 100 will finish with approximately $2.3 still in his or her IRA account and will have withdrawn and perhaps paid tax on just under $5.8 million during the 30 years. Leaving as much as possible to continue to compound in your IRA even after mandatory retirement withdrawals begin is a great way to maximize investment value and offset any impact of inflation.

IRAs—Bankruptcy and Creditors

The laws regarding the ability of creditors to access your IRA accounts vary from state to state. Many states allow some protection for IRAs against creditor's claims. The new personal bankruptcy law exempts up to $1 million of a debtor's IRA. If this issue might affect you, check with an attorney in your state. For some, this could be an additional powerful incentive to have a significant portion of their retirement funds in an IRA account.

Open an IRA

IRAs are easy to open. You can call any mutual fund family, stockbroker and most banks or other financial institutions as well. You simply tell them which IRA you want, Roth or traditional, and they will provide you with the proper forms. You fill them out, send them a check, or transfer funds, and your account is open. You then direct them to invest your funds in whatever you like, stocks, mutual funds, or bonds (see Chapter 22 for advice on specific investments).

One of my favorite ways to open an IRA is online. Most major brokerage houses and most mutual fund families will allow you to open, or download a form for mailing, an IRA account without talking to anyone. You are not embarrassed by the small amount of your first investment plus you don't have to be subject to listening to the broker's ideas on investing, usually a good thing. My best suggestion for mutual fund investments is Vanguard. They have many funds, many index funds, and are one of the least expensive fund families when it comes to fees, expenses, and charges. As we have seen in Chapter 16, for a long-term investor, even small charges against an account can amount to huge amounts over many years.

CHAPTER 18

Annuities

What Are Annuities?

Annuities are an investment that you can only make through an insurance company. Although they are technically an insurance product, they differ substantially from the other products that insurance companies sell. There are many different types of annuities that are available. Some annuities pay money back to the investor immediately. The annuity that interests a long-term investor acts as a simple investment vehicle in which the investor buys (invests in) his or her annuity, allowing the investment to grow for many years before there are any withdrawals. It is called a deferred, variable annuity. This annuity "defers" returns until some future date. It is variable since there is no predetermined rate of return. You buy annuities through insurance agents, banks, brokerage firms, mutual fund families, and others.

Annuities and Taxes

The main advantage of annuities for a long-term investor is their ability to grow and compound tax-deferred until the investor withdraws the money. Like IRAs, 401Ks, and other plans, deferred variable annuities allow the investor to get the benefits of compounding for many years without paying taxes. Taxes will be due on withdrawal, but unlike IRAs, there are no taxes on the original amount invested, only on dividends or capital gains. There is also no tax deduction for annuity investments. In fact, unlike tax-free bonds, the yearly returns in an annuity are not even reportable on your tax return.

Open an Account

You can open an annuity account at most banks, brokers, insurance agents, and many mutual funds. If you like, you can open and invest in an annuity over the Internet just like stocks. I have two annuities: one that I opened many years ago through an insurance agency and one I opened more recently at Vanguard Mutual Funds without talking to anyone. You can make one lump-sum investment or monthly or yearly investments just like an ordinary mutual fund.

Advantages

The main advantage of an annuity for a long-term investor is its tax-deferred growth. In Chapter 11, we looked at the impact of taxes on long-term investors. But another big advantage of annuities is there is no limit to the amount you can invest. You can invest $1 million or more. Many wealthy individuals place large sums of money into annuities that they leave invested tax deferred until retirement. Annuities have the same limits on withdrawals as IRAs, you cannot begin withdrawals until you reach the age of 59½ and you must begin withdrawals at age 70½.

Disadvantages

There are a few disadvantages to annuities. They are usually more limited in investment options than IRAs. They offer investors a choice of funds that invest in stocks, bonds, or money market funds. Vanguard's Variable Annuity program allows you to invest in about 15 different funds. You can put all your money on one fund or divide it among all funds in any way that you see fit. I have my money in a "Total Stock Market Fund," but you could invest it in everything from a money market fund to a bond fund to a small company growth fund. The choices are broad but not unlimited.

The second, and perhaps, most serious disadvantage of annuities is their cost. Since they are an insurance product, there are extra yearly costs to maintain your account. Again Vanguard has one of the lowest fees, averaging about half of 1% yearly. Many other annuities charge in the 2%

per year range, both have a significant impact on your total return as we learned in Chapter 16.

Annuities usually have some minimum-required investment to start and that can be a disadvantage. Vanguard wants $5,000 to start an annuity, but once established, you can add as little as $50 at a time.

Advice

Annuities are an excellent choice for investors who want the benefits of tax-deferred investing and have a significant amount of money to invest. They allow you to get around the limits on IRAs, 401Ks, and other plans.

Annuities are also an excellent choice for parents and grandparents investing for young children who have no employment earnings, no earned income. You can open a custodial account for a child of any age and contribute one lump sum or any amount monthly. As mentioned, there is no tax deduction for your investment, but the funds invested can compound tax-deferred until your child or grandchildren reaches 70½ under current law.

Annuities are also an excellent choice for investors who have an IRA or 401K, which limits the amount of money they can invest in other tax-free or tax-deferred vehicles. If you have another retirement plan, like a Roth IRA, for example, you can still open a variable annuity account.

Annuities also work for individuals who, for whatever reason, have no earned income and do not qualify for an IRA or 401K or other plan at work.

If you qualify to open a Roth IRA that would usually be my first choice for most people since the final returns are completely tax-free. But deferred, variable annuities in the four cases cited are excellent choices for long-term investors. Most insurance agents are familiar with them. Make sure that you make clear your purpose to use your annuity, as a tax-deferred investment vehicle. If your agent is not familiar with this, he or she can refer you to someone at the insurance company who is an expert to answer your questions. My first choice is to open it with Vanguard online.

A sensible plan for a parent or grandparent investing for a child, even an infant, would be to start an annuity with parent or grandparent as the custodian. Then you can switch investment strategy and start a Roth IRA when the child begins a working career. The annuity is one form of retirement plan that does not need earned income. The Roth IRA makes the most sense when the child has some income but not enough to make the tax deduction in the traditional IRA worthwhile, and you get tax-free distributions with Roth. This plan would allow the investor to take advantage of as many years of tax-free compounding as possible. Most young people do not start earning serious money until they are late teenagers, and by that time, they would have missed 17 or 18 years or more of compound investing. Chapter 9 showed that another 17 or 18 years of investing produce a significant increase in returns. Once your child or grandchild begins their own investment plan with a Roth or traditional IRA or even a 401K, you can continue contributing to his or her deferred, variable annuity if you choose to do so. My youngest daughter, age 20, has both an annuity and a Roth IRA. Annuities get you around the limits allowed under the law in most other retirement investment plans.

Gordon Williamson has authored a good book entitled, *Getting Started in Annuities*,[100] which explains in plain language the different types of annuities available and their features. He covers all kinds of annuities, including the variable deferred one that interests long-term investors.

FIGURE 18A1 Vanguard Funds[101]
March 31, 2006

Vanguard Variable Annuity Funds as of March 31, 2006
Money Market Account
Short-Term Investment Grade Bond Account
Total Bond Market Index Account
High Yield Bond Account
Balanced Account
Total Stock Market Index Account
Equity Index Account
Equity Income Account
Diversified Value Account
Growth Account
Capital Growth Account
Mid-Cap Index Account
Small Company Growth Account
REIT Index Account
International Account

CHAPTER 19

401Ks, SEPs, and other
Tax-Deferred Methods

Besides traditional and Roth IRAs and annuities, there are several other methods that allow investors to make their stock investments and compound returns tax-free until retirement. The most important and popular is the 401K.

401Ks

To take part in a 401K, your employer must have such a plan. The good news is that many employers, even small employers, have or are now starting 401Ks. 401Ks have some of the same tax-free compounding features that IRAs have. Investments made through a 401K collect tax-free until withdrawn. The same age limits on withdrawals that are in place for IRAs exist also in a 401K. You cannot withdraw funds from the plan without penalty until you reach age 59½, and you must begin withdrawals by age 70½. There is a financial hardship exception in 401Ks for withdrawals. Like a traditional IRA, all contributions to a 401K are deductible from income for tax purposes so any contributions made by investors lessen current taxes, but also like a traditional IRA, withdrawals are taxable at ordinary tax rates.

An employer may contribute to 401K plans for employees or may match employee contributions usually up to a ceiling. Employees contribute through a payroll deduction during each pay period. The

–

401K limits for contributions in 2005 is $14,000, much higher than IRA limits, and is $4,000 higher for employees over age 50, allowing them a total contribution of $18,000 per year in 2005. Employers may or may not contribute to the plan, but the maximum total employer and employee contribution is $42,000 in 2005. Self-employed people can set up a one-person 401K under certain circumstances.

Normally, in a 401K, the employer's plan does not allow the investment freedom that IRAs allow. Usually, the employer selects a plan with several mutual fund choices from which the employees can choose. Each employee can select individual funds within these limits. He or she can usually divide his or her investment selections among several different funds. If you take part in a 401K at any level, it severely restricts or limits your ability to open a traditional IRA. It also may limit or eliminate the ability of your spouse to take part in his or her own IRA.

Despite some limits, 401Ks are one of the greatest tools available to long-term investors. They allow larger contributions and usually involve employer contributions or matches that are, in essence, "free" money for the employee. And they enjoy all the same tax-free compounding benefits that IRAs enjoy.

By the year 2000, 40 million Americans took part in 401Ks with over $2 trillion dollars invested in them. But it is also clear that many Americans are either not contributing at all to plans they qualify for or are not contributing to the maximum extent possible in their plan. If your employer has a 401K plan, you should do everything possible to contribute the maximum amount allowable to the plan. Do not forgo employer matches as they are free money, and what is even better it is free money invested to compound tax-free on your behalf until your retirement. If available, select stock index mutual funds that mimic an index (see Chapter 22) and also charge much lower fees than actively managed funds.

401Ks can play a significant part in a long-term investor's plan.

SEPs

Another employee-related pension plan is an SEP, a Simplified Employee Pension Plan. In an employer setup SEP, an employer can contribute up to $42,000, or 25% of the employee's salary in 2005, into the plan. The employer's contribution is not taxable income on the employee's tax return. Self-employed individuals can set up an SEP if they are the only employee, but SEPs must cover essentially any other employees the employer has. If the employer sets up the SEP for employee contributions, employees may contribute through a salary reduction up to $14,000 to the

SEP in 2005, $18,000 for those employees that are over 50. If an employee contributes to both an SEP and 401K, the limits apply to both plans as a total.

Simple IRA

A simple IRA is a plan that a small employer may set up to allow employees to contribute to an IRA at work. The maximum contribution limits for 2005 are $10,000 for employees under 50 and $12,000 for employees over 50. To set up a Simple IRA, the employer cannot have more than 100 employees and cannot keep other retirement plans. Employers will often match employee contributions to a Simple IRA, and if the employer does match, he or she can match up to 3% of the employee's salary. Distributions rules are similar to other retirement plans, penalty-free distributions only after age 59½.

Keogh Plans

A self-employed person can set up a Keogh plan. Keogh plans involve some complications that are beyond the scope of this book. Simply put, there are two choices: a defined benefit plan and a defined contribution plan. The maximum contribution in 2005 to a Keogh plan would also be $42,000. There are many good sources available in the bookstore on Keogh plans.

All these plans allow a long-term investor to invest his or her savings in the stock market and compound without taxes, an enormous benefit as we have seen in Chapter 11. Some of the plans even allow the investor to avoid some income taxes during the year of the contribution.

Selection of Funds in 401Ks and Annuity Plans

In 401Ks and annuities, you have more limited investment selections than in IRAs. Typically, you are limited to a group of mutual funds from a mutual fund family selected by your employer. They will normally include stock, bond, and money market funds. For that portion of your funds dedicated to a retirement investment plan from this book, an investor should select stock funds. The best alternatives are broad-based index funds or total stock market funds. These will incur the lowest costs. If index funds are not available, select an equity income fund or any broad-based fund invested in large capitalization well-known companies.

I urge all long-term investors to take full advantage of these plans if they are available. Fund these plans to the maximum and invest the funds using the specific advice given in Chapter 22. Under funded, tax-deferred retirement plans are a national scandal. I am convinced that many employees would invest more in these plans if they only understood the power of long-term compounding using tax-deferred vehicles and reinvesting all distributions. Many employees do not understand that every $100, $1,000, or $5,000 that they contribute to a tax avoidance retirement plan may total over $50,000, $500,000, or $2.5 million when invested until retirement. The only serious disadvantage that these plans have is the limits on investment vehicles (fund choices) and the unavoidable yearly costs that may be much higher than with a self-directed plan. The advantages of higher limits, employer matches, and immediate income tax savings are significant.

CHAPTER 20

Legacy Investing

One possible objective for a long-term investor is legacy investing. Legacy investing is useful for a long-term investor who understands the returns available to him or her and is interested in leaving a large sum of money to future generations. Imagine, if an ancestor of yours had invested even $1 for you 200 years ago, how much it would be worth today? It turns out that a lonely dollar invested at 8% for 200 years is worth almost $5 million today and at 11.76% that dollar is worth $4.5 *billion*; yes, that is billion dollars. So an investment of $1,000, $10,000, or $100,000 could leave your distant heirs in very good shape. Most of us do not remember or have any idea who our ancestors were 200 years ago. But if one of them left you even a modest amount invested in some asset that appreciated, like real estate or stocks, you would certainly know that person now. A small amount invested now can make you a well-known and remembered person in a couple of centuries.

As many of us are living longer than our ancestors, we are living to see not only grandchildren but also great-grandchildren and some even great-great-grandchildren. This trend will undoubtedly continue to expand, leading to an increasing interest in funding legacy gifts for longer and longer periods.

Legacy investing is also a way for families to preserve wealth. The United States has traditionally tried to erode the concentration of wealth in families by punishing multigenerational wealth with high tax rates. Some wealthy families have tried to use trusts and other sophisticated techniques to preserve wealth and avoid as much tax as possible.

This topic is a little off course for this book, but I wanted to introduce it since some investors may want to pursue further. Legacy investors might want to invest for even longer periods of time than normally considered in this book.

Dynasty Trusts

Anyone seriously interested in legacy investing will need a good estate attorney who has some knowledge and experience in this field. Most estate planners are comfortable using a trust called a dynasty trust for an individual who does not want certain assets or all his or her assets distributed to his or her heirs at death. A dynasty trust can last either 21 years after an individual's death or 90 years after its formation. The 21-year limit is the "Rule against Perpetuities." Wealthy individuals use dynasty trusts to preserve assets after the individual's death.

In the last decade, a few states have passed laws removing the Rule against Perpetuities and trusts in these states may be, I caution, "may be," able to exist forever. The states that have done so are New Jersey, Delaware, Alaska, South Dakota, Wisconsin, and Idaho. Some added states may pass such laws in the next decade.

There are several new developments in this field. One is something called a revival trust. A revival trust is for an individual who plans to have his or her body frozen at death, in hopes of potential revival in future years with advances in technology. This trust holds assets after an individual's death intending to pay the funds back to the individual on revival. A few law firms and even some banks have gotten involved in this idea, and there are reports that they have created a few of them. It seems that this idea could also benefit an individual who just wants to preserve assets for many years to leave to distant heirs. There was an article in the *Wall Street Journal* in the Weekend Edition, January 21-22, 2006, about just such a trust.

In searching the Internet, it is obvious that some law firms are pursuing ideas for legal legacy trusts. One calls theirs a "Megatrust," which intends to allow for the "passage of significant wealth through multiple generations without imposing transfer taxes."[102] A long-term investor interested in legacy investing will need to do some research to find an estate attorney who is familiar with the current and evolving law. It is an emerging field.

A Note on Legacy Investing Using an IRA

There is a little known method of "stretching" an IRA that allows implementation of a legacy-type investment strategy. Internal Revenue Service rules allow any person that you name as your IRA beneficiary to extend the required distribution period using the age of the beneficiary. This allows for much lower maximum distributions for young heirs and a much longer possible holding time for investments to compound tax-deferred. Simply put, starting an IRA for a young person, say a teenager, can allow that teenager to choose a young person as his or her beneficiary, perhaps his or her future grandchild. The grandchild can inherit the IRA and use his or her youth to stretch the holding period for the IRA for many years. This can only occur once. But it can be a powerful tool in the right situation with participants of the right age. There is a good book written specifically on this topic by Ed Slott, *Parlay Your IRA into a Family Fortune*. I recommend it.

Really Long-Term Investing

What kinds of returns are available to the really long-term investor? Figure 20A1 shows the results.

FIGURE 20A1 Investment Results
Compound Returns Based on Rate and Years

	Assumed Onetime Investment						
	7%	8%	9%	10%	11%	12%	13%
Years							
50	$294,570	$469,016	$743,575	$1,173,909	$1,845,648	$2,890,022	$4,507,359
75	$1,598,760	$3,212,045	$6,411,909	$12,718,954	$25,073,988	$49,130,558	$95,693,681
100	$8,677,163	$21,997,613	$55,290,408	$137,806,123	$340,641,753	$835,222,657	$2,031,628,742
150	$255,603,415	$1,031,723,501	$4,111,257,617	$16,177,178,358	$62,870,486,067	$241,381,176,945	$915,728,060,732

I have only included a time frame up to 150 years because the numbers get so astronomical it is hard to include them in a chart. In Figure 20A1, an investor who earns a rate of return of 11% on $10,000 invested just once for 150 years ends with $62 billion. Even on an 8% return, the estimated return in the United States for 200 years produces

—

219

over $1 billion dollars for heirs. By my calculation, 150 years might be your great-great-great-grandchildren.

For those of you who want to speculate on really long-term returns, Figure 20A2 shows the results of a compound rate of return of 11% for up to 500 years. Don't ask me how much money that is, only a mathematician could tell us.

FIGURE 20A2 Really Long-Term Investing
$10,000 Invested

	Net Results Compounding 11%
50 Years	$1,845,648
75 Years	$25,073,988
100 Years	$340,641,753
150 Years	$62,870,486,067
200 Years	$11,603,680,368,011
300 Years	$395,269,801,828,840,000
400 Years	$13,464,539,808,295,200,000,000

CHAPTER 21

Ideas on Developing
Your Personal Plan

Everyone should develop his or her personal plan. It is impossible for me to advise every one of you exactly what you should do. Much depends on your personal situation. This chapter has some information that may help in developing your own plan.

Write It Down—You Will Follow It!

It is important that you write down your plan on paper or in your computer. Put down your investment goals, your savings and investment plans, and any other relevant information that relate to your plan. It is simple to develop an investment plan. How much can you start with and how much can you invest each year is a good place to begin. Using your age, or the age of the person you are investing for, you can calculate your total value at estimated retirement age using the assumptions in this book. You can use any compound rate of return that makes sense to you. I have used compound annual returns around 11-12% in much of this book. I argued that the next 60 years will probably be more like the last 60 years than it will be like the 19th century or the early part of the 20th century, but admittedly, anything can happen. If you are not comfortable with my rate of return, you can use a rate of return that makes sense to you. I used 8% in class for many years until Jeremy Siegel's book was published.

I strongly urge you to put your plan in writing. If you put it in writing, you will be much more likely to follow it. You will be more likely to invest when scheduled, and to be sure, to reinvest all distributions faithfully. There is something about having to face the stark reality of figures on a piece of paper that is powerful. Even if you feel motivated after reading this book, believe me that motivation will fade. In a year or 5 years, your memory and commitment will drift. Other opportunities, new needs, and lifestyle changes will dissipate your commitment. It is important that you put it in writing. Just like dieting, you will be much more likely to follow the plan if you have to face the reality, on paper, of not meeting your plans. For most of you, carrying out this plan will require some sacrifice, and for some of you, it requires much sacrifice. The reward is worth it. Table 21 in the appendix is a simple long-term investment plan.

Understand the Nature of Your Expected Returns (See Chapter 25)

It is important that you understand what I call the "nature and characteristic" of your return. The real challenge in this plan is to uphold your commitment over a long period of time. That is a difficult proposition. Committing to anything for a long period of time, even marriage, turns out to be difficult. Committing to this investment plan is difficult for several important reasons. First, much of the dollar amount of your return comes in the later years. Your investments in this plan are probably not going to look spectacular in the first 10, 20, or even 30 years. The big returns come later. This is simply a statistical issue. Compounding requires years to build up a large base on which to compound further. You need patience. Other investment plans may "promise" you big returns in a short period. This is not that plan. If you want spectacular results in a short period, go for it. But do it with money that you do not need to fund the retirement plan that you adopted from this book.

There is a second even more unusual issue that will test your resolve. The stock market moves up over long periods of time, but it does not move up consistently. It moves up and it moves down, and sometimes, it moves down or sideways for months, sometimes for many years. The upswings can come suddenly and during a fairly short period of time. You need be able to weather the downturns or the sideways years and keep on investing and reinvesting distributions. Cumulating larger numbers of shares during downturns becomes particularly valuable during the short or long sharp upswings that occur. I deal with this key issue in more detail in

Chapter 25. I show in Chapter 25 that the Great Depression was actually good for investors who owned companies that survived, if they continued to reinvest all distributions and held on for the long run. Their results were better than if the depression had not occurred.

There will be times when you will become weary in funding and reinvesting dividends and distributions. Results will not look good in the short run. You must understand the nature of returns in the stock market. It can be discouraging, even scary at times, and every stock market decline pushes some people to the sidelines, sometimes for the rest of their lives. That is simply the way the stock market works.

Monitor Your Result

It is a good idea to check your results periodically. I don't advise doing this too often because I don't want you obsessed with the daily or weekly speculation about current events or stock price movements. You are a long-term investor, so checking your investments once a year seems like a good idea. If that is too long a period for you, then do it once a month. Use a specific date, December 31, your birthday, or whatever and look at where your investments are, and if they are in a suitable range of results, that makes sense considering where the overall stock market is. I have been recording my net worth for 44 years and that is not long enough. But it does give me a historical perspective that is helpful, particularly during downturns. Having watched my investments during many downturns, I now have more patience and confidence in the markets capacity to return to norms.

Revise Your Plan—Rarely

In Chapter 26, I will give you my ideas on when to change course. The short answer, however, is rarely. We have already seen the large cost involved in trading. Switching investments, if you have chosen them carefully, is not something you should consider lightly. Individual investments, just like the general market, go through ups and downs, and switching out of investments can sometimes be the most costly error of all. In my own experience, I have lost more money by switching out of investments, not sticking with buy and hold, than I have ever gained through "shrewd" investment trades. Both in stocks and real estate, the worst mistakes I ever made were not in buying poor-performing investments but selling my investments too soon. AT&T is a great example. A great company but a mediocre stock at best until the

—

divestiture in 1984. Many shareholders bailed out when it became obvious the divestiture was going to occur. This was not going to be the AT&T they knew and loved, mostly for the surety of the dividends. But by selling out, they missed the boom that was to come for shareholders who held on as they received shares in all the "Baby Bells." Patience is the key word. There is a time to switch investments and investment strategy, and I will go over my ideas in Chapter 26. For now I want to stress that the best strategy is to select your investments carefully (use the advice in this book) and stick to them through thick and thin. *Don't* listen to relatives, friends, neighbors, insiders, or investment professionals, especially stockbrokers. Their interests are significantly different from yours. Make up your own mind and be willing to stick with it.

CHAPTER 22

Investment Plan Alternatives

In Chapter 7, I discussed various investment plan amounts. For illustration purposes, I am going to assume in this chapter that you will be able to gather at least $3,000 over the next few years. If you cannot plan to gather at least $3,000 in the next few years, don't lose heart; you will just have to extend your investment horizon slightly. Most mutual funds have minimum requirements for IRA investments that apply to your first investment. That amount is often $2,500 or $3,000. If you can only save $1,000 this year, you may have to invest it in an individual stock or two or save it in a money market fund until you reach $3,000.

The two basic alternative investments that long-term investors should use are individual stocks and mutual funds. If you are using annuities to make your investments or you have a company retirement fund, you are usually limited to mutual funds with that money. If you are using a Roth or traditional IRA, you have the choice. If you don't want to worry or think about it, put it all in mutual funds using suggestions in the next section.

My preferred method would be to divide your investment funds equally between index mutual funds and individual stocks. That is what I have done. You don't have to do this every year, but you should try to do it over 5 years. For instance, if you invest $3,000 this year in a mutual fund, you might want to try to invest $3,000 next year or in the next few years in individual stocks.

Mutual Fund Investment

Mutual funds are one of the easiest and best ways to invest in the stock market. A stock mutual fund buys shares of stock, and the investor buys shares in the fund. There are many mutual funds that invest entirely or partially in stocks. There are entire mutual fund families that have many funds that specialize in a range of potential stock investments. You can find a fund that specializes in almost any field that interests you, and large stock funds typically invest in hundreds of stocks. The funds charge management fees to manage the fund. The shares that you own are shares in that fund not shares in the stocks that they buy. You can usually buy and sell your shares in a mutual fund every day. Some funds trade minute to minute just like stocks. Others settle their price at the end of the trading day based on the closing price of the stocks or assets that they own.

Index Funds
What Are They?

Index mutual funds are of interest to a long-term investor. They are mutual funds that invest in stocks to try to mimic a common index. For instance, there are a number of funds that invest in essentially the same 500 stocks that comprise the Standard and Poor's 500. There are funds that try to duplicate the S&P 100, the NASDAQ composite, The Russell 1000, the Wilshire, and even a fund that invests only in the 30 stocks in the Dow. Some index funds try to duplicate the results of all stocks traded on the major exchanges. These are usually called "Total Stock Market funds." Vanguard and Fidelity are two of the biggest fund families that have a wide range of index and other funds, and each manages billions of investment dollars for investors.

Advantages and Disadvantages

Index mutual funds have both advantages and disadvantages compared with investing in individual stocks. Mutual funds give an investor an opportunity to invest in dozens, hundreds, or even thousands of stocks without investing much money. Most mutual funds do have some minimum limits for initial investments. They vary significantly from hundreds of dollars to thousands. Most of Vanguard funds have initial minimums of $3,000. The minimum investment to add funds after the first investment is only $100. Many of Fidelity's funds have $2,500 initial minimums. Fidelity even has some index funds with extremely low expenses, 0.07% yearly, that have $100,000 minimums.

Index funds give a long-term investor the chance to assure himself or herself that he or she will compound his or her investment dollars at close to the index's compound rate. There will be a slight difference in results over time because of expenses. Fidelity's Spartan 500 index fund has compounded at 8.78% yearly for the last 10 years. The S&P 500 has compounded at 8.95% yearly. Index funds give an investor instant diversification. An investment of $2,500 or $3,000 in an S&P index fund allows an investor instantly to own a share of 500 companies. Index funds, unless you direct them otherwise, will often automatically reinvest all distributions in added shares of the fund, which is what a long-term investor wants.

There are two disadvantages to owning index funds. Your return is limited to the return on the market averages, and you will incur expenses in managing the account.

Every long-term investor should have part of his or her capital invested in stock index mutual funds. Earning the market average compound rate of return is an achievement in itself. If you are investing for many years, you want to assure that your rate of return is close to the index return if the market continues to grow and compound at exceptional rates. Index funds are the perfect way to do this.

Historical Returns

I am going to concentrate on two fund families, but almost every fund family has some index funds.

Vanguard Funds

My favorite for most investors is Vanguard. They have four index funds that I would recommend an investor to consider. Figure 22A1 lists those funds. The funds listed in Figure 22A1 all have $3,000 initial minimums and $100 minimums for added investments. These four funds try to invest to match as closely as possible the results of the index of stocks they are following. Over time, their returns have been just slightly less than the real index. This difference usually reflects expenses. I discuss the impact of trading and fees in Chapter 16.

The Vanguard 500 Index fund tries to "track" the performance of the S&P 500. The Vanguard Total Stock Market Index fund tries to "track" the investment return of the overall stock market. The Vanguard Value

Index fund tries to "track" the investment return of large capitalization value stocks. The Vanguard Total International Stock Index fund tries to "track" the investment return of a combination of indexes including "Europe, Pacific, and Emerging Markets stock index funds."

FIGURE 22A1 Vanguard Index Funds[103]

Fund Name	Ticker Symbol	Comparison Years	Compound Fund Rate of Return	Comparison Index Rate of Return	Comparison Index
Vanguard 500 Index	VFINX	10	8.88%	8.95%	S&P 500
Vanguard Total Stock Market	VTSMX	10	9.06%	9.11%	Total Stock Market Index
Vanguard Value Index	VIVAX	10	9.33%	9.45%	Value Index
Vanguard Total International	VGTSX	5	10.90%	11.04%	Total International Composite

The Vanguard 500 Index fund is a good place for an investor to start. Dividing your index fund investment dollars, if you have enough, between the 500 Index Fund and the Total Stock Market Index fund also makes a lot of sense. The Vanguard Value Index makes sense for those investors who want to stick to the larger well-known names in the stock market. Many of the stocks discussed in the stock selection section of this chapter would qualify for this fund. Value means that their current price must be a reasonable multiple of earnings and dividends. The Total International fund is for investors who wish exposure to foreign markets. Dividing your funds among all four, or three of the four, would be a good strategy for a long-term investor.

The returns indicated are for the last 10 years. Three of these funds have been around for longer than 10 years and one, the 500 Index fund, started in 1976. Its compound rate of return since 1976 is 12.16%. Shiller's compound rate of return from 1976 to 2004 is 12.52%. As suggested in Chapter 29, the stock market has actually underperformed its postwar historic average compound rate of return the last 10 years.

The difference in returns in Figure 22A1 for the fund and for the index may be the impact of fees charged on the account every year. The fund managers do have to pay a commission to buy stock, but index funds do not require much trading. An individual investor has to pay a commission to buy stock as well. Vanguard charges fees on these four funds that range from 0.17% yearly on the 500 Index fund to 0.31% yearly on the Total International fund.

Fidelity Funds

The other fund family that I recommend is Fidelity. Fidelity has several index funds that work well specifically for the high net worth investor. But they also have a broad range of different kinds of funds that are perfect for an average investor. Both Fidelity and Vanguard do not assess sales charges at purchase to buy shares so the full amount of your investment goes right to work.

Fidelity has several "classes" of index funds. Their "Advantage" class has five funds, each with onetime $100,000 initial minimum and $2,500 minimums to add funds. The "Investor" class has five similar funds with $10,000 initial minimums and $1,000 minimums to add funds after the first investment. The "Advantage" class funds have extremely low expense ratios of 0.07% yearly. The "Investor" class funds have an excellent expense ratio of 0.10% yearly. The higher the initial investment minimum, the lower the expense ratio. For a long-term investor, the higher expense ratios can mount up.

FIGURE 22A2 Fidelity Index Funds[104]

Fund Name	Ticker Symbol	Comparison Years	Compound Rate of Return	Comparison Rate of Return	Comparison Index
Spartan 500 Index					
Investor	FSMKX	10	8.77%	8.95%	S&P 500
Advantage	FSMAX	10	8.78%	8.95%	S&P 500
Spartan Extended					
Market	FSEMX	5	12.50%	12.65%	DJW 4500
Investor	FSEVX	5	12.50%	12.65%	DJW 4500
Advantage					

Spartan International					
Investor	FSIIX	5	9.48%	9.86%	MS EAFE
Advantage	FSIVX	5	9.49%	9.86%	MS EAFE
Spartan Total Market					
Investor	FSTMX	5	5.82%	5.95%	DJ 5000
Advantage	FSTVX	5	5.82%	5.95%	DJ 5000
Spartan US Equity					
Investor	FUSEX	10	8.78%	8.95%	S&P 500
Advantage	FUSVX	10	8.78%	8.95%	S&P 500

The Fidelity funds incur low fees, only slightly lower for the Advantage funds than the Investor funds. The Vanguard funds performed a bit better on the one fund that is directly comparable, the 500 Index fund, despite slightly higher fees. The Spartan 500 fund attempts to copy the S&P 500. The Spartan Extended Market index fund tries to replicate the total return of all mid—to small-capitalization stocks. The Total Market fund attempts results of a broad range of the US stock market, while the US Equity Investor fund mimics the total US stock market. The International Investor Index fund uses the Morgan Stanley Index for Europe, Australasia, and the Far East. If you have $10,000 or $100,000 to invest, any of the Fidelity Index funds are attractive.

A good source on mutual funds is Morningstar. They have an informative website and publish paperbacks that list major mutual funds and ETFs. Morningstar lists the fund families in Figure 22A3 as some of the largest. All these fund families will have some index funds.

Most long-term investors should put at least half of their investment funds in index funds. Put all your investment dollars into any of these index funds or a combination of them if you don't want to select individual stocks. The returns that you will get over the long run will be slightly below the index's average return because of expenses.

FIGURE 22A3 Morningstar List of Mutual Fund Families[105]

Fund Families

⇨AIM Investments	⇨Fidelity	⇨PIMCO
		⇨Putnam Investments
⇨American Funds	⇨T. Rowe Price	
⇨American Century	⇨Franklin Temp	⇨TIAA-CREF
⇨Dodge & Cox		⇨Vanguard
	⇨Janus	
	⇨Oakmark	

Exchange-Traded Funds

What Are They?

Exchange-traded funds are one of the newer investment products on *Wall Street.* They are index mutual funds with one major exception; they trade on the exchanges all-day just like any stock. Most ETFs are index funds and thus do little trading and have low transactions costs with low stock turnover rates. There are several different types of ETFs: SPDRs, VIPERs, QUBES, IShares, PowerShares, StreetTracks, and HOLDRs. When you buy shares in an ETF, you do so through a broker so they can be good vehicles for long-term investors.

Advantages and Disadvantages

Exchange-traded funds offer investors many different specialized ways to invest. There are ETFs focusing on almost anything of interest. There are ETFs investing in utilities, health care, real estate, small or large caps, financials, energy, emerging markets, and so on. They offer limited stock trading and low trading costs and fees. They trade every minute the market is open.

The big disadvantage for long-term investors in ETFs is also one of the biggest advantages, the daily market trading. Since they trade like a

—

stock, they do not have to trade at exactly the value of the investments that they own. Often, the net asset value of the underlying stocks the fund owns is lower than the price of the fund. Because of this, a long-term investor may be paying a "premium" the equivalent of a sales charge for the fund when buying the shares. There is no guarantee that in 50 years the price of the fund will still be selling at a "premium." It might then be selling at the net asset value or even less than the net asset value. In a traditional mutual fund, an investor has to wait until the end of the day to sell his or her shares. But the price he or she receives is the net value of all the stocks and other assets the fund calculates it owns. The investor is buying shares from the fund itself instead of from another investor selling shares in the market in ETFs. I looked at Vanguard's Total Stock Market VIPER recently. If you invest $10,000 in this ETF and get an 11.76% compound rate of return for the next 60 years, an investor would receive $7,617,297. If you invested in a traditional index mutual fund that bought the same shares, your result would be $7,891,937 or almost $300,000 more. However, its expense ratio is 0.13% yearly compared to 0.17% for the Vanguard Index 500 fund. That extra 0.04% costs an investor about $115,000 over 60 years, making the net advantage for the traditional fund about $160,000. It is not a huge difference in a return of $7.8 million. A long-term investor who invests in an index fund wants to be sure that his or her return comes as close as possible to the index itself. With ETFs able to trade over or under net asset value, it is one added worry for a long-term investor.

If you like the idea of ETFs, study them carefully before investing. I use them in my own portfolio but not in my retirement fund. ETFs are new, and the history we have on them means little to a long-term investor. You can find out more about their brief history in *Morningstar ETF 100*.

When to Use Funds Instead of Stocks?

Mutual funds, particularly index funds, are good investments for long-term investors. An inexperienced investor may not want to put in the time and effort to make carefully researched stock selections. Some investors don't want to worry about the increased volatility and variability in results that can occur with individual stocks. Index funds give an investor an almost foolproof way to be sure that many years from now he or she will have achieved a result close to the index average. If the index compounds at 11%, you want to compound at 11% or 10.90% at worst. You are putting your faith in the economy as a whole instead of individual stocks.

—

Funds are also a good place to achieve some diversification. Altria may succumb to tobacco lawsuits or legal restrictions. In your portfolio, it might represent 10% or more of your holdings. In the Vanguard Total Stock Market index fund, it represents 0.71% of the assets. A bankruptcy or failure of Altria will only be a scratch for Vanguard fund shareholders.

Funds are also a great place to specialize in industries that you like but are unwilling or unable to select individual companies. If you want to invest in real estate without owning any property, you can buy Vanguard Real Estate Investment Trust Index fund. They invest in 120 companies that are in the real estate business. The largest holding in the fund represents less than 5% of their total assets. If you like health care's future, you can invest in Vanguard's Health Care fund that invests only in the health care industry. They own over 100 companies from biotechs like Amgen and Genentech to large pharmaceuticals like Pfizer, Eli Lilly, and Abbott. These are great investment opportunities, but these are not retirement fund investments. Invest in funds like these with other money.

Fund Families and Fund Selection

As I indicated, the fund families that I like the most are Vanguard and Fidelity. Vanguard is huge and a pioneer in low-cost funds. Fidelity is also huge and has a great variety of specialized funds. T. Rowe Price is another good family, and I have more investments with them than any other fund family. I have been investing with Price since the 1960s so they have been around for a long time. Fees and costs become more important the longer your time frame. I do not recommend funds with sales charges. I don't mind redemptions charges, but be sure you will stay with the fund if there are redemption charges. It really isn't necessary for a long-term investor to incur either sales or redemption charges. You can buy most no-load funds directly without any commission over the Internet or by mail from the fund family itself. Some discount brokers like Charles Schwab allow you to buy certain mutual funds in your account without commission charges.

I am not in favor of most actively managed mutual funds. My own investment experience tells me that index funds beat actively managed funds over any reasonable time frame. The information that I have studied confirms my personal judgment. Don't use them in your retirement portfolio. If you want to use them, concentrate in specific industries like health care, biotech, or information technology, but not with your retirement fund from this book.

Selecting Your Own Stocks

Advantages

There is only one reason that I can think of to select stocks yourself since, over the long run, most of the data suggests that even professional money managers cannot outperform the market averages. You have to believe that you can select stocks that will outperform the averages. You believe that you can find the next Philip Morris. And that is a good reason. You just may find it, and in this section, I am going to advise you on how to do it. I include this section because I know that many of you, like me, will want to try some stock selection on your own. Middle-aged or older investors who have less time until retirement are good candidates for stock selection since they may need to attempt a higher rate of return. Since there isn't a mutual fund yet designed explicitly for long-term investors, the choices available in the previous section on mutual funds may not be satisfying. I won't try to discourage you from trying stock selection, but I insist that you limit your own selections to less than half of your long-term investment capital.

Disadvantages

I have stated the most important disadvantage several times. If the "pros" can't outperform the market averages, then what makes you think you can? If you can't outperform the averages, then why try? Don't be fooled by claims that professionally managed funds can outperform the market. Every year some fund managers do outperform the market averages for 1 year, 2 years, or even 5 years. But they cannot do it for the long run, and that is what we want. If I believed that there was a single fund manager that could outperform the S&P for even 20 years, I would recommend him or her wholeheartedly. Warren Buffett is probably the closest, but he will likely retire in the coming years and who knows how his successor will perform.

There are a couple of other disadvantages not directly related to return that I worry about in stock selection. First, investing in individual stocks can lead you to start watching the markets too closely, day-to-day, or month-to-month like I do. While it may seem counterintuitive, this can lead to some fatal errors of judgment. Second, it may tempt you to trade the market once you start using your own judgment, particularly if you have some success. Success in investment selection is almost always temporary. Just when I think I have it figured out the stock market jumps up and kicks me in the butt. Just like gambling, some initial success in stock selection may be the worst thing that can happen to you. Investing in index funds is not emotional; daily movements in prices are smaller compared to movements in individual stock prices. It takes some of the gambling out of investing which inevitably creeps in if you select your own stocks. Stick with index funds unless you are committed to the idea of stock selection. But if you still want to pick stocks, the rest of this chapter will give you my best ideas on stock selection for the long run.

Stock Selection

Pick a Stockbroker

Selecting stocks to invest in for the long run is, to some degree, an art. There isn't a scientific method that works every time. Investors should realize that investing in index mutual funds means that, at best, you are going to get the market averages. In the S&P 500, approximately 250 stocks will achieve at higher rates of return than the market average and 250 stocks will achieve at lower rates than the market averages. You don't have to select the next Philip Morris to just do better than the averages, and there are great returns available to an investor who can improve his or her annual rate of return. I am going to offer you a couple of lists of stocks that currently meet the long-term selection criteria that I will set out in this chapter. However, note that every stock has some negative aspects to it, no matter how positive the overall seems. Nothing in life is perfect, but, as I point out later in this chapter, you don't have to pick all winners. The research in Chapter 8 shows that with a little luck even losers can sometimes turn out to be winners. All you need to become a "millionaire" at retirement is to have some winners, and this chapter will try to give you the best chance to succeed.

The first step that you need to take before investing in stocks is to open an investment account. You can do it at any stockbroker by phone, in person, or by mail. (Many banks have investment divisions that perform stockbroker functions.) You can also do it over the Internet without talking to anyone. I recommend using the Internet since the long-term, buy and hold investing that you will be doing in this account, does not appeal to most brokers. They make money on trading. Sure they like it when you do well, but only because you are likely to trade more. And you are not going to trade a lot, at least with your retirement money.

235

Opening an account at one of the discount brokers using the Internet is easy and convenient. It also brings the advantage of not having to explain yourself to a broker who always has his or her own theories about how to invest. Buy and hold for 50 years is not usually one of them, although most stockbrokers will nod their head approvingly when you describe your strategy. I have both kinds of accounts: online, where I talk to no one, and in-person, where I have to talk to a broker to carry out a trade. I am happy with the in-person brokers that I use, but I must say that it has taken me years of training to get them to stop bothering me with short-term trading tips and understand the stock investing style I want to do. If you are a novice investor, it is much more likely that they will try to talk you out of using the strategy in this book without telling you that is what they are doing.

"Thrive and Survive"

Long-term investing needs a different thinking about investments. I like to call it "thrive and survive." Long-term investors want to invest in companies that will survive 50-70 years or more and that will also thrive and do well in sales and profit growth over many years. When evaluating a stock for possible purchase, the first question that you should ask yourself is, "Will this company still be around and doing well in 50, 60, or 70 years?" That question impacts and overrides every other consideration.

Stocks That Have Lasted!

One theory is that companies that have already lasted for a longtime are more likely to last for a longtime in the future. Companies that have a long history of sales and profit growth are more likely to have a long future of sales and profit growth. So my first rule of "thrive and survive" is to pick stocks that have lasted for a long time, have performed well for a long time and, most important, continue to perform well. I consider 50 years as the minimum to qualify. The first question any long-term investor should ask himself about a stock under consideration is, "Will this company, without a doubt, survive for 50-70 years?" If that answer is yes, then you should ask, "Is it highly likely that this company will still be successful and thriving in 50-70 years?"

"Hold on," you say, "doesn't that automatically remove some of the great new high-flying technology companies of the modern era, Microsoft, Intel, Cisco, Dell, Google, Genentech, and Amgen?" Yes, I admit it. Many of these are great companies, but they are not for you in the part of your portfolio that is long-term retirement investing. The reason is simple. What kind of technology, computers and software will we be using in 50-70 years? Who knows? Obviously, there will be significant changes in the technologies that we use many years from now. Will there even be an Internet, as we know it? Will we still use what we call a computer and if so, what will it be like? Will Microsoft, Apple, Intel or Google be able to adjust to the dramatic changes in technology that will inevitably occur over a long period of time? Stock market history flows with the dead bodies of companies that had a monopoly on a new technology for a time. Railroads are a great example of a onetime great new technology sidelined on the way to the future. I am sure that some of the great technology companies of today will thrive and survive into the future, but I can't guess which ones. The big question to ask when examining potential stock investment goes something like this. Will Cisco Systems, more likely, still be selling its products in large numbers in 2065? Or will Hershey Foods, more likely, still be selling chocolates in large numbers in 2065? Which question can you answer yes with the most confidence? While nothing is for sure, I would bet the barn that Hershey's will still be successfully selling chocolate bars in 2065. I am not so sure about Cisco. Maybe they will and maybe they won't, but I am not willing to bet my retirement on maybes. If you want to invest in new technologies, it is fine with me, just not with your retirement money. I invest in them myself, but fund your retirement first. When you are certain you have completed your retirement investment goals and you still have investment dollars left over, go for it. Just remember that stock market history shows that you don't need to take the risks in the latest technology company to have spectacular returns.

FIGURE 22B1 Adapted from Siegel, *The Future for Investors*[106]
Top 50 Companies—Compound Annual Return
on Investment (1957-2003)

Company 1957	Industry	Company 2005	Compound Rate of Return 1957-2003	Result of $10,000 in 1957
Phiip Morris	Tobacco and food	Altria	19.75%	$39,872,550
Thatcher Glass	Glass	Merged—Altria	18.42%	$23,853,527
National Can	Aluminum	Merged—Pechiney	18.31%	$22,855,299
		Merged—Cadbury		
Dr Pepper	Soda	Schweppes	18.07%	$20,817,085

—

Lane Bryant	Retail	Merged—Limited	17.62%	$17,463,611
General Foods	Food	Merged—Altria	16.85%	$12,909,843
Abbott Labs	Pharmaceuticals	Abbott Labs	16.51%	$11,290,347
Warner-Lambert	Pharmaceuticals	Merged—Pfizer	16.40%	$10,810,284
Celanese	Chemicals	Merged—Aventis	16.39%	$10,767,645
Bristol-Myers	Pharmaceuticals	Bristol-Myers	16.36%	$10,640,714
Columbia Pictures	Entertainment	Merged—Coca-Cola	16.25%	$10,187,702
Tootsie Roll	Candy	Tootsie Roll	16.11%	$9,638,351
American Chicle	Pharmaceuticals	Merged—Pfizer	16.06%	$9,449,265
Pfizer	Pharmaceuticals	Pfizer	16.03%	$9,337,561
Coca-Cola	Food and sodas	Coca-Cola	16.02%	$9,300,614
California Packing	Food	Merged—Altria	16.01%	$9,263,810
Merck	Pharmaceuticals	Merck	15.97%	$9,118,013
Lorillard	Tobacco	Merged—Loew's	15.96%	$9,081,917
National Dairy	Food	Merged—Altria	15.92%	$8,938,922
Standard Brands	Food	Merged—Altria	15.90%	$8,868,253
Richardson Merrell	Food	Merged—Procter & Gamble	15.87%	$8,763,273
Houdaille Industries	Manufacturing	Went private	15.77%	$8,422,044
Reeves Brothers	Manufacturing	Went private	15.74%	$8,322,235
R. H. Macy	Retail	Went private	15.69%	$8,158,452
Stokely-Van Camp	Food	Merged—PepsiCo	15.56%	$7,747,231
PepsiCo	Food and sodas	PepsiCo	15.54%	$7,685,793
McCall	Publishing	Went private	15.34%	$7,097,045
Colgate-Palmolive	Consumer staples	Colgate-Palmolive	15.22%	$6,765,222
R. J. Reynolds	Tobacco	Merged—Altria	15.16%	$6,605,051
Crane Co.	Manufacturing	Crane Co.	15.14%	$6,552,490
Consolidated Cigar	Tobacco	Merged—Viacom	15.01%	$6,220,679
Penick & Ford	Machinery	Merged—Altria	15.00%	$6,195,847
Best Foods	Food	Merged—Unilever	14.97%	$6,121,931
Paramount Pictures	Entertainment	Merged—Viacom	14.92%	$6,000,651
General Cigar	Tobacco	Merged—Swedish Match	14.90%	$5,952,800
Virginia-Carolina Chemicals	Chemicals	Merged—Exxon	14.85%	$5,834,800
Congoleum Nairn	Carpet and linoleum	Went private	14.82%	$5,765,101
Truax-Traer Coal	Coal	Merged—DuPont	14.80%	$5,719,089

Am Agricultural		Merged—Consolidated		
Chemicals	Chemicals	Coal	14.80%	$5,719,089
Amalgamated Sugar	Sugar	Went private	14.78%	$5,673,436
Heinz	Food	Heinz	14.78%	$5,673,436
Corn Products	Food	Merged—Unilever	14.71%	$5,516,440
Wrigley	Candy	Wrigley	14.65%	$5,385,261
American Tobacco	Tobacco	Fortune Brands	14.55%	$5,173,379
Electric Auto-Lite	Automotive	Merged—Honeywell	14.52%	$5,111,420
Bohn Aluminum	Aluminum and			
and Brass	brass	Merged—Viacom	14.51%	$5,090,929
Flintkote	Building materials	Merged—British Tobacco	14.48%	$5,029,937
Quaker Oats	Food	Merged—PepsiCo	14.45%	$4,969,660
Gulf, Mobile &				
Ohio	Railroad	Merged—PepsiAmericas	14.43%	$4,929,868
Kroger	Retail	Kroger	14.41%	$4,890,388

So how do you select companies that will survive for 50-70 years? The next few figures may be of some help. Figure 22B1 lists the 50 companies with the top returns in the S&P composite from 1957 to 2003 from Jeremy Siegel's *The Future for Investors*. Long-term investors should be required to read Siegel's books. Table 22A1 in the appendix shows the same 50 companies updated to 2005 with their price at the end of 2005 and current earnings per share and dividends per share. Both Figures 22B1 and 22B2 include the theoretical result of a $10,000 investment made in each company in 1957, reinvesting all distributions in added stock, for both 2003 and 2005 respectively. Figure 22B2 includes only surviving companies in 2005.

You can use this information to help select the industry categories and individual stocks that have consistently performed well over the past 50 years. Decide if it is likely that they will perform well in the next 50 years. It is obvious from Figures 22B1 and 22B2 that all the companies listed performed well, compounding at least 14% per year for 46 or 48 years.

I look for industry categories that dominate Figure 22B1 and that do not exist in Figure 22B5, which shows the worst performing 50 companies in Siegel's S&P analysis. There are five categories that dominate Figure 22B1 that do not exist in Figure 22B5 and they are in Figure 22B3. They are consumer staples, food, candy and sodas, pharmaceuticals, and tobacco. The most important question to ask is which industries and companies in Figure 22B1 will likely still survive and thrive in 2075 and beyond. Two clear answers for industries might be food, candy and

—

soda, and pharmaceuticals. Tobacco has been historically profitable both for companies and for shareholders placing 6 companies in the top 50. Tobacco, at least in the United States, has been under attack for decades, but it still seems to thrive. There is a risk that someday politicians could decide to make it illegal to smoke here and in much of the world. I would not place all my eggs in the tobacco basket even though Philip Morris has been the star for the last 50 years and still is priced reasonably today (May 2006). But investing in one tobacco stock as part of a diversified plan of long-term investments does make sense. Most of the tobacco companies have diversified themselves into other fields, usually food, as a protection against the assault on tobacco.

FIGURE 22B2 Adapted from Siegel, *The Future for Investors*, Top 50 Survivors[107] Compound Annual Return on Investment (1957-2005)

Company 1957	Industry	Company 2005	Compound Rate of Return 1957-2005	Result of $10,000 in 1957
Philip Morris	Tobacco and food	Altria	19.78%	$57,869,112
Abbott Labs	Pharmaceuticals	Abbott Labs	15.61%	$10,551,194
Bristol-Myers	Pharmaceuticals	Bristol-Myers	15.11%	$8,589,497
Tootsie Roll	Candy	Tootsie Roll	14.90%	$7,857,789
Pfizer	Pharmaceuticals	Pfizer	14.49%	$6,612,070
Coca-Cola	Food and sodas	Coca-Cola	14.86%	$7,714,950
Merck	Pharmaceuticals	Merck	14.56%	$6,821,341
PepsiCo	Food and Sodas	PepsiCo	15.50%	$10,094,238
Colgate-Palmolive	Consumer staples	Colgate-Palmolive	14.84%	$7,661,149
Crane Co.	Manufacturing	Cran e Co.	14.89%	$7,820,029
Heinz	Food	Heinz	14.12%	$5,676,759
Wrigley	Candy	Wrigley	14.45%	$6,510,266
American Tobacco	Tobacco	Fortune Brands	14.27%	$6,034,546

FIGURE 22B3 Top 3 Industries from S&P 500 in 1957
Compound Annual Rate of Return

Industry	Companies Name in 1957	Companies Exist Name in 2005
Food, candy, and soda	Dr Pepper	
	General Foods	
	Tootsie Roll	Tootsie Roll
	Coca-Cola	Coca-Cola
	California Packing	
	National Dairy	
	Standard Brands	
	Richardson Merrell	
	Stokely-Van Camp	
	PepsiCo	PepsiCo
	Best Foods	
	Heinz	Heinz
	Corn Products	
	Wrigley	Wrigley
	Quaker Oats	
Tobacco	Philip Morris	Altria
	Lorillard	
	R. J. Reynolds	
	Consolidated Cigar	
	General Cigar	
	American Tobacco	
Pharmaceuticals	Abbott Labs	Abbott Labs
	Warner-Lambert	
	Bristol-Myers	Bristol-Myers
	American Chicle	
	Pfizer	Pfizer
	Merck	Merck

Is there any doubt that food companies and candy and soda providers will survive for the long haul? There are 15 total or partial food companies in the top 50 and 3 of them that you would classify as candy and soda, although you could easily lump them all together as food. These 15 companies have survived and thrived for 48 years in good times and in bad. What may be just as interesting is that there are no food, candy, or

—

241

soda companies in Figure 22B5. It is likely that this group will continue to perform well, and selecting any one or a group of them makes eminent sense. And 5 companies of the original 15 are still independent entities that you can invest in. The other food companies were acquired during the past 46 years.

I am also high on pharmaceuticals. They have almost everything going for them, an aging population, dramatic new cures for many diseases on the horizon, and a growing world population in which to compete. While pharmaceuticals make sense as a part of a long-term strategy, I would not gamble everything on them either. No drug is perfect or works perfectly with everyone, and the drug companies face an increasingly negative legal environment that may inhibit future drug development for fear of expensive judgments for any potential liability. The second issue that worries me is their dependence on third-party insurance payers and governments for much of their income. Health costs are climbing and will continue to do so. It is not clear that insurance companies and government insurance programs are going to be able to afford or be willing to pay for the newest and most expensive drug therapies the pharmaceuticals will develop. Government may step in some day to "take over" or more heavily regulate this industry. So include pharmaceuticals as part of your long-term investment portfolio but, like tobacco, don't bet the entire farm on them. There are only four pharmaceuticals left in Figure 22B3, and they all make sense for a long-term investor.

Consumer staples are another solid category dominated by firms that have spent billions establishing name brands that they are now aggressively marketing all over the world. Later in this chapter, I will give you my personal choices for long-term compound returns, but any of these companies listed in Figure 22B4 would be good selections for a portfolio.

Brand Names and Brand Identification

It is always a good idea to look for companies that have strong brand identification. Established brand names are like legal monopolies. Normally, no one can take those brand names away, and unlike patent protection, brand ownership is forever. The name "Coca Cola" or "Tide" are worth fortunes in and of themselves, but more important, they are insurance for a long-term investor that the company, the owner of the brand name, will likely survive or become an attractive acquisition. The emerging economies in Asia and other parts of the world are showing an uncommon interest in brand names. Many of the companies that have "survived" and "thrived" own proven brand names.

The Siegel Solution

So how do you select companies that will survive and thrive for 50-70 years? Figure 22B4 may be of some help. This figure lists the 20 companies with the top returns in the S&P 500 from 1957 to 2005 calculated by Jeremy Siegel, perhaps the premier researcher into historic stock market returns. These are 20 companies that survived in the S&P 500 since 1957 and had the best compound annual rates of return for 48 years. Selecting all or a group of stocks from Figure 22B4 is an excellent idea. There is a high likelihood that stocks that have had superior long-term performance in the past will continue to provide investors with superior performance in the future.

FIGURE 22B4 Jeremy Siegel's 20 Best Performing Stocks[108]

Company Name	Compound Annual Return, 1957-2005	Industry	Dividend Yield
Altria	19.80%	Tobacco and food	4.07%
Bristol-Myers Squibb	15.79%	Pharmaceuticals	2.87%
Abbott Labs	15.72%	Pharmaceuticals	2.25%
Merck	15.59%	Pharmaceuticals	2.37%
Coca-Cola	15.54%	Sodas and food	2.81%
PepsiCo	15.41%	Sodas and food	2.53%
Pfizer	15.30%	Pharmaceuticals	2.45%
Tootsie Roll	15.27%	Candy	2.44%
Crane	15.14%	Manufacturing	3.62%
Colgate-Palmolive	14.94%	Consumer staples	3.39%
Fortune Brands	14.22%	Consumer staples	5.31%
William Wrigley	14.12%	Food and candy	4.02%
Heinz	14.11%	Food	3.27%
Kroger	14.09%	Food retail	5.89%
Schering-Plough	14.02%	Pharmaceuticals	2.57%
Procter & Gamble	14.00%	Consumer staples	2.75%
Wyeth	13.81%	Pharmaceuticals	3.32%
Hershey Foods	13.79%	Food and candy	3.67%
Royal Dutch	13.55%	Oil and gas	5.24%
General Mills	13.39%	Food	3.20%

FIGURE 22B5 Siegel's Bottom 50 Companies, S&P 500, Compound Yearly Return[109]

Company 1957	Industry	Company 2003	Compound Return
Zenith Radio	Electronics	Complete failure	00.00%
White Motors	Automotive	"	00.00%
Vertientes-Camaguey	Sugar	"	00.00%
United States Smelting	Steel	"	00.00%
U.S. Hoffman Machinery	Machinery	"	00.00%
Airloom Carpet	Carpet	"	00.00%
Sunbeam	Home electronics	"	00.00%
Republic Steel	Steel	"	00.00%
Pan American	Airlines	"	00.00%
New York, New Haven	Railroads	"	00.00%
National Steel	Steel	"	00.00%
G. C. Murphy	Retail	"	00.00%
Minneapolis-Moline		"	00.00%
Monarch Machine Tool	Machinery	"	00.00%
Manhattan Shirt	Clothing	"	00.00%
Manati Sugar	Sugar	"	00.00%
Joy Manufacturing	Household	"	00.00%
Jaeger Machine	Machinery	"	00.00%
International Shoe	Shoes	"	00.00%
Holly Sugar	Sugar	"	00.00%
Guantanamo Sugar	Sugar	"	00.00%
W. T Grant	Retail	"	00.00%
Goebel Brewing	Beer	"	00.00%
Eastern Air Lines	Airlines	"	00.00%
Eagle-Picher	Power	"	00.00%
Cornell Dubilier	Electric	"	00.00%
Colorado Fuel & Iron	Steel	"	00.00%
American Shipbuilding	Shipping	"	00.00%
Addressograph	Business Equipment	"	00.00%
Bethlehem Steel	Steel	Still Bethlehem	–13.54%
Republic Pictures	Entertainment	Merged Tyco International	–11.50%
Wheeling Steel	Steel	Merged WHX	–8.72%

Family Finance	Finance	Merged Aristar	-8.55%
Publicker Industries		Merged Publicard	-8.07%
Reading Co	Railroad	Reading Entertainment	-7.95%
Allis-Chalmers		Still Allis-Chalmers	-6.97%
Burlington Industries	Manufacturing	Merged Burlington Ind. (new)	-6.46%
Wilson Co		Merged Tyson Foods	-6.34%
Warner Bros.	Entertainment	Merged Warnarco	-6.04%
Youngstown Steel	Steel	Merged Ling-Temco-Vought	-5.98%
Lee & Sons	Clothing	Merged Burlington Industries	-5.71%
American Export Lines	Shipping	Merged Tyson Foods	-5.18%
Jones & Laughlin	Steel	Merged Tyson Foods	-5.02%
TWA	Airlines	Merged UAL	-4.35%
Cluett Peabody		Merged WestPoint Stevens	-4.25%
Aldens		Merged Collins & Aikman	-4.01%
Stevens (JP)		Merged WestPoint Stevens	-3.89%
Van Raalte		Merged WestPoint Stevens	-3.87%
Food Fair	Supermarket	Merged Revlon	-3.44%
Northern Natural Gas	Gas	Merged Enron	-2.89%

Combine Recent History and Future Projections

This method is similar to the first. It screens stocks to look at a series of factors, including their more recent results. See if they have performed as well during the last 10 years as they did in the entire 48 years. These factors test whether a company can survive and thrive for 50 or 60 years. We may find stocks that have an overall strong performance for 48 years but have not done well in the last decade. It isn't necessary for the company to have performed exactly as well in the past 10 years as it did in the past 48, but it should be close enough. For instance, Altria has performed slightly better for stockholders in the last 10 years than it did for the entire 48, a good sign.

Long-Term Returns to Shareholders

It is simply not enough for a company to have lasted for a long time. Some companies that have lasted forever are on the way down, and you must be careful to discriminate between long-lasting companies that continue to thrive and an exhausted rooster on its last legs. Fortunately, it is not that difficult to do. The best place to start for a novice investor who does not want to do research himself or herself is Jeremy Siegel's book, *The Future for Investors.*[110] Siegel has done much of the initial work for us, and he lists in the appendix of his book the average annual compound return to shareholders of all the 500 stocks in the S&P 500 from 1957 to 2003. This return assumes all dividends and distributions reinvested in the company's stock, and the investor did not have to pay any taxes or used a tax avoidance or deferral described in Chapter 11.

Siegel lists the 500 companies in order of return, from best to worst, showing the possible total accumulation on December 31, 2003 for a single dollar invested in each stock in 1957. Our famous Philip Morris is, of course, number one. The name has changed to Altria to provide less identification with its cigarette dominated past. Figure 22B1 lists the top 50 companies in Siegel's book and updates their results to the end of 2005. The first criteria for screening that I suggest to a novice or inexperienced investor is to invest only in companies in Siegel's top 50 surviving stocks. Table 22E in the appendix also shows the top 50 with the additional screening factors that I believe are most important. They have all performed well over a long period of time. They have survived bull markets and market crashes. They have survived wars and recessions, political turmoil, and terrorism to provide their stockholders with healthy and above-average returns. Most of them, but not all, are likely to continue to do so for many years into the future.

Earnings

Stock returns to shareholders usually reflect positive earnings trends, but not always. For all kinds of reasons, a stock might go up in value even during a period when a company's earnings were not performing that well. We want to be careful in selecting companies that will most likely last for 50-70 years. In the end, the stock price and the company's dividend will eventually have to reflect the earnings trend so we want to see a positive 10-year trend in earnings. We will look at the company's earnings per share over a 10-year period and see if the earnings are steadily increasing. We want to see a yearly increase in earnings that bears some relationship to the return to shareholders in dividends and stock price. If a company's stock price is going up significantly faster than its earnings, it might be good, but it also might be a warning sign. Many companies have seen their investor's return go up faster than their earnings have in the past decade. It is not a matter for unusual concern as long as the difference between the two is not too great. I like to see at least 10% compound earnings growth during the past decade to go with the double-digit increase in shareholder return. Past earnings and dividend information is readily available from any good guide like Morningstar or Standard and Poor's in the bookstore.

Dividends

In Chapter 10, I showed that dividends were critical to a long-term investor, so in screening stocks for possible investment, we like companies that pay strong dividends. I don't have a standard of dividend payout that I want. In fact, sometimes too high a dividend can be a warning sign. I am not comfortable investing in a company that pays out all or most of its earnings in dividends. This could be a sign that the company is not faring well in general and must pay such a healthy dividend to attract investors. But as Chapter 10 showed, dividends play a significant role in total investor return, especially for long-term investors.

Earnings and Dividend Stability

A company that survives for the long haul is more likely to have steady increases in earnings and dividends rather than earnings or dividends that jump all around. A company might look good from an earnings growth standpoint considering only the beginning and ending earnings but might have had ups and downs, even losses, along the way. Ups and downs in earnings and profits are not always bad, but they do lead to some additional confusion and uncertainty about a company's future, so I like to screen also for earnings and dividend stability in my long-term portfolio. It is better to see stable trends for both, although it is not uncommon for good companies to have stable dividends coupled with some instability in earnings growth. You will see some good companies with less stable earnings growth listed in the "Silver" group.

Globalization

Much of the future success of the US economy and American companies lies in globalization. No longer can an American company survive and thrive only in the American market, and this trend will quicken in the coming decades. Many of the companies in Figures 22B1 and 22B2 already are doing more business and earning more money outside the United States than they are inside. It is easy to find out if a company is globalizing their business by searching the financial websites or the company's website. If a company does not discuss its global penetration on its website or in its annual report, be careful.

My Screening Results

FIGURE 22C1 Suggested Stock Selections Using My Screening

7 Gold Stocks	Type of Business	Siegel's 46-Year Compound Return[111]
Altria	Consumer staples/ tobacco	19.75%
Procter & Gamble	Consumer staples	14.26%
Exxon Mobil	Oil and gas	12.55%
Colgate-Palmolive	Consumer staples	15.22%
McGraw-Hill	Publishing	13.56%
General Electric	Conglomerate	14.22%
Hershey Foods	Foods/candy	14.22%

6 Silver Stocks	Type of Business	Siegel's 46-Year Compound Return
PepsiCo	Soda/food	15.54%
Chevron Texaco	Oil and gas	12.14%
General Mills	Consumer staples	13.59%
Abbott Labs	Pharmaceuticals	16.51%
Wrigley	Food/candy	14.65%
IBM	Computer	11.94%

The stocks listed in Figure 22C1 are the result of a screening that began with the top returning 250 stocks in Jeremy Siegel's *The Future for Investors*. Siegel's analysis began in 1957 and ended in 2003. Many of the original companies did not survive. They went bankrupt, went private, or were acquired by some other company. Since I only included the top 250, none of those went bankrupt, but many were acquired, and a surprising number decided to become private companies again, a trend that has become popular again. I took all the survivors and screened them for the factors discussed earlier. In Table 22D in the appendix, I include a description of my screening system. This system tries to find long-term stocks that will likely survive and thrive. Table 22E in the appendix shows the results and my screen for each of these surviving top 250 companies. This system leaves many good candidates out. For instance, to make this list, a company must have been on the S&P 500 in 1957 and must be there currently. I strongly suggest the reader put any other companies that he or she discovers through the same or a similar screening that I detail in Table 22D.

You can see in Table 22E the factors that I valued for a long-term investment. I used both long-term (46-year) compound returns to shareholders and short-term (10-year). I used both long-term and recent earning history (10-year). I used analyst's (that cover the stock) estimates of future growth. I used P/E ratios (favoring low ones), dividends, dividend yields, and dividends to earnings as well. Finally, I valued earnings and dividend stability. Most of the companies in this list did well on 10-year dividend stability, but only a few (7) did well on 10-year earnings stability. The top 3 ranked stocks all had stable 10-year earnings growth and dividend growth.

Notice, the 7 gold stocks listed in Figure 22C1 are not necessarily the top 7 stocks in Table 22E. I dropped or moved to silver some of the stocks in Table 22E if they did not meet certain minimum requirements for the gold category. To qualify as gold, the company had to have compound rates of return for Siegel's 46 years of at least 11% and compound 10-year returns of at least 10% yearly. A number of stocks that qualified statistically were dropped due to concerns about industry category discussed previously. PepsiCo fell into silver because their 10-year return was below 10% yearly. All these are still great companies. I tried to limit the number of recommendations for those of you who have limited funds to invest, but I would not object to a long-term investor investing in any of the stocks in these two categories (gold and silver). In fact, I already have personal investments in several of the silver group.

I like the partial diversity of the gold group, but I do regret not having a major pharmaceutical included. It just did not work. Abbott Labs is a great company, and I urge investors who have enough capital to consider it. All the pharmaceuticals stocks were hurt in my screening system due to weaker than normal 10-year earnings growth and shareholder return. The gold group contains 3 consumer staples, 1 food/candy, 1 oil and gas, 1 conglomerate, and a publishing company. It is a decent diversification for a small group of stocks. A close look at the seven stocks that I selected as

—

gold stocks will indicate that there is significant personal judgment about the factors used in screening. The 13 stocks listed in both the gold and silver group are all very close. Investors can use their own judgment in selecting any of these stocks for the long-term.

Investors need to use judgment about both companies and industries. Is Altria safe from growing world-wide restrictions on smoking? What will the impact of the green movement be on Exxon and Chevron who derive much of their sales and earnings from fossil fuels? Can Mc-Graw Hill's business model survive the massive move of information and even reading to the internet? These are not technical investing questions but issues for which any individual investor judgment matters.

A Three-Phase Plan

The following calculations are totally subjective and mine alone. I believe them to be reasonably good estimates of an investor's probability of achieving the specific investment goals cited in this book.

Phase One—Qualify for and open a Roth IRA, earn, save, and invest $3,000 in the Vanguard 500 Index fund.

> Odds of you becoming a millionaire by age 70-65%.
> Odds of you being worth $10 million sometime during your lifetime—30%.

Phase Two—Save and invest using your Roth IRA a second $3,000 in the Vanguard Total Stock Market Index fund.

> Odds of you becoming a millionaire by age 70-90%.
> Odds of you being worth $10 million sometime during your lifetime—75%.

Phase Three—Save and invest using your Roth IRA an additional $14,000, $1,000 each in the 13 stocks listed in Figure 22C1.

> Odds of you becoming a millionaire by age 70-99%.
> Odds of you being worth $10 million sometime during your lifetime—95%.

Diversification

Diversification is a key word in the investment community. It goes with "asset allocation," which I will discuss in Chapter 31. Diversification simply means not to put all your eggs in one basket. It implies that an investor should divide his or her investment dollars over different types of assets, different asset classes, and over different geographical areas. You should not, the theory goes, have all your money in stocks or all of it in bonds or all of it in real estate. And you should not have all your stock investment dollars in one stock or one category of stocks. Dividing your investments is less risky since a decline or an outright failure in one investment has a more limited impact on your total result. There are some good sources on the issue of diversification or asset allocation, a more sophisticated form of diversification.

I agree with the idea that diversification divides and lowers your risk, but it can also divide and lower your return. If stocks provide better returns over the long run than any other asset class, any diversification out of stock into other assets may lessen your overall return. But if you divide your money between stocks, bonds, and real estate, you will be less likely to have as severe a decline during downturns. Not all your assets will likely go down together. By mitigating this risk, you may also limit your total return. If you can find assets or asset classes that all perform equally well, and divide investment dollars over those assets only, you will probably lower your risk with the same rate of return. But that is not easy to do. Chapter 6 looked at returns to alternative investment assets and concluded that over any reasonable period of time returns to stocks were significantly higher.

It may be possible to diversify your stock investing over stock groups that all have the same chance for success. If you look at Figure 22C1, there is some modest diversification. They are all publicly traded American companies, but they are in varied types of businesses. They are not all consumer staples or oil and gas, but from varied industries.

If your investment dollars in the plan outlined in this book are not your only investment dollars, that is if you have other investment funds, then I would strongly suggest that you follow a diversification or asset allocation plan with those funds. This investment plan is specific; it is for your retirement. Stocks give you a superior opportunity to garner significant retirement funds on a small investment over the long run. The downside is you have to weather some added risk and volatility in the short run. I said in the beginning of this book that returns and risk are related. A larger return usually requires more risk. If you are investing in index funds or mutual funds, that risk boils down to two issues. First, your investment may provide volatile returns. In fact, I guarantee it. That is precisely why you are a long-term investor so you can look past the short-term volatility that invariably comes with stock investing. The second risk you must take is the risk the investment will not perform up to your expectations or the illustrations cited in Chapters 6 and 8. In Chapter 29, I detail reasons that this plan might fail, starting with your failure to follow through. Some of the risks are common to all asset classes and some more common to stocks. You can judge the likelihood that one of those risks will come to be.

This plan requires you to invest without a great deal of consideration to the idea of diversification. In fact, in some ways, non-diversification is the heart of the plan, the reason it can succeed.

The Best Companies All Have Potential Downsides

If you study individual stocks long enough, you will find faults with every one of them.

Oil and gas companies will thrive until someone comes up with the technology to bypass their function. While it may not be likely that this will happen soon, the possibility increases as the decades go by and if oil prices escalate. Giant oil companies will undoubtedly have the resources to be at the forefront of any technological change, but it is a risk.

Consumer staples are in competitive markets; they must constantly protect and enhance their valuable brands and stay on top to produce the returns that a long-term investor is expecting.

Pharmaceuticals have a huge potential market with the retiring of the baby boomers and the new technology of the biotech century in front of them. But they face competition at every step, a health care environment that is bordering on dysfunction, the Food and Drug Administration, greatly increased government involvement and regulation, and the potential of lawsuits at every turn.

Tobacco companies face both governmental and individual lawsuits and the possibility that smoking may be outlawed generally.

Every company and every industry faces challenges. It is the nature of business. It is one reason, while not a perfect standard, I favor companies that have already lasted, already weathered storms, and already met challenges. But we must recognize that the fact that a company has weathered past challenges does not guarantee that it will weather future and vastly different ones.

How Much to Invest in How Many Stocks?

If you must invest some of your retirement funds in individual stocks use the systems suggested in this chapter or develop your own system and stick to it. Don't jump to every new idea, new industry, or new initial public offering (IPO.) This is about longevity.

If your funds are limited, don't invest in an individual stock unless you have at least $1,000 to invest. You should first fund your mutual fund investment plan before investing in stocks, if that is possible. Investing $1,000 in each of the 7 gold stocks, or in all 13 gold and silver stocks in Figure 22C1, makes much sense. If you have $7,000 to invest in stocks, it is probably better to invest in 7 stocks than to put it all into one hoping that you picked the next Altria.

If you have more funds to invest and decide to include the silver stocks in Figure 22C1, you can put more of your funds into the stocks you think make the most sense (in my case the gold labeled stocks) and a lesser amount in the second-tier stocks (in my case the silver stocks).

Many investors will want to carry out their plan over several years, and you may have to buy one stock before another. Don't let that worry you. If you look at the history of stock performances, they can vary a lot over a short period, but over the long haul, the differences narrow dramatically. Some stocks that you might pick will do well right off the bat, and others will go down or move slowly for a while. Don't let that deter you. Look at some of the performances detailed in this book. Expect variation in the short run.

Why to Hold and Hold—Missing the Bull Market

Once you have made your selection, do not change your position unless you have a really good reason. In Chapter 26, I outline some good reasons to change course, but believe me from past experience, changing course is usually a mistake.

Do not try to time the market with retirement funds, getting out when the market seems about to top and getting in when the market is approaching the bottom. This is a prescription for disaster. One point is clear: to function well in any long-term system, you must be in the markets when the bulls are raging. Sometimes the markets move violently up in a short period of time. Many investors are tempted out of markets that are rising and end up missing the lion's share of the gains. At other times, the market moves up slowly over a longer period of time. If you miss any bull market or part of a bull market that occurs in the coming decades, you will dramatically lessen your rate of return. Your plan will fail. You can never be sure when the market is about to move upward or if it has already moved up just how much more will it move. Just when it looks the bleakest, when all the "experts" are predicting lower and lower prices, something happens to turn market sentiment and, before you know it, you have missed a big move. Or just when the bull market looks exhausted, all the experts are saying the bulls cannot run much longer, that is when the biggest move occurs. Don't try to guess, bet on and stay with the market, and stay long, always. It has always been the best strategy for the long run.

Industries to Highlight

I tend to like established companies in established industries. Food, sodas, and candy will probably be with us forever. Consumer staples with brand names seem like sure winners. Financial services are a very competitive market, but the future is all about financial services. I would be hesitant about industrial manufacturers, manufacturing as we know it may not last much longer. Stay away from the new technology stocks for long-term investing. Technology is the wave of the future, but it is changing so quickly that it is impossible to predict who can win in the long run. IBM was the surest technology play for 25 years, and they missed the big move into personal computers. If you want to invest in technology, try a mutual fund that specializes in the field so you get some diversification within the industry. Look for companies that pay dividends, but not all their earnings in dividends. Dividends are the backbone of a long-term investor's plan. Every investment should be with a company who, to one degree or another, is going international. The great companies of the future will be global.

International investing is acceptable but a little unwieldy at times. I have not stressed foreign stocks for a couple of reasons. Most large American companies have automatic dividend reinvestment plans, but only a few foreign companies have them. Undoubtedly, that will change with time. Also, some foreign companies are difficult and expensive to buy through American brokers. Foreign companies that trade their stock or ADRs on American exchanges work well. Use the same standards to pick international companies like Nestlé, one of my largest personal holdings.

Nobody Has All Winners

Nobody has all winners, and everyone has some losers, so expect it. In our plan, you don't need all winners to become a millionaire or more at retirement. Don't let some failure discourage you. My early investments make the point clearly. Three or four of them were total busts, but two or three of them were home runs, if I had only known to stick with them. You will not get, nor should you expect all winners, no matter what selection system you use. What you are trying to do is to select enough good stocks that have an excellent chance of succeeding to increase your probability of success. If you do that, you will achieve your goal. You may only need one winner, one big rate of return achiever to make it. Imagine an investor in 1957 that put $1,000 in 10 stocks if one of them was Philip Morris. The other 9 could have all declared bankruptcy, and our investor is still flying high. Just give yourself as many good chances as possible to insure your result and be patient. If you find one winner to invest in, you will probably find several.

Alternative View

There are so many different theories of investing strategy that it is impossible to even list them. And there are so many variations of each theory that even trying to understand them is a huge task. Once you start investing, you will find many people who will criticize your strategy. They might tell you that it is a bad idea to stick with mature, successful companies. All companies have a life cycle. Why pick one that is in midlife when you can get a youngster? Don't listen to all the random advice that you will get from everyone, especially investment professionals. If you want, develop your own system for stock investing, a variance of mine, or something different. I love it; send it to me if you want. But if you don't have much confidence in it, or in mine, then stick to index fund investing. Nothing fails more quickly than an investing system in which the investor does not have real confidence. If you have confidence in your investing plan, you will stick to it. The truth is that I have been searching my whole life for a short-term trading system that works. I haven't found it, and I doubt that anyone else has either. The only method that works consistently is compound returns and time. Stay with them.

CHAPTER 23

Depression and Inflation

I like to think of this investment plan as your personal backup plan in case other things in your life don't go as you imagined them. Call it a "Plan B" investment strategy. If you are successful in your financial life, the investment plan in this book may be only one of many investment strategies that you follow. I am not recommending that you put all your investment dollars in a long-term investment plan. Only enough that if everything else fails, you will still become a millionaire and have a prosperous retirement.

Ups and Downs in Life

If you are young, realize that like most people you will probably experience a few ups and downs in life, both personal and financial. Failed marriages, health problems, and failed business ventures are only some of the downs that you may well have to endure during a long lifetime. Success in business or investing, having children and grandchildren, and wonderful love affairs may be some of the ups that you will look back on many years from now. The truth is that life is a gamble, and one part of that gamble involves money. In my high school teaching experience, I found that young people today are often supremely confident that they will be a huge success once they leave school. Many have had years of parental reinforcement that everything they did was wonderful. But those of us that have lived a few extra years know that financial success, like any success, is difficult to achieve. If you are sure that you don't need the kind of investment plan outlined in this book because you will make all the money you need in the real world, I have news for you. Don't count on it!

You Cannot Depend on Inheritance

If you are lucky enough to be born to wealthy parents, or even upper-middle-class parents, many of you believe that you are set for life. At worst, you will inherit a sizable estate and not have to worry about your financial future or your retirement. Think again. One thing we learned from the recent dotcom collapse is that millionaires and even billionaires can become thousand-airs very quickly. You cannot depend on parents or grandparents to assure your financial future, no matter how wealthy they may be now. I have personally watched several multimillionaires lose everything in a few short months. Their children and grandchildren thought that they had the world by the tail.

Even if your relatives manage to hold on to their money, there are several pitfalls in you're getting the benefit of it. First, seniors are living longer. Parents living into their 90s and more is no longer uncommon and will likely become more widespread as years go by. Your wait for aging parents to pass on can be long. You may be a grandparent yourself when you finally reap the benefits for which you have waited so long.

In addition, elderly people often get funny ideas about who should inherit their money. They change their wills based on reasons that may be hard for you to understand and accept. A divorce, choice of careers, or even just your willingness to show up when they think you should, all can have an impact on who they choose as heirs. Elderly people are often unwilling to give up control of their investments prior to death. They tend to make poor decisions, listen to scam artists, or just fritter away much of what they worked a lifetime to create. While they may live longer, they may not live better, at least not right away. Health care costs for your aging parents or grandparents may eat up a large part of the nest egg that you hoped to inherit. Elderly medical care for simple living or common diseases of aging can cost millions. There are many stories of relatively wealthy individuals using all their funds in health care related costs during the last year or two of life fighting disease.

Wealthy parents or grandparents are great to have, but depending on their capacity to manage many years of financial health successfully is a stretch. If you do end up inheriting a bundle, then the plan in this book may be superfluous, but what if you don't? Why take the chance? It isn't necessary to depend on someone else for your retirement future.

You Cannot Depend on Your Own Innate Abilities

I mentioned another issue that I see with young people today, the tendency to believe in themselves—too much. I love self-confidence, but the "real" world is hard. It is a "dog-eat-dog" world, and no matter how successful you have been in school or other aspects of your life, success in the financial world requires some unusual skills. And there are millions of other confident people out there trying to defeat you.

I hope your personal skills will get you far, but there is no reason you should have to rely solely on them. The truth is there are many talented and smart people who never become millionaires. Any self-made millionaire will tell you that there is much luck involved in financial success. The difference between a millionaire and a middle-class existence is often just chance. You should develop and use your talents to the greatest extent possible, but there is no reason you have to depend on the combination of your abilities and luck to end wealthy. No matter how talented, fate can be perverse, and you should not stake your future on it.

Depression Experience

I am going to spend a little time talking about the Great Depression of the 1930s. It is important for those of you too young to have any memories of it to understand what it was and the impact it had on the generation that lived through it. I was born during the depression, but I have no memory of it. I do have memories of parents, relatives, and family friends who did live through it, discussing it.

The depression started in the fall of 1929, October to be exact. Business and the stock market had performed exceedingly well during most of the 1920s. The stock market had roared ahead for a decade; the Dow Jones Industrial Averages moved from around 60 to over 370 by the fall of 1929, an increase of 6 times in just 10 years. Fortunes made in stocks made millionaires common. Business was booming, and it was an era of "modern" technologies and innovative, thriving industries. Skyscrappers began to dot the skylines of major American cities for the first time. The automobile opened a new avenue of transportation for everyone. The telephone made communications instant. Radio and the motion pictures revolutionized entertainment. Life was good, and it was going to get better.

Then the depression hit. Suddenly, millions were out of work. The government's calculation of unemployment by 1932 was officially 25%, but most assumed that it was much higher in reality because of the way the government measured unemployment. The stock market declined in sudden and swift moves. It dropped about in half from October to the end of 1929. It recovered some in the spring of 1930, as it was about to do several times in the next decade, and some, including President Hoover, thought the worst was over. By 1932, the Dow had fallen to 42, an almost 90% drop from the highs of the summer of 1929. Investors attracted into the market during the boom times of the previous decade had made fortunes as the markets hit continuous new highs. Now they lost everything. They lost their investments, their business, their jobs, and often their homes all at once. People withdrew savings from their bank accounts in record numbers causing nearly half the banks in the country to fail, close their doors forever. And there was no Federal Deposit Insurance on bank accounts. If your bank went under, you lost all your deposits just when you could least afford it.

The depression seemed endless to those who lived through it. For many, it broke their spirit, their confidence in the country, its political and economic system severely shaken. Many would never recover. There were periodic upswings in both the economy and the stock market. But each time the market looked brighter, it would end in a new plunge to what seemed like lower and lower levels.

The depression clearly ended with the gigantic government spending on the military that accompanied World War II. Finally, jobs were available for all.

Those who lived through the depression had strong memories of it. Many were much more cautious with their money and investments because of it. Most of those who survived and remember the depression are either gone or retired today. Most of today's investor class knows the depression only as part of a chapter in a history test, after World War I and before World War II.

But could we have another depression? There is no easy answer to this question. Economists still don't fully understand the Great Depression and disagree on what caused it. In fact, depressions were common during the 19th century. Often, the cause was money speculation and wide currency swings or manipulations. Since 1940, we have experienced many "recessions," some of them punishing and severe. But nothing has occurred even close to the order of magnitude of the 1930s. In the modern era, we are devastated if unemployment goes above 10% and the stock market drops 20% or 25%. It is hard to imagine what would happen if we experience depression-like conditions again. The Dow at 1,500, unemployment at 25%, it is almost unimaginable. Some economists believe that another 1930s-type depression is impossible. We have insurance for bank accounts, stock market margin is 50% not 5%, and the US economy is an integral part of the world economy. I can't answer this question with authority, but I do believe that another depression is more than just a possibility. If it happens, it probably won't be like the Great Depression. It will be different, perhaps related to some currency issues, a world economic crisis, an environmental catastrophe, or related to some newfangled, difficult to understand, investment vehicle that always crowd the horizons. Maybe the government's budget shortfall will run out of control, or the trade deficit will tank the dollar. I don't know. But I believe the investment plan in this book has the capacity to survive another depression.

Can This Plan Survive and Thrive a Depression?

The million-dollar question is, literally, can this or any long-term investment plan survive a depression?

An investment analysis of stocks and mutual funds from the 1920s clearly shows that, on paper, investments in funds like the MFS fund used earlier in this book survived the depression. I say on paper because it could only survive depression conditions in theory. For most Americans, conditions in the depression were so bad that any investment funds, no matter to what level they had fallen, had to be liquidated for family survival. They had to eat and find shelter. Holding on to downtrodden mutual funds or stocks on the theory that they may recover their pre-depression levels (they did in 1954, some 25 years later) was impossible for many. The truth is that having your investments remain intact, hold and hold and reinvest distributions, would probably be physically impossible for most American families if a future depression was as severe as the 1930s. Long-term investing does work theoretically, on paper. The 1924 MFS fund still returned an over 9% compound return for anyone who was able to hold on during the devastating decade of the 1930s for the long-term.

The next depression may not be as devastating as 1929, and I am not asking you to put all your savings and investment dollars into this plan. It will take some discipline, but I am convinced that many of you could survive a mild or moderate depression with your investment plan intact. And it will be more important than ever that you do so. A depression will surely mean that your other chances for wealth and financial success will have decreased dramatically. You will depend even more on this retirement plan for a comfortable future. It may be the only thing you have left. The question to ask again is, are you willing to stick to it?

The Actual Advantages of Downturns

As I mentioned in other chapters, there are some benefits to downturns, particularly downturns in the stock market. Good companies that survive downturns do still suffer. Many of them pay annual dividends and have shareholders who depend on those dividends to live. Part of the company's stock price value, whether it is high or low, depends on those dividend payouts. Cutting dividends can have a devastating impact on shareholders and on the company's stock price. If at all possible, companies will often try to avoid cutting dividends or try to make the needed cuts as small and painless as possible. This means that for many companies, downturns mean that they simply pay out a higher percentage of their reduced earnings in dividends than they did previously. For investors in dividend-paying stocks or mutual funds who reinvest in added stock, this can actually be a great advantage. The investor who reinvests dividends in added stock when stock prices are low is getting more shares for each dividend dollar than he or she would have had the company stock remained high. With an eventual recovery of the economy and the company stock price at some future date, our consistent investor now has more shares of the company stock than he or she would have if the downturn had not occurred. Downturns, recessions, and even depressions can actually increase an investor's total value dramatically. Figure 23A1 shows the result today of a theoretical investor of $1,000 in the S&P composite in 1871 as it happened (including the dramatic stock decline in the Great Depression) and a hypothetical assumption that the Great Depression never occurred. Distributions did not change in the two examples, and final stock price was the same, but shares of stock held increased significantly because of the depression. In this case, the depression made our $1,000 investor an additional $45 million. Dollar distributions were the same in both assumptions, the actual distributions that occurred, but those dollars distributions bought more shares of stock in the depression assumption than in the non-depression assumption.

Our theoretical investor would have had to have the wherewithal to stay invested through the depression and continue to reinvest all distributions. Not an easy chore, but the results show that his or her return increased about 68% because the depression occurred. This works just as well for run-of-the-mill recessions. Assuming the company survives the downturn and returns to normalcy after the recession, reinvesting dividend dollars at lower stock prices is very profitable to long-term investors. Recessions are also scary, but they can be useful. Chapter 25 has more

—

examples of the benefits of downturns. Long-term investors do not fear downturns in the stock market.

FIGURE 23A1 Standard and Poor's Composite
Total Return, 1871-2004[112]
Comparing Depression and Hypothetical No Depression Conditions
$1,000 Investment in 1971

	Total Final Result in 2004
Actual results with depression	$110,634,735
Hypothetical results assuming no depression	$65,659,299
Percent lost if no depression	40.66%

Potential of Inflation

We cannot spend this entire chapter on depressions. We need to look a little closer at inflation. We saw in Chapter 13 that even a little of inflation every year can have a devastating impact on an investor's returns in the long-term. We have had consistent inflation, with no depressions, for the past 65 years so it is likely that we will have a continuing battle with some inflation for the next 65 years.

Runaway Inflation

We have not had anything like a runaway inflation in the United States. In the late 1970s and early 1980s, the inflation rate did hit double digits (over 10%) for a few years. The Federal Reserve Bank cranked interest rates up to historic levels, and after a few painful years and a difficult recession, the economy straightened out and inflation moderated substantially. In the past 20 years, inflation has been taming, slowing, and in recent years, it has been downright low for those of us that have long memories.

Runaway inflation has occurred in world history. Often, it is related to loss of confidence in and flights out of currencies. The most memorable was the one experienced in 1923 by Germany and Austria. It was devastating, just as bad as the depression of the 1930s, maybe even worse. It did not last as long. Runaway inflation can be devastating to business and the economy and would certainly have a negative impact on stocks. It is hard to judge how severe that impact would be. Prices of individual stocks might go up dramatically as the value of the currency went down. Higher stock prices in the face of huge inflation might not mean a lot. Our "real" return measures, what our dollars can buy in goods and services, could be decimated. If our stocks double but prices of goods and services go up 10 times, we are not better off than we were. In fact, the Internal Revenue Service would still want to tax us on our stock price increase if we sold the stock, even though we would have lost a fortune.

Runaway inflation is an ever-present risk but probably not a likely one. The Federal Reserve Bank seems intent on watching for even small signs of inflationary pressures, and this vigilance makes runaway inflation a more distant risk than a Great Depression. It is hard to advise investors what to do if runaway inflation does hit us. Unlike depression, we have little experience that tells us that an investor who continues to hold and reinvest during a runaway inflation will come out on top. Hard assets may be the best resort in a runaway inflation; gold, silver, platinum, even copper, diamonds, and precious jewels may well be the best investment in the unlikely event of uncontrollable inflation. Putting a part of your financial investments in hard assets to protect against runaway inflation is a smart idea. I have about 5% of my total investments in gold coins. Runaway inflation would be one of the few reasons that I might recommend considering a change in investment strategy.

Eat Away Inflation

The more likely inflation that you will experience we might call "eat a way" inflation. This is inflation that eats away at your results little by little each year. This might be an inflation of between 1% and 3% yearly, perhaps popping up periodically with higher inflation rates as the Federal Reserve Bank works interest rates higher until it is under control again. In Chapter 13, *The Corrosive Impact of Inflation*, we looked at the impact of this kind of inflation on stock returns. We also looked at the possibility and speculation that some inflation can be good for stock market returns.

Inflation has an important impact, but as we saw in Chapters 14 and 15, the impact of inflation on stock market returns can be moderated and even be removed with added time.

—

Can This Plan Survive and Thrive Inflation?

I think, the plan outlined in this book can survive and prosper during a modest or moderate inflation. I am not going to contend that stock prices benefit from modest inflation, but it is possible. If the FED could wave a magic wand over the economy and remove inflation, that is impose zero inflation, would stocks benefit from that environment? Possibly, but some would argue that a long-term investor will end up with better inflation-adjusted returns if there is a little inflation in the system than if we stamp it out altogether. Runaway inflation presents a different problem since we have no modern-day experience with it in the United States. It seems hard to argue that runaway inflation would do anything but harm a long-term stock market investor.

Can You Stick to It?

I always end asking some version of the same question: can you, our investor, stick to the plan?

Sticking to this plan under some inflation may be easier to do than under a depression or runaway inflation. We can hope that we will not have devastating unemployment in the next depression. If we have modest inflation rates, stocks will probably move higher, but will they move up enough to make inflation-adjusted returns positive? As long as normalcy returns to the economy at some point, long-term investors should be able to survive with their plan intact.

Plan B

Nothing is perfect in life, and the reader should not use this book as the total answer to his or her life's financial questions. As I suggested before, this is your plan "B." It should be your backup plan in case all else fails. I hope that you never need to use it, that it never matters to you since you have been so successful with your own business plans or your other investment plans. But I also hope that you can sleep a little easier at night, knowing that you have an investment plan in place that can survive most economic conditions. This plan doesn't force you to rely entirely on your own skills and luck. It will leave you, if all else fails, in a good place when you enter the twilight of your life.

CHAPTER 24

Implement the Plan Now!

To carry out any plan, you must first have a plan. To develop a plan, you will need, at the minimum, the following pieces of information:

- Your age (or the age of the person for whom the investment is intended).
- Estimated years until retirement of the plan recipient.
- Dollar goal at retirement.
- Funds available to invest within 1 year.
- Funds available to invest yearly.
- Do you (or does the plan recipient) qualify for a Roth IRA?
- Do you (or does the plan recipient) qualify for a traditional IRA if you do not qualify for a Roth?
- Are you (or is the plan recipient) employed and a participant in your employer's retirement plan?

Take a piece of paper, or if you are computer savvy, open a new document in word, and try to answer the 8 questions listed above. Table 21 in the appendix is a sample plan form.

For age, put your age if you are investing for you. If you are investing for someone else, like a child or grandchild, put both their age and your age.

For our purposes, I am going to suggest that you ignore the possibility of extended life spans. You can use the strong possibility that life spans will be longer in the 21st century as your hedge against inflation. Make

—

the rough assumption that you will counter future inflation with a longer investment period. Use 70 as your retirement age since that is the age when most tax-advantaged retirement plans first require distributions. If you are 19 now, your years until retirement for investment purposes are 51. You may actually retire before 70, but we are assuming that you will keep your investment plan in place until you are 70. If you are investing for an infant grandchild, his or her retirement years are 70.

State your dollar goal for the recipient at retirement, $1 million, $10 million in today's dollars. You can adjust this later when we will see if the funds available to you can meet your goal. Do not, at this point, try to adjust for inflation.

Put down the dollar amount of funds that you have available or that you wish to devote to this retirement investment plan immediately or within 1 year of today. If you are employed, how much can you save in the next year? If you have funds available now, perhaps invested in something else or in cash, list that amount.

Put down how much you estimate you can save each year or for the next 5 or 10 years to add to this retirement plan.

Answer whether you qualify for a Roth IRA (see Chapter 17).

Answer whether you qualify for a traditional IRA if you do not qualify for a Roth.

Answer whether you are a participant in an employer-sponsored retirement plan.

Fill out your copy of Table 21 as a starting point. Figure 24A2 is a sample investment plan. I assume that I (or the person I am investing for) am 19 years old. I have 51 years until I am 70. I want $3 million in this plan at retirement. I have or will have $3,000 available to invest this year, and I estimate that I can save about $2,000 per year after this year. I qualify for a Roth IRA and am not a participant in an employer retirement plan at my work.

Figure 24A2 allows you to calculate how much the funds that you have available to invest can produce in the required years. In the appendix, I have included tables (Tables 24A1-24A8), which allow you to calculate returns on both onetime investments and yearly investments for rates of return from 7% to 13%, including 11.76% (my preferred rate). If you are making the same investment every year, just use the right column of the appropriate table. In this case, we used the left section ($1 invested onetime for years) for a onetime investment to calculate our return on our initial $3,000 investment. It turns out that each dollar invested for 51 years at 11.76% returns $290.139. And $3,000 times $290.139 returns $870,417. Then we used the right section to calculate our return on our yearly investment of $2,000. And $1 invested every year for the next 51 years at 11.76% yearly produces $2,747.80. And $2,000 per year produces $5,495,600 (2,000 times $2,747.80) for a total return at the end of 51 years of $6,366,017, well more than our $3 million goal. It is a good idea to try to carry out a plan like this that has a significant amount of projected excess funds. This gives an investor some cushion in case the compound rate of return on the securities selected misses his or her target or as a hedge against the impact of inflation on returns.

If you come up short, you can calculate exactly how much added money you need to save and invest to meet your goal for retirement. For instance, suppose in Table 21 you had stipulated a goal of $10 million. Now you are short in Figure 24A2 by some $3.6 million. You need to either increase your initial first year investment from $3,000 to $15,752 or increase your yearly investment from $2,000 to $3,746 to meet your goal of $10,000,000 at retirement.

If you are closer than 50 years to retirement, you can also use Tables 24A1-24A8 in the appendix to calculate how much you need to invest now and for the remaining years to have a stated sum at retirement. Suppose you only have 20 years until retirement and you would like to know how much you would have to put away, at 11.76% compounded, each year to have $1 million in 20 years. Go to Table 24A1 for 11.76% and find the number that tells you how much you will have for each single dollar invested every year at 11.76% in 20 years. It turns that each dollar produces $78.32 in 20 years. And $1,000,000 divided by $78.22 equals $12,784, which is how much you must save and invest each year to be a millionaire at retirement in 20 years. Chapter 27 has more detailed information for investors who have less time left until retirement. One caution about retirement calculations when you have fewer years left until retirement: not only do you have to invest more money to reach a given goal but, in addition, the normally high likelihood that your compound rate of return will meet its target decreases substantially. As noted previously, once you get beyond 20 or 30 years, the achieved compound rate of return does not vary a lot. But if you are calculating for 20, 10, or less years, the impact of retiring in a down cycle in the market is much greater on rate of return than if you have invested for a longer time.

FIGURE 24A2 Calculation of Estimated Ending Total Value Retirement Fund

Calculation Steps	
Amount invested to start	$3,000
Amount to invest yearly	$2,000
Estimated compound rate of return	11.76%
Years until retirement or withdrawal	51
Amount in Table 24A1 (11.76%) for 51 years	290.139
Multiply 290.139 times $3,000	$870,417
Amount in Table 24A1 (11.76%) for 51 Years	2,747.80
Multiply 2,747.80 times $2,000	$5,495,600
Total estimated value at retirement	*$6,366,017*
Total dollar goal at retirement	$3,000,000
Excess retirement funds	$3,366,017
Short retirement funds	000

The Four-Step Implementation Plan

Get the Money!

The first step in implementation of your plan is to get the money for your initial investment. If you already have savings and are willing to commit them to this plan, go for it. If you have to get a job to raise the money, do it now, don't wait. Numbers are great to look at, but they are only numbers. The only way this plan will mean anything to you is if you can find the money. The hardest part of starting any investment plan is making the first investment. Once you do that, it gets easier. A very wealthy investor once told me that the hardest part of getting to $100 million is the first $10 million. And from 0 to $1 million will probably be harder than $1 million to $10 million.

Select a Tax Avoidance System

Once you have the money you must select the tax avoidance system that works best for you. If you qualify, use the Roth IRA as your initial choice unless you already have a high income. If your income is large, you may not qualify for Roth, and the tax deduction of the traditional IRA may make it more attractive. You may need to consult an accountant to help you make this decision. If your income is high to start with (over $100,000 per year), you probably already have an accountant.

For most of you, the Roth IRA will be the way to go. If you take part in a retirement plan at work, make sure that you fully fund it and make all the contributions you can within the legal limits, especially those that qualify for matching by your employer. Then select investment index funds that fit the strategy outlined in Chapter 22. Normally, this will be some total stock market fund, an S&P 500 fund, or an equity and income fund that specializes in high dividend-paying stocks.

If you take part in a retirement plan at work, you may still be able to open a Roth or traditional IRA if your regular income is not large. You need to consult with an accountant to decide if you qualify. If you do, and have the extra funds, do it now.

Young people need to understand that both traditional and Roth IRAs may not be available to them once they start to work in the business world. If you start and invest in IRAs now, you may have to stop additional investing in them once you take a job that offers you a 401K or different retirement plan. But you can keep your existing investments growing, tax-free or deferred, until age 70. It is another strong reason to start a retirement plan using an IRA early in life.

If you take part in a retirement plan at work and are not able to open any kind of IRA but you still have extra funds that you would like to put to work, consider an annuity (see Chapter 18).

Select Investment Alternatives

Next you must decide about investment alternatives. Use Chapter 22 to guide you. Do not exasperate yourself too much about this. If you use the advice in Chapter 22 and divide your investments in a reasonable manner, differences in investment selection may not make a big difference in the end. If you don't want to upset yourself about it, stick with a broad-based mutual fund with low yearly costs. You don't need to pick stocks like a pro to take part in this plan.

The most important point is to take action.

Take Action—"Get It and Forget It"

Take action today or the first day that you can. My advice is to make your investment choices, structure your investment vehicles, open your accounts, and invest. Then forget about it, at least until the next time you are required to invest according to your plan. To paraphrase the guy on TV selling those neat ovens, "Get It and Forget It."

You Don't Have to Talk to Anyone—Use the Internet

If you want to use my preferred method of opening your account using the Internet without talking to anyone, here is how to do it:

Traditional and Roth IRA:

- Open www.Vanguard.com.
- Got to "Personal Investors."
- Sign up for access by clicking on "Sign up for Access" (no cost to you).
- Click on "Account Types and Services."
- Click on "Retirement."
- Click on "Traditional IRA" or "Roth IRA."
- Read as much of the information as you need.
- Click on "Invest Now"—Read.
- Click on "Invest Now" again.
- Enter your ID and password.
- Mark in "Traditional" or "Roth" whichever applies and click on "Continue."
- Mark on "Vanguard Mutual Funds" and click on "Continue."
- Mark in "Open a New IRA for me" and click on "Continue."
- Mark a method of payment, "Bank Transfer" of "Check" and click on "Continue."
- Select the fund you wish to invest your money in (See Chapter 22), highlight and click "Continue."
- Enter the amount you intend to invest and the year of the contribution (if requested) and click on "Continue."
- *Important*—Make sure you indicate to reinvest all dividends and capital gains and click on "Continue."
- Indicate whether you wish to name a primary beneficiary and click on "Continue."
- Enter % to each beneficiary, if appropriate, and click on "Continue."
- Name a secondary beneficiary, if appropriate, and click on "Continue."
- Review your account application, if correct, and click on "Submit."

- Finish application online or by printing it for mailing with a check.

I went through this entire procedure so that you can see how easy it is. Really, you don't need my instructions, just follow the instructions on the screen. If you are using a different mutual fund family, it will be similar, just follow their instructions.

If you select the mail-in alternative, you should make a copy of your application and check and mail it in. You will then have taken the first and most critical step to financial security. I say this for a reason. The hardest thing to do is to start. Once you begin, the likelihood that you will continue investing and actually have a retirement plan at retirement goes up significantly.

If you want to buy some individual stocks, you will take a different path at "Account Types and Services." Here you will go to "General Investing" and then to "Brokerage Accounts" and continue to open a brokerage account with Vanguard. It is just as easy.

Or Call a Broker

If you would rather call a broker, he or she will ask you basically the same questions the mutual fund family will, and they will fill out the form for you based on the information you give. Have the information in the previous section handy. Many brokers are helpful, especially to young people opening their first account. They see the potential for a big investment trader down the road. Tell your broker where you want to invest your money. Use the advice in Chapter 22.

Many brokerage houses have their own mutual funds and will try to convince you to invest with them. Don't agree to this. Ask for the yearly fees and other expenses and compare them to Vanguard or the other low cost funds. In Chapter 16, we looked at the cost to investors of excessive fees and other expenses. There is no reason to incur added costs, especially if you are simply investing in an index fund.

Tell the broker that you are a long-term investor and have no interest in trading. They may nod approval, but it probably won't prevent them from trying to turn you into a trader. I have found that after a while, and my refusal of several requests for trades, the brokers get the hint and let you alone. It reminds me of all the catalogs that you get at home. If you buy something through a catalog even once, you will be hounded forever with more of them. If you agree to trade on a broker's suggestion once, he or she will come back again and again for more.

Stick to your plan; remember, stockbrokers have their own motivations that rarely are in sync with yours. Don't let a broker snow you or try to intimidate you with how smart he or she is or how rich he or she can make you. If he or she is so rich, why is he or she wasting his or her time trying to convince a small investor where to put his or her money?

If you are investing in individual stocks, the broker will probably try to steer you away from your intended investments toward the stocks he or she likes and the firm is probably pushing. This is especially true if he or she senses that you are an inexperienced stock market investor. Don't let them do this. Not with your retirement funds. Tell them firmly that these are the stocks or funds you want to invest in, and if they are not happy with that, you will take your business elsewhere.

Discount brokers, like Charles Schwab, will make trades at a lower cost per trade than full-service brokers. There are several of them, and they offer varying levels of service. Fortunately, a long-term investor doesn't require much service. All of them will let you open your account online or by talking to someone. Usually discount brokers will not try as hard to sway you to other investments, so if you want to use a "real" person to invest with, they are a good choice.

How to Stick to the Plan?

The first condition is to start. It may sound silly, but if you put off starting until next month or next year, the chances that you will ever start go way down. I would rather see you start now with a smaller amount than wait until you cumulate a larger amount later. Don't let mutual fund minimums deter you from starting. If you have to, start with a small stock investment or cumulate funds in a money market fund until you are ready.

Don't watch your investments too closely! This may sound like strange advice, but the closer you watch your returns, the more likely it is that, at some point, you will give up on your strategy. And you will be tempted to give up. Look at any of the long-term charts of returns in this book. In every one of them, including Altria, there are years when an investor was tempted to give up. The stock is down, the market is down, the returns are below my expectation, the democrats just won the White House, or whatever. There will always be times when you are tempted, and the closer you watch your investments, the more likely it is that you will fail to fulfill your plan. It would be better if you were Rip Van Winkle, made your investments, and woke up 50 years later to see what happened. Look at them once or twice a year. That is enough.

Make all additional investments on a specific day that you will not forget, your birthday, your anniversary, April fool's day, or whatever. Invest on the day in your plan. If you don't have the funds you had planned to invest, invest less but invest now. Don't wait. Time is the greatest wealth machine ever invented. Use it!

When to Fail!

Don't wait another minute! If you have the money, do it now. Don't wait for the market to drop! Don't wait so you can watch your investment selections for a while. If this is your beginning, do it right now, this day, this minute.

If you have to fail in completion of this investment plan, fail in the later years. Make sure that you get through the first 10 or 20 years without failing, that is where the lion's share of the return comes from. Figures 25B1 and 25C1 show the dramatic difference in final returns for an investment made today and the same investment made 10, 20, 30 years, or more from now. The investment you are making today will produce, by far, the biggest dollar for dollar return of all your future investments, even if you invest more in later years. These dollars, even if they are fewer, will produce bigger returns than more dollars later. Don't fail before you even implement the plan, start now!

Chapter 25

The Nature and Characteristic of Your Return

In this chapter, I want to look at the nature and characteristics of the returns that you are likely to receive so you will be prepared for whatever the stock market has to offer. I am going to look at 5 stocks and 3 mutual funds as well as the S&P composite. We will look at historic returns overall, yearly, for different holding periods, from market tops and bottoms, return variations based on rate of return, back-loaded return characteristics, and volatility. I will look at returns from the S&P composite, the Dow, two MFS funds, my Stratton Fund, Altria, AT&T, Procter & Gamble, General Electric, ExxonMobil, and DuPont. I included Stratton Growth Fund since it is the one investment that I made in which I unintentionally followed the advice I am giving in this book. I will also look at the risks to return associated with being out of the market. I selected these to give the reader comparisons to look at that include average returns, above-average returns, and below-average returns.

The chapter will make sure that the investor understands the nature of the return he or she can expect, the timing of the returns, and specifically what they should look for in deciding whether a particular investment is meeting his or her goals.

Overall Returns

Figure 25A1 shows the potential returns available for a $10,000 investment using the historic compound rates of returns for several different assets for 5 different periods. You can use this data to estimate what the return on an investment might be if the future is anything like the past. This figure assumes that you invest $10,000 once and reinvested all dividends using a tax-deferred or tax avoidance investment account. It shows what you might earn if the returns in the future are the same as they have been in the past. The S&P returned 9.05% compounded for 134 years. If that same return continues for the next 20, 35, 50, 60, or 70 years, you can see the return possible in the first four rows of Figure 25A1. Your $10,000 will produce $56,561 in 20 years and $1,809,423 in 60 years. Looking at the "star" of the stock market for the last 50-60 years, a $10,000 investment in Altria will produce $5,490,897 in 35 years if it continues to compound at the same rate of return it compounded at for the last 46 years. It will produce $4,046,278 in 35 years if Altria continues to compound at the same rate of return it compounded at for the last 34 years. It may be unlikely that Altria can reproduce this return, but who knows. I have included 3 starting periods for DuPont, which has been a below-average performer. The results show that with a $10,000 investment, you would need 60 years to become a millionaire if DuPont compounds at its 46-year average rate but only 50 years if it compounds at more recent return rates from either 1962 or 1970.

As we saw in Chapters 9 and 5, time and rate of return both have a spectacular influence on returns. If you can find a stock that outperforms the averages, your return will go up dramatically. Look at the difference for any time frame between DuPont 1957 and Altria 1957. For that matter, look at the difference if Altria compounds at its 1957-2003 rate or its 1970-2004 rate. A 1% increase in the rate of return produced almost $1.5 million extra return in 35 years.

FIGURE 25A1 Historic Returns of $10,000 Investment Example

Investment	Long-Term Rate of Return	20 Years	35 Years	50 Years	60 Years	70 Years
S&P 1870[113]	9.05%	$56,561	$207,443	$760,823	$1,809,423	$4,303,253
S&P 1946[114]	11.76%	92,412	489,806	2,596,089	7,891,937	23,990,954
S&P 1957[115]	10.85%	78,472	367,917	1,724,983	4,832,166	13,536,264
S&P 1970[116]	11.02%	80,914	388,189	1,862,349	5,297,529	15,069,041
MFS 1924[117]	9.23%	58,457	219,770	826,222	1,997,634	4,829,869
MFS 1935[118]	10.69%	76,237	349,779	1,604,794	4,431,015	12,234,525
Stratton 1972[119]	12.17%	99,434	556,782	3,117,712	9,831,124	31,000,621
Altria 1957[120]	19.75%	367,714	5,490,897	81,992,873	497,200,235	3,014,994,652
Altria 1970[121]	18.71%	308,849	4,046,278	53,010,909	294,603,769	1,637,236,240
AT&T 1957[122]	10.50%	73,662	329,367	1,472,699	3,997,023	10,848,244
DuPont 1957[123]	8.30%	49,268	162,928	538,794	1,195,935	2,654,556
DuPont 1962[124]	10.78%	77,487	359,872	1,671,352	4,652,449	12,950,760
DuPont 1970[125]	10.59%	74,872	338,887	1,533,885	4,197,121	11,484,446
Exxon 1957[126]	12.55%	106,392	626,747	3,692,113	12,042,869	39,281,219
Exxon 1970[127]	15.07%	165,699	1,360,423	11,171,350	45,470,192	185,075,068
GE 1940[128]	12.85%	112,210	687,947	4,217,724	14,128,427	47,327,050
GE 1957[129]	12.21%	100,145	563,774	3,173,789	10,043,700	31,784,060
GE 1970[130]	14.32%	145,360	1,082,125	8,055,839	30,713,757	117,099,517
PG 1957[131]	14.26%	143,842	1,062,424	7,847,133	29,761,388	112,874,381
PG 1970[132]	15.85%	189,636	1,723,302	15,660,366	68,196,532	296,976,900

Yearly Returns

The return rates for different investments varied depending on the investment but not as much as one might suppose. In the appendix are the compound rates of return based on year invested for the S&P since 1870 (Table 6A1), GE since 1940 (Figure 8A2 in Chapter 8), and the MFS fund (Table 10A1) since 1924. Figure 25A2 shows a summary of the highest and lowest returns, using a minimum investment period of 30 years for these investments. Obviously, investing during down years, like the 1973/1974 period, produces that highest compound return rate once the investment recovers and makes new highs. The S&P rate range since 1946 is fairly narrow from a high of 12.07% to a low of 10.23%, quite stable. An individual stock is likely to be more volatile than an index, but they also present opportunities to improve average return rates, which will have a significant impact on the result.

Figure 25A2 Highest and Lowest Rate of Returns

	Lowest Rate Start Year	Lowest Rate	Highest Rate Start Year	Highest Rate
S&P 1870[133]	1871	9.03%	1974	13.60%
S&P 1946[134]	1961	10.23%	1973	12.07%
GE 1940[135]	1959	11.20%	1973	14.47%

The returns rates in Figure 25A2 show that for a long-term investor the date on which you enter the market is important but not as important as entering. It is true that, as we saw in Chapter 5, small differences in return rates translate into large differences in total return. But even the lowest return rate in Figure 25A2 is significant and has the potential to make you a millionaire or more.

There are 3 main reasons I do not favor waiting for a poor stock market in hopes of maximizing your return rate. First, identifying the bottom is always obvious when looked at many years after the fact. It is usually impossible to discover the bottom while it is happening, and you run the risk of being out of the market for the short bursts upward that can make up a large percentage of your return. As pointed out earlier, there is no evidence that suggests that even market professionals can pick market tops and bottoms accurately over a long period of time. Figure 25A4 shows you the difference in total returns for an investor who was out of the market and missed some bull markets. It shows that if you missed the 3 best years of investing in the S&P in the last 60 years, your return dropped 71.2%. If you missed the 3 best years in the MFS fund since 1924, your return declined over 67%. Even missing 1 year can cost you millions. Missing the one best year in the S&P cost you around $2.6 million and almost $4 million in the MFS fund. It is not worth the risk. Even if you could tell the bottom accurately, you may have to wait years until the market hits bottom. That can dramatically reduce your return as suggested in Figure 25A3. Figure 25A3 shows the interaction between time and return for the S&P by comparing the highest return and the lowest return, assuming waiting periods of 5, 10, and 15 years. If you could time the market and select the highest return year since 1946 to begin investing in the S&P, you would have achieved higher total returns only if you could do it by waiting less than 5 years to find that high starting rate of return. If you have to wait 10 years, you only get 50 years of investing instead of 60; the lower yearly rate of return actually produces a higher total dollar return ($3.4 million versus $2.9 million for the higher rate of return for only 50 years). The breakeven point occurs somewhere between 8 and 9 years of waiting. In general, if you wait to try to find a year in which the stock market will produce the highest rate of return, you won't be better-off unless your wait is less than 8 years. It is obvious, with 20/20 hindsight that starting your investment plan in 1932, 1973, or 1982, all interim low points for the market, would have produced superior rates of return. But how much would you have lost in compounded dollar returns at a lower rate while you wait? Without the benefit of hindsight, waiting with hopes of identifying market bottoms years from now does not pay. Finally, it looks easy on paper to identify market bottoms, but you have to be able to keep disciplined and wait for years. Identifying and buying at the bottom, when everyone is pessimistic and all the experts are predicting further lows, is hard to do, and trying to time the market may make implementation of a long-term investment plan impossible. Many investors believed that the market hit its lows at the end of 1929 in the Depression after it fell almost in half in a few months only to find that it dropped almost 80% in the next three years,.

FIGURE 25A3 Total Return for a $10,000 Investment in S&P Invested in Lowest Rate of Return for 60 Years versus Highest Rate for 45, 50, and 55 Years

S&P Returns[136]	60 Years	Wait 5 Years	Wait 10 Years	Wait 15 Years
10.23%	$3,451,350			
12.07%		$5,271,270	$2,890,020	$1,086,640

FIGURE 25A4 Total Return for a $10,000 Investment in S&P for 60 Years and MFS for 80 Years (Assumes 58-Year Rate of Return for S&P of 11.76%)

	Years	Missed Best Year	Missed 3 Best Years	Percent Lost Missing 3 Best Years
S&P, 60 years[137]	$7,866,560	$5,279,420	$2,716,620	71.2%
MFS Trust A[138] 1924-2004	$11,472,953	$7,504,815	$3,757,043	67.3%

The Back-End Load of Compound Returns

The return earned by an investor is skewed toward those who stay with the investment until the last possible year. The returns in dollars are back-loaded; the biggest dollar returns occur in the last years and the smallest dollar returns in the early years. Look at Figure 25A5, which summarizes an investor's position in 10-year increments for a $2,000 per year annual investment compounded at an 11.76% annual rate of return. As you can see, the extra 10 years almost triples an investor's result. If our investor stops his or her investment plan after 60 years, he or she has a more than respectable $15 million. But hold for just another 10 years and now they have over $45 million. Returns are back-end loaded because of compounding. An investor needs to build a base to get the big dollar returns. This is one of the reasons that there are not a lot of investors following a truly long-term strategy. The early years do not produce enough return, enough action to satisfy most investors, especially those with gambling instincts. Even an 11.76% annual return doesn't look like a lot when you are compounding $2,000. But as the years go by, the investor's base increases steadily and the same 11.76% yearly return in year 71 increases total value over $5 million in that year alone compared with $235 the first year on the first $2,000 invested.

FIGURE 25A5 Total Return—10-Year Increments
$2,000 Annual Investment at 11.76% Compound Rate of Return

10 Years	$38,773
20 Years	$156,639
30 Years	$514,944
40 Years	$1,604,166
50 Years	$4,915,329
60 Years	$14,981,041
70 Years	$45,580,126

Bull/Bear Markets

Bull and bear markets are sure to occur during your investment career. I pointed out the impact of dividend reinvestment during downturns. In this section, I want to look at the impact of downturns on investors' results. Investors who buy and hold shares in dividend-paying stocks through downturns, recessions or depressions, are better off if the share price returns to new highs than if the downturn had not occurred. The unique character of dividends and dividend reinvestment is responsible for this surprising phenomenon. During downturns, many companies try to maintain their dividend rate for shareholders who depend on those dividends, and companies try to hold their dividend at pre-downturn levels. Even when they are forced to reduce their dividends, they often do so by a smaller percentage than the stock price has declined. In either case, the dividend as a percentage of the share price, often called the yield, goes up. In general, in recessions and even in depressions, dividend yield rates rise. This means that investors who reinvest dividends in added shares end with more shares than they would have if there had been no decline in the stock price. Assuming the stock price does eventually return to new highs and normal compound rates of return, the investor who held through the recession or depression is actually richer because of it.

Figure 25A6 shows the compound rates of return for the S&P for three periods in the second column. The third column shows the result in dollars for an investor of $10,000 in the S&P at the beginning of the period, if no taxes were paid and all dividends were reinvested in added shares.

FIGURE 25A6 The Impact of Depressions and Recessions on Returns[139]

Standard and Poor's	Actual Compound Rate of Return	Total Final Value	Total Final Value after Elimination of Downturn	Actual Loss in Dollars	Adjusted Compound Rate of Return
1871-2004 Period Smoothed 1929-1955	9.12%	$1,106,347,348	$494,167,393	$612,179,955	8.47%
1946-2004 Period Smoothed 1972-1979	11.58%	$5,761,360	$5,305,985	$455,375	11.42%
1929-1955 Period Smoothed Entire	5.97%	$45,136	$29,995	$15,141	4.32%

The fourth column shows a theoretical final value assuming the downturn in stock price had not occurred. This assumes the stock price in 1929 never dropped and increased evenly from 1929 to 1955 until it reached the actual 1955 levels. The S&P composite went from 21 in 1929 to 45 in 1955, but it stopped along the way below 7. Columns 4 and 6 assume that the market never went to 7. It just went from 21 to 45 in those 26 years in evenly spaced increments. As you can see, when we assume no downturn, the investors return dropped dramatically. Our long-term investor would have lost over half of his or her final total value in 2004 ($494 million instead of $1.1 billion) if the depression had not occurred.

I then looked at the postwar period (1946-2004) and smoothed out the weak stock market from 1972-1979 in the same manner. In this case, elimination of the 1970s recession and stock price downturn cost our investor in the S&P $455,375. Finally, I looked at the depression period alone. Stock prices did not reach their pre-depression highs until 1954.

—

I looked at the 1929-1955 period and assumed that no depression had occurred, no drop in the S&P from 21 to 7 occurred, and our investor again lost significant value, about 1/3 of his or her final value ($15,141).

Ups and downs in the stock market are hard to take, but they actually make long-term investors more money. There are only two ways downturns hurt you in the long run. First, if because of the recession or depression, the market averages or your stock picks are never able to regain the pre-downturn levels and never resume their normal appreciation toward our target rate of return. The second way, and more likely scenario, is that you the investor become frightened by the downturn, withdraw some or all your investment or, just as devastating, you refuse to reinvest dividends in added stock. Dividend reinvestment during downturns is your chance to buy added stock at bargain prices,

Don't fear downturns. They are inevitable, and they are profitable for you. You will actually be richer in 50, 60, or 70 years because of downturns.

The Importance of Early Investing

One of the critical issues that investors need to understand is the importance of early investing. The time value of money discussed in Chapter 5 will never be more obvious than in Figure 25B1. Here, we assume two grandparents who decide to invest funds for a grandchild. In the first three columns, the first grandparent invested $1,000 at his or her grandchild's birth and $1,000 for four more years. Then, for whatever reason, he or she stopped investing. With no further investments, assuming our historic post-WWII annual compound rate of return, our grandchild has just over $9.7 million at age 70. In the right three columns, we assume a different grandparent who with the same general idea begins his or her $1,000 per year investing plan at the grandchild's 21st birthday. Instead of stopping after 5 years, he or she continues contributing (probably through a trust after his or her death) every year until the grandchild reaches 70 years old. The second grandparent contributed ten times the investment funds that the first grandparent did ($50,000 versus $5,000). The grandchild of the second grandparent ends with just under $2.5 million, about 25% of the final total of the first grandchild.

The message in Figure 25B1 should be crystal clear. Early investments, in a compound rate of return environment, count much more than later investments. This applies to anyone investing; the grandparent example is just that—an example of something that applies to all of us. Often, I get high school students in economics class who listen to my pitch and then say something like, "I'm in high school, and I'll worry about saving for retirement when I start a career." I show them that waiting until they are 27 instead of starting at 17 costs them around 60% of their total long-term investment at age 70. Whether you are investing for you or for someone else, the key is to start early and get as many years to compound returns as possible. The difference in final value is dramatic.

FIGURE 25B1[140] Total Return
Early Investment/Delayed Investment Compared

Grandparent 1			Grandparent 2		
Compound	Annual Return	11.76%	Compound	Annual Return	11.76%
Age	Investment	Total Value	Age	Investment	Total Value
1	$1,000	$1,118	1	$0	$-
2	$1,000	$2,367	2	$0	$0
3	$1,000	$3,763	3	$0	$0
4	$1,000	$5,323	4	$0	$0
5	$1,000	$7,066	5	$0	$0
6		$7,897	6	$0	$0
7		$8,826	7	$0	$0
8		$9,864	8	$0	$0
9		$11,024	9	$0	$0
10		$12,320	10	$0	$0
11		$13,769	11	$0	$0
12		$15,388	12	$0	$0
13		$17,198	13	$0	$0
14		$19,220	14	$0	$0
15		$21,481	15	$0	$0
16		$24,007	16	$0	$0
17		$26,830	17	$0	$0
18		$29,985	18	$0	$0
19		$33,511	19	$0	$0
20		$37,452	20	$0	$0
21		$41,857	21	$1,000	$1,118
22		$46,779	22	$1,000	$2,367
23		$52,280	23	$1,000	$3,763
24		$58,429	24	$1,000	$5,323

—

25	$65,300	25	$1,000	$7,066
26	$72,979	26	$1,000	$9,015
27	$81,561	27	$1,000	$11,192
28	$91,153	28	$1,000	$13,626
29	$101,872	29	$1,000	$16,346
30	$113,853	30	$1,000	$19,386
31	$127,242	31	$1,000	$22,784
32	$142,205	32	$1,000	$26,581
33	$158,929	33	$1,000	$30,824
34	$177,619	34	$1,000	$35,567
35	$198,507	35	$1,000	$40,867
36	$221,851	36	$1,000	$46,791
37	$247,941	37	$1,000	$53,411
38	$277,099	38	$1,000	$60,809
39	$309,686	39	$1,000	$69,078
40	$346,105	40	$1,000	$78,319
41	$386,806	41	$1,000	$88,647
42	$432,295	42	$1,000	$100,190
43	$483,133	43	$1,000	$113,090
44	$539,949	44	$1,000	$127,507
45	$603,447	45	$1,000	$143,619
46	$674,413	46	$1,000	$161,626
47	$753,723	47	$1,000	$181,751
48	$842,361	48	$1,000	$204,243
49	$941,423	49	$1,000	$229,379
50	$1,052,134	50	$1,000	$257,472
51	$1,175,865	51	$1,000	$288,868
52	$1,314,147	52	$1,000	$323,957
53	$1,468,691	53	$1,000	$363,171
54	$1,641,409	54	$1,000	$406,998
55	$1,834,439	55	$1,000	$455,979
56	$2,050,169	56	$1,000	$510,719
57	$2,291,268	57	$1,000	$571,897
58	$2,560,722	58	$1,000	$640,270
59	$2,861,862	59	$1,000	$716,683
60	$3,198,417	60	$1,000	$802,083
61	$3,574,551	61	$1,000	$897,526

62	$3,994,919	62	$1,000	$1,004,192
63	$4,464,721	63	$1,000	$1,123,403
64	$4,989,772	64	$1,000	$1,256,633
65	$5,576,569	65	$1,000	$1,405,530
66	$6,232,374	66	$1,000	$1,571,938
67	$6,965,301	67	$1,000	$1,757,916
68	$7,784,421	68	$1,000	$1,965,764
69	$8,699,868	69	$1,000	$2,198,056
70	$9,722,973	70	$1,000	$2,457,665

The Advantage of Yearly Investments

Steady, year-by-year investment plans are superior to onetime investments. There are many reasons for yearly investments. It obviously increases your total return by increasing your total investment, but it also forces continued attention and commitment to the original plan.

But don't let the idea of yearly investments confuse the issue of time. Early investments are worth much more than later ones. At 11%, a onetime investment of $10,000 is just about equal, in 70 years, to an investment of $1,000 every year. They both total right around $15 million. Obviously, a $10,000 investment every year is worth significantly more, $150 million.

My point here is that you should tailor your investments in whatever manner is most suitable for you. I like the yearly investment plan since it is likely that as a young person grows older, he or she will find it easier to save the needed investment dollars. But don't put off early investments, even smaller amounts, on the theory that large investments in later years will make up the difference. They probably will not do the job. Figure 25C1 shows the return results for both onetime and yearly investments at different rates of return. Figure 25C2 shows the difference in returns between investments made in 10-year intervals.

FIGURE 25C1 Total Return—One Time and Every Year
Investments Compared
Assumed 70 Years

Investment $	9% Return	10% Return	11% Return	12% Return
$1,000 Onetime	$416,730	$789,747	$1,488,091	$2,787,800
$1,000 Every year	$5,034,953	$8,676,217	$15,005,375	$26,010,132
$2,000 Onetime	$833,460	$1,579,494	$2,976,038	$5,575,600
$2,000 Every year	$10,069,907	$17,351,433	$30,010,750	$52,020,263
$5,000 Onetime	$2,083,650	$3,948,735	$7,440,096	$13,938,999
$5,000 Every year	$25,174,766	$43,380,083	$75,026,824	$130,050,659

FIGURE 25C2 Total Return to a One Time $10,000 Investment
Full 70 Years and Delayed Start

Begin Investment	9% Return	10% Return	11% Return	12% Return
Year 1—Full 70 Years	$4,167,301	$7,897,470	$14,880,191	$27,877,998
Delay Start—10 Years	$1,760,313	$3,044,816	$5,240,572	$8,976,969
Delay Start—20 Years	$743,575	$1,173,909	$1,845,648	$2,890,022
Delay Start—30 Years	$314,094	$452,593	$650,009	$930,510

Figure 25C1 clearly shows the rewards available for the consistent yearly investor. Investing every year instead of one time gives an investor 10 times the final return. At an 11% compound annual rate of return, investing $5,000 every year produces just over $75 million compared with $7.4 million for a onetime investor. Assuming lower return rates produces an even higher multiple of total return. At 9% a $2,000 onetime investor finishes with $833,460, but a $2,000 every year investor finishes with slightly more than $10 million. Figure 25C2 shows the added rewards for those who start their investment plan quickly and the penalties for those who delay. Every 10 years delayed loses about two-thirds of your final value. An investor who achieved 11% compounded for 70 years ended with just under $15 million for his or her onetime $10,000 investment. If he or she delayed that investment just 10 years, his or her return drops to $5.2 million and a delay of 20 years reduces it just over $1.8 million.

These figures illustrate two key points. The first point is that an investor should invest early, invest as much as he or she can, and if possible do it immediately. The second point is there are multiple returns possible for an investor who can manage a yearly investment plan.

286

CHAPTER 26

When to Change Course?

I am tempted to answer the question in the title of this chapter by simply saying "Never." The more I study historical returns for stocks, stock market averages, and funds, the less confidence I have that any of us can figure out when to change course. The question itself infers that something has happened to make the future fundamentally different from the present or the past. If something like that happens, it might pay to give up on this plan and try to find another one. But don't do it lightly.

Jeremy Siegel recently published some results that confirm this advice. Siegel studied the S&P averages for nearly 50 years, and I have used the results of some of his research throughout this book. His latest study was an attempt at analyzing the results if an investor had simply invested in the original 500 stocks in the S&P index and held them from 1957 until 2003. Or if the investor had adjusted his or her investment every time, Standard and Poor's changed the stocks comprising the 500 index. Standard and Poor's uses certain criterion to decide if a stock qualifies to belong or if an existing S&P member should be dropped. On average, they make about 20 changes a year in the index. Mutual funds that index their result to the S&P 500 must sell their shares in any companies that are dropped from the index and buy shares in any companies that are added. Stocks must meet earnings and liquidity standards. Most "experts" would argue that this is a good thing since certain industries go into decline and others unexpectedly develop. New companies like Microsoft, Cisco, and Intel were not in existence in 1957 and would not be able to join the index if the S&P did not update the members. Siegel compared returns from the original index members, assuming no adjustment (no deletions and no additions) to the adjusted S&P. He found, much to everyone's surprise, that an investor in the original S&P with no adjustments performed slightly better over the 46 years than an investor in the adjusted S&P.

This is not a big surprise to me. My personal experience (anecdotal as it may be) suggests that I would have been better off to hold my original stock selections many years ago instead of the multiple changes of strategy that I did pursue in reality. The inability of investment professionals to outperform the market averages over any reasonable period of years only confirms this conclusion.

Investment "experts" will try to convince you that you should trade stocks or try to time the market and that investing for the long run needs active stock selection management. My general advice is don't believe it. Stick it out, stay with your original selections in almost every case. I will go over some possible reasons to change course in the next section.

What if the plan seems to be working but one or all your investments is not performing up to par? Again, I would advise you to change course only after careful consideration and because of some fundamental change. In researching my own investment history, I made far more mistakes switching out of investments that I gave up on too early than I did by poor investment decisions to start. I gave you a little flavor of that in Chapter 1. I would have been much richer today if I had never looked at a *Wall Street Journal* or *Barron's*, if I had just held my first inclinations until today. The best you can do is to use the best information to make the best selections and let them alone. Don't hover over your stocks; don't jump at every piece of good information or every bad earnings report. Over a long period of time, every company and every fund will experience some good times and some not-so-good times. Expect it.

Changes to Worry About

Changes in Global Situation (Wars, Terrorism, Natural Disasters)

Global changes might make fulfillment of the investment plan in this book impossible. Nuclear war, out-of-control terrorism, or some natural disaster (asteroid hits the earth) would change everything. If something that big occurs, then all bets are off. We might all be dead anyway so it won't matter. My attitude is that if something this big so severely damages our country, the world, or our economy, there won't be many other

Chapter 27

What If I Don't Have Enough Time?

Not Enough Time—What If I Am 30, 40, 50, 60, or More?

A couple of questions that I get all the time from friends and relatives when I talk to them about long-term investing: Is there anything I can do if I don't have 50-80 years left? What if I am already 40, 50, or 60 years old? This chapter is for you!

Yes, there are several things that you can do, but remember, this is a book about long-term investing, and there are several factors that we cannot alter once we lessen the investment holding period.

Once we start looking at investing for 10 or 20 years, many of the assumptions that we made earlier are not as dependable. The shorter the period, the less you can count on a specific compound rate of return to meet their long-term historic averages. In a shorter period, the rates may exceed or fall short of the long-term averages.

Time is the key in our investment plan, and the less you have of it, the less years that you have to compound rates. We looked several times at the difference between 50 and 60 years or 60 and 70 years. Every 10 years multiplied dollar return significantly. The difference between a grandparent investing for a grandchild at birth and a 20-year-old beginning his or her investment plan today is enormous, and we can't repeal Einstein's Rule of 72. Believe me, if there was a way to repeal it, to get those long-term returns in a shorter period, I would have figured it out.

But don't lose heart. There are some things you can do.

Reduce Your Goals? No

There are only a couple of ways for a middle-aged or older investor to counter the loss of compounding returns over extended periods of time. One of the least appealing is to reduce your goals. Give up becoming a millionaire or more and settle for what you can make with the years left. If you are not willing to give up so easily (I agree with you), then you can look at three other choices.

Increase Your Investment Dollars

Many of us who have reached middle age have been fortunate to accumulate some investment funds. Many of us already have investments in the market, in stocks, bonds, CDs, or savings accounts. I have been using $10,000 as my standard investment amount, sometimes I use $1,000, but every time you increase your beginning investment dollars, you automatically increase your final return. Figure 27A1 looks at higher first investments with a shorter duration. Remember though, Figure 27A1 assumes an 11.76% compound annual rate of return, and assuming any rate in shorter than a 20—or 30-year time frame makes me uncomfortable. But it is worth a look. Here is what you would achieve after 10, 20, or 30 years of investing using the plan in this book and assuming a continuation of the post-WWII average compound rate of return of 11.76%.[141]

Figure 27A1 shows some real potential for middle-aged investors with added money to invest. Remember, to achieve these returns, you still need to invest based on the principles outlined in this book. You need to avoid taxes until retirement and reinvest all distributions and dividends in added stock. Those factors may be slightly less important, but they are still a critical part of your success.

**FIGURE 27A1 Results Based on Dollars Invested at 11.76%
Compound Rate of Return and Years Left Until Retirement**

Dollars Invested	10 Years Left	20 Years Left	30 Years Left
$25,000	$75,998	$231,030	$702,315
$50,000	$151,997	$462,059	$1,404,630
$100,000	$303,993	$924,119	$2,809,259
$200,000	$607,986	$1,848,238	$5,618,518
$500,000	$1,519,966	$4,620,595	$14,046,295
$1,000,000	$3,039,932	$9,241,189	$28,092,591

Figure 27A1 shows that it is possible to amass significant added retirement dollars if you have some investment dollars already amassed. For instance, if you have $200,000 to invest and 20 years left, an investment in an S&P index fund might just return you over $1.8 million. This assumes the S&P is going to grow at its historic 11.76% rate for the next 20 years. There is a good chance that this might happen, but you must accept the odds of achieving any yearly rate of return are much greater for someone with 40, 50, or 60 years of investing remaining. The good news is that you are just as likely to achieve a higher-than-average return as you are to achieve a lower one. If you have 30 years left, you might still end with over $5.5 million.

Earn a Higher Rate of Return

Older investors can try to offset the fewer years left by looking for a higher-than-average rate of return by investing in individual stocks. I looked at some of the companies we examined earlier in this book to see how a short-term investor might have fared over the last 10, 20, or 30 years. Figure 27A2 shows the 10-, 20—and 30-year returns for onetime investments of $10,000 or $100,000. In this figure, you can see the big difference in results even over shorter periods of time. If Altria repeats its past 30-year performance, a 40-year-old who invests $10,000 will have $1.9 million when he or she is 70, and if he or she can invest $100,000 today, he or she will have over $19 million.

**FIGURE 27A2 Actual Achieved Individual Stock Returns
for 10, 20, and 30 Years
Ending in 2004**

Stock	Assumes $10,000 Invested			Assumes $100,000 Invested		
	10 Years	20 Years	30 Years	10 Years	20 Years	30 Years
Boeing	$15,790	$109,983	$891,988	$157,905	$1,099,827	$8,919,882
Caterpillar	$58,387	$293,144	$285,840	$583,873	$2,931,443	$3,858,403
Disney	$21,433	$301,503	$963,603	$214,330	$3,015,034	$9,636,027
DuPont	$44,720	$221,199	$610,997	$447,202	$2,211,988	$6,109,967
Exxon	$43,298	$189,187	$1,085,099	$432,978	$1,891,969	$10,850,992
GE*	$49,131	$233,001	$1,185,859	$491,309	$2,330,014	$11,858,592
IBM	$57,419	$57,946	$347,303	$574,194	$579,461	$3,473,031
P&G*	$42,244	$230,747	$497,605	$422,445	$2,307,475	$4,976,051
Altria	$50,584	$417,283	$1,931,083	$506,835	$4,172,833	$19,310,834
Nestlé	$35,740	$118,212	$506,663	$357,395	$1,182,124	$5,066,632

*GE = General Electric, P&G = Procter & Gamble.

An investor who has $100,000 to invest but only 10, 20, or 30 years until retirement might invest in a basket of stocks, like these, that have outperformed the market averages in the past. Chapter 22 details my favorite selections. Again, the risk of the markets or individual stocks under performing their long-term average annual rate of return goes up substantially with fewer years. And remember that you still must follow the system by reinvesting all distributions and finding a way to either avoid all taxes or pay the taxes with other funds. But one advantage may be that the risk you take in stock or fund selection may be somewhat smaller with less years than the risk you take over longer time periods. Companies that are performing well now will probably continue to perform well for some years into the future. Altria's success is much more likely to continue over 10 or 20 years than over 50 or 60 years.

An investor who has less time and is looking to secure an above-average rate of return might try to get James O'Shaughnessy's book *What Works on Wall Street* and select one of O'Shaughnessy's top-ranked stock selection strategies. O'Shaughnessy has done the most extensive and thorough job of analyzing dozens of strategies in stock investing. You will have to devote more time to it, but it holds the promise of producing above-average rates of return that just might achieve your dollar goal over a shorter period of time.

Take More Time—Keep Your Investment Dollars Working

The last method I am going to suggest is to simply to take more time. Extending your retirement age or investment holding period just 5 or 10 years produces large increases in your returns. I have documented in a few chapters, Chapter 9 in particular, the dramatic impact of extra time on returns. An extra 10 years of investing at an 11.76% compound rate of return just about triples your total return. You can either postpone your retirement or you might retire at your normal age and simply keep your investment dollars working after retirement. This latter plan may just work for many older, near-retirement investors. If you can survive an extra 5 or 10 years in retirement without using the investment dollars in your investment account, you can achieve a bigger return and still retire on time. This may mean that you will need other sources of income along with social security to get you through those years. An investor who can avoid using his or her investment dollars can use time to his or her advantage. Don't stop your investment plan at retirement. Keep it going as long as you can. Maybe you will have to scrimp a little for a few years, but remember, it can triple your result every 10 years.

Stock Selection Advice for Investors with 20, 30, 40, 50 Years until Retirement

Investors with less time until retirement will need to select a combination of stocks and funds that produce a superior rate of return. But we know that a given rate of return earned over a long period of time is much less dependable the shorter the time period we examine. Despite this fact, we can try and select combinations of stocks that have produced superior returns in the past and hope that they continue to produce these returns in the future. An investor might avoid index funds and select a combination of high returning stocks from Siegel's best performing stock list in Figure 22B4, invest as much as possible, and hope for the best.

A sample $50,000 portfolio for a 50-year-old investor with 20 years left until retirement might look like Figure 27B1. This portfolio assumes that these five stocks will achieve the same rate of return during the next 20 years that they have for the last 48 years.

—

FIGURE 27B1 Sample Portfolio, $50,000 Investment, 20 Years to Retirement

Company Name	Investment	Compound Rate of Return[142]	20-Year Potential Return
Altria	$10,000	19.80%	$370,798
Bristol-Myers Squibb	$10,000	15.79%	$187,881
Abbott Labs	$10,000	15,72%	$185,425
Merck	$10,000	15.59%	$181,303
Coca-Cola	$10,000	15.54%	$179,741
Total	$50,000		$1,105,148

Picking these stocks to perform as well in the next 20 years may be something of a stretch. It is highly likely that they will perform either better or worse so it is unlikely that an investor will achieve exactly the return indicated in Figure 27B1. Investors need to understand that both the actual results and the variance of that result is more inconsistent with only 20 years left until retirement. But it does give you a chance, an opportunity to turn $50,000 into $1 million or more before you retire. Remember again that these returns are calculated on the assumption that an investor will use a tax-deferred vehicle to make his or her investments and will reinvest all dividends and distributions in added stock. If it is difficult or impossible to use a tax-deferred vehicle for a $50,000 investment in specific stocks, an investor should be prepared to pay the taxes out of other funds.

Three of the five selections in Figure 27B1 are large pharmaceutical companies, leaving an investor with a highly concentrated portfolio, not a diversified one. Some investors might want to select the top 5 targets in Figure 22B4, including only one pharmaceutical and one soda stock. Figure 27B2 shows the results of 5 top selections from Siegel's top performers with a more diversified selection. Figure 27B2 is a sample portfolio for a $50,000 investment for 30 years, and Figure 27B3 is a sample portfolio for a $50,000 investment for 40 years. Both portfolios attempt some industry diversification.

FIGURE 27B2 Sample Portfolio, $50,000 Investment, 30 Years to Retirement

Company Name	Investment	Compound Rate of Return[143]	30-Year Potential Return
Altria	$10,000	19.80%	$2,257,899
Bristol-Myers Squibb	$10,000	15.79%	$813,817
Coca-Cola	$10,000	15.54%	$762,028
Tootsie Roll	$10,000	15.27%	$710,377
Crane	$10,000	15.14%	$686,731
Total	$50,000		$5,230,612

FIGURE 27B3 Sample Portfolio, $50,000 Investment, 40 Years to Retirement

Company Name	Investment	Compound Rate of Return[144]	40-Year Potential Return
Altria	$10,000	19.80%	$13,749,051
Bristol-Myers Squibb	$10,000	15.79%	$3,522,428
Coca-Cola	$10,000	15.54%	$3,230,684
Tootsie Roll	$10,000	15.27%	$2,942,061
Crane	$10,000	15.14%	$2,812,218
Total	$50,000		$26,256,442

The data in Figures 27B2 and 27B3 show the potential return if all five stocks continue to produce, for the next 30 or 40 years, the same rate of return that they have for the past 48 years. Obviously, with less time, there is a significant chance that the results depicted will not be met. But you have a decent chance and even if some of them come close, an investor will still finish well even though he or she did not have 50, 60, or 70 years left.

It is entirely possible that the returns an investor gets might just be better in the next 20, 30, or 40 years than in the past 50 years. But Figure 27B4 shows an investor's final result assuming that the average returns for the five stocks in Figures 27B2 and 27B3 are less than past returns. The average compound rates of return calculate at 16.77% per year in Figure 27B2 and 16.95% per year in Figure 27B3. Figure 27B4 assumes that the actual returns are 1%, 2%, 3%, or 4% less than the historic average.

**FIGURE 27B4 Calculation of Reduced Returns for
Figures 27B2 and 27B3**

Compound Rate of Return	30-Year Example	40-Year Example
Total return in Figures 27B2 and 27B3	$5,230,612	$26,256,442
Minus 1% annually	$4,044,371	$18,612,303
Minus 2% annually	$3,177,608	$13,162,216
Minus 3% annually	$2,397,744	$9,279,898
Minus 4% annually	$1,839,829	$6,522,580

Figure 27B4 shows the reduced returns to investors in both the 30-and 40-year investment scenario assuming reduced rates of return. A 40-year investor of $50,000 who achieves a compound rate of return that is 3% per year below the 48-year historical return will still finish with $9,279,898 instead of $26,256,442. A 30-year investor who achieves a rate of return 1% below the 48-year historic return will finish with $4,044,371 instead of $5,230,612.

Investors with more or less than $50,000 to invest can easily calculate their returns. Simply multiply the returns shown by the multiple of $50,000 that you are investing. For example, $100,000 initial investments will double all the projected returns in Figures 27B1-27B4. A $25,000 beginning investment will half all the projected returns.

This is a book about time and compound rates of return. But an investor with less time left isn't totally lost. He or she has several options to attempt to finish big at retirement. The return rates achievable may be more uncertain, but with a larger initial dollar investment, a more aggressive selection of investments, or a longer holding period, strong returns are still possible.

CHAPTER 28

How to Finish with $10 Million or $100 Million?

Finishing Big

Some of you may have greater ambitions than to retire with $1 million. What if you would like to finish life with $10, $50, or even $100 million dollars? It is possible, even if you are not wealthy right now. Of course, if you have some investment dollars already, you are ahead of the game and may be in a better position to finish big than someone who has no investment funds to work with.

Let's look at how much you would need to invest, both onetime and yearly, to finish with this big of a return. Figure 28B1 shows you how much money you would need to invest, onetime, right now to have $10,000,000, $50,000,000, or $100,000,000 after 50, 60, 70, or 80 (don't forget potential life extension) years. For example, it would need a onetime investment of $54,182 now to allow you to have $10 million at retirement in 50 years, assuming an 11% compound rate of return. If you assume some serious life extension, or if you are investing for a child or grandchild, you would have to invest only $2,367 once to give them $10 million in 80 years. If, in 80 years, people are living just 20 years longer than today (a conservative assumption, see Chapter 12), 80 might just be the normal retirement age. If you want $100 million, you will have to invest $346,018 today at 12% for 50 years, but only $35,871 if you have 70 years remaining on your investment time horizon. A young person today could invest with an 80-year time horizon and potentially end with $10 million for a onetime investment of $1,155. He or she might end with $50 million for a onetime investment of $5,775 and $100 million for a onetime investment of $11,549, assuming a 12% compound rate of return, just slightly above the post-WWII average of 11.76%.

FIGURE 28B1 Required One Time Investment to Finish Really Big Rate of Return/Years—$10 Million, $50 Million, $100 Million

$10,000,000	Onetime			
Return	50	60	70	80
9%	$134,485	$56,808	$23,996	$10,136
10%	$85,186	$32,843	$12,662	$4,882
11%	$54,182	$19,082	$6,720	$2,367
12%	$34,602	$11,141	$3,587	$1,155
13%	$22,186	$6,536	$1,925	$567

$50,000,000	Onetime			
Return	50	60	70	80
9.00%	$672,427	$284,040	$119,982	$50,682
10.00%	$425,928	$164,214	$63,311	$24,409
11.00%	$270,908	$95,409	$33,602	$11,834
12.00%	$173,009	$55,704	$17,935	$5,775
13.00%	$110,930	$32,679	$9,627	$2,836

$100,000,000	Onetime			
Return	50	60	70	80
9.00%	$1,344,854	$568,081	$239,963	$101,363
10.00%	$851,855	$328,427	$126,623	$48,819
11.00%	$541,815	$190,819	$67,203	$23,668
12.00%	$346,018	$111,409	$35,871	$11,549
13.00%	$221,859	$65,357	$19,253	$5,672

The most practical way for most investors to finish with a real fortune is with investments made every year. Figure 28B2 shows the yearly investment that it would take to finish with $10, $50, or $100 million by compound rate and years. At 12%, it takes only $1,079 a year to finish with $10 million in 60 years and only $112 per year if you think you may have 80 years left. And $100,000,000 would need a yearly investment of $10,792 for 60 years at 12% and $1,118 a year for 80 years.

Most of these plans are practical and potentially doable depending on your age, your financial situation, and your discipline and patience. If you are trying really big finishes, you should select your notch from one of these charts, preferably the yearly chart, and plan to make the yearly contribution needed. Always have in mind the opportunity to make extra contributions to your investment plan. Extra contributions give you a cushion against inflation or the possibility that your rate of return turns out to be less than planned, especially any extra contributions in the early years. For instance, suppose you are on a path to have $10 million in 60 years and are assuming an aggressive 12% return compound yearly. You need to invest $1,079 yearly. If you find some extra money during the first 10 years of your investment plan, say an extra $5,000 over 10 years, and you invest it as added funds, you will have given yourself a cushion in case the slightly higher than historic rate doesn't happen. With the extra $5,000, you will be able to have your return slip to 11.40% from 12% and still achieve the same result.

FIGURE 28B2 Required Yearly Investment to Finish Really Big Rate of Return/Years—$10 Million, $50 Million, $100 Million

$10,000,000	Yearly			
Return	50	60	70	80
9.00%	$10,386	$4,356	$1,834	$774
10.00%	$7,155	$2,745	$1,056	$407
11.00%	$4,909	$1,723	$606	$213
12.00%	$3,359	$1,079	$347	$112
13.00%	$2,294	$675	$199	$59

$50,000,000	Onetime			
Return	50	60	70	80
9.00%	$51,932	$21,778	$9,171	$3,869
10.00%	$35,773	$13,726	$5,282	$2,035
11.00%	$24,547	$8,617	$3,032	$1,067
12.00%	$16,795	$5,396	$1,736	$559
13.00%	$11,468	$3,374	$993	$293

$100,000,000	Onetime

—

Return	50	60	70	80
9.00%	$103,864	$43,557	$18,343	$7,738
10.00%	$71,547	$27,452	$10,564	$4,070
11.00%	$49,094	$17,235	$6,063	$2,134
12.00%	$33,591	$10,792	$3,472	$1,118
13.00%	$22,936	$6,747	$1,987	$585

If we look at the past, we can calculate which companies in Siegel's S&P survivors would have produced $50 million or $100 million based on dollars invested, return, and time. Figures 28B3 and 28B4 look at onetime investments of $10,000, $20,000, and $50,000. Assuming each company compounds at the same rate of return they achieved from 1957 to 2005 for the next 50 or 60 years, Figure 28B3 lists companies that would have achieved at least $50 or $100 million.

Figure 28B3 shows that only Altria would have achieved at least $50 or $100 million based on a onetime investment of $10,000, $20,000, or $50,000 for 50 years. Six additional companies would have made our investor at least $50 million on a onetime investment of $50,000 for 50 years. Extending the time frame to 60 years in Figure 28B4 gives us more options. All 14 companies produced at least $50 or $100 million with onetime investments of $20,000 or $50,000. Altria qualified in all categories, and two additional companies, Abbott Labs and PepsiCo, got us to $50 million on a $10,000 investment and to $100 million on a $20,000 investment.

FIGURE 28B3 Companies Achieving $50 or $100 Million after 50 Years
One Time Investment of $10,000, $20,000, or $50,000

50 Years	Investment $10,000 Result $50 Million	Investment $10,000 Result $100 Million	Investment $20,000 Result $50 Million	Investment $20,000 Result $100 Million	Investment $50,000 Result $50 Million	Investment $50,000 Result $100 Million
	Altria	Altria	Altria	Altria	Altria	Altria
					Abbott Labs	
					PepsiCo	
					Bristol-Myers	
					Tootsie Roll	
					Crane	
					Coca-Cola	

FIGURE 28B4 Companies Achieving $50 or $100 Million after 60 Years
One Time Investment of $10,000, $20,000, or $50,000

60 Years	Investment $10,000 Result $50 Million	Investment $10,000 Result $100 Million	Investment $20,000 Result $50 Million	Investment $20,000 Result $100 Million	Investment $50,000 Result $50 Million	Investment $50,000 Result $100 Million
	Altria	Altria	Altria	Altria	Altria	Altria
	Abbott Labs		Abbott Labs	Abbott Labs	Abbott Labs	Abbott Labs
	PepsiCo		PepsiCo	PepsiCo	PepsiCo	PepsiCo
			Bristol-Myers		Bristol-Myers	Bristol-Myers
			Tootsie Roll		Tootsie Roll	Tootsie Roll
			Crane		Crane	Crane
			Coca-Cola		Coca-Cola	Coca-Cola
			Colgate-Palmolive		Colgate-Palmolive	Colgate-Palmolive
			Merck		Merck	Merck
			Pfizer		Pfizer	Pfizer
			Wrigley		Wrigley	Wrigley
			Fortune B		Fortune B	Fortune B
			Heinz		Heinz	Heinz

FIGURE 28B5 Companies Achieving $50 or $100 Million after 50 Years
Yearly Investment of $5,000, $6,500, or $7,500

50 Years	Investment $5,000 Yearly Result $50 Million	Investment $5,000 Yearly Result $100 Million	Investment $6,500 Yearly Result $50 Million	Investment $6,500 Yearly Result $100 Million	Investment $7,500 Yearly Result $50 Million	Investment $7,500 Yearly Result $100 Million
	Altria	Altria	Altria	Altria	Altria	Altria
	Abbott Labs		Abbott Labs		Abbott Labs	
			PepsiCo		PepsiCo	
			Bristol-Myers		Bristol-Myers	
			Tootsie Roll		Tootsie Roll	
			Crane		Crane	
			Coca-Cola		Coca-Cola	
			Colgate-Palmolive		Colgate-Palmolive	
					Merck	
					Pfizer	
					Wrigley	

—

FIGURE 28B6 Companies Achieving $50 or $100 Million after 50 Years
Yearly Investment of $1,500, $2,000, or $3,500

60 Years	Investment $1,500 Yearly Result $50 Million	Investment $1,500 Yearly Result $100 Million	Investment $2,000 Yearly Result $50 Million	Investment $2,000 Yearly Result $100 Million	Investment $3,500 Yearly Result $50 Million	Investment $3,500 Yearly Result $100 Million
	Altria	Altria	Altria	Altria	Altria	Altria
	Abbott Labs		Abbott Labs		Abbott Labs	Abbott Labs
	PepsiCo		PepsiCo		PepsiCo	PepsiCo
	Bristol-Myers		Bristol-Myers		Bristol-Myers	Bristol-Myers
			Tootsie Roll		Tootsie Roll	Tootsie Roll
			Crane		Crane	Crane
			Coca-Cola		Coca-Cola	Coca-Cola
			Colgate-Palmolive		Colgate-Palmolive	Colgate-Palmolive
			Merck		Merck	
			Pfizer		Pfizer	
			Wrigley		Wrigley	
					Fortune	
					Heinz	

Figures 28B5 and 28B6 calculate the companies that will make our investor at least $50 or $100 million, assuming yearly investments using their historic 48-year compound rate of return for the next 50 or 60 years. A $1,500 yearly investment in Altria might make an investor worth $100 million after 60 years if Altria can continue to compound at 19.78% yearly, an aggressive assumption. But a number of other companies qualify for superrich status with fairly modest yearly investments if they can maintain their historic compound rates of return. Figures 28B3-28B6 all assume that the named companies all maintain the same compound rate of return in the future as they did from 1957 to 2005. It may be a stretch to imagine that you can pick which company or companies can maintain these high rates of return in the future, but the illustrations show that it is possible to become superrich with a little luck and 50-60 years. As usual, remember that this assumes that our investor uses a tax avoidance or deferral investment strategy and reinvests all distributions in additional stock.

One other comment on big money returns and investing that you should keep in mind. IRAs, both traditional and Roth, have limits ($4,500 per person today). If you need to invest more than the current limits, you may have to have multiple investments, perhaps an IRA and an annuity (see Chapters 17-19), or invest in multiple IRAs over a number of years. Keep in mind that annuities will probably return less than your IRA, even if it were possible to invest in the same mutual fund, because of higher annuity costs. You should scale back your rate of return calculation to account for this.

You can use Figures 28B1 and 28B2 in a couple of ways. One way would be to start with the amount you would like to have at some point distant in the future, assume a rate of return, and then look up the needed onetime investment or yearly investment. See if that amount seems possible based on your own finances, your income, and your savings. Or you can start with your own finances, figure out how much you can possibly invest yearly and then, assuming a rate of return (11% or 12% should do it), figure the years of investing you will likely have and see where you will finish. I think everyone should start with the $100 million charts and see if it can work. Drop to $50 million or $10 million only if it looks impossible. Think big. Or pick one or two companies that have already demonstrated their capability to produce these kinds of returns. The more companies you can afford to put in play the higher the likelihood that at least one of them will perform according to these projections. Once armed with information, there is nothing to stop you.

Patience

One of the key messages in this book is a simple idea—patience. Besides making the right investments, investing in the correct way, and reinvesting all distributions, the most critical requirement to the success of your investment plan is your capacity to be patient. And your patience will be tested. If you hold mutual funds or stocks over many years, there will be periods in which the stock market will look like the worst investment imaginable. As an example, look at the 1965-1974 nine-year period. Even if our investor reinvested all dividends and paid zero taxes, the best an investor in the S&P 500 could do during the 9-year time frame was to break even in nominal dollars. The worst news was that adjusted for inflation, adjusted for what his or her dollars could buy at the mall, our investor lost 40% of his or her capital in those 9 years. In more recent times, an investor in the S&P in 1999 found that he or she had lost 38% of his or her capital by 2002. You have to be able to weather these kinds of markets, both physically and emotionally, and from my own perspective, it is easier to write about it than to experience it. When markets go south, it almost always seems there is no possible recovery and there is no end. The temptation is to forget about investment plans and do something else with your money, spend it or put it into real estate. The stock markets seem in a conspiracy to discourage investors, and sometimes, it takes years until investors are willing to come back into the market in large numbers. No matter what happens, keep investing and keep reinvesting dividends. I warn you that your confidence in this investment plan will surely be tested. Your ability to achieve the kinds of returns identified in this book will depend largely on how patient you are willing to be.

If you are adopting a multiyear investment plan, which I imagine is the majority, you must remain committed to continue your investment program through thick and thin. We have seen how important continued investment and reinvestment is during downturns. Downturns in the stock market are the best time for investors to accumulate large amounts of stock through added investing or reinvesting distributions. They are a great opportunity for you, but it won't seem that way when it happens. But you have to stick with it when all the experts are pessimistic and when all your friends and relatives are bragging about how they got out of the market 1,000 points higher than it is today. Can you do this? The real issue is confidence. If you are confident in this long-term plan, you will be much more likely to be patient and to succeed. It is one reason I urged you earlier to try to reproduce the returns, calculate them yourself on your own computer. I want you to reproduce the calculations, not to check on my accuracy, but to develop a richer and deeper understanding of the numbers and more confidence in the result. Then it will become your plan. If you do find mistakes in some of my numbers, that's great, let me know so I can correct them. But the real benefit will be that you will have a new and deeper confidence in the long-term investment returns possible. Confidence translates into patience.

The penalties that you will pay if you fail to display patience are varied and substantial. If you make withdrawals from your investment account, every dollar withdrawn will cost you many multiples at retirement. If you fail to follow through on your investment plan or fail to invest and reinvest in down markets, you will suffer even larger losses from your final goal. If you fail to wait long enough or reinvest dividends, the results are enormous. Many charts and tables in this book show the penalty you will pay, but Figure 28C1 tries to summarize just a few of the most prominent possible failures.

—

FIGURE 28C1 Examples of Plan Failures

Failure	Estimated Result
Failure to continue planned investments	$1,000 failure in a $10,000 plan
	Loss of $417,000
Early withdrawals	20% withdrawal after 20 years in $10,000 plan
	Loss of $126,000
Failure to reinvest dividends	Loss of 93-99% of total return
Failure to continue investments or reinvest dividends in a bear market	Loss of 65% of total return in 1968-1981 bear market
Failure to avoid or defer taxes	Loss of 88.7% of total return in post-WWII S&P 500
Failure to maintain investments	Loss of 67% of total return for 10 years

—

CHAPTER 29

What Might Prevent This Plan from Working?

It may surprise you that I am including a chapter in this book on what might make the plan presented fail. No matter how encouraging the prospects for long-term investing, there is always the possibility that this plan will not work.

Nothing in Life Is Foolproof

We can study the past as much as we want, but we know, intuitively, the past is not always a good model for the future. There are a few things that could happen that would derail your investment plans. No plan in life is foolproof, and all we can do is to use our current knowledge and the information available to us to plan for the future and hope for the best. I am personally convinced that the advice in this book is highly likely to produce the results described, and I have personally been investing for years based on its principles. But I understand, and the reader should understand, there are several possibilities, some remote, that might derail our plans. My advice: read this chapter and keep alert just in case.

Fail to Follow Through

Believe it or not, my number one fear that will prevent this plan from working is you. You can fail in several ways. Let's look at them.

- The biggest chance for failure is that you simply fail to start a plan.
- You fail to continue or complete your investment plans.
- You fail to complete the investment plan amounts.
- You fail to use a tax avoidance scheme as recommended in Chapters 17-19.
- You fail to reinvest all dividends, capital gains, and other distributions in added shares.
- You fail to make investments that achieve market average returns.
- You fail to continue the plan for the planned number of years. You fail to take advantage of time and compound returns.

One aspect of failing that I would like to pay some extra attention is the timing of your investments. Early investments are worth much more than later investments, so if you must fail, fail later in the plan not early in the plan. Figure 29A1 shows the final return from a $2,000 yearly investment in 10-year intervals for 70 years compounded at 11.76%. Each return in this figure is the return achieved by the one $2,000 investment for that year. The early investments are worth much more than the later investments. One $2,000 investment at 11.76% compounded in the first year of a 70-year plan is worth $4.7 million. One investment made in the 60th year of a 70-year plan is worth $6 thousand. Figures 29A1 and 29A2 show the impact of time on investments. Figure 29A2 shows how much more an investor has to invest to make $4.7 million (return on a 70-year investment) if he or she waits 10, 20, 30, 40, or 50 years to invest. The required investment dollars to produce the same result triple every 10 years. A $2,000 investment delayed for 10 years requires a $6,000 investment to produce the same results. Delayed for 30 years, it would take over $55,000 invested to produce the same result as $2,000 would today. If you wait until your 60th year, it will take over $1.5 million to get the same result as a $2,000 investment would now—a powerful incentive for beginning your investment program now.

FIGURE 29A1 Total Return on $2,000 Investments
Compounding at 11.76%[145]
One Investment Made in Year 1-60 with Years Left

Year of Investment	Years Left	Total Return Only on This Investment
Year 1	70	$4,798,191
Year 10	60	$1,578,387
Year 20	50	$519,218
Year 30	40	$170,799
Year 40	30	$56,185
Year 50	20	$18,482
Year 60	10	$6,080

FIGURE 29A2 Required Investment to Produce $4.7 Million
after 70 Years
One $2,000 Investment Delayed for 10-60 Years
Compound Rate of Return of 11.76% Yearly

Year of Investment	Years Left	Investment Required to Produce $4.7 Million
10th Year	60 Years	$6,000
20th Year	50 Years	$18,200
30th Year	40 Years	$55,300
40th Year	30 Years	$168,000
50th Year	20 Years	$509,000
60th Year	10 Years	$1,550,000

You may fail to invest based on the principles described or you may fail to follow through on a multiyear investment plan. It takes discipline! Don't even start unless you can commit to do what it takes. You will only become more frustrated. For some, it would be better not to read this book and understand the power of compound rates of return. Now that you are aware of what is possible, you will kick yourself in later years if you could have, but did not, taken advantage of this opportunity. Don't delay and follow the advice in Chapter 26, which will help you avoid the pitfalls of poor follow through.

US Economy

The U.S. economy could fail. It could fail, and a new economic system might replace it, probably some form of socialism or extensive government control of economic affairs. If this happens, it increases the probability that your investment plan will fail as well. I do think that this is a significant possibility, although it is a remote one. It is one reason that I do not recommend taking all your investment funds and putting them into a long-term retirement fund. If I could be 100% positive the future will be like the past, it would be easy for me to tell you invest only based on the long-term strategy that I recommend here. If the U.S. economy fails, there are not many investment strategies that will survive. Perhaps government bonds would be the best place to park your money, but it depends on the type of economic failure. The government might not be a good place to invest if it is going to run most of the economy. Investments in countries with a long history of stable low-impact government like Switzerland might end being the best investment. I own some Swiss securities as a hedge against possible economic chaos in the United States. (I pay taxes on the dividends I receive and none of the stocks I own have a dividend reinvestment plan.) It is not clear that a U.S. economic failure would not doom most foreign investments as well.

**FIGURE 29B1[146] Annual Compound Rates of Growth,
the United States
Gross Domestic Product and Personal Income
1929-2000**

1929-2000	GDP	Personal Income
Nominal compound annual growth rate	6.61%	6.69%
Nominal per capital compound annual growth rate	5.37%	5.43%
"Real" compound annual growth rate	3.04%	3.11%
"Real" per capital compound annual growth rate	1.83%	1.90%

The US economy could fail to grow at its historic rate. During most of the 20th century (from 1929 to 2000), the average annual inflation-adjusted growth rate for the GDP was 3.04% per year. Personal income grew yearly by a similar but slightly higher percentage, 3.11%. The Standard and Poor's composite grew at an inflation-adjusted compound annual rate of return of 6.93% per year. This data is adjusted for inflation

—

but not for population growth. Obviously, continued positive growth in the stock market for investors is going to depend on continued growth of the US economy. The inflation-adjusted growth rate per person was 1.83% annually from 1929 to 2000. If the US economy survives, but grows at a much slower pace, say a compound rate of 1% per year, then it is logical to assume that gains in the stock market will also be moderate. Of course, the American economy easily could grow faster than 1.83% yearly in the next 100 years. Technology, international trade, productivity gains, and population growth might all lead to faster economic growth in the 21st century and better stock market returns than in the 20th century. The reasons that I worry might lead to slower growth are:

- Higher taxes, particularly on investors with higher capital gains and dividend taxes.
- Slower productivity growth.
- Less competitive markets.
- The United States backs away from free trade.
- Government entitlements choke economic system.
- Heavy government regulation slows the economic system.
- More than moderate inflation eats away at nominal gains.
- Liability lawsuit costs threaten to every major American industry.
- Immigration swamps US labor markets.
- Baby boom retirement bankrupts the US government.

Figure 29B2 projects the per capita personal income forward 100 years in nominal and inflation-adjusted "real" terms. If personal income per capita continues to grow at the same compound annual rate that it did from 1929 to 2000, average per capita income in the United States in 2100 will be $638,447 per year. Adjusted for inflation (assuming the same inflation rate) that average income would translate into $196,094 in 2000 dollars (actual per capita personal income in 2000 was $29,857 per person). If growth in personal income slows or speeds up, the results are dramatic. If the United States stagnates at a growth of 1% per year less than the 1929-2000 average, inflation-adjusted incomes drop to about 37% of what it otherwise might have been. If, on the other hand, personal income growth rates speed up to grow 1% faster in the 21st century than in the 1929-2000 period, then per capita inflation-adjusted income grows almost 2.7 times more than it otherwise might have grown. Obviously, the rate of growth of the economy and thus the rate of growth of personal income will be a significant determinant in how prosperous citizens and investors in the United States turn out to be at the end of this century.

—

FIGURE 29B2 Projected Personal Income per Person in the United States—2100
Assuming Annual Growth Rate 1929-2000, Higher and Lower Rates
Per Capital Yearly Income in 2000 = $29,857

Compound Annual Growth Rate	Average Personal Income (Nominal)	Average Personal Income ("Real")
Slower annual growth (–1.0%)	$240,921	$73,141
Slower annual growth (–0.5%)	$392,658	$119,906
Same annual growth	$638,447	$196,094
Faster annual growth (+0.5%)	$1,035,651	$319,920
Faster annual growth (+1.0%)	$1,676,065	$520,695

Long-Term Worldwide Depression

The potential for a 1930s style long-term depression is always present. We have not had a major depression in almost 70 years, and some would argue that we are due. Depressions occur, some argue, when the generation that lived through the depression passes on. With the depression generation fast disappearing, it may be that another long major depression awaits us. The statistics in this book show clearly that a stock market investor who was able to continue to save and invest through the depression prospered once the depression ended. This assumes that his or her investment choices were able to survive the long depression. Part of the advice given in Chapter 22 is an attempt to get investors in a position to "survive" a depression. If the depression is serious, then continuing an investment program through the depression may become impossible. But if an investor can survive it and select investment strategies that survive it, the 1930s experience shows us that stock market investing still paid handsome returns when the depression ended.

The biggest fear may be a depression that does not end. It has not happened in American history, but that is not to say that it could not happen in the future. An endless depression might lead to all kinds of unanticipated outcomes, both economically and politically. It is impossible to predict the impact on your retirement investment plan, but there is no plan that will account for all possibilities.

I do consider a depression as a possibility, even a probability. I don't believe that an endless depression is likely.

—

315

Baby Boom Retirement Disaster

One of the big fears for the 21st century is the baby boom generation's retirement and its potential impact on our economy, our retirement programs, and the government. With such a huge population bulge beginning retirement around 2012, the impact on the markets is hard to predict. Some argue that the baby boomers will not have enough income to support the retirement that they expect and that they will sell assets, homes, stocks, and bonds to support their retirement needs. If this turns out to be the case, the markets could be in for a rough road for a decade or even two.

I do worry about this problem, but not excessively so. Our economy is an international one and is growing more so every year. The baby boomer's retirement will have less of an impact on an internationally based economy. It is not clear that baby boomers will sell assets in large amounts to support retirement. They may reduce their lifestyle, moving into booming retirement communities, so their need to tap their investments may not be as dramatic and sudden as some assume. If this is a problem, it will probably not affect a long-term investor looking at returns for 50-80 years. Just like the depression, the baby boomer's retirement will be survivable for investors who stay committed to their plan.

Globalization Derailed

A real fear for long-term investing is that globalization and the post-WWII movement toward free trade will be derailed. Free trade in the long run is a big win for the overall economy. If we allow politics to derail trade with China and India, we will be making a historic mistake that will lead to slow economic growth and a permanent noncompetitive position in the world that will harm American investors. If we retreat from free trade, it will have a domino effect on the rest of the world. Everyone may back off from trade, and economic growth will slow to a snail's pace. In addition, developing countries will be stymied in their thirst for economic success. Investors should not fear developing countries, like China, India, and others. In the long run, if they develop their economies on free trade principles, they will be booming markets for American companies to sell their products. In fact, Professor Siegel has argued that it is China's and India's growing economies that will mitigate the impact of the baby boomer's retirement.

I believe that retreating from free trade is one of the more realistic fears for the future. There already is a growing and dogged movement

—

to stop free trade. Free trade does lead to dual results. Some are hurt by free trade and many benefit from free trade. In a democratic system, those that are injured seek redress using the political system, and it is tempting for politicians to try to restrict trade, particularly imports, to try to help constituents that are aggrieved. Unfortunately, the long-term impact of limits on trade will hurt all Americans and most investors, including long-term investors.

This is one phenomenon to watch for.

Terrorism and Economic Disruption

Of course, it is always possible that terrorism could so severely disrupt our economic system that returns to stockholders are disrupted. There are many number of ways in which terrorists could disrupt the US economic system. We have already seen the impact terrorists can have on our air transport system, but they have not had much impact on the rest of our economy so far. We will see if terrorists try to mount attacks that have a long-term impact on our economy and thus an impact on long-term investors.

Runaway Inflation

Runaway inflation, such as hit Germany and Austria in 1923, is a potentially devastating phenomenon. It ruined economies and forced them to almost start over from scratch. Modest inflation can be countered; some even argue that it is favorable for stock investors. But runaway inflation would probably be so disastrous for the entire economic system that stock market investors would undoubtedly suffer dearly. I don't think that runaway inflation is as likely as depression, if we look at the two extreme economic disasters. The Federal Reserve Bank has proven its ability to get inflation under control several times. The current FED seems committed to controlling and slowing inflationary factors wherever they may surface. If the FED maintains this vigilance, runaway inflation is a remote possibility. However, the Federal Reserve Bank ability to stimulate the economy out of a deep recession or depression is much more doubtful. I worry more about the potential for a depression the FED could not prevent or relieve more than I do about an inflation, which the FED has shown both the ability and determination to control.

Mean Reversion

One of the common concepts that is in vogue about today's stock prices is an idea called mean reversion.[147] The advocates of this theory point to the tendency for stock prices to overshoot and then return to historic levels over time. Based on their historical analysis of stock prices, many believe that current stock prices are significantly overvalued, and they have been overvalued for some time. The significance of this idea is the presumption that stocks have advanced more than their historic average in recent times and that stock prices will have to return to their long-run historic average values. Stock prices will have to decline absolutely or increase substantially less than average for some years to come.

There are some ways to develop historical stock price averages, but two are most commonly used: the average price to earnings ratio (called the P/E ratio) and the average yield (or rate) paid on dividends. By whatever measure one employs, it is clear the price the average stock sells for today is higher, relative to their earnings and dividends, than they have been historically. As I look in the paper today, the Dow Jones Industrial Averages show a P/E ratio of 18.24 to 1. That means that an investor in the entire 30 Dow stocks is paying a price of a little over $18 for each $1 of yearly earnings the Dow 30 achieved. If we look at a broader index, the Standard and Poor's 500 Index, the ratio is slightly higher, 19.85 to 1. Most long-term studies conclude that, while P/E ratios can vary significantly, their average over a long period of time has been somewhere between 13 and 14 times earnings.

The other measure that is often used is dividend yield. This is the percentage of a stock price that is paid out to its investors as dividends during a year. We have already analyzed the importance and power of dividends to a long-term investor in Chapter 10. Currently, the Dow Industrials are paying an average of 2.38% per year in dividends and the S&P 500 are paying an even smaller 1.84% in dividends. The average dividend paid by stocks since 1925 is around 4.5%.

Since the P/E ratio is higher than "normal" and the dividend yield is "lower" than normal, the mean reversion theory would require lower stock prices to redress the imbalances. Prices would have to fall to bring the P/E ratio and the dividend yield back to their historic average. If the mean reversion theorists are correct, we may be in far below-average stock market returns like the 1929-1954 period or like the 1965-1982 period.

—

We cannot reject this theory easily. However, there are two responses that have been advanced against mean reversion that are relevant for us. The first is that we may be in a new era of investing that justifies higher P/E ratios and lower dividend payouts. The averages the mean reversion proponents use were collected over long periods of time and are heavily weighted by the past. We may be creating new means (averages) for a new era. Look at a longtime successful company like Coca-Cola. The end of the Cold War, years of prosperity, opening global markets, and growing third world economies all over the world have made the prospects for a company like Coca-Cola better than ever in its history. Like many companies, Coca-Cola has been expanding its distribution all over the world for years. No longer limited to North America and Europe, Coke's potential future earnings growth is better today than at any time in its past, justifying higher stock prices relative to current earnings or dividends. Stock prices reflect the future not the past. If Coke's (or any other company's) future is significantly brighter than 10, 20, 30, 40, or 50 years ago, why should that not justify higher current P/Es? We would like to be able to calculate Coke's P/E based on its future earnings not its past. If we could know the future and Coke does grow earnings more rapidly in the future than it did in the past, its current P/E might in fact look low. But all we have is the past P/Es, and the difficulty is that Coke's stock price is based on investor's evaluation of Coke's future.

Many refuse to believe in this new era idea. We have heard it before. The data presented on long-term returns to stocks in Chapter 6 clearly showed that over many years the significance of entering the stock market by buying a stock during high stock price years versus low stock price years is fairly modest. If you are investing for 5, 10, or 15 years, the difference can be significant. But if you are investing for 50-70 years, which is the focus of this book, slightly below-average returns immediately following an investment may not mean a significant difference in compound return over many years. In Chapter 6, I presented data on compound long-term returns based on year of investment. Despite the devastating 90% drop in stock prices from 1929 to 1932, an investor who invested $1,000 in the best years of the booming 1920s would still have achieved a compound rate of return of 11.5% per year. An investor who had the courage to invest his or her $1,000 in 1932 at the bottom of the stock market crash would have earned only a slightly higher compound return of 12.13% per year. Even if mean reversion works and we revisit the historic ratios with a period of below-average stock returns, a long-term investor has little to fear from the mean reversion theory. The power of long-term compound rates of return over time dwarf the decline in stock prices in the greatest depression in history.

Mean Reversion in Reverse

Despite all the talk about bubbles and high stock prices, the compound rate of return for stocks has been below its post-WWII average for the past 10 years. The S&P composite showed an 11.76% compound rate of return for 58 years from 1946 to 2004. In the last 10 years, ending in the spring of 2006, the S&P 500 index has returned an annual compound rate of 9.35% a year. If any mean reversion is to occur, it might be in the other direction. Look at Table 6A1 in the appendix. The last column shows the annual compound rate of return from any starting year 1871 to ending year 2004. If you launched an investment in any single year from 1946 to 1994, the worst your annual compound rate of return could have been was 10.23%, starting in 1961. Mean reversion could also mean the 9.35% annual return for the last 10 years must at least eventually exceed 10.23%. To carry out this for an investor in 1995, the coming years will have to return significantly more than 10.23%. I calculate that for a 1995 investor's return to just equal the worst annual average return in 48 years, the next 10 years will have to return at least 11.12%. And that just gets them to the worst long-term return in the past half-decade.

Assume that investments made in 1995 will eventually meet the postwar average of 11.76%. Figure 29C1 shows us that the S&P will have to average 14.22% compounded over the next 10 years if we are to meet the postwar average for the full 20-year period. And $100,000 invested in the S&P in 1995 was worth $244,225 at the end of 2004 and will have to be worth either $701,449 to match the worst postwar compound return or $924,119 to match the average compound return. The S&P returned slightly more than 3% plus dividends in 2005, so if mean reversion, calculated this way, is to work, it will have to make a move.

—

FIGURE 29C1 Calculation of Required Compound Rate of Return
S&P 500, 2005-2025 to Match Mean and Lowest Post-WWII Return

	If Return Reverts to S&P Mean	S&P 500 Index	Compound Rate of Return	Result of $100,000 Invested in 1995
S&P 1995		616		$100,000
S&P 2005		1,250	9.35%	$244,225
S&P 2015	10.23%	2,652	11.12%	$701,449
S&P 2015	11.76%	2,957	14.22%	$924,119

I am not a fan of mean reversion, but by selecting the starting and ending points with care, you can use it to justify 2006 as a good time to start a long-term retirement investment program.

What Didn't We Think Of?

The truth is that we can't anticipate everything. Things happen in history that no one could have imagined, both great things and awful things. We are not soothsayers and cannot expect to accurately predict the future. We are captured by our own history. We look at dangers from the standpoint of history and that may be all we can do. There will be things that happen in the 21st century that no one has anticipated today. Many of them will be wonderful; a few hold the potential for disaster. All you can do is to try your best to prepare yourself for the future and hope for the best. Don't worry about the unknown. What is the worst that could happen? Perhaps an asteroid hits the earth and destroys all life. What good were your investments anyway? No sense in worrying about it now.

While there are all kinds of disastrous futures possible, what is the most likely probability? In my opinion, it is the economy and the American economic system, which has shown so much resilience over generations, will continue to survive and thrive. I think the higher likelihood is that our economy, our stock market and our system, will perform better in the 21st century than it did in the 20th century. Every disaster imagined or unimagined is possible, no matter how low the likelihood, but don't let the disaster predictors deflect you from pursuing your retirement goals. I believe that it is much more likely that you will prosper in the next 100 years with even greater stock market returns than those achieved in the 20th century.

—

CHAPTER 30

What You Should Do
and Not Do—Now!

Things I Don't Like to Hear

"I want to spend the money on something else!"

I can understand anyone and especially a teenager who really wants something. We all have experienced these feelings. I am not going to tell you to sacrifice everything for your investments. I don't think that is a good way to live, although it is a good way to invest for the long run. But if your financial condition at retirement is important to you, and it should be, sacrificing something now to insure a more comfortable retirement should not be too much to ask. You have a simple choice, are you willing to make some sacrifice for a large return years from now?

"They should do it themselves."
"I don't want to spoil my kids or grandkids."

Parents and grandparents often take the understandable attitude that young children should do it for themselves. I can appreciate this attitude, but often, the same parents and, particularly, grandparents will spoil grandkids with wasteful expenditures that mean little to them in the long run. This plan is not "wasting" money on a multitude of toys for Christmas or the latest in music technology. It is planning for your child's retirement. Most young children and even teens are usually not in a position to understand the issues and often not in a position to fund an investment anyway. It is only parents or grandparents who have the wherewithal and understanding to carry out an investment plan. If you wait until the kids are old enough to be in a position to understand and implement it themselves, a lion's share of the returns is gone.

"I'm too young to worry about money"—"I think about it when I am 25 (35) (45)!"

"I will make it on my (their) own."

In Chapter 25, I detailed the direct answer to this response. Waiting is costly, extremely costly. Figure 25A5 shows exactly why waiting is so punishing. Most kids, particularly teenagers, don't want to have to start worrying about retirement at age 16 or 17. But they need to understand the cost involved in waiting. This is where a parent or grandparent can step in and help them, at least, to get started. Once they embark on an investment plan, it is much more likely that they will continue it. The first investment is the key.

The other attitude among teens that I have faced is a kind of supreme self-confidence. Many believe that they will be hugely successful in the business world and worrying about squirreling away rather small amounts of money at their current age is unnecessary. Chapter 3 details how hard it is to save much money and get rich on your own. The odds are against you, no matter how smart, slick, or quick thinking. There is a lot of luck involved. You don't have to make investing an obsession at an early age, just start a modest investment plan, and it will relieve your mind. *It's almost like buying an insurance policy.*

"I just don't want to think about it."

The comments in the previous section apply here. There are many things we don't want to be bothered with, and investing for your future may be one of them. You, or they, need to realize the potential cost involved. Much of this book showed you the cost of not carrying out an investment plan at the earliest possible time.

"I am too dumb." "I don't understand investments in the stock market. I might make a fool of myself."

This is a common attitude especially with young people who have had no exposure to investing. It is also common of adults who have not had some exposure themselves. It is a shame that many people feel that they have to have knowledge and experience to be able to invest. My attitude is that for long-term investing, a lack of experience may just be a good. There is no magic in investing. Sure, it helps to have some knowledge and experience, but, believe me, there is no magic formula the smart Harvard and Princeton educated elite know about. The truth is the average consumer's judgment about companies and their products are often better than the judgment of the smartest PhD at an Ivy League University. You are not too dumb, and you won't make a fool of yourself. You can use some of the advice that I have offered in previous chapters to structure investments, but I encourage even the most inexperienced investor to use their judgment. Don't be afraid, and don't feel stupid. Sure you will find many people in the investment community who will try to give the impression that they are knowledgeable and know all the answers. If they had the answers, they would be busy investing based on it rather than trying to impress you.

Keep It Simple

Keep your plan simple. Don't get too sophisticated and complicated. The main idea is to stick to it. Find a way to insure that you will not deviate from your commitment to your plan.

Separate This Plan from Other Investments

I strongly advise you to keep this plan separate from any other investing that you do. I love investing, all kinds of investing including what many would call speculation. No matter how caught up in your life that you get with investing and speculating, separate this retirement plan from everything else and always, always fund this first. If you want to speculate on biotech or nanotech or whatever the new fad is, go ahead, but only after you have first funded your retirement investment plan. Only use money that is not needed to complete your plan from this book. If you think about this as a separate plan, keep separate records on it, or open a different investment account, and do not mix it in with your other investing; you will be much more likely to complete the plan. No matter how excited about this plan you might be right now, remember that 5 or 10 years from now you will probably be living a different life with new concerns and new interests. Separating your plans will help you to preserve the determination to be rich at retirement that you have right now.

Review—The Devastating Impact of Waiting

Review Chapter 25 periodically, particularly the devastating impact of waiting. Review it every time you find yourself tempted to put off a planned investment or you are tempted to take that dividend this year and go on a vacation instead of reinvesting it in added stock. Keep Figures 25A5 and 25B1 firmly in your mind. Refresh yourself about how much you will lose if you don't fully complete the plan. Small dollars now translate into huge returns years from now.

How to Handle Takeovers—What If Your Stock Gets Acquired?

Don't panic if a company that you invested in gets acquired or merges with another company. Sometimes it is the best thing that can happen to you. If your company is bought for cash, you will simply have to figure out a new investment vehicle. You can pick a new stock or add to your existing investments in stocks or mutual funds. Just reapply the screening technique described in Chapter 22. If you have structured your investment correctly, any capital gain on which you would normally have to pay tax is either deferred or avoided. You have the full proceeds to reinvest.

It is likely that your company will be acquired for stock and you get stock in the acquiring company in exchange for your stock. Simply take a careful look at the acquirer to see if they fit or come close to fitting the investment screening techniques that you are applying. If you have a tax-advantaged account, you have the choice of selling your new stock and investing the funds in something else that fits your long-term goals, without paying any immediate tax. All your funds can go to work compounding in your new investment.

Looking at some of the best 46-year rates of return in Jeremy Siegel's book, *The Future for Investors,* a number of the most successful investments did not achieve their success on their own but made a huge amount of money for investors after the company was bought by an even more successful company. Companies like Kraft Foods, General Foods, and Rexall drugstores were eventually acquired by Philip Morris, soon to become Altria, the best performing stock of the last 50 years. Lane Bryant, a sleepy mature woman's retail store, was acquired by the Limited in 1982 and is fifth on the list of top performers in Siegel's book. A stock that I owned as a young man, Celanese, was acquired by Horchst AG in 1987 and then by Aventis in 1999 and then was partially spun off as Celanese AG. Had I held it, I would have had the ninth best performer, compounding at 16.39% for 46 years. Columbia Pictures, Nabisco, Smuckers, and Quaker Oats all returned over 15% compound annual rate of return while being acquired and sometimes acquired again. A takeover can lead to good things. Don't panic, just look at the acquiring company as if you were thinking of buying the stock on your own. Does it fit your long-term parameters?

Why Not Use "Excess" Money (Give Up a Latte or a Frozen Coke or (God Forbid) That New Flat Screen HDTV)

One way to look at investing for the long-term is to think about what you would have to give up to have millions at retirement. Could you give up your morning grande soy latte at Starbucks, currently $3.55 at my Starbucks? If you only give it up for 1 year, it alone would make you a millionaire if invested at 11.76% for 60 years. If you give it up forever, it produces over $9.7 million at the same return. Consider a frozen coke at the movies, $4.75 at my local theater. If you go to the movies twice a week, that money invested would produce $3.7 million after 60 years. Want a new flat screen TV that cost $3,000? I hope you want it a lot since the opportunity cost to you if you invest the money now in a tax-advantaged account compounding at 11.76% for 60 years is over $2.3 million. It is a nice TV, but an expensive one at retirement.

The Loose Change System

The loose change system is one that works well if you can just discipline yourself to implement it. A number of authors have suggested the idea. Get a big jar and throw all your loose change in it every day. Try to cumulate loose change by never paying for anything with change. Every time you buy something use dollar bills. Just keep all your change from each cash payment that you make for coffee, movies, a newspaper, or whatever. *You never spend your change.* At the end of the year, just take the jar to a bank and cash it in for dollars that you put into your *Roth* IRA or annuity. Most people that try this system find that it is easy to collect $2 in change on average each day. Two bucks a day is worth over $6 million dollars in 60 years (Figure 30A1).

FIGURE 30A1 The Loose Change System Invested at 11.76% Compound Annual Rate of Return in a Tax-Advantaged Account

Loose Change Saved per Day	50 Years	60 Years	70 Years
50 Cents	$495,902	$1,511,048	$4,597,021
$1	$991,805	$3,022,096	$9,194,043
$1.50	$1,487,707	$4,533,144	$12,791,064
$2	$1,983,610	$6,044,191	$18,388,086
$3	$2,975,415	$9,066,287	$27,582,128
$4	$3,967,220	$12,088,383	$36,776,171
$5	$4,959,025	$15,110,479	$45,970,214

Loose change can make you rich so cumulate as much as possible in that big jar. Figure 30A2 shows how much loose change you would need to collect each day to have a million dollars in 30, 40, 50, 60, or 70 years. Believe it or not, 11 cents a day gets you there in 70 years.

FIGURE 30A2 Loose Change per Day Required to Accumulate $1 Million

Years Until Retirement	Loose Change Required per Day
30 Years	$9.59
40 Years	$3.08
50 Years	$1.01
60 Years	33 Cents
70 Years	11 Cents

The 5% Solution

Another system that I wholeheartedly recommend I call the 5% path. Save and invest 5% of your income for the rest of your life, and you will be a millionaire at retirement. Figure 30A3 shows what an average American with an average American income could accumulate at retirement. The mean household income in the United States was $37,800 according to the Federal Reserve Bank Survey of Consumer Finances. Assume that

—

our average American's annual income was $37,800 his or her entire life and that he or she saved and invested 5% of that income in the plan in this book. Figure 30A3 shows what our "average" investor might amass by years left to retirement.

FIGURE 30A3 5% Investment Plan
Result at Retirement, 11.76% Compound Annual Rate of Return

Years to Retirement	Total at Retirement
10 Years	$36,640
20 Years	$148,024
30 Years	$486,622
40 Years	$1,515,937
50 Years	$4,644,986

Any investor under the age of 40 could assure themselves of millionaire status at retirement if they just committed to save 5% of their income every year. Most Americans have rising incomes the older they get. Figure 30A3 makes the unrealistic assumption that income remains static for an entire lifetime. The 5% investment plan, if implemented on the very first job, could make virtually every person in the United States a millionaire at retirement.

Figure 30A4 shows how much the average American starting an investment plan at different ages must save in order to be a millionaire by the time they are 70. It also shows the average income by age from the recent Federal Reserve Bank survey and how much saving 5% of income produces. Assuming he or she never gets a raise, a 25-year-old needs to save 2.38% of his or her income to become a millionaire at age 70. A 35-year-old needs to save 4.66%, and a 45-year-old needs to save 14.11% to become millionaire at retirement.

FIGURE 30A4 Required Yearly Savings to Become Millionaire at Age 70
Federal Reserve Bank Reserve Survey of Consumer Finance Data

Age of Investor	Average Income	5%	Savings Required	Saving % Required
25	$31,500	$1,575	$750	2.38%
35	$47,200	$2,360	$2,200	4.66%
45	$49,600	$2,480	$7,000	14.11%

The 2% System

If the "average" American (according to the Federal Reserve Bank survey data) saved exactly 2% of his or her income every year and invested it at 11.76% per year, reinvesting all dividends and using an IRA, he or she would have $1,046,121 at age 65 and $1,823,955 at age 70. This assumes that they started their working career at age 21, ended it at age 65, and earned exactly the mean income by age groups identified in the FED survey.

Stop Spending and Start Investing

Americans are addicted to spending. It is one reason our economy is so dynamic. So how do you, a typical American addicted to spending, stop spending and start investing? The best idea that I know of is one idea that is taught in economics classes all over the world. It is called opportunity cost. Without getting technical, the idea is that each time you make a decision, say a spending decision, you are also choosing to give up other alternatives that you could have selected. If you spend $100 on an expensive sweater at the mall today, you gained a sweater but you also gave up all the other things that you might have bought at the mall but didn't. So the opportunity cost is something that you do not get because you spent your $100 on a sweater. Every time you spend money on something when you could have saved and invested it, there is an opportunity cost. In our case, every dollar you spend now that you could have put into a retirement plan cost you $790 out of your retirement fund in 60 years. Figure 30A5 shows you the opportunity cost of spending on various items in lost retirement funds in 50, 60, or 70 years. When you think about the new sweater and realize that this sweater is going to cost you $78,919 out of your retirement money, you had better really like the sweater. How about the $30,000 you were going to spend on a new car? It will cost you $71 million in 70 years. The data in Figure 30A5 are onetime investments only. I am not asking you to give up buying cars or sweaters or lattes for the rest of your life. That's no way to live. But maybe you could give up one thing here and there and build a better life for yourself when you are older. I hope using the idea of opportunity cost will motivate you to forgo certain spending so you can improve your investments and make your retire richer.

FIGURE 30A5 Opportunity Cost in Retirement Funds
of Various Purchases
Assumes, Compound Rate of Return of 11.76%

Item Purchased	Cost	Cost in 50 Years	Cost in 60 Years	Cost in 70 Years
Grande soy latte[148]	$3.55	$921	$2,802	$8,517
1 Movie ticket	$9.50	$2,466	$7,497	$22,791
1 CD	$14.95	$3,881	$11,798	$35,866
Dinner at	$50	$12,980	$39,460	$119,955
exclusive rest				
1 Sweater	$100	$25,961	$78,919	$239,910
New bike	$500	$129,804	$394,597	$1,199,548
New computer	$1,000	$259,609	$789,194	$2,399,095
Wide-screen TV	$3,000	$778,827	$2,367,581	$7,197,286
New car	$30,000	$7,788,268	$23,675,810	$71,972,862

Motivation—How Badly Do You Want to Become a Millionaire?

It really comes down to the question of how badly do you want to assure yourself of being able to retire rich. The opportunity is there for you to grab. If you don't care that much, then maybe this plan is not for you. I think that this book has proven that you don't have to make huge sacrifices, that you don't have to become an "expert" in investing, and that structuring your account to get the maximum out of it is really simple. If the potential returns and ease of accomplishing them are not enough motivation, there is not much that I can say except "good luck."

Make More Decisions Independent of Money
(or Retirement Worries—Get More Out of Life!)

There is another more subtle advantage to building a retirement fund now. With the confidence that you will be where you want to be, financially, at retirement, you may just find that making other decisions in life becomes both clearer and easier. Decisions about careers may now lead you into something that you love to do instead of something that will get you the most immediate dollars. You may get more out of life without retirement worries hanging over you for years and years. Maybe I am overstating it, but having fulfilled a retirement plan that leaves you rich or well off just might change the way you live the rest of your life.

CHAPTER 31

Specific Topics

Asset Allocation

Asset allocation is like the bible in the investment community today. Every major investment firm has an asset allocation system or model and advises clients on the importance of asset allocation. Many believe it is the most important theoretical tool in investments. The ideas of asset allocation and portfolio strategy began back in the 1950s. But they really took hold in the 1980s when many of the major investment houses realized that it was more than a potent investment tool. It was a great marketing strategy to sell wealthy investors on their services.

Asset allocation is a system that divides your investment dollars over asset classes. It tries to achieve a given rate of return while reducing the risk. A simple form of asset allocation might involve analyzing 10 different stocks that all promised an 11% annual compound return. An investor might put all his or her money into one of these stocks or he or she could divide his or her funds in all 10. The promised return of all investments is identical. But what if, while achieving the 11% overall return, 1 of the 10 stocks failed and went bankrupt. Assume the other 9 companies each achieved slightly more than 11% so the investor who invested in all 10 received his or her desired 11% return overall. An investor who put all his or her money in one stock takes the risk the company that failed was the one he or she selected and the entire investment failed. The same estimated return, but the 10-stock plan reduced the investor's risk.

There are many different forms of asset allocation. It can require an investor to divide his or her investment dollars over asset classes like stocks, bonds (short, medium, and long-term), cash, real estate, precious metals, and so forth. The idea is that investing in diverse assets can produce a rate of return objective with reduced risk. If the stock market goes down, the bond market is likely to go up. The idea is to have asset classes that have what allocation theorists call a low correlation. Investments in asset classes should be made so the asset classes offset one another in up or down markets. By reducing the risk of loss (as in the previous example), asset allocation can also lessen the risk of volatility.

Many asset allocation models want investors to "allocate" investments geographically, as well as among asset classes. We live in a world economy and having investments in other parts of the world may provide more risk reduction for a total portfolio.

Asset allocation models adjust the proportion of investments among asset classes based on investor's age. A younger investor will have more money allocated to stocks and less to bonds. An older investor, who may not be in a position to withstand a short-term drop in stock prices, may have more money allocated to bonds and less to stocks. Younger invests can more likely survive a deep recession or depression with investments more often than a retired investor living off investment income.

Asset allocation models also divide investment dollars among different size companies; "small cap," "medium cap," and "large cap" are terms that distinguish companies that have a small, medium, or large market capitalization. Market capitalization is the total value of all the shares of stock that a company has issued determined by its current trading price. A company with 1 million shares outstanding and a $50 per share price has a market capitalization of $50 million.

Asset allocation is used within stock investing groups. It is not a good idea to put all your money into oil and gas stocks even if you think they have good prospects for the coming years. A sudden change in technology making the use of fossil fuels obsolete could drive many oil and gas producers out of business. Asset allocation models recommend the investor divide that portion of his or her investment dollars devoted to stocks among different types of stocks.

I use asset allocation to manage my own investments. Any investor who has significant funds invested should use it. There are many good sources that are available on the subject. I allocate over both asset classes and geographically as protection against a sharp or prolonged decline in prices of any group of assets. I live off investment income. I could invest all my money in dividend-paying stocks and receive income and the potential of large long-term returns. My bond investments give me some protection against a "bear" market in stocks. But I do not believe that allocating investments in this manner is improving my overall return in the long run. My statistical life expectancy is about 16 years. I hope to live another 20 or 25 years, and I am sure that my total net worth would likely be substantially higher in 20 or 25 years if I invested all my money in the stocks or stock funds recommended in Chapter 22. I also know that I will face some periods in the next 20 or 25 years when my net worth and income might decline substantially if I fully invest in the stock market. I am not willing to risk the chance that I would have to downsize my lifestyle in the short run to end a richer man. But in my case, asset allocation is not improving my overall return.

Every situation is different. A young person reading this book with zero investment dollars wants to start an investment plan with $2,000 earned in a summer job. Asset allocation makes little sense to this person. He or she can't divide $2,000 efficiently over many asset classes. For a middle-aged person with some investment dollars already, dividing your assets using an asset allocation model begins to make sense. If you are older, or retired, it is important that you follow an asset allocation plan. You do not have to pay an investment adviser to do a model for you. For instance, I recently picked up Richard Ferri's *All about Asset Allocation* in the bookstore in paperback. There are good sources on the topic for an inexperienced investor.

How does the advice in this book fit into asset allocation? For investors who already have significant investment dollars using an asset allocation model, this plan fits into the stock-investing portion of that model. If you have significant investment dollars, I do not recommend putting all those dollars into the plan in this book. For an investor with enough years left, my advice would be to allocate the funds necessary to meet your retirement investment goals. Then you can use other investment funds or savings to develop your asset allocation model in the years ahead. Young people starting an investment program should keep asset allocation in mind for the future. It is not something to worry about now.

If, as recommended, you are carrying out an investment plan with index mutual funds, you are performing some asset allocation over stock classes immediately. These funds invest in many stocks in different industries and fit asset allocation models for the stock-investing portion of your model. If you are stock selecting for all or part of your retirement fund, you should avoid putting all your money into one stock, like Altria, or one industry, like oil and gas or pharmaceuticals. Over your investment years, divide your money in several different companies in different industries. The stocks listed as "gold" and "silver" stocks in Chapter 22 provide enough alternatives to carry out a reasonable stock asset allocation as a start.

Many asset allocation models want investors to invest in foreign stocks. I have had an investment account in a foreign country for the last 30 years. There are many foreign companies that have return potential that are as good or better than American companies. I am a longtime investor in the Swiss company, Nestlé. As noted in Chapter 8, Nestlé's long-term performance has been good but slightly below market average. I do not recommend overseas investing for amateur investors. Investing outside the United States can be tricky. But many foreign companies do trade their shares on American exchanges. The shares are ADRs. The information available for foreign companies is often limited. It is more difficult for investors to decide if a foreign company meets the standards set out in Chapter 22. Timely information can be critical to your investment success. If you are inexperienced or have only a limited fund of investment dollars, stick to American companies. Most of them are diversifying out of the country anyway.

For a wealthier, experienced investor, putting a part of his or her portfolio in foreign stocks does make sense. Use my system or any system that you devise to make your selections. If you have trouble getting the needed information, stay away. The trading costs for investing in foreign stocks are often higher than that in domestic stocks. One way to get exposure to foreign investing is through mutual funds. Almost every mutual fund family has some funds that invest outside this country. Fees in these funds tend to be higher than on many domestic funds.

Speculative Investing

I love speculative investing. I do it all the time. I invest in biotech's, precious metals, the futures and options markets, and even nanotechnology stocks. I know that part of the attraction to investing for many investors is the same attraction that many of us get in Las Vegas or Atlantic City in the casinos. I am not going to preach to you about the evils of speculative investing. Speculators perform an important function in many markets. The most money I ever made in an investment idea was speculating in gold and silver futures' contracts in 1978 and 1979. *But*, and this is a big but, you don't speculate with your retirement fund. Like gambling in the casinos, you only speculate with money that you can afford to lose.

It is critical that you develop a way of thinking about your investments that allows you to allocate your investments just like the asset allocation crowd. Retirement investments are not the same animal as speculative investing even if occasionally you invest in similar assets. Fund your retirement plan first, and always fund it. If you have excess funds and you want to speculate, be my guest. For many of you, a retirement plan will let you feel freer to speculate and risk other funds. You know that you have a strong retirement plan in place. The older you are, the less you should speculate. It must represent a smaller and smaller part of your investment portfolio as you age. Ironically, when you were young, you had less investment funds, and this is the most suitable time for speculation. As you get older and gather more savings and investment funds, your speculative funds might remain the same in dollars, but they should be a smaller and smaller part of your total asset structure.

Dogs of the Dow and High Dividend Strategy

One investment strategy is an old favorite, the "Dogs of the Dow" strategy. There are books written about it and even some websites devoted to it. The theory uses the 30 stocks in the Dow Jones Industrial Averages to start. These stocks pay differing dividends; the dividend yields differ from stock to stock. Dividend yield is the dividend divided by the stock's price. The strategy is that you pick a date, usually they use Jan 1 or Dec 31, and list the 30 Dow stocks by dividend yield from highest to lowest. Then buy the Dow stocks with the highest dividend yield. You rebalance your portfolio once every year, selling any stocks that are no longer "high dividend" yielding stocks and buying new entrants. The reason a stock falls out of the high dividend category is usually not because it reduced its dividend. Most fall out because their stock price went way up making the dividend, as a percentage of stock price, lower. If you bought it last year when the dividend yield was high and the price went up, you have a nice profit.

The reason investors call the high dividend yield stocks "Dogs" is that their stock price is low relative to their dividend, so they are temporarily out of favor with the market, a "dog." The advocates of this theory can produce evidence to show that over many years, this strategy outperforms the market averages. James O'Shaughnessy, whose work I trust, did an extensive analysis of the Dogs of the Dow strategy from 1928 to 2003. He found that the Dog strategy outperformed the S&P 500 significantly (a 12.24% annual compound return for the Dogs versus 9.70% compound return for the S&P). Careful readers of this book know what

—

a dramatic difference those rates translate to in return over many years. O'Shaughnessy also found that the Dogs had less downside risk in "bear" markets. In 2006, the "Dogs of the Dow" returned a 24.8% return for the year compared to 18.2% for the entire Dow and 16.3% for the S&P. Figure 31A1 shows the results of the Dogs of the Dow (10 highest yielding Dow stocks) strategy compared with all 30 Dow stocks for the previous 5 years.

FIGURE 31A1 Dogs of the Dow Strategy[149]
Recent Results

Year	Dogs of the Dow	Dow 30
2005	−8.9%	−1.1%
2004	+.05%	+4.4%
2003	+23.6%	+28.7%
2002	−12.2%	−18.6%
2001	−7.8%	−7.3%
10 Years	12.9%	14.0%

The Dog strategy has not performed as well in the last 10 years as it has for a much longer time. Even so, I like strategies like Dogs of the Dow that promote dividend-paying stocks.

The Use of Leverage

Leverage is a financial term that means multiplying your results usually using borrowed money. In stock investing, an investor can purchase more stock than he or she has cash. The broker will loan him or her the added money and charge the investor interest. If the investor's investments are profitable, he or she may earn a much greater return at a fairly low cost. I do not advise long-term investors to use leverage in an attempt to increase returns. All brokers require something called "margin" when an investor leverages his or her investments and borrows money from the broker. A typically levered stock position might find an investor with $10,000 worth of stock but only investing $5,000 of his or her own money. If the stock appreciates over the years, an investor can profit from leverage. But we know that markets are susceptible to inevitable downturns. When stock prices turn down, the investor must continually put up additional funds to maintain the margin, in the example 50%. The investor must keep 50% of the market value of the stock in cash. If the price of the stock drops 10%, it is now worth only $9,000. Our investor's cash position is now $4,000. (He or she lost $1,000 when the price of the stock declined.) The broker requires 50% of $9,000 or $4,500 as his or her margin requirement. The investor must deposit an additional $500 to bring his or her margin up to 50%. If he or she does not or cannot, the broker will (according to the rules of the exchanges) liquidate enough of the investor's position to place the margin back to 50%. So investors in a margined, leveraged, position must be able to make additional cash deposits in the event of a temporary downturn in the stock's price. We saw in Chapter 8 how the stellar performer of the past 50 years, Altria, lost over 50% of its market value in 1 year. A fully leveraged investor would be wiped out under those circumstances. Altria recovered the following year and went on to post new highs each of the next 6 years, but our leveraged investor lost everything. This only has to happen once in 60 or 70 years for an investor to lose everything. Long-term investors do not need to leverage their investments to earn spectacular returns, and I strongly advise against it.

Price Earnings Ratio

The price-earnings ratio is the most commonly used statistical technique in analyzing stock prices. It is a simple calculation that divides the current price of a stock for 1 share by its earnings for the year for 1 share. Earnings are usually quoted per share since some multimillion dollar number has little meaning for an average investor. If the company reports earnings per share of $1 for the year and the price of the stock is $20 per share, the P/E ratio is 20 (20 to 1). There are many different theories about P/E ratios; they should be low, they should be high, or they should bear some relationship to historic P/Es for that particular stock. Many analysts and economists have studied P/E ratios over a long period of time and worry about current P/E ratios. If you simply average the yearly P/E ratios for the S&P 500 for the 134 years of its existence, it turns out that the average P/E ratio for the S&P is 14.88. That means on average the price of an S&P stock was about 15 times its earnings at the end of an average year. The range on the P/E ratio in history has been a low of 5.31 in 1917 to a high of 46.37 in 2001. Some argue that low P/Es are the time to buy stocks, and when P/Es are high, it is the time to sell stocks. The P/E ratio was 20.48 at the end of 2004 on the S&P 500. Maybe it was a good time to sell until either stock prices fell below the historic average of 15 or earnings increases brought the average down to 15 or less. But P/E ratios are tricky. Only 1 year since 1989 has the P/E ratio dropped

—

below 15. And that was to 14.88, which is exactly the historic 134-year average. An investor using historic P/E ratios would have missed a good stock market for the last 15 years.

A high P/E ratio for a stock or for the entire market can mean several things besides just the idea that stocks might be "overpriced." For instance, high P/E ratios might mean that company prospects for the future are better than normal. Rational investors see this and bid the price higher to reflect the improved economic conditions or prospects for future earnings. So there is no easy answer to the P/E question and much is in the eyes of the beholder.

The real question is not whether P/E ratios are higher or lower than average but will your future returns go down if you buy stocks during high P/E years rather than low P/E years? I looked at this in Figure 31B1. I divided investments into 4 classifications; P/E ratios lower than 10, P/E ratios between 10 and 15, P/E ratios between 15 and 20 and P/E ratios over 20. And I looked at compound returns for each classification for 5 different time frames, 5 years, 10 years, 20 years, 50 years and returns to 2004. The results are in Figure 31F1. Looking at the long-term, up to 134 years, it turns out the low P/E ratio years did compound at a higher rate of return than average. What seems surprising for those that believe in investing only in low P/E years, the highest P/E classification of over 20 produced the second best results. The 10-15 and 15-20 P/E ratio years were both slightly below average. I am not recommending using this as an investment tool, but if you did, you would only invest in years in which the P/E ratio was either low or high. You will notice that in 4 of the 5 time frames the same pattern held. Investments in high and low P/E years produced better returns than those closer to average. The under 10 P/E ratio produced a better return in 4 of the 5 time frames, and I would discount any results from a 5-year time frame for a long-term investor. It is correct that an investor who invested only in low P/E years would have produced better compound rates of return. The problem with trying to use this information for a long-term investor is the last time an opportunity to invest with an average P/E under 10 occurred 23 years ago. Long-term investors also understand the role of time in investing success, and 23 years are a lot of years lost compounding dividends.

If we look at the high P/E ratio category (over 20), we find that in 4 of the 5 time periods, investment in high P/E periods produced better than average returns. And only in onetime period (20 years) did an investment in a high P/E year produce below-average returns. It seems the most attractive time to invest is during high or low P/E ratio years.

FIGURE 31B1 Price/Earnings Ratios and Historical Returns
S&P 500, 1870-2004

Compound Yearly Return	P/E Ratio			
	Less than 10	10-15	15-20	More than 20
To December 31, 2004	11.57%	10.52%	10.42%	10.60%
For 50 years	10.77%	8.83%	8.65%	9.70%
For 20 years	11.74%	8.42%	8.71%	8.05%
For 10 years	13.72%	9.02%	7.20%	9.84%
For 5 years	14.49%	9.20%	5.96%	15.46%

Nothing in Figure 31B1 would deter me from encouraging you to begin an investment program right now. If you wait until the P/E ratio on the S&P 500 is below 10, you may wait 20 years or more or forever. The compound rate of return you could have earned even at a reduced rate would not be recaptured. P/E ratios have their place in investment analysis, and if you ever get the opportunity to invest in stocks when the average P/E is less than 10, go ahead. Increase your investment if possible. But Figure 25C2 shows that waiting years for an average P/E to fall into the low teens or to the historic average of 15 may not make sense. Even if you earn a higher compound rate, you will have lost added compounding years during the waiting period. Remember time is your ally.

CHAPTER 32

Conclusion

I want to apologize for some of the repetitive material and advice that I emphasized over and over again in this book. The issues are so critical that I wanted to be sure that the reader realized how important they really are.

I summarize a few of the critical points that require this emphasis in this book in Figures 32A1 and 32A2. In Figures 32A1 and 32A2, I am going to assume that a fairly wealthy family in 1940 had quintuplets: Johnny, Jamie, Joey, Jimmy, and Jerry. Mom and Dad knew a little bit about compound rates of return and decided to fund an investment account for each of the kids at birth. They liked General Electric and invested $10,000 for each child in General Electric stock in 1940. Each child received exactly the same number of shares at the same cost. However, for some inexplicable reason, the accounts were set up in different ways and the investment strategy differed slightly for each.

Johnny's investment in GE stock was made through a Roth IRA. (There was no such thing as a Roth IRA or any IRA in 1940, but I am going to assume there was for illustrative purposes. Today, Roth IRAs are common.) Johnny reinvested all dividends and distributions that he received from GE in additional stock in his Roth IRA account. Because he had an IRA, he paid no taxes when those distributions were made and was able to reinvest the full amount of dividends that GE paid. By the time Johnny was 65 years old, his investment in GE stock was worth $22,943,292. He can now remove and use all or some of this money from his account at any time and will pay *zero* taxes.

Jamie's investment in GE stock was made in exactly the same way as Johnny's, a Roth IRA, reinvesting all distributions without paying taxes. Jamie wanted to retire early, and so she closed her account at age 55, liquidated her stock, and took the money to live on 10 years earlier than Johnny. (For purposes of illustration I am going to assume that there is no penalty for early withdrawal. In fact, as discussed in Chapter 17 on IRAs, there is such a penalty for anyone withdrawing funds from an IRA before the age of 59½.) By the time Jamie was 55 years old, her investment in GE stock was worth $4,763,121. Although Jamie did everything else right, she suffered a loss of almost 80% compared to Johnny for choosing to terminate her investment 10 years earlier than Johnny.

Joey's investment in GE stock was made through a regular brokerage account, probably the only method actually available in 1940. Joey reinvested all his dividends and other distributions, but because this was not a tax-sheltered investment account, Joey had to pay taxes each year on the distributions before he could reinvest them. I am assuming that Joey paid the maximum Federal tax rate on dividends then in force each year. Joey held his investment for the full 65 years, and Joey's investment in GE stock was worth $5,639,009. (If we assume that Joey paid taxes each year at half of the maximum rate, his final total was $11,548,162, still a loss of 50%.) Although Joey held his investment for the full 65 years, reinvested all distributions, he suffered a loss of just over 75% compared to Johnny because the account in which the investment was set up required him to pay taxes on the distributions.

Jimmy's investment in GE stock was made through a Roth IRA. However, in Jimmy's account, dividends and distributions were not reinvested in additional GE stock; they were simply held in cash in the account. Jimmy held his investment for the full 65 years, and his investment in GE stock plus cash from dividends was worth $6,641,221, a loss of more than 71% compared to Johnny's account. (Jimmy could have improved his return by investing his distributions in anything that produced a return, stocks, bonds, CDs, etc.)

Finally, Jerry's investment in GE stock was made through a regular brokerage account like Joey's, but Jerry did not reinvest any distributions or dividends, and he simply took the distributions and spent them each year. Jerry did hold his investment for the full 65 years. By the time Jerry was 65 years old, his investment in GE stock was worth $3,240,595, a whopping loss of over 85% compared to Johnny's.

Five accounts, the same dollar investment, all invested in the same stock, but look at the difference in final results. Long-term investors need to look carefully at how their investments are structured, how long they last, and how they manage any distributions along the way.

FIGURE 32A1 $10,000 Investment for Each of Five Quintuplets Born in 1940
General Electric Stock in 1940
Different Results Based on Structure of Investment

Quintuplets	Investment Conditions	Final Total	Percent Lost	Compound Rate
Johnny	Roth IRA, reinvest all, held for 65 years	$22,943,292	—	12.64%
Jamie	Roth IRA, reinvest all, held for 55 years	$4,763,121	79.24%	11.86%
Joey	Regular account, reinvest all, held for 65 years	$5,639,009	75.43%	10.24%
Jimmy	Roth IRA, no reinvestment, hold distributions, 65 years	$6,641,221	71.06%	10.51%
Jerry	Regular account, no reinvestment, spend dividends, 65 years	$3,240,595	85.88%	9.30%

Now let us use the same quintuplets and make some new assumptions. Let's assume that our parents invested $10,000 for each child in 5 different stock investments. But this time let us assume that all the accounts were structured correctly to get the maximum return. All the accounts were Roth IRAs, all reinvested all distributions and dividends, and all of them held their accounts for 65 years until they were 65 and ready to retire.

However, in a distorted attempt at diversification, the parents invested Johnny's $10,000 in GE stock, Jamie's $10,000 in the Dow Chemical stock, Joey's $10,000 in Standard and Poors Composite, Jimmy's $10,000 in Zenith Radio (later Zenith Electronics), and Jerry's $10,000 in Bethlehem Steel. Figure 32A2 shows the various results.

Five different investments used the same structure to get the maximum return. Two of the kids lost everything since Zenith and Bethlehem Steel went under. The S&P composite result was great but not as spectacular as the GE investment, and Dow Chemical performed fairly well, although it clearly lagged the overall market average.

Long-term investors also need to be careful in selecting their investment portfolio. The message in these two figures is clear. Both investment selection and investment structure are critically important.

—

Making good investment decisions is critical, but it is only one side of the coin. Investors must also structure their investments properly in order to get the maximum return that is available. I hope that this book will help you accomplish both.

FIGURE 32A2 $10,000 Investment for Each of Five Quintuplets
Born in 1940
Different Results Based on Different Investments
Investment Structure Identical

Quintuplets	Investment	Final Total	Percent Lost	Compound Rate
Johnny	General Electric Stock	$22,943,292	—	12.64%
Jamie	Dow Chemical	$2,886,798	87.42%	9.26%
Joey	S&P Composite	$12,482,186	54.40%	11.78%
Jimmy	Zenith Electronics	$0	100.0%	0%
Jerry	Bethlehem Steel	$0	100.0%	0%

Finally, a Simple Plan to End Rich

Get a job. Earn at least $3,000.
Put $3,000 in a Roth IRA (I assume that you qualify).
Invest the $3,000 once in your IRA in the Vanguard 500 Index fund.
Forget About It!

Results for a 15-year-old assuming an 11.76% compound rate of return.
At age 70, you will have $1,357,916 in your Roth IRA account
Assume you retire at age 70 and live to 100 and you take the minimum mandatory withdrawals required in the traditional IRA.

At age 100, your Roth IRA will be worth over $3 million and you will have withdrawn and spent over $7.7 million between age 70 and age 100.

All for earning and investing a onetime $3,000 now!

APPENDIX

TABLE 5A1 Nominal Dollar Returns by Rate and Years

				Return			
Rate	8.00%	9.00%	10.00%	11.00%	12.00%	13.00%	14.00%
$1,000							
Years							
20	$4,661	$5,604	$6,727	$8,062	$9,646	$11,523	$13,743
30	$10,063	$13,268	$17,449	$22,892	$29,960	$39,116	$50,950
40	$21,725	$31,409	$45,259	$65,001	$93,051	$132,782	$188,884
50	$46,902	$74,358	$117,391	$184,565	$289,002	$450,736	$700,233
60	$101,257	$176,031	$304,482	$524,057	$897,597	$1,530,053	$2,595,919
70	$218,606	$416,730	$789,747	$1,488,019	$2,787,800	$5,193,870	$9,623,645
80	$471,955	$986,552	$2,048,400	$4,225,113	$8,658,483	$17,630,940	$35,676,982
90	$1,018,915	$2,335,527	$5,313,023	$11,996,874	$26,891,934	$59,849,416	$132,262,467
$10,000							
Years							
20	$46,610	$56,044	$67,275	$80,623	$96,463	$115,231	$137,435
30	$100,627	$132,677	$174,494	$228,923	$299,599	$391,159	$509,502
40	$217,245	$314,094	$452,593	$650,009	$930,510	$1,327,816	$1,888,835
50	$469,016	$743,575	$1,173,909	$1,845,648	$2,890,022	$4,507,359	$7,002,330
60	$1,012,571	$1,760,313	$3,044,816	$5,240,572	$8,975,969	$15,300,535	$25,959,187
70	$2,186,064	$4,167,301	$7,897,470	$14,880,191	$27,877,998	$51,938,696	$96,236,450
80	$4,719,548	$9,865,517	$20,484,002	$42,251,128	$86,584,831	$176,309,405	$356,769,818
90	$10,189,151	$23,355,266	$53,130,226	$119,968,738	$268,919,342	$598,494,155	$1,322,624,674

TABLE 5A2 Simple and Compound Returns Illustrated

Year	Simple Interest Rate of Return			Compound Rate of Return		
	Investment	Return	Total	Investment	Return	Total
1	$1,000	$110	$1,110	$1,000	$110	$1,110
2	$0	$110	$1,220	$0	$122	$1,232
3	$0	$110	$1,330	$0	$136	$1,368
4	$0	$110	$1,440	$0	$150	$1,518
5	$0	$110	$1,550	$0	$167	$1,685
6	$0	$110	$1,660	$0	$185	$1,870
7	$0	$110	$1,770	$0	$206	$2,076
8	$0	$110	$1,880	$0	$228	$2,305
9	$0	$110	$1,990	$0	$253	$2,558
10	$0	$110	$2,100	$0	$281	$2,839
20	$0	$110	$3,200	$0	$5,222	$8,061
30	$0	$110	$4,300	$0	$14,828	$22,889
40	$0	$110	$5,400	$0	$42,102	$64,991
50	$0	$110	$6,500	$0	$119,546	$184,537
60	$0	$110	$7,600	$0	$339,443	$523,980
70	$0	$110	$8,700	$0	$963,819	$1,487,799

TABLE 6A1 Standard and Poor's Composite Returns

Stock Market Data Used in Robert J. Shiller's *Irrational Exuberance* updated					
Amount Invested	$10,000				
Year	S&P Composite Price	Dividends per Share	Shares Owned	Value	Compound Yearly Rate of Return From Year to End
			2,252.25	$10,000	9.05%
1871	4.74	0.26	2,375.79	$11,261	9.03%
1872	5.07	0.3	2,516.37	$12,758	9.00%
1873	4.42	0.33	2,704.25	$11,953	9.12%
1874	4.54	0.33	2,900.81	$13,170	9.11%
1875	4.37	0.3	3,099.95	$13,547	9.16%
1876	3.58	0.3	3,359.72	$12,028	9.34%
1877	3.25	0.19	3,556.14	$11,557	9.45%
1878	3.45	0.18	3,741.68	$12,909	9.43%
1879	4.92	0.2	3,893.78	$19,157	9.17%
1880	5.84	0.26	4,067.13	$23,752	9.06%
1881	6.01	0.32	4,283.68	$25,745	9.06%
1882	5.84	0.32	4,518.41	$26,387	9.12%
1883	5.34	0.33	4,797.63	$25,619	9.22%
1884	4.34	0.31	5,140.32	$22,309	9.43%
1885	5.2	0.24	5,377.57	$27,963	9.30%
1886	5.64	0.22	5,587.33	$31,513	9.27%
1887	5.27	0.25	5,852.38	$30,842	9.38%
1888	5.14	0.23	6,114.26	$31,427	9.44%
1889	5.32	0.22	6,367.11	$33,873	9.46%
1890	4.6	0.22	6,671.62	$30,689	9.64%
1891	5.41	0.22	6,942.92	$37,561	9.53%
1892	5.51	0.24	7,245.34	$39,922	9.56%
1893	4.41	0.25	7,656.07	$33,763	9.82%
1894	4.3	0.21	8,029.97	$34,529	9.89%
1895	4.32	0.19	8,383.14	$36,215	9.94%
1896	4.22	0.18	8,740.72	$36,886	10.02%
1897	4.75	0.18	9,071.94	$43,092	9.95%
1898	5.65	0.2	9,393.07	$53,071	9.84%
1899	6.02	0.21	9,720.74	$58,519	9.83%

—

1900	6.87	0.3	10,145.23	$69,698	9.75%
1901	7.95	0.32	10,553.59	$83,901	9.65%
1902	8.05	0.33	10,986.22	$88,439	9.69%
1903	6.57	0.35	11,571.48	$76,025	9.96%
1904	8.25	0.31	12,006.29	$99,052	9.77%
1905	9.54	0.33	12,421.60	$118,502	9.67%
1906	9.84	0.4	12,926.54	$127,197	9.70%
1907	6.57	0.44	13,792.25	$90,615	10.19%
1908	9.03	0.4	14,403.20	$130,061	9.88%
1909	10.3	0.44	15,018.48	$154,690	9.79%
1910	9.05	0.47	15,798.45	$142,976	9.99%
1911	9.11	0.47	16,613.52	$151,349	10.04%
1912	9.38	0.48	17,463.68	$163,809	10.06%
1913	8.04	0.48	18,506.28	$148,791	10.29%
1914	7.35	0.42	19,563.79	$143,794	10.45%
1915	9.48	0.43	20,451.17	$193,877	10.21%
1916	9.8	0.56	21,619.81	$211,874	10.22%
1917	6.8	0.69	23,813.59	$161,932	10.68%
1918	7.9	0.57	25,531.78	$201,701	10.53%
1919	8.92	0.53	27,048.80	$241,275	10.43%
1920	6.81	0.51	29,074.49	$197,997	10.82%
1921	7.31	0.46	30,904.07	$225,909	10.78%
1922	8.78	0.51	32,699.18	$287,099	10.59%
1923	8.55	0.53	34,726.15	$296,909	10.69%
1924	10.16	0.55	36,606.01	$371,917	10.51%
1925	12.46	0.6	38,368.74	$478,074	10.30%
1926	13.49	0.69	40,331.26	$544,069	10.26%
1927	17.46	0.77	42,109.90	$735,239	9.97%
1928	23.15	0.85	43,656.05	$1,010,638	9.65%
1929	21.4	0.97	45,634.85	$976,586	9.83%
1930	15.51	0.98	48,518.30	$752,519	10.36%
1931	8.44	0.82	53,232.16	$449,279	11.29%
1932	6.82	0.5	57,134.81	$389,659	11.68%
1933	9.97	0.44	59,656.30	$594,773	11.19%
1934	9.26	0.45	62,555.37	$579,263	11.40%
1935	13.04	0.47	64,810.05	$845,123	10.96%
1936	17.06	0.72	67,545.29	$1,152,323	10.63%

1937	11.02	0.8	72,448.76	$798,385	11.40%
1938	12.69	0.51	75,360.41	$956,324	11.28%
1939	12.37	0.62	79,137.57	$978,932	11.42%
1940	10.53	0.67	84,172.92	$886,341	11.78%
1941	8.76	0.71	90,995.15	$797,118	12.17%
1942	9.52	0.59	96,634.56	$919,961	12.12%
1943	11.48	0.61	101,769.32	$1,168,312	11.89%
1944	13.1	0.64	106,741.25	$1,398,310	11.76%
1945	17.33	0.66	110,806.42	$1,920,275	11.38%
1946	15.13	0.71	116,006.19	$1,755,174	11.76%
1947	15.03	0.84	122,489.57	$1,841,018	11.88%
1948	15.19	0.93	129,988.93	$1,974,532	11.96%
1949	16.54	1.14	138,948.26	$2,298,204	11.89%
1950	19.75	1.47	149,290.23	$2,948,482	11.60%
1951	23.41	1.41	158,282.09	$3,705,384	11.35%
1952	26.04	1.41	166,852.66	$4,344,843	11.24%
1953	24.83	1.45	176,596.37	$4,384,888	11.45%
1954	34.97	1.54	184,373.28	$6,447,533	10.84%
1955	45.37	1.64	191,037.86	$8,667,388	10.40%
1956	46.44	1.74	198,195.61	$9,204,204	10.49%
1957	40.33	1.79	206,992.29	$8,347,999	10.96%
1958	53.49	1.75	213,764.33	$11,434,254	10.45%
1959	59.06	1.83	220,387.91	$13,016,110	10.38%
1960	56.8	1.95	227,954.05	$12,947,790	10.64%
1961	71.74	2.02	234,372.60	$16,813,891	10.23%
1962	62.64	2.13	242,342.17	$15,180,314	10.75%
1963	74.17	2.28	249,791.82	$18,527,059	10.49%
1964	83.96	2.5	257,229.64	$21,597,000	10.34%
1965	91.73	2.72	264,857.07	$24,295,339	10.29%
1966	81.33	2.87	274,203.44	$22,300,965	10.82%
1967	95.3	2.92	282,605.05	$26,932,262	10.56%
1968	106.5	3.07	290,751.51	$30,965,036	10.44%
1969	91.11	3.16	300,835.74	$27,409,145	11.14%
1970	90.05	3.14	311,325.74	$28,034,883	11.42%
1971	99.17	3.07	320,963.43	$31,829,944	11.35%
1972	117.5	3.15	329,567.99	$38,724,238	11.04%
1973	94.78	3.38	341,320.89	$32,350,394	12.07%

1974	67.07	3.6	359,641.37	$24,121,147	13.60%
1975	88.7	3.68	374,562.23	$33,223,670	12.85%
1976	104.7	4.05	389,051.03	$40,733,643	12.52%
1977	93.82	4.67	408,416.50	$38,317,636	13.26%
1978	96.11	5.07	429,961.31	$41,323,581	13.48%
1979	107.8	5.65	452,496.39	$48,779,111	13.30%
1980	133.5	6.16	473,375.62	$63,195,646	12.67%
1981	123.8	6.63	498,726.84	$61,742,382	13.37%
1982	139.4	6.87	523,305.41	$72,948,774	13.16%
1983	164.4	7.09	545,873.75	$89,741,645	12.71%
1984	164.5	7.53	570,861.17	$93,906,662	13.13%
1985	207.3	7.9	592,616.13	$122,849,323	12.26%
1986	248.6	8.28	612,354.10	$152,231,230	11.65%
1987	241	8.81	634,739.33	$152,972,179	12.34%
1988	276.5	9.73	657,075.73	$181,681,439	11.95%
1989	348.6	11.05	677,903.86	$236,317,286	10.84%
1990	328.75	12.1	702,854.85	$231,063,531	11.84%
1991	388.51	12.2	724,925.91	$281,640,965	11.10%
1992	435.64	12.38	745,526.83	$324,781,306	10.75%
1993	465.95	12.58	765,655.01	$356,756,952	10.84%
1994	455.19	13.18	787,824.51	$358,609,837	11.92%
1995	614.57	13.79	805,502.07	$495,037,407	9.35%
1996	743.25	14.9	821,650.04	$610,691,394	7.71%
1997	962.37	15.5	834,883.60	$803,466,927	4.68%
1998	1,190.05	16.2	846,248.76	$1,007,078,338	1.58%
1999	1,428.68	16.48	856,010.34	$1,222,964,860	−1.98%
2000	1,330.93	16.27	866,474.67	$1,153,217,137	−1.03%
2001	1,144.93	15.74	878,386.59	$1,005,691,159	3.23%
2002	899.18	16.07	894,084.97	$803,943,327	17.31%
2003	1,080.64	17.39	908,472.87	$981,732,124	12.69%
2004	1,199.21	18.6	922,563.48	$1,106,347,348	

Table 6A2 Return Calculation Formulas
(For Excel Worksheets)

Calculate Ending Value **Given:**	A = Amount invested (single onetime investment) B = Years to maturity C = Compound annual rate of return Ending value = $A*((1 + C)B)$
Calculate Rate of Return **Given:**	A = Amount invested (single onetime investment) B = Years to maturity C = Ending value Rate of return = *Rate* (B,,-A,C)
Calculate Ending Value **Given:**	A = Initial investment (single onetime investment) B = Years to maturity C = Compound annual rate of return D = Additional yearly investments (identical amounts) Ending value = $(A*((1 + C)B) - (FV(C,B,D,0,1))$

TABLE 10A1 MFS Mass Investors Trust A

MFS Trust A		1924	Distribution Reinvestment Model		
	Beginning Year	Cumulative Distribution Reinvested	End Year	Capital Appreciation	Total Value
1924	$10,000	$0	$10,760	$760	$10,760
1925	$10,760	$699	$13,607	$2,148	$12,908
1926	$13,607	$751	$15,085	$727	$13,635
1927	$15,085	$808	$19,951	$4,058	$17,693
1928	$19,951	$1,173	$25,649	$4,525	$22,218
1929	$25,649	$1,009	$23,503	-$3,155	$19,063
1930	$23,503	$1,012	$17,290	-$7,225	$11,838
1931	$17,290	$928	$9,820	-$8,398	$3,440
1932	$9,820	$573	$9,479	-$914	$2,526
1933	$9,479	$543	$12,490	$2,468	$4,994
1934	$12,490	$598	$13,902	$814	$5,808
1935	$13,902	$653	$18,501	$3,946	$9,754
1936	$18,501	$1,667	$24,008	$3,840	$13,594
1937	$24,008	$925	$16,201	-$8,732	$4,862
1938	$16,201	$716	$20,130	$3,213	$8,075
1939	$20,130	$790	$19,810	-$1,110	$6,965
1940	$19,810	$958	$17,990	-$2,778	$4,187
1941	$17,990	$1,034	$16,455	-$2,569	$1,618
1942	$16,455	$965	$18,904	$1,484	$3,102
1943	$18,904	$1,001	$23,586	$3,681	$6,783
1944	$23,586	$1,138	$28,491	$3,767	$10,550
1945	$28,491	$1,874	$37,705	$7,340	$17,890
1946	$37,705	$2,377	$35,801	-$4,281	$13,609
1947	$35,801	$1,722	$36,629	-$894	$12,715
1948	$36,629	$2,059	$37,054	-$1,634	$11,081
1949	$37,054	$2,216	$44,599	$5,329	$16,410
1950	$44,599	$2,938	$56,893	$9,356	$25,766
1951	$56,893	$5,169	$69,949	$7,887	$33,653
1952	$69,949	$4,538	$80,256	$5,769	$39,422
1953	$80,256	$3,709	$80,534	-$3,431	$35,991
1954	$80,534	$6,587	$123,116	$35,995	$71,986

1955	$123,116	$8,958	$153,679	$21,605	$93,591
1956	$153,679	$7,764	$171,030	$9,587	$103,178
1957	$171,030	$8,706	$151,003	-$28,733	$74,445
1958	$151,003	$8,070	$216,469	$57,396	$131,841
1959	$216,469	$10,231	$236,247	$9,547	$141,388
1960	$236,247	$10,716	$234,293	-$12,670	$128,718
1961	$234,293	$17,958	$294,770	$42,519	$171,237
1962	$294,770	$13,725	$266,362	-$42,133	$129,104
1963	$266,362	$14,864	$319,983	$38,757	$167,861
1964	$319,983	$13,418	$371,101	$37,700	$205,561
1965	$371,101	$24,221	$409,344	$14,022	$219,583
1966	$409,344	$28,923	$377,970	-$60,297	$159,286
1967	$377,970	$40,805	$454,244	$35,469	$194,755
1968	$454,244	$44,338	$501,889	$3,307	$198,062
1969	$501,889	$32,176	$477,978	-$56,087	$141,975
1970	$477,978	$47,905	$482,280	-$43,603	$98,372
1971	$482,280	$79,246	$526,136	-$35,390	$62,982
1972	$526,136	$43,335	$584,882	$15,411	$78,393
1973	$584,882	$24,869	$511,211	-$98,540	-$20,147
1974	$511,211	$19,606	$380,035	-$150,782	-$170,929
1975	$380,035	$27,193	$505,911	$98,683	-$72,246
1976	$505,911	$31,109	$625,462	$88,442	$16,196
1977	$625,462	$32,615	$556,273	-$101,804	-$85,608
1978	$556,273	$36,487	$602,306	$9,546	-$76,062
1979	$602,306	$53,962	$734,757	$78,489	$2,427
1980	$734,757	$98,928	$959,704	$126,019	$128,446
1981	$959,704	$110,945	$912,820	-$157,829	-$29,383
1982	$912,820	$133,225	$1,085,280	$39,235	$9,852
1983	$1,085,280	$174,536	$1,311,994	$52,178	$62,030
1984	$1,311,994	$105,346	$1,350,514	-$66,826	-$4,796
1985	$1,350,514	$195,577	$1,682,213	$136,122	$131,326
1986	$1,682,213	$304,487	$1,971,695	-$15,005	$116,321
1987	$1,971,695	$295,746	$2,118,821	-$148,620	-$32,299
1988	$2,118,821	$230,128	$2,338,812	-$10,137	-$42,436
1989	$2,338,812	$357,258	$3,183,633	$487,563	$445,127
1990	$3,183,633	$298,988	$3,180,490	-$302,131	$142,996
1991	$3,180,490	$459,303	$4,060,471	$420,678	$563,674

—

1992	$4,060,471	$766,697	$4,360,301	-$466,867	$96,807
1993	$4,360,301	$737,897	$4,797,550	-$300,648	-$203,841
1994	$4,797,550	$556,443	$4,748,663	-$605,330	-$809,171
1995	$4,748,663	$614,642	$6,616,924	$1,253,619	$444,448
1996	$6,616,924	$803,499	$8,330,655	$910,232	$1,354,680
1997	$8,330,655	$844,486	$10,970,839	$1,795,698	$3,150,378
1998	$10,970,839	$768,176	$13,488,722	$1,749,707	$4,900,085
1999	$13,488,722	$454,196	$14,427,023	$484,105	$5,384,190
2000	$14,427,023	$592,176	$14,377,917	-$641,282	$4,742,908
2001	$14,377,917	$138,908	$12,042,968	-$2,473,857	$2,269,051
2002	$12,042,968	$48,695	$9,393,444	-$2,698,219	-$429,168
2003	$9,393,444	$66,503	$11,472,953	$2,013,006	$1,583,838
2004	$11,472,953	$110,237	$12,793,272	$1,210,082	$2,793,920
2005	$12,793,272				

TABLE 12A1 Sources—Life Extension

Michael Fossel, *Reversing Human Aging*, William Morrow & Company.
Marvin Cetron and Owen Davies, *Probably Tomorrows*, St. Martin's Press.
Christopher Meyer and Stan Davis, *It's Alive*, Crown Business.
Ray Kurzweil, *The Age of Spiritual Machines*, Penguin Press.
Jeremy Rifkin, *The Biotech Century*, Putnam.
Douglass Mulhall, *Our Molecular Future*, Prometheus Books.
K. Eric Drexler, *Engines of Creation*, Anchor Press.

Websites

http://www.foresight.org/
http://nano.xeros.com/nanotech/feynman.html
http://sandbox.xerox.com/nano
http://www.extropy.org

TABLE 13A1 Inflation Factor by Inflation Rate and Year

				Impact of Inflation on Return by Rate and Years				
Inflation Rate	0.500%	1.000%	1.500%	2.000%	2.500%	3.000%	3.500%	4.000%
Year	1	1	1	1	1	1	1	1
1	0.995	0.990	0.985	0.980	0.975	0.970	0.965	0.960
2	0.990	0.980	0.970	0.960	0.951	0.941	0.931	0.922
3	0.985	0.970	0.956	0.941	0.927	0.913	0.899	0.885
4	0.980	0.961	0.941	0.922	0.904	0.885	0.867	0.849
5	0.975	0.951	0.927	0.904	0.881	0.859	0.837	0.815
6	0.970	0.941	0.913	0.886	0.859	0.833	0.808	0.783
7	0.966	0.932	0.900	0.868	0.838	0.808	0.779	0.751
8	0.961	0.923	0.886	0.851	0.817	0.784	0.752	0.721
9	0.956	0.914	0.873	0.834	0.796	0.760	0.726	0.693
10	0.951	0.904	0.860	0.817	0.776	0.737	0.700	0.665
11	0.946	0.895	0.847	0.801	0.757	0.715	0.676	0.638
12	0.942	0.886	0.834	0.785	0.738	0.694	0.652	0.613
13	0.937	0.878	0.822	0.769	0.720	0.673	0.629	0.588
14	0.932	0.869	0.809	0.754	0.702	0.653	0.607	0.565
15	0.928	0.860	0.797	0.739	0.684	0.633	0.586	0.542
16	0.923	0.851	0.785	0.724	0.667	0.614	0.566	0.520
17	0.918	0.843	0.773	0.709	0.650	0.596	0.546	0.500
18	0.914	0.835	0.762	0.695	0.634	0.578	0.527	0.480
19	0.909	0.826	0.750	0.681	0.618	0.561	0.508	0.460
20	0.905	0.818	0.739	0.668	0.603	0.544	0.490	0.442
21	0.900	0.810	0.728	0.654	0.588	0.527	0.473	0.424
22	0.896	0.802	0.717	0.641	0.573	0.512	0.457	0.407
23	0.891	0.794	0.706	0.628	0.559	0.496	0.441	0.391
24	0.887	0.786	0.696	0.616	0.545	0.481	0.425	0.375
25	0.882	0.778	0.685	0.603	0.531	0.467	0.410	0.360
26	0.878	0.770	0.675	0.591	0.518	0.453	0.396	0.346
27	0.873	0.762	0.665	0.580	0.505	0.439	0.382	0.332
28	0.869	0.755	0.655	0.568	0.492	0.426	0.369	0.319
29	0.865	0.747	0.645	0.557	0.480	0.413	0.356	0.306
30	0.860	0.740	0.635	0.545	0.468	0.401	0.343	0.294
31	0.856	0.732	0.626	0.535	0.456	0.389	0.331	0.282
32	0.852	0.725	0.617	0.524	0.445	0.377	0.320	0.271
33	0.848	0.718	0.607	0.513	0.434	0.366	0.309	0.260

—

34	0.843	0.711	0.598	0.503	0.423	0.355	0.298	0.250
35	0.839	0.703	0.589	0.493	0.412	0.344	0.287	0.240
36	0.835	0.696	0.580	0.483	0.402	0.334	0.277	0.230
37	0.831	0.689	0.572	0.474	0.392	0.324	0.268	0.221
38	0.827	0.683	0.563	0.464	0.382	0.314	0.258	0.212
39	0.822	0.676	0.555	0.455	0.373	0.305	0.249	0.204
40	0.818	0.669	0.546	0.446	0.363	0.296	0.240	0.195
41	0.814	0.662	0.538	0.437	0.354	0.287	0.232	0.188
42	0.810	0.656	0.530	0.428	0.345	0.278	0.224	0.180
43	0.806	0.649	0.522	0.419	0.337	0.270	0.216	0.173
44	0.802	0.643	0.514	0.411	0.328	0.262	0.209	0.166
45	0.798	0.636	0.507	0.403	0.320	0.254	0.201	0.159
46	0.794	0.630	0.499	0.395	0.312	0.246	0.194	0.153
47	0.790	0.624	0.491	0.387	0.304	0.239	0.187	0.147
48	0.786	0.617	0.484	0.379	0.297	0.232	0.181	0.141
49	0.782	0.611	0.477	0.372	0.289	0.225	0.175	0.135
50	0.778	0.605	0.470	0.364	0.282	0.218	0.168	0.130
51	0.774	0.599	0.463	0.357	0.275	0.212	0.163	0.125
52	0.771	0.593	0.456	0.350	0.268	0.205	0.157	0.120
53	0.767	0.587	0.449	0.343	0.261	0.199	0.151	0.115
54	0.763	0.581	0.442	0.336	0.255	0.193	0.146	0.110
55	0.759	0.575	0.436	0.329	0.248	0.187	0.141	0.106
56	0.755	0.570	0.429	0.323	0.242	0.182	0.136	0.102
57	0.751	0.564	0.423	0.316	0.236	0.176	0.131	0.098
58	0.748	0.558	0.416	0.310	0.230	0.171	0.127	0.094
59	0.744	0.553	0.410	0.304	0.225	0.166	0.122	0.090
60	0.740	0.547	0.404	0.298	0.219	0.161	0.118	0.086
61	0.737	0.542	0.398	0.292	0.213	0.156	0.114	0.083
62	0.733	0.536	0.392	0.286	0.208	0.151	0.110	0.080
63	0.729	0.531	0.386	0.280	0.203	0.147	0.106	0.076
64	0.726	0.526	0.380	0.274	0.198	0.142	0.102	0.073
65	0.722	0.520	0.374	0.269	0.193	0.138	0.099	0.070
66	0.718	0.515	0.369	0.264	0.188	0.134	0.095	0.068
67	0.715	0.510	0.363	0.258	0.183	0.130	0.092	0.065
68	0.711	0.505	0.358	0.253	0.179	0.126	0.089	0.062
69	0.708	0.500	0.352	0.248	0.174	0.122	0.086	0.060
70	0.704	0.495	0.347	0.243	0.170	0.119	0.083	0.057

TABLE 15A1 Actual Inflation-Adjusted Compound Rate of Return 8-13% Nominal Return for 60 Years

Compound Rate	0.05%	1.0%	1.5%	2.0%	2.5%	3.0%
8%	7.46%	6.92%	6.38%	5.84%	5.30%	4.76%
9%	8.46%	7.91%	7.37%	6.82%	6.28%	5.73%
10%	9.45%	8.90%	8.35%	7.80%	7.25%	6.70%
11%	10.45%	9.89%	9.34%	8.78%	8.23%	7.67%
12%	11.44%	10.88%	10.32%	9.76%	9.20%	8.64%
13%	12.44%	11.87%	11.31%	10.74%	10.18%	9.61%

TABLE 21 Simple Long-Term Investment Plan

Name _____

Age _____

Annual income $_____

Total investment and savings $_____

Planned yearly savings—10 Years $_____

Dollars desired at retirement $_____

Years until termination of plan _____

Onetime investment required to achieve goal $_____
                              Or
Yearly investment required to achieve goal $_____

My Plan

I will invest $_____ this year
                    _____ in index mutual funds
                    _____ in individual stocks

I will invest $ _____ in 2007
                    _____ in 2008
                    _____ in 2009
                    _____ in 2010
                    _____ in 2011
                    _____ in 2012
                    _____ every year after 2012

***

Estimated compound rate of return
Years to withdrawal
Onetime investment this year _____
Final result from Table 22B2 (multiply by factor) $_____

Annual investments every year   _____
Final result from Table 22B3 (multiply by factor) $_____
Total estimated at retirement $_____

TABLE 22A1 Top 50 Companies—Siegel
Compound Rate of Return

Company 1957	Industry	Company 2005	2005 Price per share	2005 Earnings per share	2005 Dividends per share
Philip Morris	Tobacco and food	Altria	$74.42	$4.99	$3.20
Thatcher Glass	Glass	Merged—Altria	$74.42	$4.99	$3.20
National Can	Aluminum	Merged—Pechiney			
Dr Pepper	Soda	Merged—Cadbury Schweppes	$38.29	$2.10	$0.91
Lane Bryant	Retail	Merged—Limited	$22.35	$1.66	$0.60
General Foods	Food	Merged—Altria	$74.42	$4.99	$3.20
Abbott Labs	Pharmaceuticals	Abbott Labs	$39.43	$2.16	$1.18
Warner-Lambert	Pharmaceuticals	Merged—Pfizer	$23.32	$1.09	$0.96
Celanese	Chemicals	Merged—Aventis	$43.90	$0.99	$0.78
Bristol-Myers	Pharmaceuticals	Bristol-Myers	$21.13	$1.51	$1.12
Columbia Pictures	Entertainment	Merged—Coca-Cola	$40.31	$2.04	$1.24
Tootsie Roll	Candy	Tootsie Roll	$28.93	$1.40	$0.32
American Chicle	Pharmaceuticals	Merged—Pfizer	$23.32	$1.09	$0.96
Pfizer	Pharmaceuticals	Pfizer	$23.32	$1.09	$0.96
Coca-Cola	Food and sodas	Coca-Cola	$40.31	$2.04	$1.24
California Packing	Food	Merged—Altria	$74.42	$4.99	$3.20
Merck	Pharmaceuticals	Merck	$31.81	$2.11	$1.52
Lorillard	Tobacco	Merged—Lowe's			
National Dairy	Food	Merged—Altria	$74.42	$4.99	$3.20
Standard Brands	Food	Merged—Altria	$74.42	$4.99	$3.20
Richardson Merrell	Food	Merged—Procter & Gamble	$57.88	$2.73	$1.24
Houdaille Industries	Manufacturing	Went private			
Reeves Brothers	Manufacturing	Went private			
R. H. Macy	Retail	Went private			
Stokely-Van Camp	Food	Merged—PepsiCo	$59.08	$2.39	$1.04
PepsiCo	Food and sodas	PepsiCo	$59.08	$2.39	$1.04
McCall	Publishing	Went private			
Colgate-Palmolive	Consumer staples	Colgate-Palmolive	$54.85	$2.43	$1.28
R. J. Reynolds	Tobacco	Merged—Altria	$74.42	$4.99	$3.20
Crane Co.	Manufacturing	Crane Co.	$35.27	$2.25	$0.50
Consolidated Cigar	Tobacco	Merged—Viacom			

—

Penick & Ford	Machinery	Merged—Altria	$74.42	$4.99	$3.20
Best Foods	Food	Merged—Unilever	$68.65	$3.28	$3.15
Paramount Pictures	Entertainment	Merged—Viacom	$0.00	$0.00	$0.00
General Cigar	Tobacco	Merged—Swedish Match	$0.00	$0.00	$0.00
Virginia-Carolina Chemicals	Chemicals	Merged—Exxon	$56.17	$5.72	$1.28
Congoleum Nairn	Carpet and linoleum	Went private	$0.00	$0.00	$0.00
Truax-Traer Coal	Coal	Merged—DuPont	$42.50	$2.07	$1.48
Am Agricultural Chemicals	Chemicals	Merged—Consolidated Coal	$0.00	$0.00	$0.00
Amalgamated Sugar	Sugar	Went private	$0.00	$0.00	$0.00
Heinz	Food	Heinz	$33.72	$1.96	$1.20
Corn Products	Food	Merged—Unilever	$68.65	$3.28	$3.15
Wrigley	Candy	Wrigley	$66.49	$1.83	$1.28
American Tobacco	Tobacco	Fortune Brands	$78.02	$4.13	$1.44
Electric Auto-Lite	Automotive	Merged—Honeywell	$37.25	$1.94	$0.91
Bohn Aluminum and Brass	Aluminum and brass	Merged—Viacom	$0.00	$0.00	$0.00
Flintkote	Building materials	Merged—British Tobacco	$45.04	$2.94	$1.65
Quaker Oats	Food	Merged—PepsiCo	$59.08	$2.39	$1.04
Gulf, Mobile & Ohio	Railroad	Merged—PepsiAmericas	$0.00	$0.00	$0.00
Kroger	Retail	Kroger	$18.88	$1.31	$0.26

TABLE 22B1 Dollar Investment Required for Given Return
Assumed Annual Compound Rate of Return
Years until Retirement
With Additional Years of Life Extension

Onetime Dollar Investment Required Today to Have $1 Million at Retirement								Rate =	8%
Years to	Assumed Additional Years of Investing								
Retirement	0	3	6	9	12	15	18	21	
10	$463,193	$367,698	$291,890	$231,712	$183,941	$146,018	$115,914	$92,016	
11	$428,883	$340,461	$270,269	$214,548	$170,315	$135,202	$107,328	$85,200	
12	$397,114	$315,242	$250,249	$198,656	$157,699	$125,187	$99,377	$78,889	
13	$367,698	$291,890	$231,712	$183,941	$146,018	$115,914	$92,016	$73,045	
14	$340,461	$270,269	$214,548	$170,315	$135,202	$107,328	$85,200	$67,635	
15	$315,242	$250,249	$198,656	$157,699	$125,187	$99,377	$78,889	$62,625	
16	$291,890	$231,712	$183,941	$146,018	$115,914	$92,016	$73,045	$57,986	
17	$270,269	$214,548	$170,315	$135,202	$107,328	$85,200	$67,635	$53,690	
18	$250,249	$198,656	$157,699	$125,187	$99,377	$78,889	$62,625	$49,713	
19	$231,712	$183,941	$146,018	$115,914	$92,016	$73,045	$57,986	$46,031	
20	$214,548	$170,315	$135,202	$107,328	$85,200	$67,635	$53,690	$42,621	
21	$198,656	$157,699	$125,187	$99,377	$78,889	$62,625	$49,713	$39,464	
22	$183,941	$146,018	$115,914	$92,016	$73,045	$57,986	$46,031	$36,541	
23	$170,315	$135,202	$107,328	$85,200	$67,635	$53,690	$42,621	$33,834	
24	$157,699	$125,187	$99,377	$78,889	$62,625	$49,713	$39,464	$31,328	
25	$146,018	$115,914	$92,016	$73,045	$57,986	$46,031	$36,541	$29,007	
26	$135,202	$107,328	$85,200	$67,635	$53,690	$42,621	$33,834	$26,859	
27	$125,187	$99,377	$78,889	$62,625	$49,713	$39,464	$31,328	$24,869	
28	$115,914	$92,016	$73,045	$57,986	$46,031	$36,541	$29,007	$23,027	
29	$107,328	$85,200	$67,635	$53,690	$42,621	$33,834	$26,859	$21,321	
30	$99,377	$78,889	$62,625	$49,713	$39,464	$31,328	$24,869	$19,742	
31	$92,016	$73,045	$57,986	$46,031	$36,541	$29,007	$23,027	$18,280	
32	$85,200	$67,635	$53,690	$42,621	$33,834	$26,859	$21,321	$16,925	
33	$78,889	$62,625	$49,713	$39,464	$31,328	$24,869	$19,742	$15,672	
34	$73,045	$57,986	$46,031	$36,541	$29,007	$23,027	$18,280	$14,511	
35	$67,635	$53,690	$42,621	$33,834	$26,859	$21,321	$16,925	$13,436	
36	$62,625	$49,713	$39,464	$31,328	$24,869	$19,742	$15,672	$12,441	
37	$57,986	$46,031	$36,541	$29,007	$23,027	$18,280	$14,511	$11,519	
38	$53,690	$42,621	$33,834	$26,859	$21,321	$16,925	$13,436	$10,666	
39	$49,713	$39,464	$31,328	$24,869	$19,742	$15,672	$12,441	$9,876	
40	$46,031	$36,541	$29,007	$23,027	$18,280	$14,511	$11,519	$9,144	
41	$42,621	$33,834	$26,859	$21,321	$16,925	$13,436	$10,666	$8,467	
42	$39,464	$31,328	$24,869	$19,742	$15,672	$12,441	$9,876	$7,840	
43	$36,541	$29,007	$23,027	$18,280	$14,511	$11,519	$9,144	$7,259	
44	$33,834	$26,859	$21,321	$16,925	$13,436	$10,666	$8,467	$6,721	
45	$31,328	$24,869	$19,742	$15,672	$12,441	$9,876	$7,840	$6,223	
46	$29,007	$23,027	$18,280	$14,511	$11,519	$9,144	$7,259	$5,762	

47	$26,859	$21,321	$16,925	$13,436	$10,666	$8,467	$6,721	$5,336
48	$24,869	$19,742	$15,672	$12,441	$9,876	$7,840	$6,223	$4,940
49	$23,027	$18,280	$14,511	$11,519	$9,144	$7,259	$5,762	$4,574
50	$21,321	$16,925	$13,436	$10,666	$8,467	$6,721	$5,336	$4,236
51	$19,742	$15,672	$12,441	$9,876	$7,840	$6,223	$4,940	$3,922
52	$18,280	$14,511	$11,519	$9,144	$7,259	$5,762	$4,574	$3,631
53	$16,925	$13,436	$10,666	$8,467	$6,721	$5,336	$4,236	$3,362
54	$15,672	$12,441	$9,876	$7,840	$6,223	$4,940	$3,922	$3,113
55	$14,511	$11,519	$9,144	$7,259	$5,762	$4,574	$3,631	$2,883
56	$13,436	$10,666	$8,467	$6,721	$5,336	$4,236	$3,362	$2,669
57	$12,441	$9,876	$7,840	$6,223	$4,940	$3,922	$3,113	$2,471
58	$11,519	$9,144	$7,259	$5,762	$4,574	$3,631	$2,883	$2,288
59	$10,666	$8,467	$6,721	$5,336	$4,236	$3,362	$2,669	$2,119
60	$9,876	$7,840	$6,223	$4,940	$3,922	$3,113	$2,471	$1,962
61	$9,144	$7,259	$5,762	$4,574	$3,631	$2,883	$2,288	$1,817
62	$8,467	$6,721	$5,336	$4,236	$3,362	$2,669	$2,119	$1,682
63	$7,840	$6,223	$4,940	$3,922	$3,113	$2,471	$1,962	$1,557
64	$7,259	$5,762	$4,574	$3,631	$2,883	$2,288	$1,817	$1,442
65	$6,721	$5,336	$4,236	$3,362	$2,669	$2,119	$1,682	$1,335
66	$6,223	$4,940	$3,922	$3,113	$2,471	$1,962	$1,557	$1,236
67	$5,762	$4,574	$3,631	$2,883	$2,288	$1,817	$1,442	$1,145
68	$5,336	$4,236	$3,362	$2,669	$2,119	$1,682	$1,335	$1,060
69	$4,940	$3,922	$3,113	$2,471	$1,962	$1,557	$1,236	$981
70	$4,574	$3,631	$2,883	$2,288	$1,817	$1,442	$1,145	$909

Onetime Dollar Investment Required Today to Have $1 Million at Retirement						Compound Rate =	9.00%
Years to	Assumed Additional Years of Investing						
Retirement	0	3	6	9	12	15	18	21
10	$422,411	$326,179	$251,870	$194,490	$150,182	$115,968	$89,548	$69,148
11	$387,533	$299,246	$231,073	$178,431	$137,781	$106,393	$82,155	$63,438
12	$355,535	$274,538	$211,994	$163,698	$126,405	$97,608	$75,371	$58,200
13	$326,179	$251,870	$194,490	$150,182	$115,968	$89,548	$69,148	$53,395
14	$299,246	$231,073	$178,431	$137,781	$106,393	$82,155	$63,438	$48,986
15	$274,538	$211,994	$163,698	$126,405	$97,608	$75,371	$58,200	$44,941
16	$251,870	$194,490	$150,182	$115,968	$89,548	$69,148	$53,395	$41,231
17	$231,073	$178,431	$137,781	$106,393	$82,155	$63,438	$48,986	$37,826
18	$211,994	$163,698	$126,405	$97,608	$75,371	$58,200	$44,941	$34,703
19	$194,490	$150,182	$115,968	$89,548	$69,148	$53,395	$41,231	$31,838
20	$178,431	$137,781	$106,393	$82,155	$63,438	$48,986	$37,826	$29,209
21	$163,698	$126,405	$97,608	$75,371	$58,200	$44,941	$34,703	$26,797
22	$150,182	$115,968	$89,548	$69,148	$53,395	$41,231	$31,838	$24,584
23	$137,781	$106,393	$82,155	$63,438	$48,986	$37,826	$29,209	$22,555
24	$126,405	$97,608	$75,371	$58,200	$44,941	$34,703	$26,797	$20,692
25	$115,968	$89,548	$69,148	$53,395	$41,231	$31,838	$24,584	$18,984
26	$106,393	$82,155	$63,438	$48,986	$37,826	$29,209	$22,555	$17,416
27	$97,608	$75,371	$58,200	$44,941	$34,703	$26,797	$20,692	$15,978
28	$89,548	$69,148	$53,395	$41,231	$31,838	$24,584	$18,984	$14,659
29	$82,155	$63,438	$48,986	$37,826	$29,209	$22,555	$17,416	$13,449
30	$75,371	$58,200	$44,941	$34,703	$26,797	$20,692	$15,978	$12,338
31	$69,148	$53,395	$41,231	$31,838	$24,584	$18,984	$14,659	$11,319
32	$63,438	$48,986	$37,826	$29,209	$22,555	$17,416	$13,449	$10,385
33	$58,200	$44,941	$34,703	$26,797	$20,692	$15,978	$12,338	$9,527
34	$53,395	$41,231	$31,838	$24,584	$18,984	$14,659	$11,319	$8,741
35	$48,986	$37,826	$29,209	$22,555	$17,416	$13,449	$10,385	$8,019
36	$44,941	$34,703	$26,797	$20,692	$15,978	$12,338	$9,527	$7,357
37	$41,231	$31,838	$24,584	$18,984	$14,659	$11,319	$8,741	$6,749
38	$37,826	$29,209	$22,555	$17,416	$13,449	$10,385	$8,019	$6,192
39	$34,703	$26,797	$20,692	$15,978	$12,338	$9,527	$7,357	$5,681
40	$31,838	$24,584	$18,984	$14,659	$11,319	$8,741	$6,749	$5,212
41	$29,209	$22,555	$17,416	$13,449	$10,385	$8,019	$6,192	$4,781
42	$26,797	$20,692	$15,978	$12,338	$9,527	$7,357	$5,681	$4,387
43	$24,584	$18,984	$14,659	$11,319	$8,741	$6,749	$5,212	$4,024
44	$22,555	$17,416	$13,449	$10,385	$8,019	$6,192	$4,781	$3,692
45	$20,692	$15,978	$12,338	$9,527	$7,357	$5,681	$4,387	$3,387
46	$18,984	$14,659	$11,319	$8,741	$6,749	$5,212	$4,024	$3,108
47	$17,416	$13,449	$10,385	$8,019	$6,192	$4,781	$3,692	$2,851
48	$15,978	$12,338	$9,527	$7,357	$5,681	$4,387	$3,387	$2,616
49	$14,659	$11,319	$8,741	$6,749	$5,212	$4,024	$3,108	$2,400
50	$13,449	$10,385	$8,019	$6,192	$4,781	$3,692	$2,851	$2,201
51	$12,338	$9,527	$7,357	$5,681	$4,387	$3,387	$2,616	$2,020
52	$11,319	$8,741	$6,749	$5,212	$4,024	$3,108	$2,400	$1,853

—

363

53	$10,385	$8,019	$6,192	$4,781	$3,692	$2,851	$2,201	$1,700
54	$9,527	$7,357	$5,681	$4,387	$3,387	$2,616	$2,020	$1,560
55	$8,741	$6,749	$5,212	$4,024	$3,108	$2,400	$1,853	$1,431
56	$8,019	$6,192	$4,781	$3,692	$2,851	$2,201	$1,700	$1,313
57	$7,357	$5,681	$4,387	$3,387	$2,616	$2,020	$1,560	$1,204
58	$6,749	$5,212	$4,024	$3,108	$2,400	$1,853	$1,431	$1,105
59	$6,192	$4,781	$3,692	$2,851	$2,201	$1,700	$1,313	$1,014
60	$5,681	$4,387	$3,387	$2,616	$2,020	$1,560	$1,204	$930
61	$5,212	$4,024	$3,108	$2,400	$1,853	$1,431	$1,105	$853
62	$4,781	$3,692	$2,851	$2,201	$1,700	$1,313	$1,014	$783
63	$4,387	$3,387	$2,616	$2,020	$1,560	$1,204	$930	$718
64	$4,024	$3,108	$2,400	$1,853	$1,431	$1,105	$853	$659
65	$3,692	$2,851	$2,201	$1,700	$1,313	$1,014	$783	$604
66	$3,387	$2,616	$2,020	$1,560	$1,204	$930	$718	$554
67	$3,108	$2,400	$1,853	$1,431	$1,105	$853	$659	$509
68	$2,851	$2,201	$1,700	$1,313	$1,014	$783	$604	$467
69	$2,616	$2,020	$1,560	$1,204	$930	$718	$554	$428
70	**$2,400**	**$1,853**	**$1,431**	**$1,105**	**$853**	**$659**	$509	$393

Onetime Dollar Investment Required Today to Have $1 Million at Retirement						Compound	Rate =	10.00%
Years to	Assumed Additional Years of Investing							
Retirement	0	3	6	9	12	15	18	21
10	$385,543	$289,664	$217,629	$163,508	$122,846	$92,296	$69,343	$52,099
11	$350,494	$263,331	$197,845	$148,644	$111,678	$83,905	$63,039	$47,362
12	$318,631	$239,392	$179,859	$135,131	$101,526	$76,278	$57,309	$43,057
13	$289,664	$217,629	$163,508	$122,846	$92,296	$69,343	$52,099	$39,143
14	$263,331	$197,845	$148,644	$111,678	$83,905	$63,039	$47,362	$35,584
15	$239,392	$179,859	$135,131	$101,526	$76,278	$57,309	$43,057	$32,349
16	$217,629	$163,508	$122,846	$92,296	$69,343	$52,099	$39,143	$29,408
17	$197,845	$148,644	$111,678	$83,905	$63,039	$47,362	$35,584	$26,735
18	$179,859	$135,131	$101,526	$76,278	$57,309	$43,057	$32,349	$24,304
19	$163,508	$122,846	$92,296	$69,343	$52,099	$39,143	$29,408	$22,095
20	$148,644	$111,678	$83,905	$63,039	$47,362	$35,584	$26,735	$20,086
21	$135,131	$101,526	$76,278	$57,309	$43,057	$32,349	$24,304	$18,260
22	$122,846	$92,296	$69,343	$52,099	$39,143	$29,408	$22,095	$16,600
23	$111,678	$83,905	$63,039	$47,362	$35,584	$26,735	$20,086	$15,091
24	$101,526	$76,278	$57,309	$43,057	$32,349	$24,304	$18,260	$13,719
25	$92,296	$69,343	$52,099	$39,143	$29,408	$22,095	$16,600	$12,472
26	$83,905	$63,039	$47,362	$35,584	$26,735	$20,086	$15,091	$11,338
27	$76,278	$57,309	$43,057	$32,349	$24,304	$18,260	$13,719	$10,307
28	$69,343	$52,099	$39,143	$29,408	$22,095	$16,600	$12,472	$9,370
29	$63,039	$47,362	$35,584	$26,735	$20,086	$15,091	$11,338	$8,519
30	$57,309	$43,057	$32,349	$24,304	$18,260	$13,719	$10,307	$7,744
31	$52,099	$39,143	$29,408	$22,095	$16,600	$12,472	$9,370	$7,040
32	$47,362	$35,584	$26,735	$20,086	$15,091	$11,338	$8,519	$6,400
33	$43,057	$32,349	$24,304	$18,260	$13,719	$10,307	$7,744	$5,818
34	$39,143	$29,408	$22,095	$16,600	$12,472	$9,370	$7,040	$5,289
35	$35,584	$26,735	$20,086	$15,091	$11,338	$8,519	$6,400	$4,809
36	$32,349	$24,304	$18,260	$13,719	$10,307	$7,744	$5,818	$4,371
37	$29,408	$22,095	$16,600	$12,472	$9,370	$7,040	$5,289	$3,974
38	$26,735	$20,086	$15,091	$11,338	$8,519	$6,400	$4,809	$3,613
39	$24,304	$18,260	$13,719	$10,307	$7,744	$5,818	$4,371	$3,284
40	$22,095	$16,600	$12,472	$9,370	$7,040	$5,289	$3,974	$2,986
41	$20,086	$15,091	$11,338	$8,519	$6,400	$4,809	$3,613	$2,714
42	$18,260	$13,719	$10,307	$7,744	$5,818	$4,371	$3,284	$2,468
43	$16,600	$12,472	$9,370	$7,040	$5,289	$3,974	$2,986	$2,243
44	$15,091	$11,338	$8,519	$6,400	$4,809	$3,613	$2,714	$2,039
45	$13,719	$10,307	$7,744	$5,818	$4,371	$3,284	$2,468	$1,854

—

46	$12,472	$9,370	$7,040	$5,289	$3,974	$2,986	$2,243	$1,685
47	$11,338	$8,519	$6,400	$4,809	$3,613	$2,714	$2,039	$1,532
48	$10,307	$7,744	$5,818	$4,371	$3,284	$2,468	$1,854	$1,393
49	$9,370	$7,040	$5,289	$3,974	$2,986	$2,243	$1,685	$1,266
50	$8,519	$6,400	$4,809	$3,613	$2,714	$2,039	$1,532	$1,151
51	$7,744	$5,818	$4,371	$3,284	$2,468	$1,854	$1,393	$1,046
52	$7,040	$5,289	$3,974	$2,986	$2,243	$1,685	$1,266	$951
53	$6,400	$4,809	$3,613	$2,714	$2,039	$1,532	$1,151	$865
54	$5,818	$4,371	$3,284	$2,468	$1,854	$1,393	$1,046	$786
55	$5,289	$3,974	$2,986	$2,243	$1,685	$1,266	$951	$715
56	$4,809	$3,613	$2,714	$2,039	$1,532	$1,151	$865	$650
57	$4,371	$3,284	$2,468	$1,854	$1,393	$1,046	$786	$591
58	$3,974	$2,986	$2,243	$1,685	$1,266	$951	$715	$537
59	$3,613	$2,714	$2,039	$1,532	$1,151	$865	$650	$488
60	$3,284	$2,468	$1,854	$1,393	$1,046	$786	$591	$444
61	$2,986	$2,243	$1,685	$1,266	$951	$715	$537	$403
62	$2,714	$2,039	$1,532	$1,151	$865	$650	$488	$367
63	$2,468	$1,854	$1,393	$1,046	$786	$591	$444	$333
64	$2,243	$1,685	$1,266	$951	$715	$537	$403	$303
65	$2,039	$1,532	$1,151	$865	$650	$488	$367	$276
66	$1,854	$1,393	$1,046	$786	$591	$444	$333	$251
67	$1,685	$1,266	$951	$715	$537	$403	$303	$228
68	$1,532	$1,151	$865	$650	$488	$367	$276	$207
69	$1,393	$1,046	$786	$591	$444	$333	$251	$188
70	$1,266	$951	$715	$537	$403	$303	$228	$171

Onetime Dollar Investment Required Today to Have $1 Million at Retirement Compound Rate = 11.00%							
Years to	Assumed Additional Years of Investing						
Retirement	0	3	6	9	12	15	18	21
10	$352,184	$257,514	$188,292	$137,678	$100,669	$73,608	$53,822	$39,354
11	$317,283	$231,995	$169,633	$124,034	$90,693	$66,314	$48,488	$35,454
12	$285,841	$209,004	$152,822	$111,742	$81,705	$59,742	$43,683	$31,940
13	$257,514	$188,292	$137,678	$100,669	$73,608	$53,822	$39,354	$28,775
14	$231,995	$169,633	$124,034	$90,693	$66,314	$48,488	$35,454	$25,924
15	$209,004	$152,822	$111,742	$81,705	$59,742	$43,683	$31,940	$23,355
16	$188,292	$137,678	$100,669	$73,608	$53,822	$39,354	$28,775	$21,040
17	$169,633	$124,034	$90,693	$66,314	$48,488	$35,454	$25,924	$18,955
18	$152,822	$111,742	$81,705	$59,742	$43,683	$31,940	$23,355	$17,077
19	$137,678	$100,669	$73,608	$53,822	$39,354	$28,775	$21,040	$15,384
20	$124,034	$90,693	$66,314	$48,488	$35,454	$25,924	$18,955	$13,860
21	$111,742	$81,705	$59,742	$43,683	$31,940	$23,355	$17,077	$12,486
22	$100,669	$73,608	$53,822	$39,354	$28,775	$21,040	$15,384	$11,249
23	$90,693	$66,314	$48,488	$35,454	$25,924	$18,955	$13,860	$10,134
24	$81,705	$59,742	$43,683	$31,940	$23,355	$17,077	$12,486	$9,130
25	$73,608	$53,822	$39,354	$28,775	$21,040	$15,384	$11,249	$8,225
26	$66,314	$48,488	$35,454	$25,924	$18,955	$13,860	$10,134	$7,410
27	$59,742	$43,683	$31,940	$23,355	$17,077	$12,486	$9,130	$6,676
28	$53,822	$39,354	$28,775	$21,040	$15,384	$11,249	$8,225	$6,014
29	$48,488	$35,454	$25,924	$18,955	$13,860	$10,134	$7,410	$5,418
30	$43,683	$31,940	$23,355	$17,077	$12,486	$9,130	$6,676	$4,881
31	$39,354	$28,775	$21,040	$15,384	$11,249	$8,225	$6,014	$4,397
32	$35,454	$25,924	$18,955	$13,860	$10,134	$7,410	$5,418	$3,962
33	$31,940	$23,355	$17,077	$12,486	$9,130	$6,676	$4,881	$3,569
34	$28,775	$21,040	$15,384	$11,249	$8,225	$6,014	$4,397	$3,215
35	$25,924	$18,955	$13,860	$10,134	$7,410	$5,418	$3,962	$2,897
36	$23,355	$17,077	$12,486	$9,130	$6,676	$4,881	$3,569	$2,610
37	$21,040	$15,384	$11,249	$8,225	$6,014	$4,397	$3,215	$2,351
38	$18,955	$13,860	$10,134	$7,410	$5,418	$3,962	$2,897	$2,118
39	$17,077	$12,486	$9,130	$6,676	$4,881	$3,569	$2,610	$1,908
40	$15,384	$11,249	$8,225	$6,014	$4,397	$3,215	$2,351	$1,719
41	$13,860	$10,134	$7,410	$5,418	$3,962	$2,897	$2,118	$1,549
42	$12,486	$9,130	$6,676	$4,881	$3,569	$2,610	$1,908	$1,395
43	$11,249	$8,225	$6,014	$4,397	$3,215	$2,351	$1,719	$1,257
44	$10,134	$7,410	$5,418	$3,962	$2,897	$2,118	$1,549	$1,132
45	$9,130	$6,676	$4,881	$3,569	$2,610	$1,908	$1,395	$1,020

—

46	$8,225	$6,014	$4,397	$3,215	$2,351	$1,719	$1,257	$919
47	$7,410	$5,418	$3,962	$2,897	$2,118	$1,549	$1,132	$828
48	$6,676	$4,881	$3,569	$2,610	$1,908	$1,395	$1,020	$746
49	$6,014	$4,397	$3,215	$2,351	$1,719	$1,257	$919	$672
50	$5,418	$3,962	$2,897	$2,118	$1,549	$1,132	$828	$605
51	$4,881	$3,569	$2,610	$1,908	$1,395	$1,020	$746	$545
52	$4,397	$3,215	$2,351	$1,719	$1,257	$919	$672	$491
53	$3,962	$2,897	$2,118	$1,549	$1,132	$828	$605	$443
54	$3,569	$2,610	$1,908	$1,395	$1,020	$746	$545	$399
55	$3,215	$2,351	$1,719	$1,257	$919	$672	$491	$359
56	$2,897	$2,118	$1,549	$1,132	$828	$605	$443	$324
57	$2,610	$1,908	$1,395	$1,020	$746	$545	$399	$292
58	$2,351	$1,719	$1,257	$919	$672	$491	$359	$263
59	$2,118	$1,549	$1,132	$828	$605	$443	$324	$237
60	$1,908	$1,395	$1,020	$746	$545	$399	$292	$213
61	$1,719	$1,257	$919	$672	$491	$359	$263	$192
62	$1,549	$1,132	$828	$605	$443	$324	$237	$173
63	$1,395	$1,020	$746	$545	$399	$292	$213	$156
64	$1,257	$919	$672	$491	$359	$263	$192	$140
65	$1,132	$828	$605	$443	$324	$237	$173	$127
66	$1,020	$746	$545	$399	$292	$213	$156	$114
67	$919	$672	$491	$359	$263	$192	$140	$103
68	$828	$605	$443	$324	$237	$173	$127	$93
69	$746	$545	$399	$292	$213	$156	$114	$83
70	$672	$491	$359	$263	$192	$140	$103	$75

Onetime Dollar Investment Required Today to Have $1 Million at Retirement Compound Rate = 11.76%							
Years to	Assumed Additional Years of Investing						
Retirement	0	3	6	9	12	15	18	21
10	$328,955	$235,655	$168,818	$120,937	$86,636	$62,064	$44,461	$31,851
11	$294,340	$210,858	$151,054	$108,211	$77,520	$55,533	$39,783	$28,499
12	$263,368	$188,671	$135,159	$96,825	$69,363	$49,690	$35,597	$25,501
13	$235,655	$168,818	$120,937	$86,636	$62,064	$44,461	$31,851	$22,817
14	$210,858	$151,054	$108,211	$77,520	$55,533	$39,783	$28,499	$20,416
15	$188,671	$135,159	$96,825	$69,363	$49,690	$35,597	$25,501	$18,268
16	$168,818	$120,937	$86,636	$62,064	$44,461	$31,851	$22,817	$16,346
17	$151,054	$108,211	$77,520	$55,533	$39,783	$28,499	$20,416	$14,626
18	$135,159	$96,825	$69,363	$49,690	$35,597	$25,501	$18,268	$13,087
19	$120,937	$86,636	$62,064	$44,461	$31,851	$22,817	$16,346	$11,710
20	$108,211	$77,520	$55,533	$39,783	$28,499	$20,416	$14,626	$10,478
21	$96,825	$69,363	$49,690	$35,597	$25,501	$18,268	$13,087	$9,375
22	$86,636	$62,064	$44,461	$31,851	$22,817	$16,346	$11,710	$8,389
23	$77,520	$55,533	$39,783	$28,499	$20,416	$14,626	$10,478	$7,506
24	$69,363	$49,690	$35,597	$25,501	$18,268	$13,087	$9,375	$6,716
25	$62,064	$44,461	$31,851	$22,817	$16,346	$11,710	$8,389	$6,009
26	$55,533	$39,783	$28,499	$20,416	$14,626	$10,478	$7,506	$5,377
27	$49,690	$35,597	$25,501	$18,268	$13,087	$9,375	$6,716	$4,811
28	$44,461	$31,851	$22,817	$16,346	$11,710	$8,389	$6,009	$4,305
29	$39,783	$28,499	$20,416	$14,626	$10,478	$7,506	$5,377	$3,852
30	$35,597	$25,501	$18,268	$13,087	$9,375	$6,716	$4,811	$3,447
31	$31,851	$22,817	$16,346	$11,710	$8,389	$6,009	$4,305	$3,084
32	$28,499	$20,416	$14,626	$10,478	$7,506	$5,377	$3,852	$2,759
33	$25,501	$18,268	$13,087	$9,375	$6,716	$4,811	$3,447	$2,469
34	$22,817	$16,346	$11,710	$8,389	$6,009	$4,305	$3,084	$2,209
35	$20,416	$14,626	$10,478	$7,506	$5,377	$3,852	$2,759	$1,977
36	$18,268	$13,087	$9,375	$6,716	$4,811	$3,447	$2,469	$1,769
37	$16,346	$11,710	$8,389	$6,009	$4,305	$3,084	$2,209	$1,583
38	$14,626	$10,478	$7,506	$5,377	$3,852	$2,759	$1,977	$1,416
39	$13,087	$9,375	$6,716	$4,811	$3,447	$2,469	$1,769	$1,267
40	$11,710	$8,389	$6,009	$4,305	$3,084	$2,209	$1,583	$1,134
41	$10,478	$7,506	$5,377	$3,852	$2,759	$1,977	$1,416	$1,014
42	$9,375	$6,716	$4,811	$3,447	$2,469	$1,769	$1,267	$908
43	$8,389	$6,009	$4,305	$3,084	$2,209	$1,583	$1,134	$812
44	$7,506	$5,377	$3,852	$2,759	$1,977	$1,416	$1,014	$727
45	$6,716	$4,811	$3,447	$2,469	$1,769	$1,267	$908	$650

46	$6,009	$4,305	$3,084	$2,209	$1,583	$1,134	$812	$582
47	$5,377	$3,852	$2,759	$1,977	$1,416	$1,014	$727	$521
48	$4,811	$3,447	$2,469	$1,769	$1,267	$908	$650	$466
49	$4,305	$3,084	$2,209	$1,583	$1,134	$812	$582	$417
50	$3,852	$2,759	$1,977	$1,416	$1,014	$727	$521	$373
51	$3,447	$2,469	$1,769	$1,267	$908	$650	$466	$334
52	$3,084	$2,209	$1,583	$1,134	$812	$582	$417	$299
53	$2,759	$1,977	$1,416	$1,014	$727	$521	$373	$267
54	$2,469	$1,769	$1,267	$908	$650	$466	$334	$239
55	$2,209	$1,583	$1,134	$812	$582	$417	$299	$214
56	$1,977	$1,416	$1,014	$727	$521	$373	$267	$191
57	$1,769	$1,267	$908	$650	$466	$334	$239	$171
58	$1,583	$1,134	$812	$582	$417	$299	$214	$153
59	$1,416	$1,014	$727	$521	$373	$267	$191	$137
60	$1,267	$908	$650	$466	$334	$239	$171	$123
61	$1,134	$812	$582	$417	$299	$214	$153	$110
62	$1,014	$727	$521	$373	$267	$191	$137	$98
63	$908	$650	$466	$334	$239	$171	$123	$88
64	$812	$582	$417	$299	$214	$153	$110	$79
65	$727	$521	$373	$267	$191	$137	$98	$70
66	$650	$466	$334	$239	$171	$123	$88	$63
67	$582	$417	$299	$214	$153	$110	$79	$56
68	$521	$373	$267	$191	$137	$98	$70	$50
69	$466	$334	$239	$171	$123	$88	$63	$45
70	$417	$299	$214	$153	$110	$79	$56	$40

| Onetime Dollar Investment Required Today to Have $1 Million at Retirement   Compound Rate = 12.00% | | | | | | | |
| Years to | Assumed Additional Years of Investing | | | | | | |
Retirement	0	3	6	9	12	15	18	21
10	$321,973	$229,174	$163,122	$116,107	$82,643	$58,823	$41,869	$29,802
11	$287,476	$204,620	$145,644	$103,667	$73,788	$52,521	$37,383	$26,609
12	$256,675	$182,696	$130,040	$92,560	$65,882	$46,894	$33,378	$23,758
13	$229,174	$163,122	$116,107	$82,643	$58,823	$41,869	$29,802	$21,212
14	$204,620	$145,644	$103,667	$73,788	$52,521	$37,383	$26,609	$18,940
15	$182,696	$130,040	$92,560	$65,882	$46,894	$33,378	$23,758	$16,910
16	$163,122	$116,107	$82,643	$58,823	$41,869	$29,802	$21,212	$15,098
17	$145,644	$103,667	$73,788	$52,521	$37,383	$26,609	$18,940	$13,481
18	$130,040	$92,560	$65,882	$46,894	$33,378	$23,758	$16,910	$12,036
19	$116,107	$82,643	$58,823	$41,869	$29,802	$21,212	$15,098	$10,747
20	$103,667	$73,788	$52,521	$37,383	$26,609	$18,940	$13,481	$9,595
21	$92,560	$65,882	$46,894	$33,378	$23,758	$16,910	$12,036	$8,567
22	$82,643	$58,823	$41,869	$29,802	$21,212	$15,098	$10,747	$7,649
23	$73,788	$52,521	$37,383	$26,609	$18,940	$13,481	$9,595	$6,830
24	$65,882	$46,894	$33,378	$23,758	$16,910	$12,036	$8,567	$6,098
25	$58,823	$41,869	$29,802	$21,212	$15,098	$10,747	$7,649	$5,445
26	$52,521	$37,383	$26,609	$18,940	$13,481	$9,595	$6,830	$4,861
27	$46,894	$33,378	$23,758	$16,910	$12,036	$8,567	$6,098	$4,340
28	$41,869	$29,802	$21,212	$15,098	$10,747	$7,649	$5,445	$3,875
29	$37,383	$26,609	$18,940	$13,481	$9,595	$6,830	$4,861	$3,460
30	$33,378	$23,758	$16,910	$12,036	$8,567	$6,098	$4,340	$3,089
31	$29,802	$21,212	$15,098	$10,747	$7,649	$5,445	$3,875	$2,758
32	$26,609	$18,940	$13,481	$9,595	$6,830	$4,861	$3,460	$2,463
33	$23,758	$16,910	$12,036	$8,567	$6,098	$4,340	$3,089	$2,199
34	$21,212	$15,098	$10,747	$7,649	$5,445	$3,875	$2,758	$1,963
35	$18,940	$13,481	$9,595	$6,830	$4,861	$3,460	$2,463	$1,753
36	$16,910	$12,036	$8,567	$6,098	$4,340	$3,089	$2,199	$1,565
37	$15,098	$10,747	$7,649	$5,445	$3,875	$2,758	$1,963	$1,398
38	$13,481	$9,595	$6,830	$4,861	$3,460	$2,463	$1,753	$1,248
39	$12,036	$8,567	$6,098	$4,340	$3,089	$2,199	$1,565	$1,114
40	$10,747	$7,649	$5,445	$3,875	$2,758	$1,963	$1,398	$995
41	$9,595	$6,830	$4,861	$3,460	$2,463	$1,753	$1,248	$888
42	$8,567	$6,098	$4,340	$3,089	$2,199	$1,565	$1,114	$793
43	$7,649	$5,445	$3,875	$2,758	$1,963	$1,398	$995	$708
44	$6,830	$4,861	$3,460	$2,463	$1,753	$1,248	$888	$632
45	$6,098	$4,340	$3,089	$2,199	$1,565	$1,114	$793	$564

—

46	$5,445	$3,875	$2,758	$1,963	$1,398	$995	$708	$504
47	$4,861	$3,460	$2,463	$1,753	$1,248	$888	$632	$450
48	$4,340	$3,089	$2,199	$1,565	$1,114	$793	$564	$402
49	$3,875	$2,758	$1,963	$1,398	$995	$708	$504	$359
50	$3,460	$2,463	$1,753	$1,248	$888	$632	$450	$320
51	$3,089	$2,199	$1,565	$1,114	$793	$564	$402	$286
52	$2,758	$1,963	$1,398	$995	$708	$504	$359	$255
53	$2,463	$1,753	$1,248	$888	$632	$450	$320	$228
54	$2,199	$1,565	$1,114	$793	$564	$402	$286	$204
55	$1,963	$1,398	$995	$708	$504	$359	$255	$182
56	$1,753	$1,248	$888	$632	$450	$320	$228	$162
57	$1,565	$1,114	$793	$564	$402	$286	$204	$145
58	$1,398	$995	$708	$504	$359	$255	$182	$129
59	$1,248	$888	$632	$450	$320	$228	$162	$115
60	$1,114	$793	$564	$402	$286	$204	$145	$103
61	$995	$708	$504	$359	$255	$182	$129	$92
62	$888	$632	$450	$320	$228	$162	$115	$82
63	$793	$564	$402	$286	$204	$145	$103	$73
64	$708	$504	$359	$255	$182	$129	$92	$66
65	$632	$450	$320	$228	$162	$115	$82	$59
66	$564	$402	$286	$204	$145	$103	$73	$52
67	$504	$359	$255	$182	$129	$92	$66	$47
68	$450	$320	$228	$162	$115	$82	$59	$42
69	$402	$286	$204	$145	$103	$73	$52	$37
70	$359	$255	$182	$129	$92	$66	$47	$33

Onetime Dollar Investment Required Today to Have $1 Million at Retirement Compound Rate = 13.00%							
Years to	Assumed Additional Years of Investing						
Retirement	0	3	6	9	12	15	18	21
10	$294,588	$204,165	$141,496	$98,064	$67,963	$47,102	$32,644	$22,624
11	$260,698	$180,677	$125,218	$86,782	$60,144	$41,683	$28,889	$20,021
12	$230,706	$159,891	$110,812	$76,798	$53,225	$36,888	$25,565	$17,718
13	$204,165	$141,496	$98,064	$67,963	$47,102	$32,644	$22,624	$15,680
14	$180,677	$125,218	$86,782	$60,144	$41,683	$28,889	$20,021	$13,876
15	$159,891	$110,812	$76,798	$53,225	$36,888	$25,565	$17,718	$12,279
16	$141,496	$98,064	$67,963	$47,102	$32,644	$22,624	$15,680	$10,867
17	$125,218	$86,782	$60,144	$41,683	$28,889	$20,021	$13,876	$9,617
18	$110,812	$76,798	$53,225	$36,888	$25,565	$17,718	$12,279	$8,510
19	$98,064	$67,963	$47,102	$32,644	$22,624	$15,680	$10,867	$7,531
20	$86,782	$60,144	$41,683	$28,889	$20,021	$13,876	$9,617	$6,665
21	$76,798	$53,225	$36,888	$25,565	$17,718	$12,279	$8,510	$5,898
22	$67,963	$47,102	$32,644	$22,624	$15,680	$10,867	$7,531	$5,219
23	$60,144	$41,683	$28,889	$20,021	$13,876	$9,617	$6,665	$4,619
24	$53,225	$36,888	$25,565	$17,718	$12,279	$8,510	$5,898	$4,088
25	$47,102	$32,644	$22,624	$15,680	$10,867	$7,531	$5,219	$3,617
26	$41,683	$28,889	$20,021	$13,876	$9,617	$6,665	$4,619	$3,201
27	$36,888	$25,565	$17,718	$12,279	$8,510	$5,898	$4,088	$2,833
28	$32,644	$22,624	$15,680	$10,867	$7,531	$5,219	$3,617	$2,507
29	$28,889	$20,021	$13,876	$9,617	$6,665	$4,619	$3,201	$2,219
30	$25,565	$17,718	$12,279	$8,510	$5,898	$4,088	$2,833	$1,963
31	$22,624	$15,680	$10,867	$7,531	$5,219	$3,617	$2,507	$1,737
32	$20,021	$13,876	$9,617	$6,665	$4,619	$3,201	$2,219	$1,538
33	$17,718	$12,279	$8,510	$5,898	$4,088	$2,833	$1,963	$1,361
34	$15,680	$10,867	$7,531	$5,219	$3,617	$2,507	$1,737	$1,204
35	$13,876	$9,617	$6,665	$4,619	$3,201	$2,219	$1,538	$1,066
36	$12,279	$8,510	$5,898	$4,088	$2,833	$1,963	$1,361	$943
37	$10,867	$7,531	$5,219	$3,617	$2,507	$1,737	$1,204	$835
38	$9,617	$6,665	$4,619	$3,201	$2,219	$1,538	$1,066	$739
39	$8,510	$5,898	$4,088	$2,833	$1,963	$1,361	$943	$654
40	$7,531	$5,219	$3,617	$2,507	$1,737	$1,204	$835	$578
41	$6,665	$4,619	$3,201	$2,219	$1,538	$1,066	$739	$512
42	$5,898	$4,088	$2,833	$1,963	$1,361	$943	$654	$453
43	$5,219	$3,617	$2,507	$1,737	$1,204	$835	$578	$401
44	$4,619	$3,201	$2,219	$1,538	$1,066	$739	$512	$355
45	$4,088	$2,833	$1,963	$1,361	$943	$654	$453	$314

46	$3,617	$2,507	$1,737	$1,204	$835	$578	$401	$278
47	$3,201	$2,219	$1,538	$1,066	$739	$512	$355	$246
48	$2,833	$1,963	$1,361	$943	$654	$453	$314	$218
49	$2,507	$1,737	$1,204	$835	$578	$401	$278	$193
50	$2,219	$1,538	$1,066	$739	$512	$355	$246	$170
51	$1,963	$1,361	$943	$654	$453	$314	$218	$151
52	$1,737	$1,204	$835	$578	$401	$278	$193	$133
53	$1,538	$1,066	$739	$512	$355	$246	$170	$118
54	$1,361	$943	$654	$453	$314	$218	$151	$105
55	$1,204	$835	$578	$401	$278	$193	$133	$92
56	$1,066	$739	$512	$355	$246	$170	$118	$82
57	$943	$654	$453	$314	$218	$151	$105	$72
58	$835	$578	$401	$278	$193	$133	$92	$64
59	$739	$512	$355	$246	$170	$118	$82	$57
60	$654	$453	$314	$218	$151	$105	$72	$50
61	$578	$401	$278	$193	$133	$92	$64	$44
62	$512	$355	$246	$170	$118	$82	$57	$39
63	$453	$314	$218	$151	$105	$72	$50	$35
64	$401	$278	$193	$133	$92	$64	$44	$31
65	$355	$246	$170	$118	$82	$57	$39	$27
66	$314	$218	$151	$105	$72	$50	$35	$24
67	$278	$193	$133	$92	$64	$44	$31	$21
68	$246	$170	$118	$82	$57	$39	$27	$19
69	$218	$151	$105	$72	$50	$35	$24	$17
70	$193	$133	$92	$64	$44	$31	$21	$15

TABLE 22B2 One Time Dollar Investment for Given Return
Assumed Annual Compound Rate of Return
Years until Retirement

Result of 1$ Onetime Investment to Retirement

Years to Retirement	Compound Annual Rate of Return							
	7%	8%	9%	10%	11%	11.76%	12%	13%
10	$2	$2	$2	$3	$3	$3	$3	$3
11	$2	$2	$3	$3	$3	$3	$3	$4
12	$2	$3	$3	$3	$3	$4	$4	$4
13	$2	$3	$3	$3	$4	$4	$4	$5
14	$3	$3	$3	$4	$4	$5	$5	$6
15	$3	$3	$4	$4	$5	$5	$5	$6
16	$3	$3	$4	$5	$5	$6	$6	$7
17	$3	$4	$4	$5	$6	$7	$7	$8
18	$3	$4	$5	$6	$7	$7	$8	$9
19	$4	$4	$5	$6	$7	$8	$9	$10
20	$4	$5	$6	$7	$8	$9	$10	$12
21	$4	$5	$6	$7	$9	$10	$11	$13
22	$4	$5	$7	$8	$10	$12	$12	$15
23	$5	$6	$7	$9	$11	$13	$14	$17
24	$5	$6	$8	$10	$12	$14	$15	$19
25	$5	$7	$9	$11	$14	$16	$17	$21
26	$6	$7	$9	$12	$15	$18	$19	$24
27	$6	$8	$10	$13	$17	$20	$21	$27
28	$7	$9	$11	$14	$19	$22	$24	$31
29	$7	$9	$12	$16	$21	$25	$27	$35
30	$8	$10	$13	$17	$23	$28	$30	$39
31	$8	$11	$14	$19	$25	$31	$34	$44
32	$9	$12	$16	$21	$28	$35	$38	$50
33	$9	$13	$17	$23	$31	$39	$42	$56
34	$10	$14	$19	$26	$35	$44	$47	$64
35	$11	$15	$20	$28	$39	$49	$53	$72
36	$11	$16	$22	$31	$43	$55	$59	$81
37	$12	$17	$24	$34	$48	$61	$66	$92
38	$13	$19	$26	$37	$53	$68	$74	$104
39	$14	$20	$29	$41	$59	$76	$83	$118
40	$15	$22	$31	$45	$65	$85	$93	$133
41	$16	$23	$34	$50	$72	$95	$104	$150

—

42	$17	$25	$37	$55	$80	$107	$117	$170
43	$18	$27	$41	$60	$89	$119	$131	$192
44	$20	$30	$44	$66	$99	$133	$146	$216
45	$21	$32	$48	$73	$110	$149	$164	$245
46	$22	$34	$53	$80	$122	$166	$184	$276
47	$24	$37	$57	$88	$135	$186	$206	$312
48	$26	$40	$63	$97	$150	$208	$230	$353
49	$28	$43	$68	$107	$166	$232	$258	$399
50	$29	$47	$74	$117	$185	$260	$289	$451
51	$32	$51	$81	$129	$205	$290	$324	$509
52	$34	$55	$88	$142	$227	$324	$363	$576
53	$36	$59	$96	$156	$252	$362	$406	$650
54	$39	$64	$105	$172	$280	$405	$455	$735
55	$41	$69	$114	$189	$311	$453	$509	$830
56	$44	$74	$125	$208	$345	$506	$570	$938
57	$47	$80	$136	$229	$383	$565	$639	$1,060
58	$51	$87	$148	$252	$425	$632	$716	$1,198
59	$54	$94	$161	$277	$472	$706	$801	$1,354
60	$58	$101	$176	$304	$524	$789	$898	$1,530
61	$62	$109	$192	$335	$582	$882	$1,005	$1,729
62	$66	$118	$209	$368	$646	$986	$1,126	$1,954
63	$71	$128	$228	$405	$717	$1,102	$1,261	$2,208
64	$76	$138	$248	$446	$796	$1,231	$1,412	$2,495
65	$81	$149	$271	$490	$883	$1,376	$1,582	$2,819
66	$87	$161	$295	$539	$980	$1,538	$1,772	$3,185
67	$93	$174	$322	$593	$1,088	$1,719	$1,984	$3,600
68	$100	$187	$351	$653	$1,208	$1,921	$2,222	$4,068
69	$107	$202	$382	$718	$1,341	$2,147	$2,489	$4,596
70	$114	$219	$417	$790	$1,488	$2,399	$2,788	$5,194

TABLE 22B3 One Dollar Investment Every Year for Given Return
Assumed Annual Compound Rate of Return
Years until Retirement

Result of 1$ Investment Every Year to Retirement

Years to Retirement	Compound Annual Rate of Return							
	7%	8%	9%	10%	11%	11.76%	12%	13%
10	$17	$18	$19	$20	$21	$22	$23	$24
11	$19	$20	$22	$23	$25	$26	$27	$28
12	$21	$23	$25	$27	$29	$30	$31	$33
13	$24	$26	$28	$30	$33	$35	$36	$39
14	$27	$29	$32	$35	$38	$40	$41	$45
15	$30	$32	$36	$39	$43	$46	$47	$52
16	$33	$36	$40	$44	$49	$53	$54	$60
17	$36	$40	$45	$50	$55	$60	$62	$69
18	$40	$44	$50	$56	$62	$68	$70	$79
19	$44	$49	$55	$62	$70	$77	$80	$90
20	$48	$54	$61	$70	$79	$88	$90	$103
21	$52	$59	$68	$78	$89	$99	$102	$118
22	$57	$65	$75	$87	$100	$112	$116	$134
23	$62	$72	$83	$96	$112	$126	$131	$152
24	$67	$78	$92	$107	$126	$142	$148	$173
25	$73	$86	$101	$119	$141	$160	$166	$197
26	$79	$94	$111	$132	$157	$180	$187	$224
27	$86	$102	$122	$146	$176	$202	$211	$254
28	$93	$112	$134	$162	$196	$227	$237	$288
29	$101	$122	$147	$179	$219	$255	$267	$327
30	$109	$132	$162	$198	$244	$286	$300	$370
31	$117	$144	$177	$219	$272	$320	$337	$420
32	$127	$157	$195	$242	$303	$359	$379	$475
33	$137	$170	$213	$268	$337	$402	$426	$538
34	$147	$185	$233	$296	$375	$451	$478	$609
35	$159	$201	$256	$326	$418	$505	$536	$690
36	$171	$218	$280	$360	$465	$565	$602	$781
37	$184	$237	$306	$397	$517	$633	$675	$883
38	$198	$257	$335	$438	$575	$709	$757	$999
39	$213	$278	$366	$483	$639	$793	$849	$1,130

—

40	$229	$302	$400	$532	$711	$887	$952	$1,278
41	$246	$327	$437	$586	$790	$993	$1,068	$1,446
42	$264	$354	$477	$646	$878	$1,111	$1,197	$1,635
43	$283	$383	$521	$712	$976	$1,243	$1,342	$1,848
44	$304	$415	$569	$784	$1,084	$1,390	$1,504	$2,090
45	$327	$449	$622	$864	$1,205	$1,554	$1,685	$2,362
46	$351	$486	$679	$951	$1,338	$1,738	$1,889	$2,671
47	$376	$526	$741	$1,047	$1,487	$1,944	$2,116	$3,019
48	$404	$570	$808	$1,153	$1,651	$2,174	$2,371	$3,413
49	$433	$616	$882	$1,270	$1,834	$2,430	$2,657	$3,857
50	$464	$667	$963	$1,398	$2,037	$2,717	$2,977	$4,360
51	$498	$721	$1,051	$1,539	$2,262	$3,038	$3,335	$4,928
52	$534	$780	$1,146	$1,694	$2,512	$3,396	$3,737	$5,570
53	$572	$843	$1,250	$1,864	$2,789	$3,797	$4,186	$6,295
54	$614	$912	$1,364	$2,051	$3,097	$4,244	$4,690	$7,114
55	$658	$986	$1,488	$2,258	$3,439	$4,745	$5,254	$8,040
56	$705	$1,066	$1,623	$2,485	$3,819	$5,304	$5,885	$9,087
57	$755	$1,152	$1,770	$2,734	$4,240	$5,929	$6,593	$10,269
58	$809	$1,245	$1,930	$3,009	$4,707	$6,627	$7,385	$11,605
59	$867	$1,346	$2,105	$3,311	$5,226	$7,407	$8,272	$13,115
60	$928	$1,455	$2,296	$3,643	$5,802	$8,280	$9,266	$14,821
61	$994	$1,572	$2,504	$4,008	$6,442	$9,255	$10,379	$16,749
62	$1,065	$1,699	$2,730	$4,410	$7,151	$10,344	$11,625	$18,927
63	$1,141	$1,836	$2,977	$4,852	$7,939	$11,562	$13,022	$21,389
64	$1,222	$1,984	$3,246	$5,338	$8,813	$12,922	$14,585	$24,171
65	$1,308	$2,144	$3,539	$5,873	$9,784	$14,443	$16,337	$27,314
66	$1,401	$2,316	$3,859	$6,462	$10,861	$16,143	$18,298	$30,866
67	$1,500	$2,503	$4,207	$7,109	$12,057	$18,042	$20,495	$34,880
68	$1,606	$2,704	$4,587	$7,821	$13,385	$20,165	$22,956	$39,415
69	$1,720	$2,921	$5,001	$8,604	$14,858	$22,538	$25,711	$44,540
70	$1,841	$3,156	$5,452	$9,466	$16,493	$25,189	$28,798	$50,332

TABLE 22D Screening Rules for Stock Ratings

- All companies had to be in the S&P 500 in 1957 (Jeremy Siegel) and continue to be in the S&P 500 today.
- Only companies that had a compound rate of return in the top 250 out of 500 in the S&P 500, as calculated by Siegel, qualified.
- Only companies that survived intact qualified.

Rules for Rating Number Calculation:

- Multiply Siegel's 1957-2003 compound return rate by 500—add result.
- Multiply the current 10-year return rate by 300—add result.
- Multiply the 10-year earnings growth rate by 200—add result.
- Multiply the analyst's 5-year growth estimate rate by 500—add result.
- P/E ratio—subtract the number.
- If earnings growth is stable, add 10 points.
- If dividend growth is stable, add 10 points.
- Multiply the dividend yield by 500—add result.
- Subtract 10-year earnings growth rate from the 10-year actual return and multiply by 150—subtract result.
- Multiply the dividend/earnings ratio by 40—subtract result.

Comments:

The 46-year and 10-year compound returns, 10-year earnings growth, and analyst's 5-year growth estimates are weighted and added to ratings.

P/E ratio is subtracted. Higher the P/E, the bigger the subtraction, favors a lower P/E.

Earnings and dividend stability each add 10 points. This covers 1996-2005 and generally means steady increase in dividends or earnings each year.

Higher dividend as a proportion of stock price is rewarded and the lower the ratio of dividends to earnings is rewarded. I like companies that have much higher earnings than dividends. They can increase dividends easily and have lots of room for earnings to fall before they have to reduce dividends.

I punish companies whose actual return to shareholders grows faster than their earnings. Altria would be higher than fourth except their 10-year compound return to shareholders is almost double their earnings growth.

TABLE 22E My Rating System

Siegel Survivors			Actual Return	Stocks Rated				
				Actual No.	Actual No.	Analyst at	Number at	
Stock	Symbol	Type of Business	3/1/57-12/31/03	10-Year Return	10-Year Earn	5-Year Est.	Analysts	P/E Ratio at
Citigroup	C	Financial Services	13.02%	16.78%	15.04%	10.00%	18	10.17
United Technologies	UTX	Aerospace	11.93%	15.97%	13.42%	10.00%	19	19.47
General Dynamics	GD	Aerospace	10.57%	14.81%	12.93%	10.00%	18	18.41
Altria	MO	Consumer staples/tobacco	19.75%	12.55%	6.90%	8.50%	9	13.76
Procter & Gamble	PGL	Consumer staples	14.26%	11.17%	9.82%	11.00%	16	20.55
Conoco Philips	COP	Oil and gas	10.76%	14.38%	14.43%	7.00%	19	7.16
Exxon Mobil	XOM	Oil and gas	12.55%	12.12%	14.25%	7.00%	19	10.86
CVS	CVS	Retail drug	13.46%	11.84%	10.59%	14.00%	10	20.9
PepsiCo	PEP	Soft drinks	15.54%	7.85%	12.75%	10.00%	16	24.3
Chevron Texaco	CVX	Oil and gas	12.14%	9.71%	12.58%	6.50%	19	9.07
Motorola	MOT	Communications equipment	13.03%	2.56%	11.14%	10.00%	26	13.29
Eaton	ETN	Machinery	12.48%	10.35%	8.80%	10.50%	18	14.54
ITT Corp	ITT	Industrial	11.75%	16.98%	7.52%	12.00%	18	28.46
Colgate-Palmolive	CL	Consumer staples	15.22%	11.83%	6.87%	10.50%	18	23.17
McGraw-Hill	MHP	Publishing	13.56%	18.83%	5.95%	11.50%	11	26.59
General Mills	GIS	Consumer staples	13.59%	8.77%	9.33%	8.10%	14	14.24
Abbott Labs	ABT	Pharmaceutical	16.51%	7.56%	5.97%	10.00%	13	19.08
Caterpillar	CAT	Industrial	10.55%	15.31%	8.60%	10.00%	14	18.9
Wrigley	WWY	Food	14.65%	10.72%	6.34%	11.00%	11	24.91
IBM	IBM	Computer	11.94%	10.87%	6.65%	10.50%	20	17.09
General Electric	GE	Conglomerate	12.21%	10.98%	7.76%	11.00%	17	21.98
Hershey Foods	HSY	Food	14.22%	11.98%	8.38%	10.00%	17	25.45
Kroger	KR	Retail food	14.41%	12.73%	7.10%	8.00%	7	15.1
Minnesota Mining and Manufacturing	MMM	Conglomerate	12.35%	9.96%	8.51%	10.50%	12	19.81
Boeing	BA	Aerospace	12.31%	5.72%	7.24%	12.50%	20	25.71
Fortune Brands	FO	Consumer staples	14.55%	8.07%	3.74%	12.00%	9	18.87
Schlumberger	SLB	Oil and gas	13.02%	9.55%	0.44%	17.50%	20	35.47

Wyeth	WYE	Pharmaceuticals	11.61%	6.83%	6.20%	8.00%	19	17.08
Archer Daniels Midland	ADM	Staples/agricola	12.59%	6.44%	4.85%	9.00%	8	23.34
Pfizer	PFE	Pharmaceuticals	16.03%	7.82%	8.10%	5.40%	18	22.87
Entergy	ETR	Electric utilities	10.28%	13.67%	8.64%	7.00%	6	16.18
Kimberly-Clark	KMB	Consumer staples	12.68%	5.60%	2.83%	7.80%	17	17.56
Coca-Cola	KO	Soft drinks	16.02%	0.22%	3.84%	8.00%	17	20.16
Pitney Bowes	PBI	Services and supplies	12.68%	7.46%	3.82%	8.00%	5	18.73
Union Pacific	UNP	Railroads	10.73%	3.44%	1.37%	14.10%	12	24.93
Bristol-Myers Squibb	BMY	Pharmaceuticals	16.36%	1.84%	0.62%	5.00%	21	16.16
Merck	MRK	Pharmaceuticals	15.97%	1.53%	2.81%	3.30%	20	16.38
Heinz	HNZ	Food	14.78%	4.34%	1.24%	7.00%	13	19.13
Southern	SO	Electric utilities	11.03%	8.59%	2.40%	5.00%	5	15
Consolidated Edison	ED	Utility	11.80%	9.55%	0.03%	3.50%	7	14.29
PPG Industries	PPG	Chemicals	10.93%	3.48%	-1.26%	8.20%	13	18.1
Campbell Soup	CPB	Food	11.58%	0.84%	0.60%	7.00%	18	16.62
Raytheon	RTN	Aerospace	11.85%	-0.35%	-5.01%	12.00%	16	23.37
Dow Chemical	DOW	Chemicals	10.59%	8.34%	-5.24%	8.00%	14	8.63
Exelon	EXC	Electric utilities	10.72%	18.22%	2.04%	9.00%	9	37.85
Deere	DE	Industrial	12.76%	7.24%	-6.76%	8.00%	9	14.27
Cooper Industries	CBE	Electrical equipment	11.49%	8.96%	-5.19%	12.30%	11	49.51
Peoples Energy	PGL	Gas utility	11.50%	5.40%	-3.61%	4.90%	3	38.44
Ford Motor	F	Automotive	11.64%	-10.44%	-11.88%	5.00%	16	6.99
AT&T	T	Telecommunications	10.50%	4.62%	-18.92%	8.00%	22	17.92

	Dividend at	Dividend Yield at	Dividend/ Earnings	Earnings Stability	Dividend Stability	My Rating
Citigroup	$1.96	4.10%	0.41	Yes	Yes	188.54
United Technologies	$1.06	1.90%	0.35	Yes	Yes	162.82
General Dynamics	$1.84	2.90%	0.25	Yes	Yes	160.42
Altria	$3.20	4.60%	0.64		Yes	160.12
Procter & Gamble	$1.03	2.10%	0.38	Yes	Yes	157.08
Conoco Philips	$1.44	2.10%	0.15		Yes	157.00
Exxon Mobil	$1.28	2.10%	0.22		Yes	155.28
CVS	$0.16	0.50%	0.11			154.31
PepsiCo	$1.04	1.80%	0.44		Yes	147.78
Chevron Texaco	$1.80	3.10%	0.28		Yes	144.51
Motorola	$0.16	0.70%	0.09		Yes	143.27
Eaton	$1.40	1.90%	0.27		Yes	141.18
ITT Corp	$0.44	1.60%	0.12		Yes	140.27
Colgate-Palmolive	$1.28	2.30%	0.63	Yes	Yes	138.51
McGraw-Hill	$0.73	1.30%	0.33		Yes	136.97
General Mills	$1.36	2.80%	0.40		Yes	134.50
Abbott Labs	$1.18	2.80%	0.55		Yes	132.24
Caterpillar	$1.00	1.30%	0.25		Yes	130.93
Wrigley	$1.28	2.70%	0.70	Yes	Yes	130.72
IBM	$0.80	1.00%	0.16		Yes	130.64
General Electric	$1.00	3.00%	0.65	Yes	Yes	129.73
Hershey Foods	$0.98	1.90%	0.49		Yes	128.95
Kroger	$0.26	1.30%	0.20			128.84
Minnesota Mining and Manufacturing	$1.84	2.30%	0.45		Yes	127.71
Boeing	$1.20	1.40%	0.38		Yes	118.97
Fortune Brands	$1.44	1.90%	0.35			118.84
Schlumberger	$0.50	0.80%	0.28			106.90
Wyeth	$1.00	2.20%	0.37		Yes	106.68
Archer Daniels Midland	$0.40	1.10%	0.25		Yes	105.49
Pfizer	$0.96	3.90%	0.88		Yes	105.45
Entergy	$2.16	3.20%	0.52			102.93
Kimberly-Clark	$1.96	3.40%	0.60	Yes	Yes	101.70
Coca-Cola	$1.24	3.00%	0.61		Yes	100.39
Pitney Bowes	$1.28	3.00%	0.56		Yes	97.69
Union Pacific	$1.20	1.30%	0.31			86.51
Bristol-Myers Squibb	$1.12	4.70%	0.74		Yes	84.99
Merck	$1.52	4.50%	0.72		Yes	83.47
Heinz	$1.20	3.20%	0.61			78.99
Southern	$1.49	4.70%	0.70		Yes	77.56

Consolidated Edison	$2.30	5.50%	0.78	Yes	68.36
PPG Industries	$1.88	3.10%	0.54	Yes	67.93
Campbell Soup	$0.68	2.20%	0.40		63.36
Raytheon	$0.96	2.20%	0.50	Yes	62.41
Dow Chemical	$1.50	3.70%	1.00	Yes	51.59
Exelon	$1.60	3.10%	1.17		48.79
Deere	$1.56	1.80%	1.00	Yes	44.15
Cooper Industries	$1.48	1.70%	0.86	Yes	33.10
Peoples Energy	$2.18	6.10%	1.06	Yes	19.90
Ford Motor	$0.40	5.40%	0.38		14.92
AT&T	$1.33	5.20%	0.94		−14.58

TABLE 24A1 Investment Factor for 11.76% Annual Compound Rate of Return

$1 Invested One Time for Years				$1 Invested Every Year for Years			
$1	11.76%			$1	11.76%		
Years	Result	Years	Result	Years	Result	Years	Result
1	$1.118	41	$95.443	1	$1.12	41	$897.53
2	$1.249	42	$106.667	2	• $2.37	42	$1,004.19
3	$1.396	43	$119.211	3	$3.76	43	$1,123.40
4	$1.560	44	$133.230	4	$5.32	44	$1,256.63
5	$1.744	45	$148.898	5	$7.07	45	$1,405.53
6	$1.949	46	$166.408	6	$9.01	46	$1,571.94
7	$2.178	47	$185.978	7	$11.19	47	$1,757.92
8	$2.434	48	$207.848	8	$13.63	48	$1,965.76
9	$2.720	49	$232.291	9	$16.35	49	$2,198.06
10	$3.040	50	$259.609	10	$19.39	50	$2,457.66
11	$3.397	51	$290.139	11	$22.78	51	$2,747.80
12	$3.797	52	$324.259	12	$26.58	52	$3,072.06
13	$4.243	53	$362.392	13	$30.82	53	$3,434.46
14	$4.743	54	$405.010	14	$35.57	54	$3,839.46
15	$5.300	55	$452.639	15	$40.87	55	$4,292.10
16	$5.924	56	$505.869	16	$46.79	56	$4,797.97
17	$6.620	57	$565.359	17	$53.41	57	$5,363.33
18	$7.399	58	$631.845	18	$60.81	58	$5,995.18
19	$8.269	59	$706.150	19	$69.08	59	$6,701.33
20	$9.241	60	$789.194	20	$78.32	60	$7,490.52
21	$10.328	61	$882.003	21	$88.65	61	$8,372.52
22	$11.543	62	$985.726	22	$100.19	62	$9,358.25
23	$12.900	63	$1,101.648	23	$113.09	63	$10,459.90
24	$14.417	64	$1,231.202	24	$127.51	64	$11,691.10
25	$16.112	65	$1,375.991	25	$143.62	65	$13,067.09
26	$18.007	66	$1,537.807	26	$161.63	66	$14,604.90
27	$20.125	67	$1,718.654	27	$181.75	67	$16,323.55
28	$22.492	68	$1,920.767	28	$204.24	68	$18,244.32
29	$25.137	69	$2,146.649	29	$229.38	69	$20,390.97
30	$28.093	70	$2,399.095	30	$257.47	70	$22,790.06
31	$31.396	71	$2,681.229	31	$288.87	71	$25,471.29
32	$35.088	72	$2,996.542	32	$323.96	72	$28,467.83
33	$39.215	73	$3,348.935	33	$363.17	73	$31,816.77
34	$43.827	74	$3,742.770	34	$407.00	74	$35,559.54
35	$48.981	75	$4,182.919	35	$455.98	75	$39,742.46
36	$54.741	76	$4,674.831	36	$510.72	76	$44,417.29
37	$61.178	77	$5,224.591	37	$571.90	77	$49,641.88
38	$68.373	78	$5,839.003	38	$640.27	78	$55,480.88
39	$76.413	79	$6,525.669	39	$716.68	79	$62,006.55
40	$85.400	80	$7,293.088	40	$802.08	80	$69,299.64

—

TABLE 24A2 Investment Factor for 7% Annual Compound Rate of Return

	$1 Invested One Time for Years				$1 Invested Every Year for Years		
$1	**7.00%**			**$1**	**7.00%**		
Years	Result	Years	Result	Years	Result	Years	Result
1	$1.070	41	$16.023	1	$1.07	41	$229.63
2	$1.145	42	$17.144	2	$2.21	42	$246.78
3	$1.225	43	$18.344	3	$3.44	43	$265.12
4	$1.311	44	$19.628	4	$4.75	44	$284.75
5	$1.403	45	$21.002	5	$6.15	45	$305.75
6	$1.501	46	$22.473	6	$7.65	46	$328.22
7	$1.606	47	$24.046	7	$9.26	47	$352.27
8	$1.718	48	$25.729	8	$10.98	48	$378.00
9	$1.838	49	$27.530	9	$12.82	49	$405.53
10	$1.967	50	$29.457	10	$14.78	50	$434.99
11	$2.105	51	$31.519	11	$16.89	51	$466.50
12	$2.252	52	$33.725	12	$19.14	52	$500.23
13	$2.410	53	$36.086	13	$21.55	53	$536.32
14	$2.579	54	$38.612	14	$24.13	54	$574.93
15	$2.759	55	$41.315	15	$26.89	55	$616.24
16	$2.952	56	$44.207	16	$29.84	56	$660.45
17	$3.159	57	$47.302	17	$33.00	57	$707.75
18	$3.380	58	$50.613	18	$36.38	58	$758.36
19	$3.617	59	$54.156	19	$40.00	59	$812.52
20	$3.870	60	$57.946	20	$43.87	60	$870.47
21	$4.141	61	$62.003	21	$48.01	61	$932.47
22	$4.430	62	$66.343	22	$52.44	62	$998.81
23	$4.741	63	$70.987	23	$57.18	63	$1,069.80
24	$5.072	64	$75.956	24	$62.25	64	$1,145.76
25	$5.427	65	$81.273	25	$67.68	65	$1,227.03
26	$5.807	66	$86.962	26	$73.48	66	$1,313.99
27	$6.214	67	$93.049	27	$79.70	67	$1,407.04
28	$6.649	68	$99.563	28	$86.35	68	$1,506.60
29	$7.114	69	$106.532	29	$93.46	69	$1,613.13
30	$7.612	70	$113.989	30	$101.07	70	$1,727.12
31	$8.145	71	$121.969	31	$109.22	71	$1,849.09
32	$8.715	72	$130.506	32	$117.93	72	$1,979.60
33	$9.325	73	$139.642	33	$127.26	73	$2,119.24
34	$9.978	74	$149.417	34	$137.24	74	$2,268.66
35	$10.677	75	$159.876	35	$147.91	75	$2,428.53
36	$11.424	76	$171.067	36	$159.34	76	$2,599.60
37	$12.224	77	$183.042	37	$171.56	77	$2,782.64
38	$13.079	78	$195.855	38	$184.64	78	$2,978.50
39	$13.995	79	$209.565	39	$198.64	79	$3,188.06
40	$14.974	80	$224.234	40	$213.61	80	$3,412.30

—

TABLE 24A3 Investment Factor for 8% Annual
Compound Rate of Return

$1 Invested One Time for Years				$1 Invested Every Year for Years			
$1	8.00%			$1	8.00%		
Years	Result	Years	Result	Years	Result	Years	Result
1	$1.080	41	$23.462	1	$1.08	41	$303.24
2	$1.166	42	$25.339	2	$2.25	42	$328.58
3	$1.260	43	$27.367	3	$3.51	43	$355.95
4	$1.360	44	$29.556	4	$4.87	44	$385.51
5	$1.469	45	$31.920	5	$6.34	45	$417.43
6	$1.587	46	$34.474	6	$7.92	46	$451.90
7	$1.714	47	$37.232	7	$9.64	47	$489.13
8	$1.851	48	$40.211	8	$11.49	48	$529.34
9	$1.999	49	$43.427	9	$13.49	49	$572.77
10	$2.159	50	$46.902	10	$15.65	50	$619.67
11	$2.332	51	$50.654	11	$17.98	51	$670.33
12	$2.518	52	$54.706	12	$20.50	52	$725.03
13	$2.720	53	$59.083	13	$23.21	53	$784.11
14	$2.937	54	$63.809	14	$26.15	54	$847.92
15	$3.172	55	$68.914	15	$29.32	55	$916.84
16	$3.426	56	$74.427	16	$32.75	56	$991.26
17	$3.700	57	$80.381	17	$36.45	57	$1,071.65
18	$3.996	58	$86.812	18	$40.45	58	$1,158.46
19	$4.316	59	$93.757	19	$44.76	59	$1,252.21
20	$4.661	60	$101.257	20	$49.42	60	$1,353.47
21	$5.034	61	$109.358	21	$54.46	61	$1,462.83
22	$5.437	62	$118.106	22	$59.89	62	$1,580.93
23	$5.871	63	$127.555	23	$65.76	63	$1,708.49
24	$6.341	64	$137.759	24	$72.11	64	$1,846.25
25	$6.848	65	$148.780	25	$78.95	65	$1,995.03
26	$7.396	66	$160.682	26	$86.35	66	$2,155.71
27	$7.988	67	$173.537	27	$94.34	67	$2,329.25
28	$8.627	68	$187.420	28	$102.97	68	$2,516.67
29	$9.317	69	$202.413	29	$112.28	69	$2,719.08
30	$10.063	70	$218.606	30	$122.35	70	$2,937.69
31	$10.868	71	$236.095	31	$133.21	71	$3,173.78
32	$11.737	72	$254.983	32	$144.95	72	$3,428.76
33	$12.676	73	$275.381	33	$157.63	73	$3,704.15
34	$13.690	74	$297.412	34	$171.32	74	$4,001.56
35	$14.785	75	$321.205	35	$186.10	75	$4,322.76
36	$15.968	76	$346.901	36	$202.07	76	$4,669.66
37	$17.246	77	$374.653	37	$219.32	77	$5,044.32
38	$18.625	78	$404.625	38	$237.94	78	$5,448.94
39	$20.115	79	$436.995	39	$258.06	79	$5,885.94
40	$21.725	80	$471.955	40	$279.78	80	$6,357.89

—

TABLE 24A4 Investment Factor for 9% Annual Compound Rate of Return

	$1 Invested One Time for Years				$1 Invested Every Year for Years		
$1	9.00%			$1	9.00%		
Years	Result	Years	Result	Years	Result	Years	Result
1	$1.090	41	$34.236	1	$1.09	41	$402.53
2	$1.188	42	$37.318	2	$2.28	42	$439.85
3	$1.295	43	$40.676	3	$3.57	43	$480.52
4	$1.412	44	$44.337	4	$4.98	44	$524.86
5	$1.539	45	$48.327	5	$6.52	45	$573.19
6	$1.677	46	$52.677	6	$8.20	46	$625.86
7	$1.828	47	$57.418	7	$10.03	47	$683.28
8	$1.993	48	$62.585	8	$12.02	48	$745.87
9	$2.172	49	$68.218	9	$14.19	49	$814.08
10	$2.367	50	$74.358	10	$16.56	50	$888.44
11	$2.580	51	$81.050	11	$19.14	51	$969.49
12	$2.813	52	$88.344	12	$21.95	52	$1,057.83
13	$3.066	53	$96.295	13	$25.02	53	$1,154.13
14	$3.342	54	$104.962	14	$28.36	54	$1,259.09
15	$3.642	55	$114.408	15	$32.00	55	$1,373.50
16	$3.970	56	$124.705	16	$35.97	56	$1,498.21
17	$4.328	57	$135.928	17	$40.30	57	$1,634.13
18	$4.717	58	$148.162	18	$45.02	58	$1,782.30
19	$5.142	59	$161.497	19	$50.16	59	$1,943.79
20	$5.604	60	$176.031	20	$55.76	60	$2,119.82
21	$6.109	61	$191.874	21	$61.87	61	$2,311.70
22	$6.659	62	$209.143	22	$68.53	62	$2,520.84
23	$7.258	63	$227.966	23	$75.79	63	$2,748.81
24	$7.911	64	$248.483	24	$83.70	64	$2,997.29
25	$8.623	65	$270.846	25	$92.32	65	$3,268.13
26	$9.399	66	$295.222	26	$101.72	66	$3,563.36
27	$10.245	67	$321.792	27	$111.97	67	$3,885.15
28	$11.167	68	$350.753	28	$123.14	68	$4,235.90
29	$12.172	69	$382.321	29	$135.31	69	$4,618.22
30	$13.268	70	$416.730	30	$148.58	70	$5,034.95
31	$14.462	71	$454.236	31	$163.04	71	$5,489.19
32	$15.763	72	$495.117	32	$178.80	72	$5,984.31
33	$17.182	73	$539.678	33	$195.98	73	$6,523.98
34	$18.728	74	$588.249	34	$214.71	74	$7,112.23
35	$20.414	75	$641.191	35	$235.12	75	$7,753.42
36	$22.251	76	$698.898	36	$257.38	76	$8,452.32
37	$24.254	77	$761.799	37	$281.63	77	$9,214.12
38	$26.437	78	$830.361	38	$308.07	78	$10,044.48
39	$28.816	79	$905.093	39	$336.88	79	$10,949.57
40	$31.409	80	$986.552	40	$368.29	80	$11,936.13

—

TABLE 24A5 Investment Factor for 10% Annual Compound Rate of Return

\$1 Invested One Time for Years				\$1 Invested Every Year for Years			
\$1	10.00%			\$1	10.00%		
Years	Result	Years	Result	Years	Result	Years	Result
1	\$1.100	41	\$49.785	1	\$1.10	41	\$536.64
2	\$1.210	42	\$54.764	2	\$2.31	42	\$591.40
3	\$1.331	43	\$60.240	3	\$3.64	43	\$651.64
4	\$1.464	44	\$66.264	4	\$5.11	44	\$717.90
5	\$1.611	45	\$72.890	5	\$6.72	45	\$790.80
6	\$1.772	46	\$80.180	6	\$8.49	46	\$870.97
7	\$1.949	47	\$88.197	7	\$10.44	47	\$959.17
8	\$2.144	48	\$97.017	8	\$12.58	48	\$1,056.19
9	\$2.358	49	\$106.719	9	\$14.94	49	\$1,162.91
10	\$2.594	50	\$117.391	10	\$17.53	50	\$1,280.30
11	\$2.853	51	\$129.130	11	\$20.38	51	\$1,409.43
12	\$3.138	52	\$142.043	12	\$23.52	52	\$1,551.47
13	\$3.452	53	\$156.247	13	\$26.97	53	\$1,707.72
14	\$3.797	54	\$171.872	14	\$30.77	54	\$1,879.59
15	\$4.177	55	\$189.059	15	\$34.95	55	\$2,068.65
16	\$4.595	56	\$207.965	16	\$39.54	56	\$2,276.62
17	\$5.054	57	\$228.762	17	\$44.60	57	\$2,505.38
18	\$5.560	58	\$251.638	18	\$50.16	58	\$2,757.01
19	\$6.116	59	\$276.801	19	\$56.27	59	\$3,033.82
20	\$6.727	60	\$304.482	20	\$63.00	60	\$3,338.30
21	\$7.400	61	\$334.930	21	\$70.40	61	\$3,673.23
22	\$8.140	62	\$368.423	22	\$78.54	62	\$4,041.65
23	\$8.954	63	\$405.265	23	\$87.50	63	\$4,446.92
24	\$9.850	64	\$445.792	24	\$97.35	64	\$4,892.71
25	\$10.835	65	\$490.371	25	\$108.18	65	\$5,383.08
26	\$11.918	66	\$539.408	26	\$120.10	66	\$5,922.49
27	\$13.110	67	\$593.349	27	\$133.21	67	\$6,515.83
28	\$14.421	68	\$652.683	28	\$147.63	68	\$7,168.52
29	\$15.863	69	\$717.952	29	\$163.49	69	\$7,886.47
30	\$17.449	70	\$789.747	30	\$180.94	70	\$8,676.22
31	\$19.194	71	\$868.722	31	\$200.14	71	\$9,544.94
32	\$21.114	72	\$955.594	32	\$221.25	72	\$10,500.53
33	\$23.225	73	\$1,051.153	33	\$244.48	73	\$11,551.69
34	\$25.548	74	\$1,156.269	34	\$270.02	74	\$12,707.95
35	\$28.102	75	\$1,271.895	35	\$298.13	75	\$13,979.85
36	\$30.913	76	\$1,399.085	36	\$329.04	76	\$15,378.93
37	\$34.004	77	\$1,538.993	37	\$363.04	77	\$16,917.93
38	\$37.404	78	\$1,692.893	38	\$400.45	78	\$18,610.82
39	\$41.145	79	\$1,862.182	39	\$441.59	79	\$20,473.00
40	\$45.259	80	\$2,048.400	40	\$486.85	80	\$22,521.40

—

TABLE 24A6 Investment Factor for 11% Annual Compound Rate of Return

\$1 Invested One Time for Years				\$1 Invested Every Year for Years			
\$1	11.00%			\$1	11.00%		
Years	Result	Years	Result	Years	Result	Years	Result
1	\$1.110	41	\$72.151	1	\$1.11	41	\$717.98
2	\$1.232	42	\$80.088	2	\$2.34	42	\$798.07
3	\$1.368	43	\$88.897	3	\$3.71	43	\$886.96
4	\$1.518	44	\$98.676	4	\$5.23	44	\$985.64
5	\$1.685	45	\$109.530	5	\$6.91	45	\$1,095.17
6	\$1.870	46	\$121.579	6	\$8.78	46	\$1,216.75
7	\$2.076	47	\$134.952	7	\$10.86	47	\$1,351.70
8	\$2.305	48	\$149.797	8	\$13.16	48	\$1,501.50
9	\$2.558	49	\$166.275	9	\$15.72	49	\$1,667.77
10	\$2.839	50	\$184.565	10	\$18.56	50	\$1,852.34
11	\$3.152	51	\$204.867	11	\$21.71	51	\$2,057.20
12	\$3.498	52	\$227.402	12	\$25.21	52	\$2,284.61
13	\$3.883	53	\$252.417	13	\$29.09	53	\$2,537.02
14	\$4.310	54	\$280.182	14	\$33.41	54	\$2,817.20
15	\$4.785	55	\$311.002	15	\$38.19	55	\$3,128.21
16	\$5.311	56	\$345.213	16	\$43.50	56	\$3,473.42
17	\$5.895	57	\$383.186	17	\$49.40	57	\$3,856.61
18	\$6.544	58	\$425.337	18	\$55.94	58	\$4,281.94
19	\$7.263	59	\$472.124	19	\$63.20	59	\$4,754.07
20	\$8.062	60	\$524.057	20	\$71.27	60	\$5,278.12
21	\$8.949	61	\$581.704	21	\$80.21	61	\$5,859.83
22	\$9.934	62	\$645.691	22	\$90.15	62	\$6,505.52
23	\$11.026	63	\$716.717	23	\$101.17	63	\$7,222.23
24	\$12.239	64	\$795.556	24	\$113.41	64	\$8,017.79
25	\$13.585	65	\$883.067	25	\$127.00	65	\$8,900.86
26	\$15.080	66	\$980.204	26	\$142.08	66	\$9,881.06
27	\$16.739	67	\$1,088.027	27	\$158.82	67	\$10,969.09
28	\$18.580	68	\$1,207.710	28	\$177.40	68	\$12,176.80
29	\$20.624	69	\$1,340.558	29	\$198.02	69	\$13,517.36
30	\$22.892	70	\$1,488.019	30	\$220.91	70	\$15,005.37
31	\$25.410	71	\$1,651.701	31	\$246.32	71	\$16,657.08
32	\$28.206	72	\$1,833.388	32	\$274.53	72	\$18,490.46
33	\$31.308	73	\$2,035.061	33	\$305.84	73	\$20,525.53
34	\$34.752	74	\$2,258.918	34	\$340.59	74	\$22,784.44
35	\$38.575	75	\$2,507.399	35	\$379.16	75	\$25,291.84
36	\$42.818	76	\$2,783.213	36	\$421.98	76	\$28,075.05
37	\$47.528	77	\$3,089.366	37	\$469.51	77	\$31,164.42
38	\$52.756	78	\$3,429.196	38	\$522.27	78	\$34,593.62
39	\$58.559	79	\$3,806.408	39	\$580.83	79	\$38,400.03
40	\$65.001	80	\$4,225.113	40	\$645.83	80	\$42,625.14

TABLE 24A7 Investment Factor for 12% Annual Compound Rate of Return

	$1 Invested One Time for Years				$1 Invested Every Year for Years		
$1	**12.00%**			**$1**	**12.00%**		
Years	**Result**	**Years**	**Result**	**Years**	**Result**	**Years**	**Result**
1	$1.120	41	$104.217	1	$1.12	41	$963.36
2	$1.254	42	$116.723	2	$2.37	42	$1,080.08
3	$1.405	43	$130.730	3	$3.78	43	$1,210.81
4	$1.574	44	$146.418	4	$5.35	44	$1,357.23
5	$1.762	45	$163.988	5	$7.12	45	$1,521.22
6	$1.974	46	$183.666	6	$9.09	46	$1,704.88
7	$2.211	47	$205.706	7	$11.30	47	$1,910.59
8	$2.476	48	$230.391	8	$13.78	48	$2,140.98
9	$2.773	49	$258.038	9	$16.55	49	$2,399.02
10	$3.106	50	$289.002	10	$19.65	50	$2,688.02
11	$3.479	51	$323.682	11	$23.13	51	$3,011.70
12	$3.896	52	$362.524	12	$27.03	52	$3,374.23
13	$4.363	53	$406.027	13	$31.39	53	$3,780.25
14	$4.887	54	$454.751	14	$36.28	54	$4,235.01
15	$5.474	55	$509.321	15	$41.75	55	$4,744.33
16	$6.130	56	$570.439	16	$47.88	56	$5,314.76
17	$6.866	57	$638.892	17	$54.75	57	$5,953.66
18	$7.690	58	$715.559	18	$62.44	58	$6,669.22
19	$8.613	59	$801.426	19	$71.05	59	$7,470.64
20	$9.646	60	$897.597	20	$80.70	60	$8,368.24
21	$10.804	61	$1,005.309	21	$91.50	61	$9,373.55
22	$12.100	62	$1,125.946	22	$103.60	62	$10,499.49
23	$13.552	63	$1,261.059	23	$117.16	63	$11,760.55
24	$15.179	64	$1,412.386	24	$132.33	64	$13,172.94
25	$17.000	65	$1,581.872	25	$149.33	65	$14,754.81
26	$19.040	66	$1,771.697	26	$168.37	66	$16,526.51
27	$21.325	67	$1,984.301	27	$189.70	67	$18,510.81
28	$23.884	68	$2,222.417	28	$213.58	68	$20,733.22
29	$26.750	69	$2,489.107	29	$240.33	69	$23,222.33
30	$29.960	70	$2,787.800	30	$270.29	70	$26,010.13
31	$33.555	71	$3,122.336	31	$303.85	71	$29,132.47
32	$37.582	72	$3,497.016	32	$341.43	72	$32,629.48
33	$42.092	73	$3,916.658	33	$383.52	73	$36,546.14
34	$47.143	74	$4,386.657	34	$430.66	74	$40,932.80
35	$52.800	75	$4,913.056	35	$483.46	75	$45,845.85
36	$59.136	76	$5,502.623	36	$542.60	76	$51,348.48
37	$66.232	77	$6,162.937	37	$608.83	77	$57,511.41
38	$74.180	78	$6,902.490	38	$683.01	78	$64,413.90
39	$83.081	79	$7,730.788	39	$766.09	79	$72,144.69
40	$93.051	80	$8,658.483	40	$859.14	80	$80,803.18

TABLE 24A8 Investment Factor for 13% Annual Compound Rate of Return

\$1 Invested One Time for Years				\$1 Invested Every Year for Years			
\$1	13.00%			\$1	13.00%		
Years	Result	Years	Result	Years	Result	Years	Result
1	\$1.130	41	\$150.043	1	\$1.13	41	\$1,295.53
2	\$1.277	42	\$169.549	2	\$2.41	42	\$1,465.08
3	\$1.443	43	\$191.590	3	\$3.85	43	\$1,656.67
4	\$1.630	44	\$216.497	4	\$5.48	44	\$1,873.16
5	\$1.842	45	\$244.641	5	\$7.32	45	\$2,117.81
6	\$2.082	46	\$276.445	6	\$9.40	46	\$2,394.25
7	\$2.353	47	\$312.383	7	\$11.76	47	\$2,706.63
8	\$2.658	48	\$352.992	8	\$14.42	48	\$3,059.63
9	\$3.004	49	\$398.881	9	\$17.42	49	\$3,458.51
10	\$3.395	50	\$450.736	10	\$20.81	50	\$3,909.24
11	\$3.836	51	\$509.332	11	\$24.65	51	\$4,418.57
12	\$4.335	52	\$575.545	12	\$28.98	52	\$4,994.12
13	\$4.898	53	\$650.366	13	\$33.88	53	\$5,644.48
14	\$5.535	54	\$734.913	14	\$39.42	54	\$6,379.40
15	\$6.254	55	\$830.452	15	\$45.67	55	\$7,209.85
16	\$7.067	56	\$938.410	16	\$52.74	56	\$8,148.26
17	\$7.986	57	\$1,060.404	17	\$60.73	57	\$9,208.66
18	\$9.024	58	\$1,198.256	18	\$69.75	58	\$10,406.92
19	\$10.197	59	\$1,354.030	19	\$79.95	59	\$11,760.95
20	\$11.523	60	\$1,530.053	20	\$91.47	60	\$13,291.00
21	\$13.021	61	\$1,728.960	21	\$104.49	61	\$15,019.96
22	\$14.714	62	\$1,953.725	22	\$119.20	62	\$16,973.69
23	\$16.627	63	\$2,207.710	23	\$135.83	63	\$19,181.40
24	\$18.788	64	\$2,494.712	24	\$154.62	64	\$21,676.11
25	\$21.231	65	\$2,819.024	25	\$175.85	65	\$24,495.13
26	\$23.991	66	\$3,185.498	26	\$199.84	66	\$27,680.63
27	\$27.109	67	\$3,599.612	27	\$226.95	67	\$31,280.24
28	\$30.633	68	\$4,067.562	28	\$257.58	68	\$35,347.81
29	\$34.616	69	\$4,596.345	29	\$292.20	69	\$39,944.15
30	\$39.116	70	\$5,193.870	30	\$331.32	70	\$45,138.02
31	\$44.201	71	\$5,869.073	31	\$375.52	71	\$51,007.09
32	\$49.947	72	\$6,632.052	32	\$425.46	72	\$57,639.15
33	\$56.440	73	\$7,494.219	33	\$481.90	73	\$65,133.36
34	\$63.777	74	\$8,468.467	34	\$545.68	74	\$73,601.83
35	\$72.069	75	\$9,569.368	35	\$617.75	75	\$83,171.20
36	\$81.437	76	\$10,813.386	36	\$699.19	76	\$93,984.59
37	\$92.024	77	\$12,219.126	37	\$791.21	77	\$106,203.71
38	\$103.987	78	\$13,807.613	38	\$895.20	78	\$120,011.32
39	\$117.506	79	\$15,602.602	39	\$1,012.70	79	\$135,613.93
40	\$132.782	80	\$17,630.940	40	\$1,145.49	80	\$153,244.87

—

Notes

1. Derived from Jeremy J. Siegel, *Stocks for the Long Run* (New York: McGraw-Hill, 2002).

2. Merrill Lynch and Capgemini, *2004 World Wealth Report*, available at http://www.ml.com/index.asp?id=7695_7696_8149_6261_14832_14938

3. Post-gazette.com Business News, *Ranks of Millionaires Hit New High1*, available at http://www.post-gazette.com/pg/05145/510108.stm

4. TNS Financial Services, *Millionaires Once Again on the Rise Reports New Study from TNS*, available at http://www.marketresearchworld.net/index.php?option=content&task=view&id=336&Itemid=

5. Merrill Lynch and Capgemini, *2004 World Wealth Report*, available at http://www.ml.com/index.asp?id=7695_7696_8149_6261_14832_14938

6. Thomas J. Staley, *The Millionaire Mind* (Kansas City, MO: Andrews McMeel Publishing, 2001), 185.

7. Ibid., 75.

8. Ibid., 6-10.

9. *Forbes* Magazine, *The World's Billionaires*, available at http://www.forbes.com/billionaires/

10. Federal Reserve Bank Bulletin, *Recent Changes in US Family Finances*, available at http://www.Federal Reserve Bankeralreserve.gov/pubs/bulletin/2006/financesurvey.pdf

11. Shiller's data.

12. Jeremy J. Siegel, *Stocks for the Long Run* (New York: McGraw-Hill, 2002), 41.

13. James K. Glassman and Kevin A. Hassett, *Dow 36,000* (New York: Random House, 1999).

14. Morningstar, *Hypothetical Portfolio Illustration*, Courtesy MFS Financial.

15. Ibid.

16. Stratton Mutual Fund, *Annual Report, 2006*.

17. James P. O'Shaughnessy, *What Works on Wall Street*, 3rd ed. (New York: McGraw-Hill, 2005), 54.

18. Jeremy J. Siegel, *Stocks for the Long Run* (New York: McGraw-Hill, 2002), 41.

19. Dow Jones Indexes, available at http://www.djindexes.com/mdsidx/downloads/xlspages/high_low_lights.xls

20. Jeremy J. Siegel, *Stocks for the Long Run* (New York: McGraw-Hill, 2002), 13.

21. Ibid.

22. Ibid.

23. O'Shaughnessy, *What Works on Wall Street*, 51.

—

24.   Robert J. Shiller, website.

25.   US Department of Commerce, *Historical Statistics of the United States*, Colonial Times to 1970, Bicentennial Edition (Washington, DC: US Bureau of the Census), 199-202.

26.   US Census Bureau, *Statistical Abstract of the United States, 2001* (Washington, DC: US Census Bureau), 451.

27.   Robert J. Shiller, *Stock Market Data*, available at http://www.djindexes.com/mdsidx/downloads/xlspages/high_low_lights.xls

28.   Ibid.

29.   Jeremy J. Siegel, *The Future for Investors* (New York: Crown Business, 2005), 36.

30.   Shiller, derived from *Stock Market Data*.

31.   Ibid.

32.   Siegel, *The Future for Investors*, 36.

33.   Shiller, derived from *Stock Market Data*

34.   Ibid.

35.   Ibid.

36.   O'Shaughnessy, *What Works on Wall Street*, 358.

37.   Jeremy J. Siegel, *Stocks for the Long Run* (New York: McGraw-Hill, 2002), 13.

38.   Ibid.

39.   US Census Bureau, *Statistical Abstract of the United States, 2001* (Washington, DC: US Census Bureau), 599.

40.   Robert J. Shiller, *Irrational Exuberance* (Princeton, NJ: Princeton University Press, 2005), 27.

41.   Shiller, derived from Stock Market Data.

42.   US Census Bureau, *Statistical Abstract of the United States, 1965* (Washington, DC: US Census Bureau), 755.

43.   Shiller, derived from *Stock Market Data*.

44.   Ibid.

45.   Data courtesy of General Electric Investor Relations.

46.   Ibid.

47.   Ibid.

48.   The share price in the second column and the shares purchased are not the actual price or shares that an investor could have bought GE stock in 1940. These are the shares and share price adjusted for all GE stock splits where investors received additional shares of stock for no added investment. The total value in the far right column is the actual total value the investor would have achieved each year.

49.   Yahoo, derived from http://finance.yahoo.com/q/hp?s=MO

50.   Ibid.

—

51. Yahoo, derived from http://finance.yahoo.com/q/hp?s=DOW
52. Courtesy of Urs Frei, Banca Credito.
53. Ibid.
54. Yahoo, derived from http://finance.yahoo.com/
55. Jeremy J. Siegel, The Future for Investors (New York: Crown Business, 2005), 264-291.
56. James K. Glassman and Kevin A. Hassett, *Dow 36,000* (New York: Random House, 1999).
57. Charles W. Kadlec, *Dow 100,000 Fact or Fiction* (New York: New York Institute of Finance, 1999).
58. Derived from Benjamin Graham, David Dodd, and Sidney Cottle, *Securities Analysis* (New York: McGraw-Hill, 1962), 537.
59. Shiller, derived from *Stock Market Data.*
60. Ibid.
61. Shiller, derived from *Stock Market Data.*
62. Jeremy J. Siegel, *Stocks for the Long Run* (New York: McGraw-Hill, 2002), 13.
63. Ibid.
64. Shiller, derived from *Stock Market Data.*
65. Stratton Mutual Fund, *Annual Report.*
66. Shiller, derived from *Stock Market Data.*
67. Ibid.
68. Ibid.
69. Massachusetts's Financial Services.
70. Derived from MFS data.
71. Ibid.
72. Ibid.
73. Ibid.
74. Shiller, derived from *Stock Market Data.*
75. Derived from Yahoo data, http://finance.yahoo.com/q/hp?s=GE
76. Derived from Yahoo data, http://finance.yahoo.com/q?s=mo
77. Derived from Yahoo data, http://finance.yahoo.com/q/hp?s=AA
78. http://www.morganstanleyindividual.com/investmentproducts/equities/why/ibbotson_chart.pdf
79. Shiller, derived from *Stock Market Data.*
80. Ibid.
81. Derived from data courtesy of General Electric Investor Relations.
82. US Census Bureau, *Statistical Abstract of the United States, 1965 & 2001* (Washington, DC: US Census Bureau), 73 and 55.
83. Ibid.
84. Jay Palmer, "Live to 150," *Barron's*, April 17, 2006, 27.

—

85. Michael Fossel, *Reversing Human Aging* (New York: William Morrow and Company, 1997).

86. Shiller, derived from *Stock Market Data*.

87. Ibid

88. Derived from data courtesy of General Electric Investor Relations.

89. US Department of Commerce, *Historical Statistics of the United States: Colonial Times to 1970*, Bicentennial Edition (Washington, DC: US Bureau of the Census), 199-202.

90. Derived from US Department of Commerce, *Historical Statistics of the United States: Colonial Times to 1970*, Bicentennial Edition (Washington, DC: US Bureau of the Census), 199-202.

91. Ibid.

92. Yahoo, derived from http://finance.yahoo.com/

93. Derived from US Census Bureau, *Statistical Abstract of the United States, 2001* (Washington, DC: US Census Bureau), 451.

94. Jeremy J. Siegel, *Stocks for the Long Run* (New York: McGraw-Hill, 2002), 13.

95. O'Shaughnessy, *What Works on Wall Street*, 51.

96. Shiller, derived from *Stock Market Data*.

97. Shiller, derived from *Stock Market Data*.

98. Morningstar website.

99. Derived from Morningstar, *Hypothetical Portfolio Illustration*, Courtesy MFS.

100. Gordon K. Williamson, *Getting Started in Annuities*, (New York: John Wiley & Sons, 1999).

101. http://flagship5.vanguard.com/VGApp/hnw/FundsVVABByType

102. http://www.mbscott.com/dynasty.htm

103. http://flagship5.vanguard.com/VGApp/hnw/FundsIndexOnly

104. http://personal.fidelity.com/products/funds/content/browse.shtml.cvsr?refpr=ipmf1

105. http://www.morningstar.com/Cover/Funds.html?pgid=hetabfunds

106. Jeremy J. Siegel, *The Future for Investors* (New York: Crown Business, 2005), 264-291.

107. Ibid.

108. Siegel, *The Best Stocks for the Long-Term*, Thursday, April 20, 2006 column.

109. Ibid.

110. Jeremy J. Siegel, *The Future for Investors* (New York: Crown Business, 2005), 264-291.

111. Ibid.

112. Shiller, derived from *Stock Market Data*.

113. Ibid.

114. Ibid.

—

115. Ibid.
116. Ibid.
117. Morningstar, Hypothetical Portfolio Illustration, Courtesy MFS.
118. Ibid.
119. Stratton Mutual Fund, Annual Report.
120. Yahoo, derived from http://finance.yahoo.com/q/hp?s=MO
121. Ibid.
122. Derived from http://att.sbc.com/gen/investor-relations?pid=5675
123. Yahoo, derived from http://finance.yahoo.com/q/hp?s=DD
124. Ibid.
125. Ibid.
126. Yahoo, derived from http://finance.yahoo.com/q/hp?s=XOM
127. Ibid.
128. Derived from data courtesy of General Electric Investor Relations.
129. Ibid.
130. Ibid.
131. Yahoo, derived from http://finance.yahoo.com/q/hp?s=PG
132. Ibid.
133. Shiller, derived from *Stock Market Data.*
134. Ibid.
135. Derived from data courtesy of General Electric Investor Relations.
136. Shiller, derived from *Stock Market Data.*
137. Ibid.
138. Morningstar, *Hypothetical Portfolio Illustration*, Courtesy MFS.
139. Shiller, derived from *Stock Market Data.*
140. The idea for a chart like this was suggested by David Bach in his excellent book *Automatic Millionaire.* It illustrates perfectly the importance of early investing even if only small amounts.
141. Shiller, derived from *Stock Market Data.*
142. Jeremy J. Siegel, *The Future for Investors* (New York: Crown Business, 2005), 264-291.
143. Ibid.
144. Ibid.
145. Shiller, derived from *Stock Market Data.*
146. Derived from US Department of Commerce, Bureau of Economic Analysis, available at http://www.bea.gov/
147. Investopedia, http://www.investopedia.com/terms/m/meanreversion.asp
148. Suggested by David Bach, *The Automatic Millionaire* (New York: Broadway Books, 2004), 31.
149. http://www.dogsofthedow.com/dogs2001.htm